Celebrity and Glamour in Contemporary Russia

This is the first book to explore the phenomenon of glamour and celebrity in contemporary Russian culture, ranging across media forms, disciplinary boundaries and modes of inquiry, with particular emphasis on the media personality.

The book demonstrates how the process of 'celebrification' in Russia coincides with the dizzying pace of social change and economic transformation, the latter enabling an unprecedented fascination with glamour and its requisite extravagance; how in the 1990s and 2000s, celebrities – such as film or television stars – moved away from their home medium to become celebrities straddling various media; and how celebrity is a symbol manipulated by the dominant culture and embraced by the masses. It examines the primacy of the visual in celebrity construction and its dominance over the verbal, alongside the interdisciplinary, cross-media, post-Soviet landscape of today's fame culture.

Taking into account both general tendencies and individual celebrities, including pop-diva Alla Pugacheva and ex-President and current Prime Minister Vladimir Putin, the book analyses the internal dynamics of the institutions involved in the production, marketing, and maintenance of celebrities, as well as the larger cultural context and the imperatives that drive Russian society's romance with glamour and celebrity.

Helena Goscilo is Professor and Chair of Slavic at the Ohio State University, USA. Her recent publications include (as co-editor) *Preserving Petersburg: History, Memory, Nostalgia* and *Cinepaternity: Fathers and Sons in Soviet and Post-Soviet Film.*

Vlad Strukov is an Assistant Professor in the Department of Russian, and the Centre for World Cinemas, at the University of Leeds, UK. He is the founding editor of *Digital Icons: Studies of Russian, Eurasian and Central European New Media.*

BASEES/Routledge Series on Russian and East European Studies

Series editor:
Richard Sakwa
Department of Politics and International Relations, University of Kent

Editorial Committee:

Julian Cooper
Centre for Russian and East European Studies, University of Birmingham
Terry Cox
Department of Central and East European Studies, University of Glasgow
Rosalind Marsh
Department of European Studies and Modern Languages, University of Bath
David Moon
Department of History, University of Durham
Hilary Pilkington
Department of Sociology, University of Warwick
Stephen White
Department of Politics, University of Glasgow

Founding Editorial Committee Member:

George Blazyca
Centre for Contemporary European Studies, University of Paisley

This series is published on behalf of BASEES (the British Association for Slavonic and East European Studies). The series comprises original, high-quality, research-level work by both new and established scholars on all aspects of Russian, Soviet, post-Soviet and East European Studies in humanities and social science subjects.

Celebrity and Glamour in Contemporary Russia

Shocking chic

Edited by Helena Goscilo and Vlad Strukov

Routledge
Taylor & Francis Group

LONDON AND NEW YORK

First published 2011
by Routledge
2 Park Square, Milton Park, Abingdon, Oxon, OX14 4RN

Simultaneously published in the USA and Canada
by Routledge
711 Third Avenue, New York, NY 10017

Routledge is an imprint of the Taylor & Francis Group, an informa business

First issued in paperback 2012

Typeset in Times New Roman by
Pindar NZ, Auckland, New Zealand

British Library Cataloguing in Publication Data
A catalogue record for this book is available from the British Library

Library of Congress Cataloging in Publication Data
Glamour and celebrity in contemporary Russia : shocking chic / edited by
Helena Goscilo and Vlad Strukov.
    p. cm. — (Basees/Routledge series on Russian and East European
    studies)
    "Simultaneously published in the USA and Canada"—T.p. verso.
    Includes bibliographical references and index.
    1. Popular culture—Russia (Federation) 2. Popular culture—
Russia (Federation)—Moscow. 3. Glamour—Social aspects—Russia
(Federation) 4. Glamour—Social aspects—Russia (Federation)—Moscow.
5. Celebrities—Russia (Federation)—Biography. 6. Celebrities—Russia
(Federation)—Moscow—Biography. 7. Social change—Russia (Federation)
8. Social change—Russia (Federation)—Moscow. 9. Russia (Federation)—
Social life and customs. 10. Moscow (Russia)—Social life and customs.
I. Goscilo, Helena, II. Strukov, Vlad,
    DK510.32.G55 2010
    305.5'20947—dc22   2010007301

ISBN 13: 978-0-415-587655 (hbk)
ISBN 13: 978-0-415-62543-2 (pbk)
ISBN 13: 978-0-203-84503-5 (ebk)

To Mark Lipovetsky and Serguei Oushakine,
with affectionate gratitude for years of intellectual stimulation.
–HG

To Pittsburgh,
a city of little glamour but with a lot of generosity.
–VS

Contents

Figures

Contributors

Brian James Baer is Associate Professor of Russian at Kent State University, the author of *Other Russias: Homosexuality and the Crisis of Post-Soviet Identity* (2009), and the founding editor of the journal *Translation and Interpreting Studies* (*TIS*).

Darra Goldstein is Francis Christopher Oakley Third Century Professor of Russian at Williams College and Founding Editor of *Gastronomica: The Journal of Food and Culture*. She also serves as food editor of *Russian Life* magazine and series editor of *California Studies in Food and Culture* from the University of California Press.

Helena Goscilo is Professor and Chair of Slavic at the Ohio State University. She writes primarily on gender and visual culture in Russia – art, graphics, film, and gesture. Her recent publications include *Preserving Petersburg: History, Memory, Nostalgia* (2008), co-edited with Stephen M. Norris, and *Cinepaternity: Fathers and Sons in Soviet and Post-Soviet Film* (2010), co-edited with Yana Hashamova.

Nadezhda Korchagina is a PhD student in the Department of Modern Languages and Cultural Studies at the University of Alberta. She holds an MA in Russian-English Translation from Kent State University. She is currently writing her dissertation on Vladimir Nabokov's self-translation of the novel *Lolita*.

Michelle Kuhn is a graduate student in the Department of Slavic Languages and Literatures at the University of Pittsburgh. Her dissertation treats issues of urbanism and modernity in Soviet films of the 1920s through 1940s.

Tatiana Mikhailova, Instructor of Russian Studies at the University of Colorado-Boulder, is the author of several articles on gendered aspects of Soviet and post-Soviet culture. Her main scholarly interests focus on the cultural representation of strong women in Russo-Soviet literature and film.

Jeremy Morris, DPhil (Sussex, 2003), has written on Soviet nonconformist literature and contemporary Russian popular culture and national identity. He is now carrying out ethnographic research on workers and margins in Russia. He is an Assistant Professor at CREES, University of Birmingham, UK.

Stephen M. Norris is Associate Professor of History and Director of Film Studies at Miami University (OH) and author of *A War of Images* (2006). He is presently finishing a book entitled *Blockbuster History: Movies, Memory, and Patriotism in the Putin Era.*

Olga Partan is a Visiting Assistant Professor at the College of the Holy Cross. Her research focuses on the history of Russian and Western performing arts and the concept of theatricality in Russian culture. She is currently completing a manuscript titled *Recurring Masks: The Impact of the Italian Commedia dell'Arte on the Russian Artistic Imagination.*

Oxana Poberejnaia, DPhil (Manchester, 2007), has been a Research Associate on the project 'An Analysis of Post-Soviet Russian Television Culture' and a project manager on the project 'European Television Representations of Islam as Security Threat: A Comparative Study'. She also taught Comparative Eastern European politics and Russian language at the University of Manchester, UK.

Vlad Strukov is an Assistant Professor at the University of Leeds (the Department of Russian, and the Centre for World Cinemas). He has published on contemporary Russian film, animation, digital media, especially the internet, and popular culture. He is the editor of *Digital Icons: Studies of Russian, Eurasian and Central European New Media.*

Preface

Conceived by Vlad Strukov as early as 2006, our plan for a volume on the cultural construction of glamour and celebrity in contemporary Russia immediately raised two insoluble dilemmas: first, the complications and contradictions – familiar to any Slavist specializing in gender/women's studies during the 1980s – of examining a phenomenon widespread in the West and theorized by sundry Western commentators but never subjected to sustained scholarly scrutiny in the Soviet Union or post-Soviet Russia; second, the *bête noire* of selection that dogs any collection of articles by various authors and chiefly arises from the practical consideration of length. The latter inevitably forced us to exclude sundry genres of celebrity and their individual incarnations. Viewing our foray into new territory as merely an introduction to a vast, largely unexplored topic, however, we anticipate that future studies of glamour and celebrity will include journalists, newscasters, astronauts, inventors, movie and television stars, radio personalities, models and fashion designers, sports icons, classical musicians and singers, and rock performers.

Throughout we have followed the Library of Congress (LoC) transliteration system, except in those cases where names have acquired a standard alternative established by Anglophone publications: for instance, Yeltsin, not El'tsin; Yuri Luzhkov, not Iurii Luzhkov. The scholarly apparatus, however, adheres faithfully to the LoC system. All dollar currency discussed is in US dollars unless otherwise specified.

Acknowledgements

We thank (1) our contributors for their work, collegial cooperation, and stoic patience; (2) the various entities that granted permission to reproduce the visuals included in the volume; (3) the Research Office of the College of the Arts and Humanities at the Ohio State University for the grant that underwrote the illustrations for Chapters 1 and 10; (4) friends and colleagues who generously sent materials pertinent to our project; and (5) the personnel at Routledge for all stages of the publication process.

Introduction

Surface as sign, or the cultural logic of post-Soviet capitalism

Celebrity and Glamour in Contemporary Russia: Shocking Chic focuses on the culture of glamour and the phenomenon of post-Soviet celebrity, two interrelated concepts that have come to symbolize the era of Vladimir Putin's leadership, both as Russia's president (2000–8) and as prime minister (2008–present).[1] After the hungry, chaotic, and humiliating years of Yeltsin's government, the growing prosperity of Russian citizens in the first decade of the millennium has led to an impression of stability, even well-being. The economic boom stemming from the high price of natural resources, especially oil and gas, and the rationalization of the Russian economy after the financial crisis of 1998, enabling Russia in 2007 to pay off all foreign debts accrued in the 1990s, predictably fanned the country's ambitions on the international political arena. As a new member of major international organizations, Russia now exercises greater influence in world politics, and that status has prompted efforts by Putin's government to transform Russia's image at home and abroad. The project of re-branding the nation – and particularly its leadership – has entailed various initiatives, including the launch of the first Russian English-speaking digital television channel, Russia Today; the organization of the Moscow Biennale of Contemporary Art; Moscow's hosting of the Eurovision Song Contest in 2009; and the choice of Sochi as the venue for the 2014 Olympic Winter Games.

There have been significant changes on the ground, too: Russia has seen a dramatic upsurge in consumerism, with an unprecedented variety of goods available in all corners of the country. A leisure industry has emerged, with world-class facilities attracting diverse crowds to the glitz of nightclubs, cinemas, and cafés, especially at weekends. The tradition of summer holidays by the Black Sea has returned to the nation's cultural horizon, and hordes of Russian tourists have become commonplace in Turkey, France, and Great Britain. Nevertheless, the cult of conspicuous consumption and the celebration of the economic success on television and in popular media have hardly masked the hardships of Russia's non-privileged citizens. The country still has one of the lowest life expectancy rates in the developed world – for men, 59 years (Harding 2007). Given the demographic crisis looming over the nation and the scant achievements so far of the health and education reforms, the discrepancy between the social reality and its projected image is striking, rendering the temptation to invoke the tired trope of the Potemkin village irresistible. What is the purpose and function of the purported façade of life in contemporary Russia? With no immediate need to impress foreign dignitaries, is Russia's current glitz a form of self-delusion? Or do the glamorous new surfaces correspond to a genuine economic transformation and reflect a new cultural depth?

Celebrity and Glamour in Contemporary Russia: Shocking Chic aims to answer these and other questions pertaining to Russian culture of the 2000s. Celebrity studies, which constitute a relatively recent academic discipline in the West, have confined themselves to Western capitalist societies. The present volume, which approaches its subject from an interdisciplinary perspective, is the first to explore the culture of glamour and fame in a post-totalitarian state. In addressing key issues in the production, circulation, and consumption of fame and glamour, as well as their manifestations in both contemporary and historical contexts, this volume, optimally, affords a foundation for Slavic celebrity studies, stimulating further scholarship that will extend other, more traditional disciplines researching the Russian Federation and other post-communist societies.

Pace the tendency in analyses of Western societies to distinguish between the discourses of glamour and celebrity, we maintain that treating celebrity, glamour, and fame as imbricated categories allows for an accurate account of developments in the political, economic, and cultural domains in post-Soviet Russia. The culture of glamour and celebrity is a visible index not only of increased affluence but also of state allegiance to capital and its need to produce cultural symbols that, on the one hand, carry the ideologemes of capitalism and individualism, and, on the other, serve the political and economic agenda of Russia's new elite. It is therefore not surprising that the new cohort of Russian celebrities has been drawn partly from political echelons (for example, Vladimir Putin and Kseniia Sobchak,[2] daughter of Leningrad's former mayor) or that celebrities such as film director Nikita Mikhalkov and sculptor Zurab Tsereteli have occupied governmental positions, as Duma representative, and as ambassador and member of the Public Chamber of the Russian Federation, respectively. An analysis of celebrity culture in contemporary Russia therefore facilitates an exploration of Russia's political power, which is hugely invested in creating glamorous new symbols.

Grammar of glamour

A recent import into Russian vocabulary, the word *glamur* was first used in the 1990s, shortly after another lexical novelty, *imidzh*, meaning "an image, a public persona," gained currency. Insofar as *glamur* conjures up images of something different, flamboyant, and intentionally bombastic, it belongs to the rhetoric of excess in contemporary Russian culture. *Glamur* and its derivative *glamurnyi* signal admiration and the effects of grandiloquent application, but, depending on the circumstances of their usage, may also convey skepticism, disapproval, or sarcasm. While *glamurnyi* is fairly neutral, *glamurnen'kii*, with its diminutive suffix, designates petty glamour or the failed attempt to achieve "the real thing." In the Russian context, whereas *glamurnyi* refers to some form of beauty, *glamurnen'kii* evokes its opposite – *poshlost'*. Rendered famous by Vladimir Nabokov's lengthy disquisition on it, *poshlost'* – normally and imprecisely translated as "vulgarity" – is both nuanced and untranslatable, described by Nabokov as "[c]orny trash, vulgar clichés, Philistinism in all its phases, imitations of imitations, bogus profundities, crude, moronic, and dishonest pseudoliterature" (Nabokov 1967). As both "pseudo" and simulant, *poshlost'* functions as the gaudy antipode of glamour. An intellectual and ideological concept of transgression and aberration, *poshlost'* permits individuals to achieve notoriety. Therefore, *glamurnyi* (high glamour) and *glamurnen'kii* (low glamour) account for the difference between celebrity and notoriety, whereby the former usually refers to favorable public acclaim, while the latter is associated with opprobrious public recognition. The fine line between "high" and "low" glamour depends on the speaker's or writer's perspective (essentially, value judgment) and tone. In Bakhtinian terms, *glamurnen'kii* carries self-referential connotations that demonstrate profound awareness of cultural discourses and signifies a relationship between the established norm and its subversive sub-categories.

The word *glamur* and its derivates are linguistic appropriations for a phenomenon that has an older Russian equivalent – *glianets* – from the German word *Glanz*. The Russian word generally means "a beam or glow of light emanating from a reflected or polished surface; a shining quality" (Kuznetsov 1998), which denotes qualities of appearance, referencing only exteriors. Originally the word was coupled not with the excesses of consumption and display, but with everyday objects (for example, *sapogi s gliantsem* [shiny boots]) or practices (for example, *nachistit' do gliantsa* [to polish an object to achieve a gloss]). *Glianets* acquired its new meaning with the sudden advent of innovative publishing techniques that utilized high-quality – "shiny" – paper to produce eye-catching images of beauty. Like other elements of everyday culture, these new *gliantsevye* or glossy magazines became a reality in Russia in the mid-1990s, resulting from the rise of advertising and the arrival of multinational publishing houses, which started operating on the Russian market (for example, the German company Burda). Therefore the Russian terms *glianets* and, eventually, *glamur*, as well as all the forms of cultural production they define, are a product of the intensive mediation (and especially mediatization) of culture in Russia that occurred during the 1990s and became extraordinarily powerful after 2000. The reflective, mirror-like surfaces of glossy magazines have occupied the visual – and visceral – spaces of Russian consumers since about 1995.[3] As glossy publications became ubiquitous, as new, glass-covered buildings materialized in Moscow and other urban centers, as capacious new shops with beckoning window displays sprang up everywhere, and as new objects with slick screens such as mobile phones, flat-screen televisions, and iPods became available for a myriad of citizens, *glamur* seemed to infiltrate the public discourse of the whole nation. Indeed, the first survey of "The Word of the Year" in Russia, conducted in 2007 by the country's philologists and subsequently reported by the Russian émigré academic Mikhail Epshtein, showed *glamur* topping the list of high-frequency words by a wide margin (Epshtein 2008).

Of the two adjectives derived from *glamur* (*glamurnyi* and *glamurnen'kii*), the first normally describes articles of clothing, makeup, entertainment, lifestyle, architecture, art, and design (for example, of Russian oligarchs' homes and yachts). *Glamurnyi* objects – and subjects, for that matter – showcase unprecedented allure and luxury. The epithet also denotes unusual qualities calculated to appeal and startle, such as a pink keyboard, which most likely would be called a *glamurnaia klaviatura* because it conspicuously departs from the standard run of keyboards.[4] In other words, *glamurnyi* stands for things ostentatiously involved in studying their own image reflected in the super-mirror of mass-produced artifacts, with what Jacques Lacan might call the purpose of staging their own identity. Narcissistic consumption, often literalized when the Russian word *shokoladnyi* (made of chocolate) substitutes for *glamurnyi*, leads to an arrogant and grandiose assumption of entitlement, creating a sense of superiority and immunity – a common cause of nationalism and political opportunism that Russia has seen in abundance under Putin. No consumer item more eloquently illustrates this phenomenon than the outrageously priced "chocolate Putin" as realized metaphor, discussed in Chapter 1.

Politics of glamour

The by-product of consumption culture, glamour in Russia is a new utopia, having replaced both the late-Soviet project of building a radiant future and the early-1990s vision of a democratic state. Not just an ephemeral vagary of the economic scene, glamour is an ideal of a social structure promulgated and promoted by Putin's regime. Like Soviet projects, the glamour utopia nurtures the aim of constructing a new being – *homo glamuricus*, to replace *homo sovieticus* – of building a new middle class, with its standard bourgeois ideology and taste. Just as the early Bolshevik regime set out to invent the Russian proletariat and bourgeoisie (Fitzpatrick 2000), the classes that were largely under-represented in Imperial Russia, Putin's regime has committed itself to consolidating and legitimizing the current era's new classes, comprising owners of economic and social wealth.[5] Similarly, just as the early Bolshevik regime strived to educate the masses by raising their class consciousness through the introduction of new everyday practices,[6] glamour is the post-Soviet didactic program intended to teach Russian citizens how to be what Thorstein Veblen's study of the late-nineteenth-century's nouveau riche, *The Theory of the Leisure Class* (1899), famously called "conspicuous consumers." The expensive glossy magazines that inundated kiosks during the 1990s served as the early primers in that education. With the aid of purported cognoscenti, they proffered advice on befitting conduct in chic restaurants, appurtenances essential to stylish home design, modes of dress for success, and techniques for achieving and dispensing sexual satisfaction – all derived from Western values and praxis (Goscilo 2000). During the anti-Western and especially anti-American 2000s, however, the array of foreign models for emulation have been supplemented and in some cases supplanted by domestic exempla: for instance, Valentin Iudashkin in addition to Armani.

The utopian nature of Russian glamour contrasts starkly with the harsh realities of average citizens' lives. In 2007, an estimated 20 percent of the Russian population subsisted on income below the official poverty line (Harding 2007). While certainly an attribute of the urban rich, glamour is unattainable for the majority of the Russian population and could hardly be more remote from the circumstances of the homeless, who have proliferated since the dissolution of the Soviet Union. Imprisoned or expelled during Soviet times, in the last two decades they have become "street people," dismissed by city administrators such as Moscow's ambitious mayor as human flotsam undermining or discrediting Russia's new image of modish plenitude. Glamour, clearly, functions as a form of social distinction, the struggle for which the sociologist Pierre Bourdieu deems fundamental to social life. Bourdieu equates distinction in spatial dispositions (habitus) with social distinction – a quality of demeanor and manners inseparable from the social arena in which the scramble after resources transpires. What legitimates social differences, according to Bourdieu, is the acquired cultural competence that defines taste, the province claimed by intellectuals as creators of symbolic power (Bourdieu 1984). While Moscow's wealthy increasingly assert their exclusive rights to its most expensive space (whether palatial residences, shops, nightclubs, or restaurants), the capital's ongoing conflict over architectural and monumental transformations between the city's wealthy and its intellectuals – as self-nominated arbiters of taste – testifies to the saliency of those distinctions in the battle over symbolic capital within the metropolis that represents Russia's public face.

In today's Moscow, "face"/surface supersedes wealth. The latter is an elementary but insufficient prerequisite for guaranteeing admittance into establishments intent on proclaiming exclusivity and thus preserving their "face," as evidenced in the "face control" practiced in the capital's snootiest nightclubs, such as Soho Rooms, Black Star Club, Rai Club (Rai meaning Paradise), and the Billionaire Club. Young men called face control directors, who police the entrances to these temples of unbridled self-presentation-masquerading-as-pleasure, turn away any hopefuls whose instantaneous first impression fails to meet the mark in looks, affluence, or attitude – what one such Petronius-*cum*-semiotician of nightclub "quick-draw aesthetics" calls "style" (Yaffa 2009). Those rejected include supermodel Natalia Vodianova and her spouse (the English-born aristocrat Justin Portman) for drunken, "completely uncultured" behavior, and a group who had deposited a cash advance of $10,000 to reserve a table at Soho Rooms (the females lacked prettiness; the males, sartorial elegance). According to face control director Pavel Pichugin, who reportedly has "worked the door at a changing roster of Moscow nightclubs" and now is a celebrity in his own right (as he revealingly puts it, "I'm like a brand"), many "people who have just made their first million and think they deserve to be in the club [... are] in fact just a bunch of miner and day laborers [... who] don't have respect or culture [sic]" (Yaffa 2009). One mark of "culture" in this milieu is the right make of car, for only the most impressively expensive models may be parked conveniently close to a club's entrance. In other words, the last decade has upped the ante for acceptance into the ever-rotating citadels of glamour on the basis of credentials, which, though individually determined, unanimously embrace appearance as their ultimate criterion. Though Moscow restaurants betray a kindred obsession with orchestrating a calculated effect certifying superiority, as argued in Chapter 11, distinction operates most intolerantly and arbitrarily in the thriving world of nightclubs.

A visitor to Russia may experience "the shock of the new" when confronted by its scale of conspicuous consumption, particularly given the Soviet history of economic hardships and consumer deprivation, as well as the fabled inefficiency of the Soviet distribution system. In addition to registering the arrival of capitalism, Russia's fixation on glamour and celebrity corroborates the existence of earlier domestic consumer models. The self-evident perversity of advertising goods in a society suffering from perennial shortages notwithstanding, Soviet commodities such as jewelry, fine cognac, and furniture were advertised with relative success within the unofficial distribution network – *blat* – accessible to highly placed functionaries that existed independently of the official system of goods exchange. Though based on different qualifications, the principle of distinction was in effect, restricting access to commodities associated with prestige. Accordingly, this volume traces the history of Soviet consumption and its impact on the post-Soviet economy of symbols by looking at such figures as Nikita Mikhalkov, Alla Pugacheva, and Zurab Tsereteli, whose success straddles and connects the Soviet past and post-Soviet present (Chapters 5, 8, and 10, respectively).

Cultural history of glamour

When writing historical accounts one assumes the artificiality of all temporal demarcations, as we do in proposing four periods in the history of glamour industries in post-Soviet Russia: 1991–4, 1995–8,[7] 2000–8, and 2008 to the present. The early 1990s witnessed a burgeoning awareness of consumer culture, manifested in the availability of various goods imported from abroad. Appearing in spring 1994, the first Russian-language version of *Cosmopolitan* ushered in the era of glamour, followed first by *Good Housekeeping* (1995), *Playboy* (Summer 1995), *Harper's Bazaar* (1996), and the startlingly named *Cult of Personality* (1998), then by analogous homegrown publications emulating the Western desiderata of glossy paper, attractive layouts, and high-definition illustrations in vivid colors, such as *Domovoi* (1994) and *Voiazh* (1998).[8] In this ad-glutted universe of spectacular promise, the primacy of gesture, stance, and display of costly or prestigious possessions – designer clothes, fabulous jewels, cars, boats, villas or palatial interiors, paintings and priceless *objets d'art* – explained the frequency with which singers, actors, models, writers, athletes, and public figures whom extraordinary success or scandal had propelled into the limelight populated the pages. They incarnated the future ideal of the moneyed but ignorant reader prepared to imbibe the lessons transmitted by these publications, one who eventually could enter the magical, glamorous dreamland of the elect.

Ironically, however, there was little "high glamour" in the glamorous life of 1995–9, except on the pages of glossies. These years witnessed the New Russians' hold on the country's political and cultural life, as they flaunted their signature "raspberry-color" [malinovye] jackets, gold chains, opulent mode of life, and egregious manners.[9] Ridiculed by the intelligentsia for their vulgarity – *poshlost'* – and remarkable ignorance, during Russia's Klondike era the suddenly affluent New Russians became the country's chief spenders both at home and abroad – uncomprehending but profligate in their expenditure of what was perceived as dubiously accumulated wealth. Despite this inauspicious beginning, mainstream publications began using the term "glamour," though still in translation or in quotation marks, and still equated with a beauty that was the stuff of dreams.

The short period of prosperity for a tiny minority of the population abruptly ended with the financial crisis of 1998, after which very few Russian citizens had the wherewithal to obtain luxury goods or advocate a lavish mode of life. Subsequently, two years of readjustment, a rationalization of the economy, and the growth of domestic markets culminated in the historic moment of Putin's election (2000) and the escalating price of oil, which created the conditions for glamour's entrance into the Russian language and its "elevation" to a household term in the Russian Federation.

Putin's election temporally coincided with the emergence of Kseniia Sobchak as Russia's arch-celebrity, which solidified the Russian perception of glamour as a corollary of a sexually liberated individual's luxurious life. Thanks to Kseniia, glamour became a form of social currency that one would strive to acquire through the symbolic exchange of cultural commodities. These stereotypes were reinforced in 2003 when *Sex and the City* (created by Candace Bushnell and Darren Star, 1998–2004, HBO) was shown on Russian television and broke all records in terms of popularity and critical acclaim. In the same year, Roman Abramovich vaulted to world notoriety by acquiring the English football club Chelsea, while Bentley opened a salon in Moscow, where it proceeded to trade more cars than anywhere else in the world. As a new market for celebrity initiatives, Moscow had no rivals. Almost immediately after *Glamour* magazine arrived in the city (2004), launching the official era of "high glamourism," glamour became a form of both cultural production and cultural critique: the first glamour novel by Oksana Robski became a bestseller; Linor Goralik released a cultural study of Barbie, who had dominated the doll market of the 1990s; the new luxury residential complex Barvikha went on sale in Moscow; and the capital hosted the international Millionaire Fair. Everyone in Russia, it seemed, was dreaming of a huge diamond. Though the global economic crisis of 2008 left deep scars on Russia's hyper-wealthy (for instance, Abramovich and Oleg Deripaska), reducing their collective fortunes by approximately $378 billion ("Forbes 100 List ..." 2008), the glamour industry has continued to flourish, promoting ever more exclusive images of extravagant, media-disseminated flair.

Unsurprisingly, the historical trajectory of Russian glamour shows a close link between the rise of Russian capitalism and the production and consumption of glamour. It also reveals a reorientation of the post-1998 Russian market to production of goods as well as symbols for domestic consumption. What characterizes Putin's economy is not only the assimilation of petrodollars but also the adaptation of global trends to local uses, instanced by the publication of bona fide Russian glamour magazines instead of the earlier Russian translations or adaptations of original Western versions. In addition, Putin's state has been preoccupied with marking its new political and economic territory by signposting the bottom of the

Arctic Ocean (2007) and by establishing the presence of Russian capital abroad: the Chelsea mania includes the prestigious Russian Economic Forum in London. Finally, a historical outline reveals the emergence and uses of glamour as a life-style, as well as a form of political discourse, artistic production, and cultural critique. Examined in Chapter 4 as a novelty on the book market, Robski's debut novel, *Casual* (2005), pioneered the genre of "the glam narrative," subsequently seized upon by other, attention-seeking authors. Striking in its imperviousness to anything outside of gloss, *Casual* charts the process of securing a higher social status through the consumption and display of glamour that has replaced the Soviet grand narratives of collective progress and individual perfection.

Industries of glamour and celebrity

The influence of celebrity and glamour has been especially pronounced on cer-tain kinds of Russian media, particularly those purveying visual stimulation. Both phenomena are increasingly significant components of news and current affairs programs on television, and fundamental to the format of such talk shows as NTV's *Voskresnyi vecher s Vladimirom Solov'evym* [Sunday Evening with Vladimir Solov'iov] and the immensely popular *K bar'eru!* [To the Barrier!] – likewise hosted by the prize-winning journalist Solov'ev. They are also an ultimate object-ive for confession and scandal shows such as RTR's *Odin den' iz zhizni zvezdy* [One Day in the Life of a Star], reality shows such as *Fabrika Zvezd* [Factory of Stars] on the all-Union Channel One and *Dom-2* [House-2] on the TNT channel, plus numerous lifestyle shows demonstrating the shopping, leisure, and fashion routines of various celebrities. Furthermore, glamour has become a major trait of so-called "concerts," a type of television show encompassing performances of both song and dance, stand-up comedy, short satirical sketches, and other modes of celebratory display. Such concerts have invaded all Russian television channels, becoming a mega-form of televisual glorification and endorsement of glamour and celebrity. Normally dedicated to a public holiday, a cultural occasion or, most commonly, an anniversary of a public or private event or persona (for example, the sixtieth anniversary of Victory Day or Pugacheva's sixtieth jubilee, respectively), they constitute the only available form of engagement with public and private his-tories. Distracting the public from serious debate of genuine social and political issues – a widespread tendency analyzed in Chapter 6 – they create the illusion of an ongoing celebration, an eternal carnival.

Needless to say, some television shows explicitly appeal to glamour consumers, focusing on ranks and charts to affirm the ostensible importance of events, such as *The Most Fashionable Designer of the Year* and *The Actress of the Year*. These and similar programs have become part of the grand style characterizing celebrification of the everyday. In their function they have replaced the Soviet television programs featuring the life of ordinary workers, whose extraordinariness was certified by the mediation of their achievements. Unlike the Soviet programs, which paraded the hardships of labor, however, contemporary glamour and celebrity programs high-light ease, light-heartedness, and nonchalance. Ultimately, glamour and celebrity are constructed as socially significant occupations and as a career path, glorified in a number of programs, including *Glamour* magazine nominations. The format of television talk shows, award ceremonies, and programs affording glimpses of celebrities' lives are duplicated and endlessly recycled in other media, including radio, print media, and the internet. In fact, the inclusion of celebrity gossip and glamour news often proceeds from an editorial strategy in response to falling circulation and competition from international and national glossy weeklies or monthlies. A paradoxical consequence of such maneuvers is not only the "tabloidization" or even "dumbing-down" of the weak Russian public sphere, but also the development of that very sphere, potentially providing opportunities for expression by marginalized and undisciplined voices.

Even a serious publication like *Kommersant* annually tracks celebrities. In 2007, its summary of a tripartite survey of the perceived elite (national, business, social-*cum*-political) – which the report identifies as "the best and worthiest representatives of Russian society" – for the sixth year in a row showed Putin far outstripping all other contenders in the first two categories. Pop diva Pugacheva ("a multiple vice-champion of the annual elite rating") was his runner-up in the national ratings, but dropped to thirty-eighth in business, where Moscow Mayor Luzhkov and Mikhalkov occupied second and fourth place, respectively. The overall preponderance of middle-aged celebrities in the ranking, especially considering *Kommersant*'s statement that it polled "1,600 Russians of different age, sex, social and financial standing, from different parts of the country," implies the easy transfer of Soviet popularity to the post-Soviet era (Alexeev 2007). An intriguing disclaimer appended as a footnote to the report eliminates those respondents (demographic data unspecified) "who did not answer the question or said that there is no elite in Russia" (Alexeev 2007). Given Russia's current addiction to glamour, celebrities, and its eagerness to be counted among international glitterati, one can only conclude that such refusals came from a miniscule number of those canvased, or that some distinguish between glamour and the elite. Of particular relevance to this volume, of course, is the inclusion among the elite of the personae we chose to analyze as the *sine qua non* representatives of glamour and celebrity: Putin, Pugacheva, Mikhalkov, Luzhkov, and Zadornov. The conspicuous absence of Tsereteli, who appeared on the roster several years earlier, warranted commentary by the paper and undoubtedly betrays the broad-based animus against his public persona and overweening monuments.

Stakhanovites of the glamour industry

The demise of the Soviet Union wrought a stunning change in the access to and packaging of fame. During the Soviet era fame invariably was grounded in the ideological domain. Whether official (the record-breaking pilot Chkalov under Stalin, for example) or unofficial (Vysotsky, the celebrated singer of the Stagnation period), it was an extension of the industry of political culture – part of the Soviet system, which often operated through symbols competing for dominance and ideological approval. In post-Soviet Russia, despite the public's political apathy, the glamour and celebrity phenomenon maintains its political, hierarchical aspect: political figures perform as stars and overtly exert a powerful economic influence as part of their notoriety, while *Kulturarbeiter* seek political ties that confer honorary titles, contracts, and positions that enhance their status as stars. The symbiosis between politics and fame endures, with the difference that contemporary celebrities and icons have displaced the Soviet ideological pantheon of shock workers, achievers, and heroes.

One of the most notorious figures of Russian glamour is Kseniia Sobchak. Daughter of the former mayor of St. Petersburg, Anatolii Sobchak (1937–2000), and Liudmila Narusova (b. 1951), a member of the Federation Council of Russia, Kseniia (b. 1981) is a "larger than life" phenomenon on the Russian cultural scene, with a colorful presence in television, film, fashion, music, and other industries. After her father's death she moved to Moscow and continued her education at one of Russia's most prestigious universities – MGIMO, which trains Russian diplomats and policymakers. Her political career was soon eclipsed by her participation in Russian reality television shows,[10] including *Dom-2*, a franchise of *Big Brother*. Rapidly transformed into a television star, she appeared in numerous programs on the entertainment network TNT and on Channel One, as well as Muz-TV, a Russian alternative to MTV, and on many radio stations. Often compared to Paris Hilton, Kseniia is a Russian socialite who exploits her excellent pedigree, attractive appearance, and knowledge of the Russian media. Her reputation rests in part on her sarcastic and cynical remarks, sexist attitude, and sexually aggressive behavior: "First, I need to rape a man's brain and only then can sex follow as the grandiose finale of the relationship"[11] ("Ksiusha in da hous!"); "I consider capitalism the best contraceptive. If you have a normal life, a job, education, money, and opportunities, you don't wish to waste your life on diapers, borsch, and other pleasures"[12] ("U Ksenii Sobchak …" 2008). She epitomizes the odd post-Soviet conundrum of sexual liberation and gender enslavement, whereby she can make an assault, for example, on the Russian media, with its patriarchal convention of depicting women as objects of men's gaze precisely because she meets the criteria of institutionalized gender stereotypes. Appearing in extravagant poses in *Playboy* and kindred Russian publications such as *Maksim*, Kseniia constructs her personal brand as an independent and sexually audacious subject, even as she undermines her own power by adhering to the traditional discourse of marriage and family.

Kseniia exemplifies the post-Soviet trajectory of glamour accreditation, having gained access to the highest echelons of Russian society thanks solely to the political and economic connections of her father, who provided a blueprint for transmuting the public self when at the end of the 1980s he succeeded in converting himself from a member of the Soviet nomenclature into the ideological "father" of perestroika. In this regard, Kseniia sublimely epitomizes the merger of political power and capitalism (Kseniia met Vladimir Putin when she was just a child[13]), with glamour serving as a means of mediation between the institutions of political and economic power. To sustain her spot in the limelight, Kseniia fully invests herself in Russia's glamour industry, ensuring her constant presence in major printed and electronic media outlets. While many detest her egoism (for example, the wife of the Russian oligarch Sergei Radionov has disparaged her repeatedly, referring to her as a useless "night potty" [chamber pot] ["Zhena oligarkha ..." 2009]), others value her as an indefatigable worker (see, for example, her show on Radio Mayak); while some blog online about her fashion items, others attend such "pseudo-events" (Boorstin 1961) as an exhibition of her shoes (the 450 pairs recalling Imelda Marcos's collection) at Vinzavod, Moscow's main stage for contemporary art and glamour. With her excessive sexualization, excessive media presence, and equally excessive workaholism, Kseniia personifies the excessive nature of Russian glamour, whereby quantity trumps quality, while repetition and recycling provide the requisite gloss – *glianets*.

A quintessential glamour/celebrity figure, Kseniia has achieved her celebrity status by exploiting glamour culture and maintains her glamorous lifestyle thanks to that status. The double-speak of her persona, anchored in a dual construction of gender (her liberatory, taboo-challenging posture, paradoxically, resting on gender stereotypes), positions Kseniia at the crossroads of glamour and celebrity phenomena, making her an ideal object of study. Yet we have excluded her from this volume largely because her omnipresence and the nature of her notoriety, which has polarized Russian audiences, render her a too-obvious case. Instead, we focus on other stars and glamour practices that illuminate the politics of gender, class, ethnicity, and creative production in more complex ways. In exploring wider issues of glamour/celebrity and identity formation in the context of a post-totalitarian state, this volume adopts the identity/personality optic to trace metamorphoses in the cultural sphere at the level of individual histories. In other words, we analyze case studies that symptomize prevailing tendencies. Our more ambitious aim is to investigate phenomena that are difficult to objectify and quantify, hence fall out of the standard realm of celebrity studies: namely, the role of popular memes constructed and circulated by means of the internet, and, more broadly, digital technologies, as well as the modification of adopted identities – including those of class and gender – in such genres as performance, popular music, literature, film, art, and architecture. This volume's emphasis falls on the mediation and consumption of glamour and celebrity figures, for we are less interested in the publicity machine that usually occupies Western commentators, inasmuch as the contemporary Russian celebrity as a reprocessed identity is a striking, unpredictable outcome of the political and cultural zigzags characterizing perestroika and the Yeltsin period.

Glamour and gender

Post-Soviet Russia's discourse of glamour and celebrity was indispensable to the legitimation of new concepts of gender in reaction to the social turmoil of the 1990s, which precipitated a crisis in gender identities, and particularly masculinity. As the economy seesawed and employment plummeted, publications discouraged women from competing for jobs with men, whose ability to maintain their standing as (at least the nominal) head of the family was decreed a national priority. Items in the press urged women to coddle the fabled "stronger sex," who, despite copious empirical indications to the contrary, fantasized their identity as primary breadwinners while floundering in an unfamiliar environment ruled by financial considerations.

A mandate of the new glossy magazines overrunning kiosks in the 1990s was to teach post-Soviet masculinity, limning models of manhood exteriorized in specific behavior, appearance, and appropriate possessions. Counsel about correct etiquette in public venues, familiarity with desirable labels and brands, acquisition of sleek, "sexy" cars, choice of correct – that is, "exclusive" and "exotic" – vacation spots, and directions for giving women sexual pleasure filled glossies intended to boost men's morale while supplying guidelines for their image construction in the brave new world of market machismo. Several such publications opted for disingenuously blunt titles: *Supermen*, unsmilingly subtitled "a magazine for real men,"[14] *MaKhaON* (for HE-men; printed in Finland),[15] *ND Novyi Dzhentl'men* [New Gentleman {misspelled}], *Dzhentl'MAN* [Gentleman], and *Medved'* [Bear]. To varying degrees, all included photos of nude or skimpily clad women and endorsed imported alcohol, lavish Italian bathroom furnishings, expensive vehicles, and the other instantly recognizable signs of an elitism founded on moneyed panache. Tellingly, a segment of this flourishing magazine industry equated masculine success and wealth with the perceived sartorial style of the Italian mafia, projected in ads and images of dark suits, shirts, ties, and hats worn by icy-eyed male personifications of another neologism of the 1990s – *krutoi*, meaning "tough," derived from the word's literal meanings of "hard-boiled" and "steep." Like so many linguistic novelties of the nineties, the term, which liberally peppered pulp action of the decade, reeked of criminality,[16] reflecting a key feature of the Yeltsin era.

A relative latecomer on the scene, *Men's Health* (1998) anomalously reinforced, rather than countered, the macho ideal by dwelling primarily on men's sexual prowess. Its sagacious advice regarding sexual technique chiefly comprised prohibitions, cautioning men who had managed to entice women into their bedrooms not to "talk dirty," not to wear flowered underwear, and not to mimic film sex scenarios. The anticipated readership could be inferred not only from such nuggets of wisdom, but also from articles like "Seks-Mashina" (Sex-Machine/Sex-Car), which belabored the presiding metaphor of the penis as stick-shift while ruminating on the hydraulics of male arousal and performance (Goscilo 2000: 36). In fact, most male-oriented magazines of the nineties projected the ideal New Russian (and new Russian man) as a paradoxical composite of macho, crime-friendly tough, fabulously wealthy sybarite, and self-confident, glamorous man of the world. Yet the very instructions purveyed by such publications presupposed his complete ignorance of sophistication and glamour.

Glossy publications left little doubt about the disorientation and desperation of Russian masculinity confronting radical transformation. Yet the majority of Russian men felt crushed, not redeemed, by the cynosure-obsessed New Russians' machismo. In a decade when ownership of one or more Mercedes-Benzes, holidays in the Côte d'Azur, and having offspring enrolled in prestigious schools abroad signaled post-Soviet "success" for a tiny percent of the population, the formerly privileged male intelligentsia lost incalculable ground, while the average Russian man simply struggled to find a tenable place within a new socio-economic order.

With intellect rendered irrelevant by the market-dictated principle of "finances make the man," those members of the intelligentsia who had agitated for greater freedom in creative activity experienced the symbolic castration of failure in a world of new values.

Glossies and pulp fiction of the 1990s corroborated a gender reorientation, whereby women's ascribed identity not only as the major consumers of mass culture, but as consumers *tout court*, lost conviction under the onslaught of advertisements peddling cars, technology, weapons, and male fashion. An incisive chapter signally titled "Mass Culture as Woman: Modernism's Other" in Andreas Huyssen's *After the Great Divide* (1986: 44–62) challenges the gendered attribution of mass culture to women as its reputed consumers, in contrast to the male domain of high-culture "thinkers."[17] Huyssen contends that the "universalizing ascription of femininity to mass culture always depended" not only on nineteenth-century prejudicial stereotypes, but also on "the very real exclusion of women from high culture and its institutions," which he hyperbolically declares "a thing of the past" (Huyssen 1986: 62). Post-Soviet Russia, in fact, transparently invalidated the gendered twinning of women and mass culture by revealing its male citizens' avid enthusiasm for such popular genres as crime fiction, pulp action, and "dimestore" magazines, as well as Sylvester Stallone screen vehicles and beefcake posters.[18] Moreover, the collapse of the male-dominated Soviet cultural infrastructure loosened men's stranglehold on the production and dissemination of verbal, visual, and aural high culture. Not high-ranking position in influential administrative entities, but market forces dictated success. This *volte-face* rapidly reconfigured the constellation of Russian "literary stars," propelling Aleksandra Marinina, author of gynocentric detective novels, and Ludmila Ulitskaia, whose sensitive chronicles of individual lives explore women's experience, into the limelight and the category of bestsellers. Sales now determined status, and while the altered conditions opened up new opportunities for women, they did little to boost men's self-confidence.

Women weathered Russia's profound sea change in the 1990s much better than their male counterparts. With the shift of priorities to a glamorous appearance, the insistent initial sexualization of female images in women's magazines, which, teemed with ads and advice about makeup, clothes, plastic surgery, and modes of maintaining an enticing figure, had its positive counterpart in the area of employment: women entered the business world as beauty consultants, owners of companies selling makeup, and partners in increasingly prestigious beauty salons. Russian models now could negotiate their own contracts with the West, eventually creating a sensation on the catwalk and amassing fortunes. Talented tennis players such as Anna Kournikova and Maria Sharapova could parley their physical prowess and endowments into lucrative contracts with Western advertisers and magazines. In short, the emphasis on looks ultimately enhanced attractive, ambitious young Russian women's career options in the transition to a market economy and its commodification of the *imidzh*.

Some aspects of the 1990s intensified in the succeeding decade, while others petered out. For instance, the Russian man of the 2000s still displays features of the traditional Slavic macho, most prominently represented by Putin and no longer in risibly crude form. A new, more effeminate type, however, that of the Moscow metrosexual, has invaded more recent Russian fashion magazines. Cross-gender identities are in the public eye, too, conferring fame and celebrity status, as Jeremy Morris demonstrates in Chapter 9 on Verka Serdiuchka. Some feminization of men on the television screen – the extreme case being the musical performer Filipp Kirkorov, Pugacheva's latest ex-husband, fond of cosmetics and Liberace-style outfits – is counterbalanced by the impeccable machismo of Putin's and other politicians' mode of visible self-presentation. These new identities emerged during the development of a men's style press in the Russian Federation, which established the image of the "new man." And media in the new millennium have learned to delectate the public with a genuine novelty in the Russian context: the sexualization of men through representative strategies previously applied only to women. Putin himself is a major – indeed, perhaps the ultimate – sex symbol and unquestionably the country's premier celebrity, emitting the aura of limitless power that for many is synonymous with sexual potency.

Celebrity and history

Chris Rojek identifies three historical processes that account for the birth of celebrity as a public preoccupation: the democratization of society, the decline in organized religion, and the commodification of everyday life (Rojek 2001: 13–17). These historical factors may explain why celebrities have always existed in Russia, even under the heavy constraints of the totalitarian Soviet regime, but they do not fully account for the surge in celebrity culture after the dissolution of the USSR, and especially under Putin. Admittedly, the increasing democratization of Russian society enabled the current decade's infatuation with celebrity. Yet, paradoxically, the rise of celebrity simultaneously has decreased the opportunities for social mobility owing to the consolidation of centralized power and the establishment of new political and economic elite. In light of these developments, Russians' preoccupation with celebrity manifests aspirations generally unrealizable in real life.

The Russian Federation inherited a largely atheistic society as a legacy of the Soviet project of enforced secularization. Though organized religion was not explicitly criminalized in the USSR, copious restrictions imposed by the state minimized its social impact. As Soviet graphics, art, and innumerable speeches of the era amply attest, the Communist Party and its leaders appropriated the role of moral compass and spiritual leader, creating their own ideological cults, complete with "commandments," icons, and rituals. After the dissolution of the USSR and the concomitant collapse of official ideology, the ban on religion evaporated, creating a void that various interest groups rushed to fill. Not only Putin-endorsed Orthodoxy, but an entire range of semi-religious, semi-ideological movements suddenly (re)surfaced, including the neo-paganism explored in Chapter 6 on Mikhail Zadornov. In a sense, the discourse of glamour and celebrity has assumed the function of official ideology, with adulatory rituals replicating those of religious cults. Celebrity creates its own religious rites and scripted procedures played out in (normally mediated) sacred places and supports a whole morphology of events, objects, and functions to buttress the notion of extraordinary experiences, or "pseudo-events." If Yeltsin's role was to deconstruct Soviet discourse, Putin's has been to implement reconciliatory strategies, with the cult of celebrity serving to legitimize the regime's needs and the public's populist aspirations. As Oxana Poberejnaia demonstrates, the worshipping potential in this process draws on a mixture of comedy and shamanism. Therefore, on one level, celebrity culture in the Russian context is a secular society's rejoinder to the decline of magic and religion, not unlike that of Western societies as defined by Neal Gabler in his book *Life: The Movie* (1998). On another level, the Russian obsession with celebrity is a natural if surrogate component of religion's revitalization after seventy years of Soviet oppression.

Rojek posits the commodification of everyday life as the third historical founding block of celebrity culture. Indeed, the arrival of capitalism in Russia altered the ways in which the public, or, rather, the consumers, perceive their everyday activities. While social distinctions based on commodity have always existed in Russia despite the Soviet state's alleged equality, the growth of markets in the 1990s – as Darra Goldstein emphasizes in Chapter 11 – designated new social strata and new forms of distinction achieved through the ownership and consumption of commodities. Furthermore, the commodification of everyday life under Yeltsin and especially under Putin transformed the everyday practices of Russian citizens, who now faced the problem not of product shortages, but of choice. The profound effects of Russia's troubled adoption of capitalism included the demarcation of new forms of being and functioning in public and private spheres alike. Under these conditions, glamour became a symbol of success and new excesses.

Few, if any, would dispute that the abundance of commodities in the Russian Federation resulting from the country's embrace of capitalism is salutary. Yet the dissolution of the Soviet Union also has had deleterious consequences, chief among them the disintegration of social bonds: the reconfiguration of borders between the former Soviet republics divided some families, while friendships, marriages, and other forms of personal and social relationships foundered under the pressure of economic reforms and the social restructuring that accompanied them.[19] Popular culture, including the wave of *chernukha* films in the 1990s,[20] eloquently captured the profound isolation and loneliness experienced by many Russians, irrespective of age and gender. In such bleak circumstances, with meager prospects of improvement, glamour and the cult of celebrity represent salvation. While the first offers escape, the second unifies fans, affirming their membership in a larger social unit founded on positive sentiments – admiration, enthusiasm, optimistic fantasies – and creates a sense of belonging and recognition (Rojek 2001: 53). It also serves as a common currency in a society that has lost all other forms of social cohesion and has to rely on new, largely commercial forms of socialization. Celebrity provides a form of para-social interaction in situations where actual physical contact is restricted or impossible, and fans strive for validation and completeness in the imaginary (virtual) realm. This volume distinguishes between older media (such as television), which promote one-to-many, center-periphery channels of communication and celebrity formation, and more recent, so-called "new media" (for example, the internet and social networking sites), which facilitate many-to-many, decentralized, and dispersed modes of interaction that create a different set of celebrities and role models.

Chapter 7 of this volume explores the role of new media in fostering and expanding the cult of celebrity and glamour in contemporary Russia. The chapter also treats the internet as a unique environment for creating its own items and modes of celebrification that outstrip other existing forms of creating and disseminating symbols of glamour and celebrity. Vlad Strukov argues that the spread of new digital technologies in Russia is a sign of the country's entry into the global communication space. Celebrity culture is a manifestation of Russia's encounter with global capitalism, which posits celebrity and glamour as a *sui generis* system of values and meanings that has supplanted traditional notions of the self, including such social identities as class, gender, and sexuality.

Russian troika: new celebrities

Celebrity and Glamour in Contemporary Russia coheres as a volume not only because the eleven chapters address a common topic, draw on shared theoretical concepts, and restrict their temporal purview to two decades, but also because various points of intersection link the chapters, in some cases even leading to a slight overlap. Gender and gender differences are focal concerns throughout, with the exception of Chapters 3 and 6. Several entries engage issues of class (Chapters 4, 5, 9, and 10), ethnic identity (Chapters 9 and 10), and "family benefits" gained through blood-kinship or matrimony (Chapters 2, 4, 5, 8, and 10). And the haemorrhaging of the Soviet past into the post-Soviet present inevitably recurs as a leitmotif in the entire collection. On the basis of these commonalities, one could easily rearrange the sequence of chapters in clusters different from those dictated by editorial preferences and sense of logic.

This volume studies three types of celebrities as mapped by Rojek: ascribed, achieved, and attributed. Ascribed celebrity is based on lineage or marriage, and three chapters of the book specifically weigh the significance of family pedigree or "patronage" in the construction of celebrity status. Michelle Kuhn's "The Mistress of Moscow" (Chapter 2) traces the rise to notoriety of Russia's only female billionairess, Elena Baturina, a corporate celebrity whose formidable wealth and reputation, Kuhn maintains, depend on power wielded by her husband, the mayor of Moscow. Chapter 5 investigates the forces deployed by Nikita Mikhalkov – scion of a renowned artistic dynasty and son of the children's poet who authored the lyrics to the Soviet national anthem – in his determination to reign as unchallenged sovereign over the Russian film industry. By contrast, Chapter 8 probes the personal and professional dynamic between the stage performer Kristina Orbakaite, daughter of Russia's most famous female veteran of *estrada* (varieté), and the perennially popular Alla Pugacheva. The three chapters look at how symbols of celebrity are negotiated between family members, focusing specifically on transpositions in celebrity status generated by the social reforms of the 1990s. Thus Olga Partan contrasts the achieved celebrity of Pugacheva, acclaimed as a star during the

Soviet era, to her daughter's ascribed celebrity, in the process elucidating the differences between the Soviet perception of popular music and stage performers, on the one hand, and, on the other, the current reception of fame-mediated personalities.

Achieved celebrities, however, dominate the study: the cases of Boris Akunin, Vladimir Putin, Verka Serdiuchka, Zurab Tsereteli, and Mikhail Zadornov variously illustrate how celebrification in contemporary Russian culture proceeded from the increased opportunities for social mobility originating in the reforms of the 1990s. The chapters on Akunin and Serdiuchka (Chapters 3 and 9, respectively) explore the peculiar phenomenon of individuals achieving celebrity status while concealing their true identity: Akunin is the pseudonym of a Russified Georgian scholar and translator from Japanese, while Serdiuchka is the cross-gendered stage identity of the Ukrainian performer Andrei Danilko. Adopting an alternate identity in order to satirize popular discourses – of gender in Serdiuchka's case and of genre in Akunin's – each qualifies as what Rojek calls a *celeactor*, "a fictional character who is either momentarily ubiquitous or becomes an institutionalized feature of popular culture" (Rojek 2001: 23). Their creative strategy instances the dramatic split between a private and a public self. As the American social psychologist George Herbert Mead argued in *Mind, Self and Society* (1934), this division is generally perceived as the human condition, acknowledged since time immemorial. In the post-Soviet context, however, this fracture evidences a crisis in both public and private identities that occurred en masse in the aftermath of the demise of the Soviet Union.

The split between the "veridical" self and the *Me* (the self as seen by others, in Mead's terms) reflects not only identity confusion and the public persona's colonization of the private self, but also the collapse of the entire system of cultural discourses necessary for expressing and mediating the self. It testifies to the complete disorientation of Russian subjects after 1991, whereby adopting a new identity – whether public or private, or even both – was the main means of surviving through the crisis. This phenomenon is epitomized by Vladislav Mamyshev, who never appears as himself in public, but invariably as the photographed reincarnation of famous historical and mythical figures ranging from Hitler, Joan of Arc, Liubov' Orlova, and Napoleon to Dracula and Jesus Christ. His original impersonation of Marilyn Monroe in the 1990s earned him the sobriquet Vlad Monro(e), his equivalent of Akunin and Serdiuchka. The inspirational nature of his photo exhibits may be inferred from the more recent project of Ekaterina Rozhdestvenskaia, who adopted but trumped his stratagem by assembling a collection of photographs featuring current celebrities metamorphosed into notable personages (for example, Beethoven, Lomonosov, Pavel Tret'iakov) as they appeared in their portraits, and individuals in renowned paintings such as Botticelli's *Venus and Mars* and Henri de Toulouse-Lautrec's *Absinthe Drinker*. While it may seem far-fetched to diagnose the multiple mediation in these meticulous recreations as a symptom of multiple personality disorder, it requires little insight to attribute the entire project, which hinges on surface appearance alone, to the current excesses in commodification, consumption, and flamboyant self-display. Russia's celebrity culture does not shrink from feeding off the personal traumas of Russian citizens, having placed in the spotlight doubles of many Russian celebrities who appear in the Russian media, continuing the work of the originals, as, for example, Andrei Malakhov's popular television show *Pust' govoriat!* [Let Them Talk!], which features doubles of Kseniia Sobchak and other famous personae.

Attributed celebrity, the third type theorized by Rojek, relies on the sensationalism of mass media and the pseudo-events they propagate, and though these factors are inseparable from all modes of celebrity (Cashmore 2006: 203–4), only two chapters (Chapters 7 and 11) focus entirely on this category. Vlad Strukov's analysis of celebrities created on the internet and Darra Goldstein's of recent trends in Russian fine dining explore the role of micro-events in the manufacture of popular trends and glamorous artifacts, rituals, and venues that maintain the celebrity status of their creators. Both chapters focus on mobilization through new media and new (or refurbished) forms of social interaction as well as the reification of cultural discourses. Celebrities of this sort emerge in the context of compressed and concentrated mediation of events, when individuals – or, as we argue, objects and phenomena – attain a moment of fame, only to disappear almost immediately from public consciousness, especially if scandal or sensationalist news coverage facilitates their nugatory "fame." Since few in this category maintain their spot in the limelight, Chapters 7 and 11 closely scrutinize not the individuals (for example, Russian celebrity blogger, Anton Nosik), but their social function and the environments in which they arise.

Among the larger questions raised by *Celebrity and Glamour in Contemporary Russia* is that of the symbiosis between celebrity culture and Russia's recent encounter with global media flows, previously hampered or disabled by the Soviet system of control over production, censorship, and signal jamming. The prefix "trans-" nicely captures the new modes and movements central to this volume. Whereas Orbakaite, Pugacheva, and Zadornov are not exportable media commodities, **trans**national figures of glamour and celebrity have emerged in the 2000s, as attested by Serdiuchka, Nosik, Akunin, and above all Putin. The first instances a **trans**position of cultural values across borders – Ukraine–Russia – whereby cross-dressing (**trans**vestism) signifies the possibility of **trans**coding and staging **trans**national identities. Nosik examples a different case of **trans**nationalism, having managed to **trans**fer the celebrity status he acquired in Israel to Russia by means of digital networks, which by definition **trans**cend borders and national dimensions of stardom. Without crossing geographical borders in person, Akunin is the only contemporary Russian author of mysteries **trans**lated regularly into English and numerous other languages, one who **trans**gresses boundaries between high and low culture and on his English-language website posts "sleuthing games" for Anglophone admirers. Finally, the figure of Putin as a global celebrity rests on his incessant media appearances, international photo-ops, and the fascination with his bifurcated persona as Russia's idol beyond the realm of politics and the West's potential nemesis.

Anti-glamur

In Russian culture of the Putin era, the prefix "anti-" has whimsically come to signify not a direct negation of a phenomenon (i.e. thesis – **anti**thesis) but, rather, an ironic engagement with it: i.e. thesis → **re**novated thesis. An aperture in Hegelian logic, "anti-" in its new meaning and function provides no proof of causal influences; instead, it interplays with the relevant discourses surrounding the issues of identity, history, and representation. "Anti-" is sooner "re-," inasmuch as it signals **re**action, **re**conceptualization, **re**vision, and **re**furbishing of the past in terms of an uncertain present and an unforeseeable future, instanced in the film industry by Egor Konchalovskii's *Anti-Killer* (2002) and Dmitrii Puchkov's *Anti-Bimmer* (2004). In *Anti-Killer*, which depicts a character released after the USSR's collapse from his Soviet-era incarceration, "anti-" tropes the new regime, a new set of rules, and new heroes; it captures not the character's rejection of the past but his existence in the present. Similarly, *Anti-Bimmer* – a parody of Petr Buslov's 2003 gangster movie *Bimmer* – **re**scripts the original's storyline, **re**imagining the identities of the characters and **re**mastering the visual paradigm. In the process Puchkov creates a new, lighter genre that retains features of the road movie familiar from *Bimmer*, but now interwoven with elements of comedy and the adventure film.

Not only cinema, but also the critical discourse of glamour in contemporary Russia follows the idiosyncratic cultural logic of "anti-." The first full-scale attack on glamour came in 1998 from Tatyana Tolstaya with the publication of her article "Ia planov nashikh lubliu glamur'ë" [I love the glamour of our plans] (Tolstaya 1998) – an ironic echo of a line from Vladimir Maiakovsky's 1927 poem *Khorosho!* [Well Done!], "Ia planov nashikh lubliu gromad'ë" [I love the grandiosity of our plans], which celebrates the massive scale of Bolshevik reforms and industrial and social projects. By citationally paralleling early Soviet modernity and post-Soviet political and cultural metamorphoses, Tolstaya emphasizes the failure of social and cultural institutions to maintain social cohesion and provide meaningful values. Written with Tolstaya's characteristic irony, the article offers a critique of glamour as a world detached from reality, a form of delusion that takes control over its subjects, "Glamour has no tearful eyes, runny noses, dismay, despair, indifference, responsibility, worry about relatives, and, finally, in the best case scenario, no death – instead, 'a living legend'"[21] (Tolstaya 1998). This somewhat scurrilous attack on glamour is delivered by a star of contemporary literature, a popular media persona, and an ascribed celebrity, inasmuch as Tolstaya traces her lineage to a number of famous authors, political figures, and distinguished scientists. Tolstaya encodes the phenomenon of glamour and celebrity as a universal model of cultural production and critique, a type of post-Soviet grand narrative that excludes any other form of presentation, mediation, and activism.

In an analogous vein, glamour appears as a despotic and corrosive force in the novel *Ampir V: Povest' o nastoiaschem sverkhcheloveke* [Empire V: A Tale about a Real Superman] (2006) by Viktor Pelevin, the internationally known author who has micromanaged his reputation as a reluctant, enigmatic celebrity. A phantasmagorical view of Putin's Russia, the work presents a world divided between two powers – vampires and khaldeis – both supporting the edifice of an anonymous empire. The book's original title relies on associations with English and Russian, the first clearly alluding to the new political regime and its imperial legacy, the second in its transposition of the letter V referencing an architectural style as well as vampires. Two phenomena convey the novel's thesis of the regime's insidious power: *glamur i diskurs*. They function as nutrients that, if read literally, are necessary for the continuation of vampires' bloodlines, so to speak; interpreted metaphorically, they account for the cultural logic of Putinism, which, according to Pelevin, rests on the proclamation of glamour as the overriding principle of the new social order.

The rhetorical device of paronomasia – which inscribes the influx of Western values in Russian culture – marks the title of another critique of glamour and celebrity, its mixture of Russian and English signaling the provenance of those categories: Sergei Minaev's *ДУXLESS: Povest' o nenastoiashchem cheloveke* [Dukhless: A Tale about a Fake Man] (2006), which stimulated heated controversy in various Russian circles. Dedicated to those born in 1970–6, the novel depicts the grotesque moral degradation of the perestroika generation. Minaev's narrative about a successful Moscow-based media maker recreates the atmosphere of glamour and celebrification in contemporary Russian only to question its ethical foundation. The title's conflation of the Russian word *dukh*, which means "soul, spirit" (thus implying morality), with the English suffix "-less" points to the dearth of such qualities in today's Russia. In addition, the use of Russian and English in a specific sequence indicates the cause of moral degradation – the import of liberal capitalism in its Anglo-American variant. Significantly, both Pelevin and Minaev derive their titles from Boris Polevoi's 1946 classic of socialist realism, *Povest' o nastoiashchem cheloveke* [A Tale about a Real Man], which codifies the exemplary Soviet hero in the aviator who loses both legs during World War II but returns to combat after undergoing a spiritual/ideological revival. Whether supermen or fake men, the new millennium's Russian protagonists lack precisely that which propelled the heroism of their literary predecessors – a moral compass that lent their actions a sense of meaning and purpose. With no intention of glorifying the achievements of late Stalinism, Pelevin and Minaev envision no alternative to either the corrupt ideology of Soviet socialism or the equally bankrupt "discourse of glamour." Thus the logic of "anti-" articulates itself as ethical and cultural impotence masked by a glamorous façade of conspicuous consumption.

While some literary figures focus on glamour as a projection of (male) moral impotence, their cinematic counterparts explore the bifurcations of (female) social pursuits. Not only literature, but also cinema currently explores the moral dysfunction of those indentured to glamour. In 2007, Andron Konchalovsky (the celebrity father of Egor Konchalovsky, director of *Anti-Killer*, and the brother of Nikita Mikhalkov, whose celebrity status Stephen Norris discusses in Chapter 5) released his new production, *Glianets* [Gloss/y]. Mimicking the trajectory of many films during the Stalin era, which charted the rewarding journey of characters from the periphery to the center and its Master, the film tracks the seamstress Galia (played by Iuliia Vysotskaia, the director's wife) as she leaves the harsh realities of the

Russian provinces (Rostov-na-Donu) for the "wonder-filled" world of Russia's capital. Konchalovsky shoots the contrasting locations in two cinematic styles so as to ironize glamour: whereas the scenes in Rostov give a nod to the gloomy naturalism of early post-Soviet *chernukha*, the Moscow segment adopts the "glossy look" of recent popular cinema: for example, Andrei Kavun's *Okhota na piran'iu* [Hunting for Piranha] (2006) and Georgii Shengeliia's *Flesh.ka* [Flash.ka] (2006). *Glianets* combines a cinematic encyclopaedia with a critique of Russian glamour and celebrity culture, which Konchalovsky condenses into onscreen collages of Moscow's luxury boutiques (for example, Max Mara, Swarovski), prominent product placement (Max Factor, Aqua Minerale), and cameo appearances by real Russian socialites (Aleksandr Peskov, Svetlana Konegen).

In an interview with *Rossiiskaia Gazeta*, Konchalovsky defined glamour as "a world where everyone is cute and fluffy. We all want to enter that world. And then we exit it and find ourselves in ... life. Glamour is hard work" (Al'perina 2006).[22] His film depicts the post-Soviet Russian citizen's world as divided between radically incompatible entities: harsh reality and glossy fantasy, the Soviet experience of a dysfunctional economy and contemporary Western models of consumer capitalism, traditional moral values and the *dukhless* (soulless) environment of contemporary life. These dualisms extend the heritage of Soviet double-speak, i.e. the distinctive voices of the official and unofficial culture, of the public ideological discourse and its private critique. It takes little imagination to detect in the universe of *glianets* the materialization of the Soviet unsaid, the release of desires repressed for seventy-odd years.

Unlike the heroines of the film's Soviet precursors, such as Evgenii Tashkov's *Prikhodite zavtra* [Come back Tomorrow] (1963), Vladimir Men'shov's *Moskva slezam ne verit* [Moscow Does Not Believe in Tears] (1979), and Tat'iana Lioznova's *Karnaval* [Carnival] (1981), Konchalovsky's Galia ultimately attains not distinction, but extinction. Whether her jealous boyfriend, Vitek, who follows her, gun raised, actually kills her at the film's conclusion (rendering her literally *dukhless* – devoid of breath) is left uncertain. The ambiguous ending, however, reinforces the director's pessimistic moral stance by implying that even if Vitek spares her life, Galia's glamorous liaison with a Russian oligarch inevitably dooms her to a spiritual death (metaphorically *dukhless*).

The disjunction between reality and fantasy, Soviet and post-Soviet, drab and glamorous accentuates an ethical void in contemporary Russian society, which perpetuates borrowed models of conspicuous consumption. The double-edged logic of "anti-" also attests the Russian intelligentsia's failure to establish genuine values, hence signifies its abrogation of the traditional self-appointed role it earlier fulfilled as the nation's moral guide and overseer.

And so ...

The study of glamour and celebrity in post-Soviet Russia illuminates the forces driving the current circulation of objects and everyday practices in a society that for decades strictly regulated not only consumption but also social and institutional behavior. Such a study necessarily reconsiders the relationship between the post-totalitarian subject and the object and habitus. Viewed as a characteristic feature of modernity, celebrity culture – especially in its postmodern forms defined by the increased technological modes of communication and grassroots processes of celebrification through social media – may serve as one of the mechanisms of mapping the territory of modernity, where Russia occupies its honorary place. Hence, celebrity helps to solve one of the paradoxes of modernization and Russia's inclusion among post-industrial states. The two most important cultural signifiers of Putin's era, glamour and celebrity, mark the victory of consumer capitalism and of post-industrial, media-saturated modernity. An analysis of celebrity in a post-totalitarian context also sheds light on the circulation of symbols in spaces no longer controlled by the government or censored/moderated by designated administrative and cultural entities. At the same time, our research indicates that the legacy of the totalitarian regime seeps into the proliferation of politically motivated celebrity figures.

The study of the discourse of glamour and celebrity also affords the opportunity to reconsider Russia's economy. The general claim is that Russia continues the economic policies of the late Soviet Union, namely its heavy reliance on the oil and gas industry and export of carbons to the West (and now the East as well). What this volume clearly demonstrates, is that Russia has emerged from the financial crisis of 1998 with a well-developed media structure whereby the production and consumption of celebrity is a booming industry targeting primarily the local consumer and aspiring to speak eventually to a wider, global audience. This volume examines traditional and new channels of constructing and consuming star identities, ranging from print media and film to television and the internet. This medium distribution signifies a change in the way celebrity symbols operate as well as a transition from the Soviet cultural and media model to a post-Soviet one, whereby the internet – and other digitally-enabled technologies – stand for the emergence of new post-Soviet identities, and result in a celebrification, if not fetishization, of the medium itself (see Chapter 7). It is therefore possible to see how Russia will soon begin capitalizing on its celebrity figures in order to fix its presence and impact on the global stage. In this case, celebrity is Russia's real hard currency that is freely exchanged and consumed on global fame-and-glamour markets. The prime example of such a phenomenon is the figure of Roman Abramovich. We can only speculate about his involvement in the promotion of the Russian state abroad; however, we are certain that his figure has been used as a metaphor for Russia's economic success in global media. Thus one of the main theoretical questions this volume poses is the use of glamour and celebrity to announce the arrival of Russia's new economic, political, and cultural elite as projected in world media.

A theoretical consideration addressed in this volume is the relationship between stardom and media, especially the new media's role in constructing new celebrities. The contributors explore the profound transformation of the media system in post-Soviet Russia, including changes in media law, ownership, and circulation, as well as their effects on identity formation. It is not unreasonable to perceive the current cult of celebrity and glamour as a mode of deflecting attention from the media's failure to secure a position in the political arena. Contemporary Russian media relentlessly cultivate celebrity culture not only because it sells, but also because the media system lacks channels necessary for real social engagement and political motivation. One can just as tenably hypothesize that celebrity discourse is a way of communicating social and political messages, which explains why political figures are constructed as celebrities. Thus this volume explores how, on one level, celebrity and glamour measure a departure from Soviet culture as everyday experience. We contend that, on another level, glamour and celebrity function as a form of mediation between the two historical periods, whereby the relevance of the past political system is defined in the ostensibly depoliticized terms of glamour and celebrity. This volume demonstrates how Soviet cultural icons have been re-branded for consumption in the post-Soviet era (e.g. Pugacheva, Mikhalkov, Zadornov), the cultural trajectories of individual stars evidencing the process of saturation of the Soviet discourse in contemporary culture. On yet another level, glamour and celebrity play a crucial part in the preservation of cultural memory: post-Soviet Russia venerates such Soviet stars as Pugacheva because they provide a symbolic link to the nation's past. In other words, they are part of the mechanism of nostalgia that enables citizens to recreate their desires in the symbolic realm.

In sum, we interpret glamour and celebrity culture as a symptom of the fundamental shift in Russia after 1991 – a shift that redefined public and private. Cultural life in contemporary Russia depends on the de-Sovietization and de-politicization of the private sphere that Gorbachev launched as part of perestroika. This process inadvertently led to the privatization of the public sphere, and the role of celebrity and glamour is to mediate the confusing identities of post-Soviet life and the tensions bred by the altered concept and role of private and public domains. In the West, so accustomed to constant change as a norm, the understanding that a social position, rank, or station is temporary has long been established. In the Russian context, the cult of celebrity mirrors the sudden, rapid social changes of the 1990s after decades of stagnation. Glamour and celebrity account for the very speed of these changes, whereby acceleration per se is a valuable commodity available to what Stendhal in a different context called "the happy few."

Notes

1 Dmitrii Medvedev's role as president since 2008 notwithstanding, we refer to the 2000s as the Putin era, for the agenda and cadres he instituted during his presidency remain in place. Moreover, as prime minister and de facto most powerful figure in Russian politics, he continues to be the dominant force in Russia's national and international decision-making.

2 The anomalous pairing recalls that of Stalin and Marilyn Monroe in Leonid Sokov's sots-art works, one of which recently sold for $44,000.

3 For an analysis of glossy new publications during this period see Goscilo (2000).

4 An obvious analogy is the recent marketing by American and European firms of laptops encased in a variety of colors, all costing more than the standard black or gray.

5 As the cases of both Boris Berezovsky and Mikhail Khodorkovsky attest, however, wealth should not provide a conduit to political power and influence, especially in challenges to state authority.

6 See, for example, Leon Trotsky's *Problems of Everyday Life: Creating the Foundations for a Society in Revolutionary Russia* (1973); the original texts were written in the late 1920s.

7 The year 1999 mysteriously falls out of our chronology of Russian glamour and celebrity because it followed the economic crisis of August 1998 and was a period of particular hardship for Russians, including the oligarchs. During that year everyone struggled to adjust to a new economic reality.

8 A supplement to the newspaper *Kommersant-Daily*, *Domovoi* patently targeted an "economically sophisticated" audience, as did *Voiazh*.

9 For the cultural significance of the New Russians, see the thematic cluster of articles by Harley Balzer, Seth Graham, Mark Lipovetsky, and Alexei Yurchak, edited by Goscilo in *Russian Review* 62, no. 1 (2003): 1–90.

10 Ellis Cashmore's monograph *Celebrity/Culture* relies on Rojek's triplex, but objects that reality television has invalidated Rojek's clear-cut differentiation between ascribed and achieved celebrity, maintaining that "there seems little to demarcate between achieved and attributed status" (Cashmore 2006: 203–4).

11 "Mne, tak skazat', vnachale nuzhno iznasilovat' mozg muzhchiny, i tol'ko posle etogo kak grandioznyi final otnoshenii nastupaet seks."

12 "Ia schitaiu, chto kapitalizm – luchshii kontratseptiv. Kogda u tebia normal'naia zhizn', rabota, obrazovanie, den'gi i vozmozhnosti, to absoliutno net zhelaniia etu zhizn' tratit' na pelenki, borshchi i prochie udovol'stviia."

13 That "privilege" evokes Dmitrii Mochalskii's famous painting of beaming children with large banners titled *After the Demonstration (They Saw Stalin)* (1949) – an ineffable experience that accounts for their depicted euphoria.

14 "Zhurnal dlia nastoiashchikh muzhchin."

15 The title evokes the word "macho," mispronounced as "makho," while the capitalized "ON" means "he" in Russian.

16 Usage of *krutoi* in reference to a macho, authoritative demeanor originated in prisons, where it also means an armed robber or racketeer. See D. S. Baldaev (1997) *Slovar' blatnogo vorovskogo zhargona* in 2 vols, Moscow: Kampana, vol. 1, 211.

17 Published the same year, Tania Modleski's "Feminity as Mas(s)querade: A Feminist Approach to Mass Culture" (in C. MacCabe (ed) *High Theory/Low Culture*, Manchester: Manchester University Press) explores the same binarism.

18 For an astute analysis of gender's role in the popular culture of the 1990s, see Eliot Borenstein (2008) *Overkill: Sex and Violence in Contemporary Russian Popular Culture*, Ithaca and London: Cornell University Press.

19 For a study of efforts to overcome the loss of traditional social ties through other forms of kinship and attachment, see Serguei Oushakine (2009) *The Patriotism of Despair: Nation, War, and Loss in Russia*, Ithaca: Cornell University Press.

20 *Chernukha*, perestroika-pioneered slang derived from *chernyi* [black or dark], may best be rendered, perhaps, as "grime and slime." It focuses in a naturalistic vein on the seamy, dispiriting, usually violent aspects of life. See Seth Graham (2000) "*Chernukha* and Russian Film," in *Studies in Slavic Cultures I*, Pittsburgh: University of Pittsburgh, pp. 9–27.

21 "V glamure net zaplakannykh glaz, khliupaiushchego nosa, unyniia, otchaianiia, naplevatel'stva, otvetstvennosti, trevogi za rodstvennikov, nakonets, net smerti, v luchshem sluchae – 'neumiraiushchaia legenda.'"

22 "Glianets eto mir, gde vse belye i pushistye. My vse khotim tuda popast'. A zatem vykhodim iz nego i okazyvaemsia v zhizni. Glianets – eto trud."
    The decision to translate "belye i pushistye" as cute and fluffy is informed by Konchalovsky's reference to a famous joke about a frog that used to be "cute and fluffy" and now is "ugly and spotty."

Bibliography

Alexeev, A. (2007) "Three Dimensions of Russian Elite," *Kommersant*, 12 Jan. Available online at: www.kommersant.com/p-98222/r_l/Kommersant_Elite_Rating/ (accessed 12 December 2009).

Al'perina, S. (2006) "Polnyi Glianets," *Rossiiskaia Gazeta*, 23 June. Available online at: www.rg.ru/2006/06/23/gljanets.html (accessed 16 December 2009).

Boorstin, D. J. (1961; 2nd edn., 1992) *The Image: A Guide to Pseudo-Events in America*, New York: Vintage Books.

Bourdieu, P. (1984) *Distinction: A Social Critique of the Judgment of Taste*, trans. of *La Distinction* (1979), trans. R. Nice, Cambridge, MA: Harvard University Press.

Cashmore, E. (2006) *Celebrity/Culture*, Abingdon, UK: Routledge.

Epshtein, M. (2008) "Glamurnyi god pod znamenem politkorektnosti. Vpervye v Rossii vybrany Slovo i Antislovo goda," *NG Ex Libris*, 17 Jan.

Fitzpatrick, S. (2000) "Ascribing Class: The Construction of Social Identity," in S. Fitzpatrick (ed.) *Russia in Stalinism: New Directions*, London: Routledge, p. 20–47.

"Forbes 100 List of Wealthiest Russians Shows Carnage from Market Turmoil of 2008" (2008), *Forbes*, 17 Apr. Available online at: http://rt.com/Business/2009-04-17/Forbes_100_list_of_wealthiest_Russians_shows_carnage_from_market_turmoil_of_2008.html (accessed 5 December 2009).

Goscilo, H. (2000) "Style and S(t)imulation: Popular Magazines, or the Aestheticization of Postsoviet Russia," *Russian Culture of the 1990s*, special issue of *Studies in 20th Century Literature* 24, no. 1 (Winter): 15–50.

Harding, L. (2007) "53 Billionaires, £100bn in the Black, but for Russia's Poor it is just Getting Worse," *Guardian*, 15 March. Available online at: www.guardian.co.uk/world/2007/mar/15/russia.lukeharding/ (accessed 14 December 2009).

——. (2008) "No Country for Old Men," *Guardian*, 11 Feb. Available online at: www.guardian.co.uk/world/2008/feb/11/russia/print (accessed 5 December 2009).

Huyssen, A. (1986) *After the Great Divide: Modernism, Mass Culture, Postmodernism*, Bloomington: Indiana University Press.

"Kseniia Sobchak v gostiakh u Kati Gordon i Dmitriia Glukhovskogo" (2008), Radio Mayak, 3 July. Available online at: www.radiomayak.ru/tvp.html?id=148730/ (accessed 13 December 2009).

"Ksiusha in da hous!" Available online at: www.maximonline.ru/girls/covergirls/224592/s_.html (accessed 27 December 2009).

Kuznetsov S. A. (ed.) (1998) *Bol'shoi tolkovyi slovar' russkogo iazyka*, St. Petersburg: Norint.

Marshall, P. D. (1997) *Celebrity and Power: Fame in Contemporary Culture*, Minneapolis: University of Minnesota Press.

——. (ed) (2006) *The Celebrity Culture Reader*, New York and London: Routledge.

Mead, G. H. (1934) *Mind, Self and Society*, Chicago: University of Chicago Press.

Nabokov, V. (1967) "The Art of Fiction No. 40," [Interview by Herbert Gold] *Paris Review*, no. 41 (Summer–Fall). Available online at: www.theparisreview.org/viewinterview.php/prmMID/4310 (accessed 1 December 2009).

Rojek, C. (2001) *Celebrity*, London: Reaktion Books.

Tolstaya, T. (1998) "Ia planov nashikh liubliu glamur'ë," *Fotozhurnal*. Available online at: http://photo-element.ru/analysis/glamour/glamour.html (accessed 4 January 2010).

Trotsky, L. (1973) *Problems of Everyday Life: Creating the Foundations for a Society in Revolutionary Russia*, London: Pathfinder.

"U Ksenii Sobchalk ne budet detei," 31 July 2008. Available online at: www.dni.ru/show-biz/2008/7/31/146510.html (accessed 27 December 2009).

Yaffa, J. (2009) "Barbarians at the Gate," *New York Times*, 27 Sept. Available online at: http://travel.nytimes.com/indexes/2009/09/27/style/index.html#pagewanted=0&pageName=27moscoww& (accessed 5 October 2009).

"Zhena oligarkha okrestila Kseniiu Sobchak 'nochnym gorshkom,'" 24 June 2009. Available online at: www.tatar-inform.ru/news/2009/06/24/173168/ (accessed 13 December 2009).

Part 1

The art of politics, and the politics of art

1 The ultimate celebrity

VVP as VIP *Objet d'Art*

Helena Goscilo (Ohio State University)

Putin is the biggest celebrity in Russia today.

Dmitry Vrubel' (2004)[1]

He's good, he's strong, he's decent, he's ours and he's president now.

Vladimir Ivchenko (2001)[2]

He is the only president I know with black belt and PhD in economics. [...] Go VVP!

Don, blogger (2002)[3]

I want a husband who'd be like Vladimir Vladimirovich.

Yulya Pipilova, 18, member of the 1,500-strong VVP Fan Club in Moscow
(2007)[4]

A man for all seasons, for all too obvious reasons[5]

In 2007 Vladimir Vladimirovich Putin (VVP) topped *Kommersant*'s annual list of Russia's elite for the seventh consecutive year, garnering 82 percent of votes among the 1,600 Russians polled (Alekseev 2007). That rating startled no one, for no Russian or Soviet head of state since Stalin has inspired the widespread hero-worship that irradiated Putin's presidency and continues to thrive today, causing Western pundits to speculate that, regardless of President Dmitrii Medvedev's *de jure* post, self-designated Prime Minister Putin remains the country's de facto leader.[6] Revered at home as the savior not only of Russia's economy, but also of its national pride and international status, Putin as president enjoyed such extraordinary popular support, with approval ratings of 70–80 percent, that the impending expiration of his second, final term reportedly plunged some members of his constituency into melancholy at his departure, anxiety regarding the nation's future, and naïve concern about his professional options in the years to come.

Indeed, a controversial, sycophantic letter signed by four *éminences grises* of contemporary culture presumptuously claiming to speak for the entire culture establishment[7] beseeched Putin to seek a third term, in flagrant violation of the constitution, "... blagodaria Vashim usiliiam byla dostignuta sotsial'naia stabil'nost' i progress, neobychaino povysilsia avtoritet nashei Rodiny vo vsem mire" ("Pis'mo" 2007) [... thanks to your efforts, social stability and progress have been achieved; the authority of our Motherland in the whole world has increased extraordinarily]. The content of this highly publicized document,[8] which evokes the visually memorable sequence in Sergei Eisenstein's *Ivan Groznyi* [Ivan the Terrible] (part 1, 1944) of multitudes supplicating Ivan to return as ruler, coincides almost verbatim with the views espoused in an interview by the spokespeople for Nashi (a nationalistic youth group-*cum*-Putin-fan-club established in 2005, most probably funded by the Kremlin and impervious to any developments in twenty-first-century Russia that counter its simplistic convictions), "Putin [...] has brought stability and the opportunity for modernization and development of the country" (Myers 2007). Such a convergence of opinion harbored by old and young generations about Putin's accomplishments characterized *vox populi* throughout his presidency, which systematically ignored, discredited, or quelled the few dissenting voices virtually drowning in the sea of hosannas. As a media celebrity Putin has no equals, and his celebrity status, unlike that of most personalities in the limelight, is ascribed (Yeltsin's chosen successor), achieved (Russia's perceived rescuer from international ignominy and financial disaster), *and* attributed (the hero relentlessly championed via Kremlin-controlled media), according to Rojek's taxonomy (Rojek 2001: 17–20).

Adulation of Putin during his presidency assumed not only ideological, but also sundry identificatory, romantic, and creative forms – all reported and disseminated in the media.[9] Doting admirers in Siberia named a kebab house and bar after him (Bar Putin), selling "vertical power" kebabs and "when Vova was little" milkshakes (White and McAllister 2003: 388), while a Siberian native adopted his surname, maintaining, "Putin is the angel who educated me spiritually" (Toomey 2003). Since 2002, the main street in the Ingush village of Olgety has borne his name (Volonikhin 2002), as have lollipops, a vodka (Putinka), an ice cream, carpets, and other products. Botanist Nikolai Egorov in Cheliabinsk even attempted to christen a frost-resistant tomato after Putin until the Kremlin curbed his horticultural exuberance (Bransten 2002; MacKinnon 2002; Toomey 2003). Rumors linked Putin romantically (and fancifully) with the Australian actress Peta Wilson ("Putin's Last Love" 2003) and the controversial Russian police lieutenant Oksana Fedorova, Miss Universe in 2002, while in the city of Iaroslavl' one of numerous moonstruck women publicly professing "mad" love for him had to be locked up in the city's psychiatric ward owing to the uncontrollable nature of her passion.[10] More recently, the tabloid *Moskovskii Korrespondent* alleged that Putin had secretly divorced his wife in early 2008 so as to marry the then 24-year-old former gymnast and Olympic medalist Alina Kabaeva (currently a deputy in the State Duma) – a provocative item that predictably led to the paper's closure ("Russia: Putin Romance ..." 2008). Though such items are standard fare for film and television stars, pop music icons, and sports heroes, political leaders rarely inspire such impassioned involvement in their love life. Even Putin's KGB/FSB past,[11] which distressed those familiar with the organization's activities, seemed to cast a haze of romantic mystery around him by analogy with Stirlitz, James Bond, and the actors who had portrayed them.[12] Such a perspective endowed a reportedly mediocre functionary treading water in Germany, who moved on to occupy his country's chief executive position, with the glamorous aura of an international spy.

Romantic and erotic fantasies woven around Putin likewise proliferated when upscale confectioner Konfael created a 12" by 19" chocolate portrait of him, weighing over three pounds and priced at approximately $700 [sic] (Figure 1.1). Considered a work of art by Konfael personnel, this "limited edition" of the edible president (only two were manufactured) went on sale in 2003. Asked what they would do if they owned such an anomalous piece of confectionary, men claimed that they probably would hang it in their offices, whereas young women wished to kiss it, while their middle-aged counterparts dreamed of eating a chocolate Putin ear (BBC Monitoring 2003c). In a no less fantastic scenario, presumably as a thera-peutic outlet for what she diagnosed as a widely shared sexual fixation on Putin, one female fan contributed to *Komsomol'skaia pravda* a needlework pattern in cross-stitch based on a widely disseminated photograph of a bare-chested Putin, sporting sunglasses and rain hat, fishing (Figure 1.2). In light of these and similar strategies for attaining virtual intimacy with Putin, it seems reasonable to conclude that the young blogger rhapsodically proclaiming her adoration of him as a "sex symbol, a real Man" [seks symbol, nastoiashchii muzhik] ("Tainstvennaia ..." 2002) summed up sentiments rampant among the female segment of the Russian population, irre-spective of age or class. For countless women Putin appears as a glamorous, elite sexual icon, whose image dominates the country's landscape yet remains elusive owing not only to the astronomical cost of high-end purchasable products imprinted

Figure 1.1 "Sweetness and light" – the chocolate Putin; 2003. Courtesy of Associated Press.

Figure 1.2 Showcasing virility (presidential pecs), religiosity (Orthodox cross), and skill in
reeling in Big Fish (rod at crotch level) by Putin on vacation in Siberia; 2009.
Courtesy of Associated Press.

with his visage, but also to the seductive remoteness of any national leader.

Eroticism played bedfellow to a mythology of ethics, for the Kremlin deployed
the media for its indefatigable campaign of projecting Putin as a paragon of civic-
minded commitment, intent not on consolidating personal power and accruing
a sizable fortune, but on restoring Russia's glory and its citizens' economic and
psychological health. According to Steve LeVine, Vladislav Surkov, Putin's chief
of domestic policy, masterminded "the transformation of the president's visage
into a savior-of-Russia icon, gargantuan and granite-faced, gazing from billboards,
television screens, and newspapers throughout Moscow" (LeVine 2008: 34). Yet
these modes of putinating the capital were only the tip of the iceberg, for Putin's
formidable virtual omnipresence during his presidency was not wholly engineered
by the Kremlin.[13] His face adorned *znachki* [pins], coins, cakes, countless T-shirts,
salt shakers, posters, postcards, playing cards (Figure 1.3), notebooks, and calen-
dars throughout the country (Figure 1.4), while portraits in oil, Swarovski crystal,
amber and semi-precious stones, copper, mosaics, and charcoal, as well as busts
and full-figure sculptures, became a booming business.

A muse for men as well as a far from obscure object of desire for women, Putin
inspired a spy thriller called *The President* by the Latvian author Alexander Olbik,

Figure 1.3 VVP as the ace, having played his cards right. Photo by Helena Goscilo.

Figure 1.4 A calendar and children's exercise book imprinted with Russia's most famous face. Photo by Helena Goscilo.

a headline-making pop song by the female duo called *Poiushchie vmeste* [Singing Together] (Leeds 2002; Suyetenko 2002),[14] and an opera by the Saratov composer Vitalii Okorokov titled *Monika v Kremle* [Monica in the Kremlin], which features Monica Lewinsky's aspirations to non-political congress with him. Like Peter the Great before him, Putin metamorphosed into a bronze monument: a bronze statue of him on horseback materialized in a Novgorod prison; in 2001 the St. Petersburg sculptor Aleksandr Palmin created a bronze bust of Putin as a tribute to his idol (Traynor 2001); and three years later a huge bronze tribute to the martial-arts president in judo garb, executed by Zurab Tsereteli, was installed in the middle of a showroom at the Zurab Tsereteli Art Gallery. For several years Putin's portraits covered a sizable part of one wall in the centrally located Moscow bookstore Biblio-Globus, across from Lubianka; in 2001 a Moscow gallery mounted an exhibition of presidential portraits titled *Nash Putin* [Our Putin] (Traynor 2001); and a bestselling loose-leaf calendar for 2002 captured a different expression on his face for each of the twelve months (skeptical in January, downcast in December), with a cover featuring Putin as "a genius of judo" in the lotus position (Sidlin 2001).[15] His deadpan visage stared impassively at shoppers from watches sold to the tune of chimes and $56 at a kiosk inside the Federation Council Building in Moscow (Goldman 2008),[16] and a wittily illustrated volume titled *Putinki: kratkii sbornik izrechenii prezidenta (Pervyi srok)* [Putinisms: A Short Collection of the President's Sayings (First Term)], published in 2004, comprised extracts from his inimitable words of wisdom uttered during the first four years "on the job," while a fan club site enabled visitors to download songs mixing techno music with Putin's distinctive speech patterns ("The Putin Cult" 2007).[17] As Putin's second term began, increasing numbers succumbed to the epidemic, which showed little sign of abating when that term expired in March 2008. Dissent had been quashed and hero-worship was in full flower.

In its comprehensiveness, the official and populist campaign to instill Putin-love in the populace left no social category unscathed. Accordingly, in October 2000, as the academic year in primary schools started, children in St. Petersburg received a booklet with snapshots from the president's childhood (Traynor 2001), and in 2008 a large, luxury photo album of the adult Putin went on sale in several major bookstores. As dictated by the protocols of canonization, even the locations Putin visited became enshrined. Upon learning that approximately six years earlier Putin in his capacity as city official had planted a maple tree by St. Petersburg's Canadian consulate, a local businessman promptly affixed a brass plaque to the tree, with the solemn words, "Planted by V Putin 7 October 1995" (Traynor 2001). The village of Izborsk outside St. Petersburg, where the presidential motorcade made an unscheduled stop in August 2000, subsequently began peddling a walking tour marking the places "where Putin bought a cucumber," "where Putin took off his jacket and tried water from a spring," and "where Putin touched a tree and made a wish" (Traynor 2001). Similarly, Magnitogorsk's city museum exhibited the overalls Putin had worn during his visit (White and McAllister 2003: 388). Though no witnesses have sighted miracles in these venues, the best-known model for such an "itinerary," *mutatis mutandis*, is Christ's Stations of the Cross, with, however, a drastically different *terminus ad quem*. Given the narrative of salvation into which many Russians conscripted Putin's "achievements," and their view of VVP as the incarnation of the New Word – Russia's unique path in a global framework – the perceived mapping of Russia's transformation requires few adjustments to conform to the Christological scenario.[18]

On the basis of celebrity conventions, one might expect this hagiographic cultural production to be occasioned by a glitzy, internationally fêted pop celebrity such as Elton John or by a Hollywood super-hero along the hypertrophied lines of Arnold Schwarzenegger, but not by a short, balding, nondescript, middle-aged erstwhile KGB agent dubbed Vova Putin by the Cheliabinsk tomato pioneer. Normally reserved for media stars, the paroxysms of swooning adoration targeting Russia's political leader throughout the 2000s bred the neologism Putin-mania and revived the ominously freighted term "cult of personality," designating a phenomenon fostered by and inseparable from Stalin, but one allegedly disavowed by VVP, who reputedly tried to check the epidemic impulse to mythologize him. Less than a year into his first term, he publicly declared, "I understand that when somebody does such things, he or she is probably guided by the best of intentions, and that he or she thinks well of me. I would like to thank them, but ask them not to do this. [But] I cannot actively stop this" (Traynor 2001).

Whether sincere or not,[19] Putin's explicit discouragement failed to subdue what created the impression of being a genuine, if frequently market-driven, love affair between the Russian population and the man it voted into office for a second time in 2004.[20] Why market-driven? Because "Putin" sells – sufficiently so for one Russian journalist, at least, to have called him "a trademark symbol of popular culture and language" (Shchuplov 2002). Fully aware of what an effective sales pitch entails, by 2003 Putin himself acutely observed, "Moe izobrazhenie i imia v sovremennykh usloviiakh iavliaiutsia raskruchennym brendom, kotorym pol'zuiutsia vse komu ne len'" (*Putinki* 2004: 71) [In contemporary conditions my image and name are a widely marketed brand used by anyone who feels like it]. Thus the political propaganda of pro-Putinists, the stratagems of profiteering entrepreneurs, and the seemingly insatiable human need to create heroes dovetailed during a period when Putin's statist ideology ensured that lucrative mega-businesses, such as Yukos and Sibneft, reverted to the state (Aron 2006)[21] and Russia's booming oil industry dramatically improved average Russians' buying power and sense of security. The Putin brand was a talisman, a symbol of the Good Life under VVP, and a sign of solidarity with his ambitious vision for the nation as a global power.

The processes set in motion were circular: the human penchant for hero-worship and collective enthusiasm fueled Putin's popularity, which in turn intensified that enthusiasm, resulting in a yet greater popularity that whipped up more enthusiasm, etc., etc. This perpetual escalation not only catapulted Putin to iconic status, but united the population in the common cause of celebrification. If, as Rojek and other theorists of celebrity culture contend, fans of celebrities find affirmation in belonging to a group devoted to the adulation of a glamorous persona, Putin as Russia's symbol bonded Russians through their support of a United Russia – precisely the party he headed.

Cult or calculation?

Those eager to court Putin's favor and express their veneration recognized few restraints. In addition to the luxurious Konstantin Palace just outside St. Petersburg renovated for his use and the billion-dollar ski-slope in Sochi masterminded for his sporting self, the extravagant gifts marking his fiftieth birthday in October 2002 staggered the wildest imagination. They did so not only because of Russia's publicized economic hardships before the petrodollars rolled in, but also because of one gift's symbolic implications. Sixty jewelers in the Ural mountains spent six months producing the item, insured for $10 million, which consists of an exact replica of the Cap of Monomakh [Shapka Monomakha],[22] the ancient ceremonial gold crown, encrusted with jewels and lined with sable, used at the coronation of Russian tsars, including Ivan the Terrible and Putin's much-admired Peter the Great. A symbol of Russian autocracy and "the succession of power from the Byzantine emperors to the Russian monarchs" (Walsh 2002c), the crown figured in newspaper caricatures of Boris Yeltsin, dubbed "Tsar Boris" for his excesses – a detail apparently forgotten or overlooked by VVP's devotees, who surely must have realized his determination to distance himself from his predecessor. Ever the opportunist, Moscow Mayor Luzhkov joined the ingratiatory birthday well-wishers by proposing to restore the statue of Feliks Dzerzhinsky, founder of the Cheka, on Lubianka Square, presumably to please the ex-KGB president (Abdullaev 2002), who, according to various estimates, during his years in office filled 25 to 50 percent of the top positions in Russia's governmental structures with his former KGB colleagues.[23]

In their own way more evocative of the Stalin cult were the $500 carpets with Putin's face emblazoned on them produced in Turkmenistan and a Kostroma textile manufacturer's undertaking of what the pertinent linen mill's chief weaver called "very responsible and labor-consuming work": the profitable business of manufacturing tapestries with Putin's portrait, based on a photograph that showed what the head of the mill's art department trustfully described, à la George Bush, as "his open look [... which] convey[s] the openness of his soul"[24] ("Russian Textile ..." 2003). The allegedly high demand for the tapestries persuaded the manufacturer to follow up with bedspreads, towels, and rugs likewise bearing the Putin image – thereby enabling enthusiasts to sleep, shower, and socialize, however indirectly, with their icon. In short, not unlike Stalin, "*Putin [vezde/vsegda] s nami*" [Putin is {everywhere/always} with us]. The frequently iterated comparison between the two inspired one tongue-in-cheek "artist," Avi Abrams,[25] to revise Vasilii Efanov's painting *Nezabyvaemoe* [An Unforgettable Meeting] (1936–7) along anachronistic lines, replacing a female delegate at the Kremlin with Putin, thus altering the significance of the momentous handshake from what under Stalin represented achievement of the ultimate goal (contact with The Leader) to a union of kindred spirits. An issue of the Russian *Newsweek* (13–19 February 2006) similarly remastered for its cover Aleksandr Gerasimov's painting *Stalin i Voroshilov v Kremle* [Stalin and Voroshilov in the Kremlin] (1938) by substituting Putin as Stalin's stroll-mate, both men symbolically joined under one umbrella.

The Kremlin's determination to control the portrayal of history, its withdrawal of various archives declassified during the 1990s, and its promotion of a study guide for high school teachers that characterizes Stalin as "one of the most successful leaders of the USSR" (Levy 2008b) rightly or wrongly strengthen the perceived parallel between the two authoritarian rulers.

What interests me here, however, is not Putin's policies or politics, but a concrete aspect of his remarkable visual celebrification: sundry images reproducing him in genres ranging from "aestheticized" photographs and paintings to carpets, bedding, busts, graphics, and performances – whether in an idolatrous, satirical, or ambiguous vein. The tradition of depicting deified leaders in twentieth-century Russia charted an uneven course. Inaugurated under Lenin, it culminated with Stalin, relentlessly mythologized on canvas and posters by Brodsky, Gerasimov, Nalbandian, Klutsis, Deni, and a host of less memorable artists. As mere mortals, Khrushchev, Andropov, Chernenko, Gorbachev, and Yeltsin were largely bypassed in that respect, and Brezhnev, despite his famous Honecker kiss, similarly inspired few painters during his lifetime and virtually none later, with the notable, ironic exception of Dmitry Prigov (1985) and prisoners who tattooed their bodies. That for some observers the obsession with pictorially immortalizing Putin implied a parallel with Stalin[26] explains why wary commentators resorted to the red-button, historically fraught label of "cult of personality" (Figure 1.5). Disclaimers voiced by Putin or leaked to the press by members of his entourage insisted on the Russian president's distaste for this diffusion of Putiniana throughout the country – a disavowal that repeatedly made news, adding modesty to the virtues constituting his public profile – and thus far no mammoth statue of him looms over the Volga-Don Canal.[27] The sheer volume and diversity of his iconographic dissemination, nonetheless, eerily recalls the artistic production of the Stalinist era, sparking exaggerated fears of political regression to fatally "jollier times" ("zhit' stalo luchshe, zhit' stalo veselee ...") – fears buttressed by the reinstatement of several Soviet practices and the Kremlin's virtually complete control of the media. Moreover, the internet facilitates broad access to those images, just as YouTube enables those outside Russia to sample clips featuring him as the protagonist of imaginary narratives, such as the ironic mini-video showing VVP as a cool, daring, Stetsoned cowboy riding the range, with music from Sergio Leone's *Man with No Name* series, starring Clint Eastwood as the fearless gunslinger even more inscrutable and macho than Putin. The analogy projected Putin as the strong, silent man of action engaged in manly pursuits – and the numerous shots of him on horseback, in helicopters, and in judo poses only consolidated that glamorous image of intrepid (self-)mastery conventionalized by Hollywood and advertisements in print and on television.[28] Putin's celebrity status rests on his mediated image of an intelligent, reserved, sober patriot of indomitable will and physical prowess, one wholly dedicated to Russia and Russians.

Especially during his first term, Putin undeniably exuded and cultivated an aura of recessiveness – of a reluctance to attract particular attention. His media-hyped kiss planted on a small boy's stomach in Red Square (2006) aside, for much of his presidency he lacked dramatic flourishes, favored a brisk and occasionally

Figure 1.5 "Mirror, mirror ..." – an ironic, admirably pithy version of the Putin-as-Stalin-legatee perspective, a caricature by John Deering, cartoonist at the *Arkansas Democrat Gazette*. Courtesy of John Deering.

opaque manner of interaction, and operated by steady, even plodding, accretion and scrupulous concern for details, often behind the scenes. His famed abstinence from alcohol and his physical appearance – not his pale basilisk gaze and uncanny resemblance to Dobby,[29] but his compact, athletic slightness – suggest the discipline and control constantly touted as his signature traits. His verbal tic of preceding official statements by a promise of laconism matches his physical shortness. Admired for his sporting skills (judo, skiing, swimming, horseback riding) and his dependability, in contrast to his predecessor's fabled expansiveness, self-indulgence, thoughtless off-the-cuff statements, and paraded emotionality, he sooner has impressed by an *absence* of qualities, as the song "A Man Like Putin" unwittingly attests,

> Moi paren' snova vlip v durnye dela, podralsia, naglotalsia kakoi-to muti. On tak menia dostal–ia ego prognala, i ia khochu teper' takogo, kak Putin! [Pripev:] Takogo, kak Putin–polnogo sil, takogo kak Putin–chtoby *ne pil*, Takogo, kak Putin–chtob *ne obizhal*, takogo, kak Putin–chtob *ne ubezhal*.[30]
> (Singing Together)

Consonant with Putin's widespread reputation of ideal masculinity, by contrasting Putin with the presumably "average male," the lyrics reveal contemporary Russia's ongoing crisis in gender identity, especially men's disorientation and instability as vestiges of the blighted 1990s.

Media and celebrification

That not all Russians sang hosannas to VVP as a model of macho probity is clear from one blogger's vehement counter-version of the song's lyrics. Slyly interpolating some of Putin's less euphemistic vocabulary, it symptomizes the oppositional view, which enjoys appreciably narrower circulation,

> takogo kak putin nuzhno dushit'
> takogo kak putin nuzhno ubit'.
> takogo kak putin nuzhno mochit'.
> takogo kak putin nuzhno udavit'
> takogo kak putin nuzhno zastrelit'
> Takogo kak putin nuzhno ebat',
> takogo kak putin nuzhno strelyat',
> takogo kak putin nuzhno vzorvat',
> takogo kak putin nuzhno zakopat'
> (*bucovin68*, blogger 2008)

Such an irreverent attitude toward Russia's major contemporary icon, however, represented a minority attitude and could not be articulated on television or in the press, but only on the internet, which to this day remains the sole channel of communication relatively free of the Kremlin's control. As one commentator notes, Russians impatient with "the absence of criticism and debate on television" increasingly have turned to the internet, which the Russian (unlike the Chinese) government does not censor (Kovalyova 2009). For instance, a television contest in December 2008 intended to identify Russia's greatest historical figures inspired a website (www.badnameofrussia.ru) asking visitors to vote for public figures who are "the disgrace of Russia" [pozor Rossii]. By 3 December 2008, Putin reportedly topped the list with 18,155 votes – more than twice the number cast for the second most "disgraceful" figure, Boris Yeltsin.[31] Astonishingly frank comments by bloggers explain the reasons for their disgust with the former president and now prime minister.[32] Though clearly many Russians' celebrity hero, Putin is more controversial than suggested in other, more traditional forms of communication.

Yet, paradoxically, the Putin cult has benefited immeasurably from the internet and other technologies, which have documented his high-profile, media-conscious international and domestic activities. In fact, Putin is the first – and thus far the only – Russian head of state to realize the enormous potential of technology to promote a painstakingly elaborated image through its dissemination around the world. International access to Russian state-controlled television channels and to YouTube make accessible to millions of viewers in the West (and beyond) the "immediacy" of Putin as Russia's revered "icon in action," in scenarios that repeatedly confirm his status as an omnipotent, charismatic star. Moreover, items posted on his website and the tradition he established while president, of annually spending several hours in telephone dialogue with Russian citizens, who call in to pose questions, seek aid or advice, and complain about their problems, create the impression of a demotic leader invested in the everyday life of "his subjects" – all, of course, captured on camera. As prime minister, Putin has maintained this annual ritual, the continuity reinforcing the general conviction that he remains the chief power in the Kremlin.

In recent years photographers have accompanied Putin not only on his visits to war zones, factories, schools, museums, and cultural events, but also on his vacations in Siberia, where a bare-chested Putin fishing, riding, and climbing trees became immortalized as a sexual commodity when snapshots of his leisurely self flooded the internet (see Figure 1.2). Putin's increased sexualization in recent years via discarded shirts, rumors of liaisons with women less than half his age, and reports of his decisive action in the midst of allegedly dangerous situations have dramatically magnified his image as the post-Soviet exemplar of seductive, reassuring virility. Reassurance also derives from Putin's projection of a dispassionate, authoritative self-confidence in his recorded confrontations with foreign dignitaries and journalists, as well as Russia's incompetent regional managers and defanged oligarchs, such as Oleg Depraska, whom he recently humiliated in public for deviousness and lack of professional responsibility (2009) – to the delight of Russian television viewers and YouTube aficionados.

Putin's acquired sophistication in public relations may be measured by the contrast between his dilatory reaction to the Kursk disaster in 2000 and his handling of the blast at the Saiano-Sushenskaia hydroelectric plant in Siberia in 2009: his prompt personal visit to the site, his expressed concern for victims of the tragedy, and above all the video conference he organized to discuss the emergency reinforced his populist image, prompting bloggers to vent their anger not at the Kremlin, but at local authorities. In doing so, they imitated Putin's strategy of faulting regional administrators for problems that reflect national inadequacies. If retrograde in his attachment to sundry Soviet-era institutions and values, Putin could hardly be more "modern" in his exploitation of technology. No other world leader in the 2000s has matched his celebrification engineered through cyber-fication.

Lack as luster?

If, as one Western commentator observed, during the early 2000s "Putin's popularity [… was] the result of anti-politics […], non-engagement" (Lavelle 2003), after the 2004 election he grew markedly less laconic and more imperial. Indeed, by the second half of the 2000s, Putin's star status and his resultant self-confidence made him less passive and decidedly more authoritarian in front of the cameras. Tellingly, a former KGB master once described Putin as a "nonentity" (Toomey 2003), while the journalist Steve LeVine noted the "complicity of his inaction" in questions of crime (LeVine 2008: 64). Lack, in short, was (and perhaps remains) Putin's strong suit, his outstanding features comprising a stylistic anodyne impassiveness and above all a certain "emptiness"; even his contradictory pronouncements ("managed democracy," a strong [i.e. imperialist] yet humanistic Russia) erase one another.

Several years ago Georgii Satarov, a political analyst and former aide to Yeltsin, maintained, "Lack of a position is part of the political style and strategy for Putin."[33] Pollster Iurii Levada nicely summed up the dynamic when he characterized Putin as a "mirror in which everyone, communist or democrat, sees what he wants to see and what he hopes for" (White and McAllister 2003: 385). Indeed, Putin's ability to seem everything to everyone raises the question of what precisely he endorses or represents. Veterans are reassured by his announced regret for the loss of the Soviet Union and his adherence to many Soviet principles; representatives of the Church applaud his seeming commitment to Russian Orthodoxy; the intelligentsia and *Kulturarbeiter* appreciate his ideological and financial support of film, art, and literature as central to Russia's cultural position in the world, publicly displayed in ritualistic ceremonies during which Putin presents awards, congratulates successful figures, and even takes part in staged events; women thrill to his physical vigor and athleticism as well as his publicized speeches on International Women's Day; children reportedly find his regular visits to schools exciting; his telephone marathons with the public assure the "man on the street" that he can get a fair hearing and help from "the man in charge"; even animals (ranging from goats to fish), with whom Putin frequently has been photographed – feeding, stroking, or kissing them – must feel safeguarded by the apparently protective affection of the nation's leader.[34] In other words, Putin "gives the public what they want" – a guaranteed stratagem to gain popularity. Yet, apart from his iterated passion for a strong Russia and his hostility toward the United States (and, more recently, the United Kingdom), one would be hard put to define Putin's political allegiances and profoundly held beliefs.

The barrage of cultural objects and gestures designed to immortalize Putin attest the rich potential of his vacuity, which allows not only for the ascription of multiple traits and the projection of myriad desires onto his persona, but also for his transformation into an art object depicted from diverse perspectives – in such genres as the official portrait, graphics, photo collage, logo, greeting card, cartoon, handicrafts, sculpture, and internet caricatures. Moreover, the register of these visuals spans the gamut from solemnity and pomp to irony, playfulness, and satire. If, as Foucault contends, we should create ourselves as a work of art (Foucault 1984: 351), others perform that task for Putin ("svita igraet korolia" [literally, the entourage plays the king]) and by constantly maintaining the spotlight on his activities, statements, and mere presence at various functions, fortify his celebrity status as the nation's White Knight.

Visualizing VVP

Folklore genres honoring Putin included a sketch of his frowning, almost chinless face by Gavriil Lubnin, accompanied by the sort of school verses that traditionally treat Russia's famous (for instance, Lev Tolstoy) in a familiar, informal mode, such as the pseudo-naïve *chastushka* quatrain, "Krasivyi muzhik Volodia / Svityi iz krepkikh zhil / Ezdit v Moskve i khodit / A ran'she v Pitere zhil."[35] Another folk genre, Russian stacking or nesting dolls (*matryoshki*), which for almost a century functioned as portable national ideology primarily targeting tourists with a weakness for souvenirs, has "embodied" virtually all Russian and Soviet heads of state, as well as its cultural luminaries, and in this regard Putin was no exception. Nor were the VVP *matryoshki* exceptional. One of them merely featured a facsimile of his face atop the national colors, with "Rossiia" splashed across them below the two-headed eagle of the Russian empire that replaced the hammer and sickle after the demise of the Soviet Union (Figure 1.6). Banal and sketchily executed, during the early 2000s these *matryoshki* symbolically equating Putin with Russia nonetheless sold for 500 rubles/$17 on the Old Arbat.[36] That equation of country and its symbol partly explains the new century's Putinmania, for a glamorous, strong leader implies Russia's recovered identity as a world power with its *sui generis* allure.

Equally conventional though more revealing is the "official" portrait in oil of *Vladimir Putin, President of the Russian Federation* (2000) by Nikas Safronov (b. 8 April 1956), a "society painter" who shares Zurab Tsereteli's penchant for courting famous subjects in the world of international politics and entertainment.[37] Numerous copies of the portrait, with the original (costing 38,400 rubles/$1,280) exhibited at the art salon on Petrovka, overran offices and Moscow's largest bookstores (Figure 1.7). Unlike another, lesser-known portrait of Putin that Safronov painted the same year, this one captured a formally attired, solemn-faced Putin in a classic ruler pose, elevated above the background of his dominion, visible from a window behind him: the Kremlin and the Moscow River, winding into the distance alongside the vast expanses that merge with the sky ("infinite Russia").

Figure 1.6 One of many Putin *matryoshkas* on Moscow's Old Arbat during the early 2000s. Photo by Helena Goscilo.

The preponderance of various shades of blue – in iconography, a color associated with tranquility – infuses the portrait with calm reassurance, which Russians in fact attributed to their leader. In other words, the portrait consolidates the image of Putin as confident and capable ruler of a huge realm.

If this rendition simultaneously conveys the salient features of self-restraint and power associated with the president, Safronov's many other portraits of Putin sooner showcase the artist's fawning flights of fancy. Following the current fashion for recasting a sitter as a notable figure from the past,[38] Safronov variously reincarnated VVP as Napoleon on a rearing steed, with uplifted hand pointing, presumably, to the field of battle; as merchant (links with capitalism), cardinal (religious orthodoxy), youthful prince (imperial but romantic leader), and the sixteenth-century monarch Francis I, generous benefactor of the arts (Fleishman 2007a). Finally, Safronov's Cubist Putin implies the latter's modern/ist credentials as reformer, patron of culture, and so forth.

Analogies with historical rulers of empires likewise clearly operated in several sculptures of Putin, less obviously in that by St. Petersburg's Aleksandr Palmin, who declared that his bronze 10" Putin was not a memorial, but "a tribute" to "a historic figure" (Traynor 2001), than in a bust costing 22,032 rubles/$734 at the Salon on Varvarka gallery, modeled on ancient sculptures of Roman emperors

Figure 1.7 Nikas Safronov's rendition of the formal President Putin against the background of his vast empire. Courtesy of Nikas Safronov.

– moreover, in ancient ceremonial garb. And when not incarnating state power, VVP appeared in the "uniform" of a judo master, as in Tsereteli's huge bronze statue (2004) (Figure 1.8) and in a doctored photograph, hawked on the Old Arbat for 150 rubles/$5, of a stern Putin in a clinch with a faceless opponent – presumably alluding to VVP's readiness to "take anyone on." The 2008 DVD *Let's Learn Judo with Vladimir Putin*, as well as his "heroic" rescue of a television crew from an escaped Siberian tiger (Faulconbridge 2008), has "enhanced his macho image" (Walker 2008), emphasized by the camouflage and desert boots Putin sported in the taiga while performing his publicized "rescue" (Faulconbridge 2008).

More ambiguous, though a Kremlin bestseller, was the 2001 calendar by Dmitrii Vrubel' and Viktoriia Timofeeva *Dvenadtsat' nastroenii prezidenta* [The President's Twelve Moods], which bordered on caricature, made no effort to idealize Putin's face, and even captured a pouty, sullen VVP with huge, protruding lips. Similarly, the couple's *Putin i chernyi kvadrat* [Putin and Black Square] (2002) depicted Putin in a deliberately crude light evoking a huckster or thug in an ill-fitting suit.[39] And an unusual caricature on sale for 500 rubles/$17 on the Old Arbat condensed a fascinating complex of ominous references (Figure 1.9): Putin's lower body and ears are those of a dragon or serpent, à la Russian fairy-tale illustrations and iconography depicting the enemy in World War I and II; the truncated middle

Figure 1.8 Russia's No. 1 celebrity in bronze at the Zurab Tsereteli Art Gallery in Moscow; December 2004, photographed October 2005. Photo by Sergei Piatakov. Courtesy of RIA Novosti.

part of his body evokes typical folkloric images of Koshchei Bessmertnyi, who repeatedly seizes defenseless women and incarcerates them; on his head Putin wears the historical *Shapka Monomakha* that was recreated for his fiftieth birthday. While the woman gripped in his right fist probably alludes to Putin's masculinist reign and stranglehold on the country, the newspaper crumpled in his left suggests the media censorship characterizing his years in office. This far from flattering depiction overturns the homogenizing idealization of canonical Putin portraits.

Equally irreverent images focused on Putin's omnipotent ubiquity, satirizing the perceived conviction that "everything is Putin" and "Putin is our all." Thus in the series of witty caricatures titled *Putin Birthday Greetings* issued by polit. ru on 7 October 2004, which include VVP as Superman and medieval despot, one "greeting" features comprehensive putination in a domestic setting: Putin sits at a table reading the book *Putin*, while his dog Koni, the king and queen on the chessboard, the cactus, and the goldfish in a bowl all have VVP's face. Though realized in another medium, the same concept animates another series: the four photographs collected under the rubric *Rebiata s nashego dvora* [Kids from Our Block] (2004) by the subversive, hilariously parodic duo of Viacheslav Mizin and Aleksandr Shaburov, known as Sinie Nosy [Blue Noses] (Figure 1.10). A typical Soviet group photograph of youths united solely by living on the same street is transformed into a series of casually dressed, close-knit male bodies, each topped by Putin's face. Exposing the political edge of the visuals, the subtitle reads "Bezlikie rossiiane v maskakh prezidenta RF Putina, kotoromu oni investirovali svoe doverie" (*Sinie Nosy/Blue Noses* 2006: 160–1) [Common[40] Russians in masks of President Putin, whom they have invested with their trust]. Likewise criticizing

Figure 1.9 An impudent caricature of Putin's wriggly power, sold on the Old Arbat in the early 2000s. Photo by Helena Goscilo.

unthinking glorification of Putin and other cultural icons, a kitschy, colorful, highly controversial "montage" titled *Gori-gori moia svecha*,[41] produced by Blue Noses the same year, bears the subtitle "Tri glavnykh polozhitel'nykh geroia rossiiskoi gosudarstvennoi mifologii – poet Pushkin, Iisus Khristos i prezident RF Putin – ne daiut pogasnut' sveche russkoi dukhovnosti"[42] (*Sinie Nosy/Blue Noses* 2006: 16–17) and depicts a haloed Christ holding a lit candle, flanked by a T-shirted Pushkin with a cigarette lighter and Putin in a bright red T-shirt warming his hand at the candle's flame (Figure 1.11).[43] Indeed, VVP's sacred status, like Pushkin's and Christ's, is protected by the powers that be in Russia, and those criticizing him, religion, and specifically Russian culture do so at their own considerable risk.

The painter Aleksandr Shednov, known as Shurik, learned as much when he attempted to beam a portrait of Putin onto the main administrative building in his home town of Voronezh on 12 June 2009 – Russian Independence Day. Charged with inappropriate behavior after his arrest and interrogation by the FSB, Shednov acknowledged that the portrait constituted a protest against Putin's return to the Kremlin for a third presidential term. Posted on the internet, the image consists of Putin's face superimposed on the body of a woman with long dark hair, in a tight, low-cut dress, huge hoop earrings in her ears, her coquettish pose matching the coyness of the words in the upper left corner supposedly spoken by him/her: "… oi, nu ia dazhe ne znaiu … tretii prezidentskii? … nu eto uzh slishkom, khotia Bog

Figure 1.10 All are Putin, having submitted to the cult and united in shared idolatry, as envisioned by Blue Noses in the series *Rebiata s nashego dvora* [Kids from Our Block]; 2004. Courtesy of Aleksandr Shaburov of Blue Noses.

Figure 1.11 The sacred trinity of contemporary Russian culture, in a multi-media work by Blue Noses titled *Gori-gori, moia svecha* [Go On Burning, My Life-Candle]; 2004. Courtesy of Aleksandr Shaburov of Blue Noses.

liubit 'Troitsy'" (Stewart 2009).[44] Shednov's aesthetic in this instance coincided with that of Blue Noses.

Like most works by Blue Noses, those portraying Putin ironize dogma and cultural conventions; their incendiary potential accounts for protests by conservative groups and for the artists' consequent reputation as hooligans. Reactions to Blue Noses' polemical depictions of VVP peaked in 2006, when Russian customs officials at Sheremet'evo Airport confiscated, among other items, their series of photographs titled *Maski-shou* [Mask Show] (2000) being exported for a gallery exhibit in London. Collating images of Bin Laden, Bush, and Putin in underwear cavorting on a couch, the works elicited outrage at their "derogatory manner" of portraying "heads of state." The widely reported incident paralleled the scandal around Vladimir Sorokin's novel *Goluboe salo* [Blue Lard],[45] and leaves no doubts that Russian airport officials, though hardly affronted by the trivialization of Bin Laden and Bush, were outraged by a less than respectful concept of their leader.

The most striking aspect of the Putiniana generated during the 2000s, however, is neither its genuflection nor its iconoclasm, but the sheer wealth and diversity of Putin images, proliferating at an accelerated rate as the decade has worn on. Only time will reveal whether that trend will abate or continue to flourish under the new president. Given Putin's hardy reputation for unique charisma, as high-powered self-appointed prime minister he has inspired several additions to the current museum of Putiniana, as instanced in the 2009 portrait of amber and pebbles presented by Yantarny Dom [Amber House] company at the Lenexpro exhibition center in St. Petersburg (Figure 1.12). And in the meantime, in January 2009 Putin turned the tables by assuming the role of artist and submitting his (doctored) painting to a charity auction of art works by celebrities in his home town. Now in its third year, the auction featured as its theme a story by Nikolai Gogol' intended to mark the two hundredth anniversary of the writer's birth, and required that each painting represent each letter of the Russian alphabet. Putin's simple watercolor of a window with red-patterned curtains, titled *Uzor* [Pattern], "will go for the most," predicted Nadezhda Anfalova, chief artist at the auction, "The buyers look at the name" (O'Flynn 2009). Indeed, at the auction in the Grand Hotel Europe that followed the exhibit, the painting, allegedly executed in twenty minutes and "filled in" by a professional artist, sold for the equivalent of $1.15 million, making it "the most expensive painting sold in Russia" ("Russian Prime Minister ..." 2009). Natal'ia Kurnikova, owner of Moscow's Our Artists art gallery, admitted that she purchased it for its uniqueness, "This picture shows an interesting side of a prominent personality. Maybe it will be the first and the last picture of its kind" (Titova 2009). Clearly, the glamorous Putin brand still sells and rules.

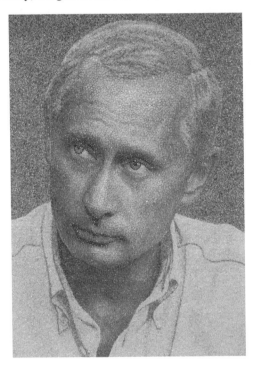

Figure 1.12 An earnest Putin in amber and pebble pieces, exhibited by the Yantarny Dom Company in St. Petersburg at the seventeenth Junmex International Jewelry Forum; 2009. Photo by Aleksei Danichev, courtesy of RIA Novosti.

Notes

1 Cited in Osipovich (2004).
2 Cited in Traynor (2001). Ivchenko is a sculptor in St. Petersburg.
3 From the blog appended to "Tainstvennaia ..." (2002).
4 Simon Osborne "We Love Putin: Meet the Russian President's Teenage Fan Club." *Independent* (21 July 2007).
5 My gratitude to Serguei Oushakine for generously sharing numerous Putin visuals with me over the years. A short, preliminary version of this chapter appeared in Russian as "VVP kak *objet d'art*," *Neprikosnovennyi zapas* 62, no. 6 (2008). Available online at: http://magazines.russ.ru/nz/2008/6/go8-pr.html (accessed 27 December 2009).
6 BBC correspondent Steven Eke has speculated that Putin's appointment of two former Kremlin aides "suggests he wants to strengthen his powers at the expense of the new presidency" (Eke 2008). Putin's live three-hour question-and-answer session on 4 December 2008, which continued the tradition of his call-in show as president, suggested that he is "the man Russians should look to in tough times," particularly since Medvedev has not orchestrated such exchanges with the public. Asked during the show what he loved most, Putin, predictably, answered, "Russia" (Isachenkov 2008b).
7 Sculptor Zurab Tsereteli and artist Takhir Salakhov, as, respectively, President and Vice President of the Russian Academy of Art; and Nikita Mikhalkov as President of the Russian Cultural Foundation, trailed by Albert Charkin, Rector of the Repin St. Petersburg State Academic Institute of Art, Sculpture, and Architecture. The institute falls under the authority of the Academy of Fine Arts, headed by Zurab Tsereteli.
8 The letter, published in *Rossiiskaia Gazeta*, prompted an instant disclaimer from those it purported to represent; 775 cultural "workers," led by Marietta Chudakova, sent their own appeal to Putin, criticizing the foursome's letter, "Takoe obrashchenie brosaet ten' ne tol'ko na tekh, kto ego podpisal, no i na Vas kak prezidenta, za gody pravleniia kotorogo vosstanovilis', k sozhaleniiu, mnogie proiavleniia stol' kharakternogo dlia sovetskikh vremen kul'ta liubogo kremlevskogo vlastitelia" (Chudakova 2007) [Such an appeal casts a shadow not only on those who signed it, but also on you as President, in the course of whose rule, unfortunately, have appeared many signs of the cult of any and all Kremlin rulers so characteristic of Soviet times].
9 Stephen White and Ian McAllister cover some of the same terrain and rely on the same sources, but only up to 2003 (White and McAllister 2003).
10 Bransten (2002), citing a report in *Pravda*.
11 Under Putin, the FSB has enjoyed enormous power, unhindered in its coercive, intimidating, and obstructionist activities, such as raiding offices of media and businesses, threatening voters, denying access to security archives, and so forth. See the series of articles in the *New York Times* punningly titled "Kremlin Rules," by Clifford J. Levy (Levy 2008a, 2008b).
12 In fact, in 2003 Putin presented Viacheslav Tikhonov, who played the cool-headed Soviet double agent (Stirlitz) operating in Nazi Germany during World War II in the TV series *Semnadtsat' mgnovenii vesny* [Seventeen Moments of Spring] (1973) with the Order of Service to the State, third degree, commending the actor for having shaped an entire generation of Soviet youth. The recent parody of *Semnadtsat'* ... by Marius Balthans/Weisberg, titled *Gitler Kaput!* (2008), reportedly prompted Communists in St. Petersburg to request that the Ministry of Culture prevent the film from opening in theaters, but without success (Barry 2008).
13 The extent to which the Kremlin orchestrated the Putin cult is impossible to determine.
14 According to several sources, rumors – a mainstay of Moscow life and journalism – indicate that the song was generated by Kremlin propaganda, for no stores carried the record, radio stations were ignorant of its provenance, and a promoter of Singing Together (a faceless duo until the song caught on) is a press secretary at the Russian Supreme Court ("The Putin Cult" 2007).

15 Printed in 1,000 copies, the calendar apparently became the most sought-after Christmas gift in the Kremlin that year. The husband-and-wife team of Dmitry Vrubel' and Viktoriia Timofeeva used photographs to produce Putin's face, varying in mood according to the month. The President's office reportedly bought the original of the calendar's cover (Owen 2001) and an exhibition titled *Putin's Twelve Moods* was arranged in downtown Moscow (Sidlin 2001). Capitalizing on his widely advertised reputation as a martial arts expert, in 2008 Putin released an instructional judo DVD, *Let's Learn Judo with Vladimir Putin*, which indubitably bolstered his public persona of intrepid "fighter" endowed with rigor and self-control. See www.guardian.co.uk/world/2008/oct/07/russia1 (accessed 23 August 2009).

16 *Ot pervogo litsa* [First Person] (2000), Putin's quasi-(auto)biography in interviews, also came out in a sizable run; a biography (2003) printed in 200,000 copies by the Lanrusinvest holding company was distributed by the publishers for free to the Russian public (BBC Monitoring 2003b). Among the ever-increasing Russian volumes devoted to VVP are Roi Medvedev's *Vladimir Putin: Chetyre goda v Kremle* [Vladimir Putin: four years in the Kremlin] and the collection titled *Chetyre goda s Putinym* [Four years with Putin], both issued by Vremia publishers in 2004. See also the irreverent two-volume collection of reports by the Kremlin correspondent Andrei Kolesnikov, *Ia Putina videl!* [I Saw Putin!] and *Menia Putin videl!* [Putin Saw Me!] (Moscow: EKSMO 2005), the titles unambiguously evoking notorious socialist realist paintings of schoolchildren and adults beatified through having seen Stalin.

17 The site, with its URL signaling Putin's Soviet-era allegiances, still exists, its owner now Prime Minister instead of President. It contains photos of a physically active Putin (occasionally topless), a family photo album, and two shots of his Labrador Koni, who figured in ads for his second presidential campaign.

18 This scenario recalls the public image of Stalin, whom propaganda portrayed as tirelessly working in the Kremlin, even at night, on behalf of the people of the USSR. See, for example, the poster by V. Govorkov, *O kazhdom iz nas zabotitsia Stalin v Kremle* [Stalin in the Kremlin is concerned about each of us] (1940). Aleksandr Solzhenitsyn ridicules this image in the eighteenth chapter of *V kruge pervom* [The first circle].

19 Astute enough to realize that popularity increases power, Putin reportedly monitored his public image on television on a daily basis and was adept at using the media, especially television, to foster his persona of a self-confident and reliable national leader. Manifestly, he was far from indifferent to Russians' perception of him.

20 In a highly critical item on Putin, Albats referred to that presidential election as a contest "between those who love Putin more than life and those who love him not quite that much" (Albats 2003).

21 According to Marshall Goldman, "Russian state control over energy assets rose from 10 per cent in 2000 to 50 per cent in 2007" (Goldman 2008).

22 On the historical and symbolic significance of the Cap, see Kollmann (2008).

23 The estimated percentage differs, depending on the source: for example Glasser cites 25 percent (Glasser 2003); Kasparov, 50 percent (Kasparov 2003). According to Ol'ga Kryshtanovskaia, Russia's premier specialist in scholarly study of the elite, during Putin's tenure military officers and the FSB (formerly KGB) leadership have accumulated substantial wealth, including shares of ownership in Russia's biggest companies (LeVine 2008: 5).

24 The words uncannily recall George Bush's gushing confession of having looked into Putin's eyes and recognized his inner worth.

25 Avi Abrams is the founder and editor of Dark Roasted Blend, a site teeming with irreverent images and much more.

26 Other developments under Putin susceptible to such an interpretation include the rise of the FSB, the elimination of a free/alternate media, Putin's iterated emphasis on the need for a strong, nationalistic Russia, the reprisal of the Soviet national anthem and

classes devoted to military strategy at schools, and the policy introduced several years ago of paying neighbors to spy and report on one another.

27 In fact, it is surprising that Tsereteli has not followed the example of Evgenii Vutetich, whose colossal monument of Stalin was completed in 1952.

28 Available online at: www.youtube.com/watch?v=ZIPCAI55JCc (accessed 13 October 2008). The numerous Putin videos on YouTube include "Putin 'the legend,'" "Terminator 2 (Putin)," and a rich assortment of often hilarious parodies.

29 The perceived resemblance between Putin and the elf from the film *Harry Potter and the Chamber of Secrets* triggered an impassioned protest from Putin's staunch defenders, who felt offended by what they denounced as a vulgar attempt to trivialize a "world leader." In fact, a Moscow law firm reportedly planned to sue the makers of the film. See Karush (2003); Smith (2003), who reported that in a BBC poll more than 7,000 stated that Dobby looked like Putin; and the sly illustration by Aleksei Merinov in *Putinki* (2004: 70).

30 Emphasis added, HG. "My guy got into some bad deal again, got into a fight, snorted some junk. / I've had it with him, I kicked him out, and now I want someone like Putin! [Refrain:] Someone like Putin, who's really strong, someone like Putin, who *won't* drink, / Someone like Putin, who *won't* do me wrong, someone like Putin, who *won't* run off." For a translation of the entire song, see Leeds (2002).

31 See www.badnameofrussia.ru (accessed 17 January 2009).

32 See www.badnameofrussia.ru/Putin-Vladimir.html#comments (accessed 17 January 2009). What motivated those who established the website (congratulated for their "daring" [smelost'] by several bloggers) and whether the numbers genuinely reflect visitors' responses is uncertain, but there can be no doubt that such a phenomenon could not appear in print, on television, or on the radio.

33 Ol'ga Kryshtanovskaia noted, in the dispassionate tone that is her trademark, "Putin is accused of lacking an ideology, but ordinary citizens themselves do not have any." Quoting a politician who claimed "Putin is neither red nor blue [...]. He is colorless," she contended, "That is what so many Russians like about the president" (Kryshtanovskaia 2003).

34 For an insightful, witty analysis of Putin's relationship with animals, see Tatiana Mikhailova, "His Family and Other Animals," unpublished paper.

35 The verses about Tolstoy run as follows, "Graf Lev Nikolaevich Tolstoi, / Pisatel' dvorianskogo klassa, / Khodil po derevne bosoi, / Ne kushal ni rybu ni miasa. / Zhena ego, Sofia Tolstaia, / Naprotiv, liubila poest'. / Ona ne khodila bosaia, / Khranila dvorianskuiu chest'. / I plakal velikii pisatel' / I kushal varenyi oves, / I roman ego *Voskresenie* / Chitat' nevozmozhno bez slez. / Ego inuiu knigu pro Annu / Ty na noch' ee ne chitai. / Ot zhizni takoi, ot paskudnoi / Popala ona pod tramvai," etc. My thanks to Nadezhda Azhgikhina and the group of women journalists who recited these verses for me many years ago.

36 Conversion into dollars of all prices in rubles reflect the exchange rates at the time of the relevant works' appearance on the market.

37 Safronov's flattering portraits include those of Yuri Luzhkov, Alla Pugacheva, and Nikita Mikhalkov (who on Safronov's website lauds the artist's Talent [sic]), many foreign heads of state, as well as George Clooney, Clint Eastwood, Mick Jagger, Sophia Loren, and Madonna.

38 See the various photo exhibits of Vladislav Mamyshev, known as Vlad Monroe, and the *Private Collection* of Ekateriana Rozhdestvenskaia, as well as the Polish Michał Pasich's *Pejzaż z portretami* [Landscape with portraits] (Kraków: The Czartoryski Museum, Conspero Foundation, 2006) and the American Eve Sussman's *89 Seconds at Alcázar* (2004), inspired by Diego Velázquez's *Las Meniñas*.

39 White and McAllister report that Putin had been called "a dark horse," "an unidentified object," and "a Malevich black square" (2003: 386).

40 *Bezlikie* would be better translated as "faceless" or "anonymous."

41 Translated as *The Candle of Our Life* (*Sinie Nosy/Blue Noses* 2006: 16), the title literally means *Go On Burning, My Life-Candle*.

42 "The three main positive heroes of Russian state mythology – the poet Pushkin, Jesus Christ, and President Putin – will never let the candle of the Russian spirit go out" (English text edited for accuracy and idiomatic usage, HG).

43 Part of the first Russian Biennale, this work was included in a criminal complaint against Marat Guelmen, the gallery owner who regularly exhibits their works, as well as that of their "mentor," Oleg Kulik, and who is perceived by some as the "ultimate agent provocateur" (FitzGerald 2006b).

44 "Oh, well, I don't know … a third presidential term? … well, that's a bit much, though God does love the 'Trinity'/three's lucky."

45 The gallerist Marat Guelman, a former political consultant for both Yeltsin and Putin, has been attacked verbally and physically for exhibiting what may be interpreted as contemporary anti-religious and anti-establishment art.

Bibliography

Abdullaev, N. (2002) "Notes from Moscow: The Bronze Chekist," *Transitions Online*. Available online at: www.tol.cz/look/TOLnew/tolprint.tpl?IdLanguage=1&IdPublicati on=4&NrIssue=38&NrSection=17&NrArticle=7395&ST1=body&ST_T1=letter&ST_ AS1=1&ST_max=1 (accessed 26 April 2005).

Albats, Y. (2003) "The West's Favorite 'Democrat,'" *Washington Post*, 24 Sept.

Alekseev, A. (2007) "VIP-parad 2007," *Kommersant* 241, no. 3817, 28 Dec. Available online at: www.kommersant.ru/doc.aspx?DocsID=840552 (accessed 5 May 2008).

Arkhangelsky, A. (2007) "The Artists' Petition," *Russia Profile*, 29 Oct. Available online at: www.russiaprofile.org/page.php?pageid=Politics&articleid=al (accessed 30 October 2007).

Aron, L. (2006) "What Does Putin Want?" *Commentary*, Dec.

Barry, E. (2008) "A Spoof Stars a Bumbling Spy, but Many Russian Moviegoers Aren't Laughing," *New York Times*, 22 Sept. Available online at: www.nytimes.com/2008/09/22/ world/europe/22iht-22spies.16359400.html (accessed 26 October 2008).

BBC Monitoring (2003a) "Russia's Putin 'No Longer in Control' of Yukos Affair–Pundit," Ekho Moskvy, 3 Oct.

——. (2003b) "Russian Firm to Distribute Putin's Biography Free at Home and Abroad," NTV, Moscow, 7 Oct.

——. (2003c) "Chocolate Putin Goes on Sale in Moscow Shops," 16 Nov.

Birch, D. (2002) "Putin's Popularity Reaches High Note," *Baltimore Sun*, 3 Sept.

——. (2003) "A Return of the People's Palace," *Baltimore Sun*, 11 May.

bucovin68 (2008) [blogger]. Available online at: www.youtube.com/comment_servlet?all_ comments=1&v=DlU3y5N1hSI (accessed 10 June 2010).

Bransten, J. (2002) "From Pop Songs to Vegetables, is a Putin Personality Cult Emerging?" *RFE/RL*, Prague, 9 Sept.

Chudakova, M. *et al.* (2007), "Otkrytoe pis'mo deiatelei kul'tury Vladimiru Putinu," Ekho Moskvy, 26 Oct. Available online at: http://echo.msk.ru/doc/622.html (accessed 31 October 2007).

Eke, S. (2008) "Putin Keeps Powerful Kremlin Aides," BBC News, 13 May. Available online at: http://newsvote.bbc.co.uk/mpapps/pagetools/print/news.bbc.co.uk/2/hi/ europe/7397809.stm (accessed 17 November 2008).

Faulconbridge, G. (2008) "Putin Saves TV Film Crew from Siberian Tiger: Reports. Former KGB Spy is Shown Striding through Forest in Camouflage, Desert Boots," Canada.com,

1 Sept. Available online at: www.canada.com/components/print.aspx?id=ce32d329–325e-44f0–9d54-fc288dfeb42@sponsor= (accessed 19 November 2008).

FitzGerald, N. (2006a) "The Pranksters of the Russian Art Scene," *International Herald Tribune*, 25 Oct. Available online at: www.iht.com/articles/2006/10/23/features/bluenose. php (accessed 1 September 2008).

—. (2006b) "Moscow Artists Strike a Rich Portrait Vein." *International Herald Tribune*, 27 Nov. Available online at: www.iht.com/bin/print.php?id=3684183 (accessed 13 March 2007).

Fleishman, J. (2007a) "Painter Has Visions of Russian, Hollywood Royalty," *Los Angeles Times*, 31 March.

—. (2007b) "Creative Expressions," *Columbia Missourian*, 21 Apr. Available online at: www.columbiamissourian.com/stories/2007/04/21/creative-expressions/print/ (accessed 12 January 2008).

Foucault, M. (1984) *The Foucault Reader*, ed. P. Rabinow, New York: Pantheon Books.

Frolov, V. (2008) "Undermining Medvedev: Western Leaders Still Ponder Who Directs Russia's Foreign Policy," *Russia Profile*, 5 Aug. Available online at: www.russiaprofile. org/page.php?pageid=International&articleid=a1217946717 (accessed 14 August 2008).

Glasser, S. (2003) "KGB Veterans Bring Tradecraft to Elected Office," *Washington Post*, 24 Sept.

Gokhman, M. (2002) "President Ubiquitous," *Moscow News*, 12–18 Feb.

Goldman, M. (2008) "Petrostate: Putin, Power, and the New Russia," *Kennan Institute Meeting Report* 26, 2. Washington, DC: Kennan Institute, Woodrow Wilson Center.

Goscilo, H. (2008) "VVP kak *objet d'art*," *Neprikosnovennyi zapas* 62, no. 6. Available online at: http://magazines.russ.ru/nz/2008/6/go8-pr.html (accessed 27 December 2009).

Isachenkov, V. (2008a) "Putin's Wife Writes Revealing Book," *Moscow AP*, 5 Sept.

—. (2008b) "Putin Hosts Live Q&A Broadcast in Russia," *Moscow AP*, 4 Dec.

Jack, A. (2002) "The Empire Strikes Back: Putin Cult Reaches New Levels," *Financial Times*, 12 Oct.

Karush, S. (2003) "Moviegoers Agree: House Elf from *Harry Potter* Looks Like Putin," *Moscow AP*, 31 Jan.

Kasparov, G. (2003) "KGB State," *Wall Street Journal*, 18 Sept.

Kollmann N. S. (2008) "The Cap of Monomakh," in V. A. Kivelson and J. Neuberger (eds) *Picturing Russia: Explorations in Visual Culture*, New Haven and London: Yale University Press, pp. 38–41.

Kots, A. (2007) "Nikita Mikhalkov – Viktoru Erofeevu: Kto tebe skazal, chto ia ratuiu za kul't lichnosti?" *Komsomol'skaia Pravda*, 27 Oct. Available online at: www.kp.ru/ daily/23992/77033/print (accessed 31 October 2007).

Kovalyova, A. (2009) "Will Internet Kill the Television Star?" *Russia Profile*, 28 May. Available online at: www.russiaprofile.org/page.php?pageid=Culture+%26+Living& articleid=a1243532864&print=yes (accessed 10 June 2009).

Kryshtanovskaia, O. (2003) "Mirror of the Nation: What the Latest Polls Reveal about President Putin," *Vedomosti*, 30 Sept.

Latynina, Y. (2003) "St. Pete's Criminal-Business-Political Elite," *Moscow Times*, 4 June.

Lavelle, P. (2003) "Putin's Popularity and Anti-Politics," Pravda.ru, 4 Sept. Available online at: http://english.pravda.ru/mailbox/22/99/391/10831_Putin.html (accessed 12 December 2009).

Leeds, L. (2002) "Pop Song 'Just Like Putin,'" 19 Sept. Available online at: www.lLeeds@post. com (accessed 25 September 2002).

LeVine, S. (2008) *Putin's Labyrinth: Spies, Murder, and the Dark Heart of the New Russia*, New York: Random House.

Levy, C. J. (2008a) "Kremlin Rules: It Isn't Magic: Putin Opponents Vanish From TV," *New York Times*, 3 June. Available online at: www.nytimes.com/2008/06/03/world/europe/03russia.html?ei= (accessed 3 June 2008).

— . (2008b) "Kremlin Rules: Nationalism of Putin's Era Veils Sins of Stalin's," *New York Times*, 27 Nov. Available online at: www.nytimes.com/2008/11/27/world/europe/27archives.html (accessed 27 November 2008).

MacKinnon, M. (2002) "A 'Personality Cult' Bedevils Wary Putin," *Globe and Mail*, 27 Sept.

Marat Guelman Gallery and State Tretyakov Gallery (2006) *Sinie Nosy/Blue Noses*, Moscow: Marat Guelman Gallery, Galerie Volker Diehl, Tomaso Renoldi Bracco Contemporary Art Vision band; State Tretyakov Gallery, Marat Guelman Foundation.

Myers, S. L. (2007) "Youth Groups Created by Kremlin Serve Putin's Cause," *New York Times*, 8 July.

"Nikas Safaronov" (2008) Peoples.ru. Available online at: www.peoples.ru/art/painter/safronov/index.html (accessed 3 May 2008).

O'Flynn, K. (2002) "Picking the Perfect Present for Putin," *Moscow Times*, 7 Oct.

— . "Putin, the Artist?" (2009) *St. Petersburg Times*, 16 Jan. Available online at: www.sptimes.ru/index.php?action_id=100&story_id=28028 (accessed 16 January 2009).

Osipovich, A. (2004) "Looks Like Celebrity," *Moscow Times*, 12 March. Available online at: http://context.themoscowtimes.com/print.php?aid=131187 (accessed 12 February 2005).

Owen, R. (2001) "President Becomes a Calendar Pin-Up," *The Times*, 5 Dec.

"Pis'mo Rossiiskoi akademii khudozhestv Vladimiru Putinu" (2007) *Rossiiskaia Gazeta*,16 Oct. Available online at: www.rg.ru/2007/10/16/pismo.html (accessed 31 October 2007).

"'Poiushchie vmeste': nash udel–bytovukha," *Ezhenedel'nik Sobesednik*. Available online at: www.sobsednik.ru/weekly/147/issue/4032.phtml (accessed 3 April 2007).

"The Putin Cult: Political Techno, Fan Clubs, and the Internet" (2007) *Perspectives on the New Russia*, 7 July. Available online at: http://putinwatcher.blogspot.com/2007/07/putin-cult-political-techno-fan-clubs.html (accessed 12 July 2008).

Putinki: Kratkii sbornik izrechenii prezidenta (pervyi srok) (2004) Illustrations by Aleksei Merinov, Moscow: Ekho Buk.

"Putin's Last Love: Foreign Actress Makes Sensational Confession" (2003) 31 July. Available online at: http://english.pravda.ru/society/stories/31-07-2003/3442-wilson-0 (accessed 4 August 2003).

Reut, A. (2002) "Putin on a Cake, on a Carpet, in a Book," *Gazeta*, 7 Oct. Available online at: www.gzt.ru/print.gzt?rubric=english&id=18050000000002986 (accessed 7 August 2004).

Rojek, C. (2001) *Celebrity*, London: Reaktion Books.

Rozhin, A. (ed.) (2000) *Contemporary Russian Artists*, [ed. of English text, G. Tchemakova] Moscow: Mikhail Afanasyev & Helen Lavrinenko, pp. 10–19.

"Russia: Putin Romance Rumors Keep Public Riveted" (2008) Radio Free Europe/Radio Liberty, 18 Apr. Available online at: www.rferl.org/content/article/1109593.html (accessed 16 June 2008).

"Russian Prime Minister Vladimir Putin's Sketch Sells for $1.15 million at Auction" (2009), 21 Feb. Available online at: www.artdaily.org/section/news/index.asp?int_sec=2&int_new=28492&int_modo=2 (accessed 21 February 2009). "Russian Textile

Mill Making Putin Tapestries" (2003) TVS (Moscow), reported by BBC Monitoring, 8 June.

Shchuplov, A. (2002) "Put a Sock in it. Vladimir Vladimirovich Putin Has Become a Folk Art Hero," *Rossiiskaia Gazeta*, 11 Oct.

Sidlin, M. (2001) "Decorate a Room with Putin's Portrait," *Nezavisimaia Gazeta*, 4 Dec.

Smith, L. (2003) "Spell of Trouble for Dobby," *Evening Standard*, 28 Jan. Available online at: www.thisislondon.co.uk/news/article-3113851-spell-of-trouble-for-dobby.do (accessed 28 January 2003).

Stewart, W. (2009) "The Portrait of Vladimir Putin as a Woman Which Got Artists Arrested by Secret Service," *Daily Mail*, 17 June. Available online at: www.dailymail.co.uk/news/worldnews/article-1193430/Artist-arrested-secret-service-portraying-Vladimir-Putin-woman.html (accessed 11 November 2009).

Suyetenko, L. (2002) "Singing Together: They Want One Like Putin" 12 Dec, trans. Vera Solovieva. Available online at: http://english.pravda.ru/main/18/90/362/4254_Putin.html (accessed 4 January 2003).

"Tainstvennaia pop-gruppa poet osanny Putinu" (2002) Translation from *Daily Telegraph*, 28 Aug. Available online at: http://Cremlin.ru/comments/00068.html (accessed 4 January 2003).

Titova, I. (2009) "Novice Painter Putin Fetches $1.1 Million for First Work," *St. Petersburg Times*, 20 Jan. Available online at: www.sptimes.ru/index.php?action_id=2&story_id=28042 (accessed 1 November 2009).

Toomey, C. (2003) "A President's Private Passions: Revealing Portraits of Vladimir Putin," *Sunday Times*, 6 Apr.

Traynor, I. (2001) "Russia Starts to Make a Legend," MSNBC.com, 11 March.

Volonikhin, I. (2002) "Russian TV Shows Ingush Village That Named its Main Street After Putin," TVS (Moscow), reported by BBC Monitoring, 10 Oct.

Walker, S. (2008) "Let's Learn Judo with Vladimir Putin," *Independent*, 8 Oct. Available online at: www.independent.co.uk/news/world/europe/lets-learn-judo-with-vladimir-putin-954578.html (accessed 2 November 2008).

Walsh, N. P. (2002a) "Putin Turns 007 in a New Thriller Novel," *Observer*, 14 July.

—— . (2002b) "Monica's Back – and This Time She's Stalking the Kremlin," *Guardian*, 18 Sept.

—— . (2002c) "Birthday Gift for Putin Casts Autocratic Shadow," *Observer*, 6 Oct.

—— . (2004) "Putin Angry at History Book Slur," *Guardian*, 15 Jan.

White, G. L. (2003) "The Secret of Putin's Success," *Wall Street Journal*, 5 Dec.

White, S. and McAllister, I. (2003) "Putin and His Supporters," *Europe-Asia Studies* 55, no. 3 (May): 383–99.

Wines, M. (2003) "Putin, Dobby and the Axis of Weirdness," *New York Times*, 2 Feb.

2 The mistress of Moscow

A case of corporate celebrity

Michelle Kuhn (University of Pittsburgh)

For the last decade the infamous Elena Baturina, one of the world's richest women (reportedly worth US$3.1 billion ["The World's Billionaires"]), has played a decisive role in changing the face of post-Soviet Moscow. Sole owner and president of the Moscow-based construction monopoly Inteko and wife of Mayor Yuri Luzhkov, Baturina enjoys not only a privileged role in the capital's recent urban development, but also relentless media attention owing to the many scandals surrounding her business dealings. As one of Moscow's most hated public figures, Baturina continues to attract the press, but has yet to be examined analytically within the framework of Russia's current boom in glamorous celebrities.

Russia's only female billionaire, the oligarchess occupies a position that simultaneously reinforces and challenges traditional gender values (on the contradictory politics of glamour and gender as applied by Kseniia Sobchak, see the Introduction). Baturina's business success derives from the political advantage of being married to Luzhkov. The power couple tag-teams its way past the competition: Luzhkov sets up the conditions for Baturina to secure contracts and execute demolitions and construction.[1] Commenting on Luzhkov's role in the husband–wife team, one critic has pointed out, "The mayor's office hands out building licenses" (Arnold 2007). In a city where bureaucratic red tape and arbitrary mandates ultimately make or break deals, the Mayor, dubbed the Master of Moscow, has served as indispensable insurance, without which Inteko, initially a manufacturer of plastic consumer goods, could not have expanded and consolidated its dominance within the construction industry[2] on the capital's mega-projects. The public and highly publicized economic benefits of Baturina's conjugal relations have repeatedly landed Baturina on the pages of newspapers and magazines, which also carry her repeated dismissal of allegations of nepotism.

Indeed, Baturina consistently asserts that she merely receives benefits guaranteed equally to all Russian businesspeople.[3] Projecting confidence in her fair business practices, she presents her successes as deriving from her exceptional business skills. She is indeed a rare creature – the only woman operating in a male market to have consolidated such a lucrative business empire. While enjoying the professional benefits of her marriage to Luzhkov, Baturina cultivates the image of a strong, independent woman whose business acumen has enabled her to break through the glass ceiling. Blogs and open internet forums show that this persona has garnered the interest of some "everywomen" aspiring to enter the business world. In the eyes of average Russian women who view her as a corporate idol, Baturina enjoys the status of a self-empowered feminist role model.

Baturina's protests against sundry allegations have themselves become a kind of meta-news, functioning as the story behind front page photographs and trumping the original news items detailing her latest business contracts or the price tags of her outings in conspicuous consumption. The *Forbes Russia* scandal of late 2006 offers an eloquent example. The magazine's December cover story detailed Baturina's rapid accumulation of wealth and her future plans for Inteko once Luzhkov stepped down as mayor, as was his announced plan prior to June 2007.[4] Objecting to a purportedly slanderous misrepresentation on the magazine cover of a statement by Baturina, Inteko lawyers insisted that *Forbes Russia* pull the story. The magazine's Russian editor, Maksim Kashulinskii, refused, but the German company, Axel Springer, the publisher holding license for *Forbes Russia*, acceded to her lawyers' demands and initially pulled the entire issue rather than simply emending the cover – a far less costly solution. Though Axel Springer later changed its decision and published the piece with a different cover, by then the story had already become a major media controversy. As Ekho Moskvy radio station editor-in-chief, Aleksei Venediktov, commented, the events ultimately strengthened Baturina's domestic reputation (Osborn 2006). The scandal not only increased her visibility, but Axel Springer's submission to her demand also seemed to confirm the formidable dimensions of her power, scoring her a victory on the international scale. The high-profile tug of war elicited USA *Forbes*' criticism of its Russian magazine for succumbing to money's censorship, thereby demonstrating the lack of freedom of the press in Russia. The parent magazine labeled Baturina's victory a battle in the war of the Russian press's freedom of speech.[5]

A corporate star is born: when money leads to fame

One might query the inclusion of Baturina in a volume about celebrities in contemporary Russia. After all, she is neither a glamorous movie star along the lines of Renata Litvinova nor a young, photogenic tennis star/model, such as Anna Kournikova or Maria Sharapova.[6] Her talent is neither aesthetic nor athletic, and she is no beauty by any standard. Though many post-Soviet celebrities boast Western-style fame by becoming promotional figures linked directly to Hollywood, or, more often, merely accumulating the signs of a Hollywood-like image, Baturina's fame only marginally intersects with this type – usually through mockery and caricature. Like Bill Gates or Donald Trump, she is a corporate celebrity, famous for her exceptional wealth as owner and head of the construction company Inteko.

Billionaire status propels people into the limelight, especially in Russia, where so many billionaires, formerly called oligarchs, are constantly in the public eye, often because of their scandalous dealings. Like many of the oligarchs who made it big in the 1990s through a variety of shady business deals and outright scams, Baturina has humble business origins. Originally a manufacturer of plastic consumer goods, she accumulated her wealth in the concrete business and eventually (in 2005) sold all her cement works to Eurocement for $800 million, a price far above the value, which nearly doubled her fortune ("The Great Fortune" 2005). In January 2008, Baturina purchased stock in Russkii Zemel'nyi Bank [Russian Land Bank], increasing her share from 20 to 90 percent ("Elena Baturina kupila" 2008). This happens to be the bank holding the Inteko accounts.

As Russia's female Trump, Baturina, who is annually featured in *Forbes Russia*'s lists of the country's wealthiest people, initially derived celebrity from her wealth, for her billionaire status attracted considerable attention in a profoundly patriarchal society. Information about Baturina's business is often published in the press, as is the case with other billionaires, such as Gates in the USA and Oleg Deripaska in Russia. It is not unusual to find new acquisitions and big contract deals written up in the business pages, and considering the high-level professional activity of Baturina and her company, her inclusion in these sections of newspapers and magazines is unsurprising. Though such coverage has a primarily informational value and thus represents perhaps the less fascinating part of Baturina's image in the press, it nonetheless is the mainstay of her public business persona. It legitimates her as a celebrity-businesswoman, and distinguishes her from other contemporary Russian female celebrities, such as Kournikova, known or lauded primarily for "secondary" forms of fame.

Like Trump, Baturina has several large markers of her presence in the capital. Securing the most lucrative construction projects in the center of Moscow – the most prized and expensive territory in all of Russia – Baturina erects buildings that are, *inter alia*, monuments to her. Functionally, these buildings usually house elite apartment complexes and commercial centers, for Baturina's products service Moscow's upper crust. In this way, wealth, glamour, and elite living remain a privilege for the few, yet a visible though ultimately intangible and certainly unrealizable dream for the masses. Whereas in the Soviet period the political elite would have occupied such buildings, today their occupants are the financially successful, a category that includes rich politicians. The "New Moscow," synonymous with wealth and hyperbolic display, carries the Baturina architectural imprimatur.[7] Her concrete giants stand in contrast to the appearance of the old center, populated by more modest pre-revolutionary and Soviet-era buildings.

Baturina, in partnership with her husband, the city's ambitious mayor, is writing only the most recent chapter in the teleological text of the city's image:[8] viewed as an heir to Stalin, Luzhkov is the next "Great Builder" to give Moscow a thorough facelift (Osborn 2006). Others have also made the connection implicitly. For instance, Pavel Baev writes, "Luzhkov has personally supervised many high-profile projects, from the rebuilding of the Cathedral of Christ the Savior to the modernization of the ring road" (Baev 2005). These happen to be two major sites in the development of the General Plan for the Reconstruction of Moscow, originally conceived in 1931 and passed in 1935: the Cathedral of Christ the Savior was demolished to make way for the Palace of Soviets, and the Garden Ring was uprooted and widened – both with Stalin's approval.

In the West, incredible wealth alone has long sufficed to make anyone a celebrity. John D. Rockefeller, also a billionaire and monopolist, was one such corporate celebrity in the late nineteenth and early twentieth centuries. Though not of Rockefeller's status, Paris Hilton is one such contemporary celebrity who earned her fame, at least initially, merely by being an heiress to her family's fortune. Her name allowed her to secure a syndicated television program and media attention, which became the "substance" of her celebrity persona. Now a professional slacker, Hilton regularly appears in the tabloids, usually for involvement in minor scandalous activities. While Baturina's profile as an older, reserved, physically unprepossessing businesswoman is obviously much more conservative than Hilton's, interest in her life in general and focus on her public appearances have boomed. Professionally she sooner resembles Rockefeller than Hilton, but the contemporary state of media and modes of expressing public opinion fostered by technology have transformed the relationship between the famous and the public so radically that it is difficult to define Baturina's fame in terms of what it was in Rockefeller's day. Like Baturina, Rockefeller became both an idol for keen supporters and the target of hostile opposition. Whereas Rockefeller's inclusion in the media involved almost exclusively newspaper and radio, today's media are significantly more image-saturated. Rockefeller may have been featured in caricatures from time to time, but Baturina makes regular appearances across the internet and in print magazines: paparazzi shots of her with Luzhkov at public events, write-ups of Baturina with her horse, artistic renderings of Baturina, amateur Photoshop work of Baturina's visage on supermodel bodies, and so on. These images, as well as broadcast and print news, are all archived on the internet and are universally accessible.

Big business Russian style, or a family affair

Though on the surface Baturina's profile appears as a model for women of self-empowerment and achievement, her story is one that reproduces traditional gender stereotypes in a new context. Awareness that her success has depended directly on her marriage to Luzhkov and the favors he regularly arranges for her through his office has prompted resentful ridicule at her expense. For instance, according to one *anekdot* (joke), Elena Baturina moves through tax inspection and shouts, "I had no dealings with your off-shore businesses! I have an honest business manufacturing plastic basins for the city of Moscow! Do you have any idea who my husband is?!" "Of course," answer the tax inspectors, "We know your business and we also recall your husband, old man Baturin."[9] The inspectors, ironically, do not know who Baturina's husband is, misguidedly assuming that she must share his surname. On the one hand, Baturina is the butt of the joke, taking for granted that everyone knows who her husband is and so understands her "untouchable" status. In the joke, as in life, Baturina relies on her husband's name to glide unimpeded through the business world. On the other hand, it is possible to understand the joke as targeting Luzhkov, whose fame in some quarters has been overshadowed by that of his wife. Such a viewpoint is adopted in a one-liner about the 2007 mayoral race, "Moscow, 2007: the election year of Elena Baturina's husband" ["Moskva 2007 goda: vybory muzha Eleny Baturinoi"] (Anekdot.ru 4).

Another *anekdot* plays on the same idea, "'Life under capitalism is simply unbearable – *blat* (the system of acquiring goods, positions, etc. through connections) no longer exists and it's not necessary,' Baturina nostalgically reminisces, having received at market price the bid for the next building project in the center of Moscow"[10] (Anekdot.ru 1). This cynical joke presents Baturina's denial of the very practice enabling her professional success.

In Russian business, money is frequently not enough for success, for even bribes can get one only so far.[11] More frequently, it is personal connections that make the difference. Having well-connected friends and acquaintances who can pull strings in the bureaucracy is often much more valuable to a businessperson. Though the continued existence of *blat* in post-Soviet Russia is disputed, there is certainly a kind of residual *blat* that has become normalized in business practice.[12] And Baturina has a built-in, never-ending supply of "favors" in her ambitious spouse.

The couple's shared values are satirized in another *anekdot*, "The strongest marriage on earth: Baturina-Luzhkov – nothing in the world draws people closer together than love for a shared billion dollars"[13] (Anekdot.ru 3). Alena Ledeneva's book *How Russia Really Works* (2006) details the unique and problematic practices that define current Russian business. One of Ledeneva's foci is "circular control" or "collective responsibility" (krugovaia poruka), a series of connections providing protection and control, often among business elite and mafia, that facilitate avoidance of bureaucratic, legal, and other perceived hindrances to successful business practices (Ledeneva 2006: 105–7). This dynamic describes the Baturina–Luzhkov "business partnership." Though they operate as a pair – she earns the billions, he navigates government channels – they are assumed to have protection through Luzhkov's alleged association with the mafia.[14]

Fame-*cum*-infamy: scandals make the celebrity world go round

Various news items about Baturina rely on shock value in addition to purportedly "unbiased" information. Baturina has often found herself at the center of scandals, many of which she has created. These scandals, not unlike those in the West accompanying Paris Hilton, Britney Spears, and various drug- or alcohol-abusing entertainers, perpetuate celebrity. Her wealth has ensured her the spotlight, but it is scandal in large part that keeps her there.

For all the adulation poured out in letters from young women hoping to emulate Baturina's successful entry into the business world (discussed below), her image in the press is that of an elite businesswoman who regularly appears at the epicenter of scandal and who simultaneously is very protective of her family and business relations. Baturina's failed quest for privacy may strike one as a way of deliberately keeping opaque her business practices, which involve both personal and professional connections. *Forbes Russia*'s intentionally ambiguous quotation of Baturina's words ("I am guaranteed protection" ["Mne garantirovana zashchita"]) on its cover (*Forbes Russia* 2006) probably reflects the reality of Baturina's situation in Russian business more closely than her claim that her business does not rely on protection from her high-level political connections. Yet that did not shield the magazine from immediate backlash: Inteko's lawsuit for one ruble per issue printed (Boronov and Chistiakova 2007) and editor Maksim Kashulinskii's resignation in protest against Axel Springer's stopping the issue's release (Tyazhlov 2006).

Another recent scandal involved a different family tie, one that disrupted the smooth functioning of her business: namely, the widely covered legal dispute between Baturina and her brother Viktor Baturin regarding his part-ownership of Inteko (Dzhemakulov 2007). Reportedly the two have resolved their differences ("Elena Baturina i ee brat" 2007), but the squabble, which suggests that the Baturins consider themselves businesspeople first and family second, inevitably provokes speculation and rumors.[15]

Not only legal spats, but disastrous building projects-gone-bad have kept Baturina's name in the media. The structure of Transvaal Water Park in Moscow is a case in point. The park's concrete roof, based on a faulty design, collapsed in 2004, killing more than two dozen visitors to the park and injuring many more. Though Baturina was the sole owner of Transvaal Water Park, she had no connection to operations and kept her name unconnected to the venture, holding her stake indirectly through a series of company fronts.[16] Ultimately, not the owners but the architects would be held responsible for the collapse. Yet it was only after Inteko's subsidiary Terra Oil acquired the abandoned, money-losing project from Sberbank and builders for remittance of debts totaling 119 billion ruble debt (Skrobot and Ukolov 2004) that cost-cutting became policy (Gizatulin 2004).

Such incidents have generated fodder for the gossip pages, which thrive on scandals of various proportions. Coverage of this sort, whether in print media or in blogs, tends to focus on Baturina's private life – her marriage to Luzhkov, her children, pastimes, and random appearances in public – thereby catering to the public's curiosity about how celebrities live at home as well as in public. This voyeuristic impulse reflects, perhaps, a need for confirmation that the wealthy are human and, like everyone else, fallible. Though Baturina belongs to the category of those celebrities people love to hate rather than to that of stars people love to emulate, readers' negative interest nonetheless keeps her name in constant circulation.

Fans (and foes): the perpetuating power of public opinion

Widespread interest in a given persona and public opinion are what sustain celebrity status. Public response to Baturina and her mode of conducting business emanates from two distinct groups. The first and by far larger group includes individuals whose opinions about Baturina range from radically negative to flattering, and usually comment on one or more recent events or actions involving her. The other group comprises mostly women, who appeal directly to Baturina for advice or with requests for financial support, and frequently do so in epistolary form, though in public forums.

The most prevalent type of reaction to Baturina usually follows news about her, in the kind of blogging encouraged in the USA press by online versions of major newspapers, such as the *New York Times*. Those reactions most frequently are negative, sometimes colored by resentment and animosity, such as "Baturina's business is long overdue for an audit," or nakedly prejudicial, such as "Thank God Baturina is not a Jew!" ("Axel Springer" 2006). One rarely encounters supportive statements. Unlike official news media, this form of public opinion usually operates free of censorship while offering the protection of anonymity. Thus, such forums permit the expression of widely held but rarely published views of Baturina. While *Forbes Russia* waded into legally dangerous waters by publishing the headline "I am guaranteed protection," the conviction that, through Luzhkov, Baturina uses questionable business practices repeatedly appears in blogs and other internet forums.

By contrast, the second type of response shows that Baturina's financial success has elevated her to the status of a role model and, apparently, of a perceived potential benefactress for other women with business aspirations. Internet forums featuring discussions about Baturina in the context of the latest news regularly include one or two "letters" addressed to her. Citing her full name and email should Baturina bite at her pitch, a certain Tat'iana writes:

> Dear Elena Nikolaevna! I have a business proposition for you. I am a woman and mother of three sons. You can image how many socks I have had to wash in my lifetime. You are probably aware that after being washed, socks inevitably get lost and can't be found. But why have the eternal question lingering every morning, "Where to come up with the socks?" And so … I have found a method how not to lose socks, not to clean them, nor touch them. It is possible to undertake on an industrial scale, but the cost of the patent is too expensive for me and the time involved too much. If this issue interests you, respected Elena Nikolaevna, then I await your response. Best regards, Tat'iana.
>
> (Liudi.ru Forum)

Another woman is less specific about her future business, but decides to try her pitch anyway:

> Hello, Elena Baturina. I am from Tashkent, I am 30 years old, raising 2 children, but still have not found my way, my career. What is the secret to your success, I really want to know? I am constantly reading about you online, I envy you in a good sense, and I want to be like you, a successful businesswoman. Respected Elena Baturina, you could help me start my business. I have considered one idea. In order to start it up I need $1,000. My only problem is the money. I'll absolutely return it to you within the year, absolutely. Please, read my letter. Help a woman who in her thirty years hasn't found her career, for the sake of my children, please. With much respect for you, Ziyoda.
>
> (Liudi.ru Forum)

Brimming with admiration and adulatory epithets, these letters customarily begin with autobiographical descriptions of women's disadvantaged lives and end with requests for start-up funds. For women trying to sell themselves as sound investments, a persuasive sales stratagem seems to bank primarily on gender solidarity in a way utterly foreign to the traditional male-run business world.

Lifestyles of the famously (nouveaux) rich(es): glam girls

Baturina's celebrity status as a billionairess, which manifests itself in various forms of visibility, includes conspicuous consumption at Sotheby's and Christie's auctions. Known as one of the major Russian collectors of art in the London art community, she regularly attends auctions at the two major houses as well as smaller ones, like MacDougall's, which is devoted entirely to Russian art (Borissova and Pyke 2004). In this respect she resembles other members of the nouveaux riches, whose ranks boast many art collectors (for instance, Roman Abramovich). Not limiting herself to the usual paintings and sculptures, on a 2008 London trip Baturina purchased the historic 65-room Witanhurst estate – second in size only to Buckingham Palace – for 50 million pounds (Neate 2008). The art world has also directly acknowledged Baturina's celebrity, and magnified it, through the work of Zurab Tsereteli, sculptor of gaudy monuments of the political and cultural elite (see Chapter 10).

Baturina enjoys a number of other glamorous privileges unattainable to the average citizen: photo-op appearances on red carpets, extravagant foreign travel, and hobnobbing with other high-profile figures are among the glitzy publicity events popularizing Baturina's image (several examples available at Liudi.ru photo-gallery and Izbrannoe [2008]). The beneficiary of VIP treatment wherever she goes, at premieres of musicals and other dramatic performances, Baturina makes Hollywood-style entrances, arriving dressed to the nines, often accompanied by Luzhkov, their daughters, and/or other elite figures. Negotiating the red carpet, she makes the requisite pit stops to strike a pose for flickering flashbulbs along the way. Along with other celebrities and on Luzhkov's arm, Baturina appeared fashionably last-minute at a 2008 Valentin Iudashkin fashion show (Gloria Mundi), and at a 2007 concert the couple presented Iosif Kobzon with a gift on stage (Bushueva 2007). She also enjoys easy access to unusual popular culture events, such as auto-touring through Italy in an antique car (Kameneva and Zorina 2008). In 2006 she spent a flashy Russian New Year celebration in London – Luzhkov opened the event – with its mayor and other politicos (Vainer 2008), and her business travels take her to elite resort locales, like Cannes (Maksimov 2008).

The primary leisurely entertainment in which Baturina actively participates, however, remains sport, of the sort traditionally associated with the rich and privileged. She recently has supplemented her longtime favorite, equestrian games, with a new favorite, golf – not incidentally, a Western import that provides an alternative deal-making arena to the conference room. Not merely hitting the links, Baturina has been instrumental in popularizing the sport in Russia. Her company Inteko's website offers information and photographs about the Inteko Russian Open Golf

Championship, which it hosted at a Moscow "kantri klab" in 2008 ("Inteko Press Release"). It features a strange "safari-style" gala, where rich, white business people were served and entertained by black Russians, an uncomfortable throwback, for Western observers, to a distinctly non-Russian colonial era.

An enthusiastic equestrian, Baturina delights in horseback riding and attending horse races as a spectator. Interviewed in *Komsomol'skaia Pravda* for a piece featuring famous Russians involved in equestrian activities, Baturina used the occasion to establish her view on gender distinctions. The interviewer noted, "In general, Baturina is sure that dealing with horses is easier for men" ["A voobshche, uverena Baturina, s loshad'mi legche muzhchinam"] (Fomina and Maksimova 2005). Speaking for herself, Baturina maintained, "They [men] have a strong hand, and it's not hard for them to stop an animal. Luzhkov can handle any horse." ["U nikh krepkaia ruka, i ostanovit' zhivotnoe truda ne sostavliaet. Vot Luzhkov mozhet spravit'sia s liuboi loshad'iu"] (Fomina and Maksimova 2005). Baturina's stereotypical perspective on masculinity posited the active, controlling man who has the power to tame unruly animals (including, presumably, women).

Tsereteli, the other infamous character responsible for the changing face of contemporary Moscow, has sculpted Baturina leading a horse, in bronze. Shown at a 2005 Manezh exhibition featuring Tsereteli's work, this naturalist composition of a billionaire businesswoman stood next to a representation of the writer Chingiz Aitmatov – new money alongside "old" literature. A statue of Luzhkov likewise was featured, in the guise of a garbage man: *Dezhurnyi po gorodu* [Caretaker of the City] clearly evokes Mikhail Cheremnykh's and Viktor Deni's 1920 famous poster of Lenin sweeping the globe clean of tsars and capitalists, *Tov. Lenin ochishchaet zemliu ot nechisti* [Comrade Lenin Cleans the Land of Impurities]. In the wake of Russia's "wild capitalism," however, Luzhkov, unlike Lenin, works hand in hand with big business to increase his own well-being. His and Baturina's bronze presence in Tsereteli's Manezh exhibition is the result of close business and personal ties. The business relationship involves both "ordinary," internationally acceptable connections – Baturina, her brother, one of Luzhkov's sons, and Tsereteli served together on the Board of Directors of Russian Land Bank ("Baturina …") – and more tenuously appropriate exchanges: Luzhkov consistently gives contracts to Tsereteli, whose monuments dominate the center of Moscow, despite strong public disapproval and the unsuitability of the monuments for the site (see Chapter 10).

Towers of power: "I have erected a monument to myself, not built by human hands"[17]

Even the "everyday" is exceptional in the lives of the elite. The trends of elite lifestyles are available only to the elite. There is very little extra-class participation. The elite have their own stores, spas, neighborhoods, parks, schools, transportation, etc. The level at which these elite institutions operate is such as makes them inaccessible to a "middle class."[18] Their cost is so high that it is rarely possible to acquire the "fixings" of an elite lifestyle one by one; the few who can afford those privileges do not need to consider the price of each. Baturina, of course, not only enjoys such a lifestyle, but also is a key enabler of it in Moscow.

Inteko and its subsidiaries have a large share in the development of the complexes Grand City, Tatiana, Shuvalovskii, and Moscow-City. The first three are residential communities that include their own schools and shops. Moscow-City shares these features, but will also house business centers and major components of the city infrastructure: the city Duma and council. There are also plans to begin modernization of public transport here. Moscow-City is by far one of the largest projects on Inteko's agenda; in fact, it is the largest project of its kind ever in all of Eastern Europe. Also significant is its location on the bank of the Moscow River within the third transport ring in the center of Moscow. As already mentioned, it is such high profile projects as Moscow-City that have helped Baturina accumulate her wealth. At the same time, she is building a legacy through them. The permanence and functionality of the buildings implicitly remind one of Baturina's empire even when she is not immediately present. They serve as mediations between a "monumental" businesswoman and everyone else. Perhaps not so surprisingly, the use value of these complexes is by and large reserved for elite communities: government officials will labor in the Administrative Complex of the Moscow Government; the very wealthy will be the only ones to afford the luxury apartments; their wealthy offspring will attend the elite schools located within the "city"; and they will be the consumers at Moscow-City's restaurants and shops.

Such places as Moscow-City will function as home, workplace, shopping center, entertainment space, and leisure space for thousands of people each day. The self-contained nature of the "city within a city" promotes the seclusion of the elite who inhabit it from the "masses," but it also increases the opportunities for contact with the builder. Through this connection, Baturina gains power, amassing properties and the elite bodies inhabiting them. At the same time, the elite living and working in these communities are privileged: they come into direct contact with Baturina's buildings, which are not equally accessible to all, hence by definition rendered elite.

Moscow-City is a project of multiplication, of Moscow and of Baturina's self as the mistress of Moscow. If Moscow is in a sense a micro-Russia, then, as Pavel Baev points out, it is a Russia more successfully centralized and autocratic compared to Putin's Russia as a whole (Baev 2005). The success of Moscow owes much to the financial resources and capital concentrated there. Moscow-City within Moscow will be an even greater concentration of resources, in particular Baturina's resources. If Luzhkov rules Moscow proper, then Moscow-City is Baturina's personal micro-empire.

It's lonely at the top: "The New Woman" as *Milliardersha/ Oligarsha*

An unusual figure, Baturina appears to have broken through the glass ceiling to become the wealthiest woman in Russia, an incredibly famous woman, who has achieved fame based on business rather than sex appeal. Yet, Baturina's successes have depended on the reproduction of stale gender models. She owns and heads

Inteko, but relies on Luzhkov to continually produce contracts for her. Her apparent power is actually shared with her husband. It is political connections more than know-how and money that make success in Russia. Without Luzhkov's influence and political position, it is doubtful that Baturina would have been able to secure so many prime jobs and amass her exceptional wealth.

Though Baturina is certainly the wealthiest case, she exemplifies a new category of woman. Today's "New Woman" is the "New Russian" house/trophy wife who has grown bored and decided to start her own business with her husband's resources. The nature of Russian business makes it very difficult for outsiders to break into its ranks, thus encouraging the ever-increasing gap between the very wealthy and everyone else in Russia. Only the already wealthy and connected are able to secure start-up funds, permits, land, etc. Baturina is no more self-sufficient than the many other elite wives who execute business plans with spousal money and connections – think Carmela Soprano and her own construction project in the *Sopranos'* final season (2007). And Baturina unabashedly seeks male support and protection outside her conjugal relationship, as well. The billionairess reportedly "feels unsafe, and has publicly demanded protection from President Putin" (Mamchur 2005).

The relationship that Baturina shares with Luzhkov is not unusual in Russia today. Using their husbands' money and connections, the wives of the Russian elite start businesses in order to escape the boredom of what often seems an otherwise vacuous life of manicures, work-out sessions, shopping, lunches, and, if they are still young enough, clubs with other elite wives. Ol'ga Slutsker and Oksana Robski are two examples of women who used start-up funds from their husbands to become entrepreneurs themselves. Slutsker opened a successful chain of gyms, and Robski is famous for her autobiographical how-to novels on catching a rich husband, the success of which led to her NTV television program *Dlia tebia* [For You].

The difference between Baturina and many of the other female entrepreneurs is that her business is not a specifically feminine one. Though Baturina in many ways reinforces old gender stereotypes, she has broken into a "man's" sphere of business. Traditional "women's jobs" are usually limited to schools, childcare, and medicine, the nurturing professions. Ownership of fitness centers catering to women and talk-show hosting are not professions so distantly removed from the old gender binary division of labor. More overtly catering to the old model is Evgeniia Steshova, with her husband Vladimir Rakovskii, who started schools for girls on how to nab a rich man (Goscilo 2007). Such businesses in part break away from the traditional feminine professions, but they fail to escape traditional gender stereotyping. These businesses focus on helping women achieve a specific image, an image that prefigures the heterosexual male as spectator/observer; they shape women to conform to male needs and desires. They also implicitly or explicitly appeal to elite Russians and cater to the image of the elite woman.

Baturina differs from them in a couple of respects. First, being no beauty, she does not use her looks as leverage in business or advertising. While she has undergone a drastic physical transformation in the last decade, dropping a lot of weight, getting a more stylish hairstyle, and dressing more neatly, she has professionalized, but not sexualized, her look. The women mentioned above each, in one way or another, have exploited their looks to business ends. Slutsker, who opened the chain of gyms, was first a professional athlete and model. Her own physique lends her legitimacy as the founder of gyms, where people will work to achieve Slutsker-like form. Baturina's business relies on no such connection between a sleek, glamorous body and the job itself. As a politician's wife and businesswoman, she seems aware that her job requires that she look tidy and conservative – an appearance that Baturina has worked at and for the most part achieved, though she continues to struggle with her fluctuating weight. She also differs from the rest in that she entered a "man's" world, the construction industry, and came out on top by playing by men's rules. Though Luzhkov served as her guide through a male industry, Baturina never was perceived as a sex-object and her business did not rely on that perception.

Furthermore, the buildings that are Baturina's "products" are functionally ungendered: both men and women inhabit them. They cater to the wealthy, and Baturina's status as a member of the class of the new rich is more important to her business than her gender identity. A large part of transcending a class boundary is to begin to "look the part," which Baturina has done by losing weight and altering her wardrobe to eliminate plump sloppiness. In fact, Baturina's status as a wealthy woman without physical appeal, paradoxically, draws considerable attention to her. The *Russia Blog* posted an entry featuring the Russian contingent of *Forbes* billionaires in March 2007, posing the question, "But who will win the swimsuit competition?" (Slepko 2007). The entry, fully entitled "The Rooskie 53 of *Forbes*: Give or Take a Billion: But Who Will Win the Swimsuit Competition?" and featuring a smiling Baturina's face atop a slim bikini model reports generally on the list of Russian billionaires, but singles out Baturina, the only female, for her appearance. Roman Abramovich and Boris Berezovsky, both on the list and not renowned for their physical beauty, did not end up with their heads pasted onto the bodies of trunk-clad supermodels. Although it is not enough for a woman to be a billionaire – she must also "look like a million bucks" – in Russia, as elsewhere, men are exempt from the requirement of attractiveness.

It would be difficult to overvalue appearance in contemporary Moscow – as in the conventions of celebrity – and Baturina's changing looks have elicited considerable commentary. One website featuring candid celebrity photographs examines "how power changes people," and pokes fun at the drastic measures taken by celebrities in order to alter their appearance ("Kak meniaet liudei vlast'"). The same site contrasts Baturina's everyday and special-occasion image, focusing particularly on her weight, makeup, and choice of clothing. It suggests that recognition of the importance and difficulty of professional stylists' work is overdue. An "image-maker" stylist clearly has had a hand in her transformation from frump to fashionista. The rise of the post-Soviet profession of *imidzhmeiker*, a kind of PR "specialist" in charge solely of clients' physical appearances, shows just how important the image is for elite Russians – and how, like the term, it has been borrowed from the Hollywood celebrity tradition. For special occasions, Baturina uses such services, and her recourse to them stimulates as much commentary as would her indifference to a glamorous image. In that sense, though Baturina possesses power as a famous billionairess, as such she is also at the mercy of public opinion, which has the power, ultimately, to determine who qualifies as a celebrity.

Luzhkov's supporters usually attribute the economic growth and facelift of Russia's capital to the mayor, who was inaugurated into office in 1992. The financial growth for which Luzhkov has been most directly responsible, however, is that of his wife, and she has become a major force not only in Moscow's economy but also in the city's physical makeover. Enabled by her ambitious and powerful spouse, Baturina's celebrification has resulted from a determined quest for money and status, tirelessly spotlighted by the media. In the process, she has forged connections with various elites, gained entry into exclusive venues reserved for the financially and politically privileged, and left a physical mark on the country's capital through her construction projects. Whether Baturina's legacy – the huge, expensive buildings that have made her extraordinarily rich – will survive her husband's tenure as mayor is uncertain, for it is not impossible that those monuments to herself, like Transvaal Water Park, will collapse or be razed by future visionary officials intent, yet again, on transforming Moscow.

Notes

1 Though many have hesitated to speak out since the *Forbes Russia* scandal, discussed in detail later in this chapter, as might be expected, the Moscow Architecture Preservation Society has no qualms about what the fearless would say is merely calling a spade a spade, "It may be a coincidence, but Mr. Luzhkov's wife, Elena Baturina, is big in the construction industry. She owns one of Russia's largest cement-makers and building companies. That must make her husband's urban planning policy – 'let's knock everything down and build something bigger and taller' – rather good for business, though she denies having that kind of influence over her spouse of 14 years" (Osborn 2005). The official website of the movement "Moscow without Luzhkov" ("Luzhkovu, net!") includes a vast collection of articles about the Luzhkov–Baturina dealings. The movement even goes so far as to dub Moscow "Baturingrad, the Capital of All Russia" ("Baturingrad, stolitsa vseia Rossii"), complementing the parody with a cartoon of Baturina enthroned on skyscrapers with the Kremlin wall and Ostankino Tower in the background. Opposite her Baturingrad cartoon on the site's header is a caricature of Luzhkov ordering bulldozers to raze more modestly sized buildings and signaling to a fleeing crowd to vacate while a line of armed personnel ensures no one will challenge the mayor's work.
2 Baturina controls "20 per cent of all construction contracts in Moscow, one of the most expensive and fastest growing cities in the world" (Mamchur 2005).
3 During the *Forbes Russia* scandal, Axel Springer released an apologetic statement explaining that its magazine's cover story misquoted Baturina: she did not say, as reported, "My protection is guaranteed," but rather, as *Kommersant* reported the correction, "I have protection secured for me and my rights as any investor does" (from Axel Springer's statement reported in Tyazhlov 2006).
4 Luzhkov had initially intended to step down at the end of 2007, but this plan changed when Putin publicly stated that he wished to appoint Luzhkov for another term. Though they have not always had the best of relations, reports back in June 2007 indicated that Putin had requested that Luzhkov remain in office an additional term – something Luzhkov had no intention of doing, according to his earlier claims (Schwirtz 2008). It did not take long for Luzhkov to be sworn in for his fifth four-year term. The event took place on 6 July 2007, and secured his wife's "guaranteed protection," the issue at stake

in the case of the unpublished *Forbes Russia* cover. The prominent speculation was that Putin feared losing Luzhkov's supporters – that is, most of Moscow – in the 2008 presidential election, and sought to capture the Moscow vote through the reinstatement and influence of the capital's popular mayor (Arnold 2007).

5 In a sense, Kashulinskii's initial refusal to pull the article upon Inteko lawyers' threat of a lawsuit was a stance against big-shot bullying of the media. The unsolved murders of journalists and other media figures in Russia in recent years are too many to enumerate. Among the highest profile cases are the murders of Paul Klebnikov (2004) and Anna Politkovskaia (2006). Their stories indicate that litigious bullying is one of the less severe punishments for uncooperative journalists and editors on the brutality spectrum. Though answers and guilt are rarely finalized in trial, the Western press and outspoken, yet-to-be-silenced journalists in Russia assign blame to big-business gangsters and high-powered politicos, the lines between whom are sometimes blurred.

6 Central to the examinations of celebrity as a cultural phenomenon have been Christine Gledhill's volume *Stardom: Industry of Desire* (1999) and James Monaco's *Celebrity: The Media as Image Makers* (1978), which focus on celebrity as an American (i.e. USA) phenomenon and, more specifically, as a Hollywood phenomenon. Movie stars, supermodels, sports figures, and select politicians form the core case studies.

7 "New Moscow" refers to the several Soviet-era "General Plans" and, of course, Aleksandr Medvedkin's film by the same title (1938), paying tribute to the 1935 version of the *Genplan* [General Plan].

8 If Iosif Stalin was the "Chief Architect" until his death in 1953, Yuri Luzhkov can accept that title today. In the post-Soviet configuration, however, Luzhkov represents himself rather than his office or a symbolic group of citizens/children: Luzhkov teams up with Baturina to build, and they share the financial prosperity. Unlike Stalin, Luzhkov cannot justify that his designs for Moscow in any way reflect the interests of the nation, or even the city.

9 "Prikhodit v nalogovuiu inspektsiiu Elena Baturina i v krik, 'Del ia nikakikh ne imela s vashimi ofshorami! U menia chestnyi biznes po proizvodstvu plastmassovykh tazikov dlia g. Moskvy! Da vy khot' znaete, kto moi muzh?' 'Konechno,' otvechaiut ei v nalogovoi inspektsii, 'biznes my vash znaem i pro muzha vashego, starika Baturina, tozhe pomnin.'"

10 "'Zhizn' pri kapitalizme prosto nevynosima – blata net i ne nado,' nostal'girovala Elena Baturina, poluchiv po skhodnoi tsene ocherednoi uchastok pod zastroiku v tsentre Moskvy."

11 Alena Ledeneva, Stephen Lovell, and Andrei Rogachevskii explain that in many situations, a combination of *blat* and bribery is necessary because bribes often involve a level of trust often obtainable only through *blat* due to the negative associations with bribes (Lovell *et al.* 2000).

12 For details on how *blat* transformed and came to be a given in Russian business and life, see Ledeneva (2000) and Lovell *et al.* (2000).

13 "Samyi krepkii brak na svete – Baturina-Luzhkov: nichto na svete ne sblizhaet sil'nee, chem liubov' k obshchemu milliardu dollarov."

14 David Satter explains in detail the connections among Luzhkov, his close friends and allies, and the Solntsevo gang (Satter 2004: 133–6).

15 Their conflict suggests a blood relationship similar to that between Daniel Plainview and his son with regard to the oil business in Paul Thomas Anderson's film *There Will Be Blood* (2007): familial affection extends only to those not perceived as harmful to the growth of the business, for the purpose of business is simply to grow, even when its gargantuan worth exceeds what one could spend in a lifetime.

16 "No one ever proved her ownership, because the paper trail got lost in over 10 shell companies related to the park. The water park was not insured for architectural mistakes, and the flawed building design was the reason for the tragedy. The families of the killed and injured never received any compensation" (Mamchur 2005).

17   "Ia pamiatnik sebe vozdvig nerukotvornyi" by Aleksandr Pushkin in 1836 (Pushkin 1982).
18   One can argue that a true middle class still does not exist in Russia.

Bibliography

Anderson, P. T. (dir.) *There Will Be Blood*, 2007.
Anekdot.ru (1) Available online at: www.anekdot.ru/an/an0612/x061224;10.html (accessed 15 August 2007).
— . (2) Available online at: www.anekdot.ru/id/211522 (accessed 15 August 2007).
— . (3) Available online at: www.anekdot.ru/id/99872 (accessed 15 August 2007).
— . (4) Available online at: http://pda.anekdot.ru/anekdots/peoples/1999-08-08 (accessed 20 December 2009).
Arnold, C. (2007) "Russia: Moscow Mayor's Power on the Wane as He Enters Fifth Term," Radio Free Europe/Radio Liberty, 24 July. Available online at: www.rferl.org/featuresar ticle/2007/07/4602e891-a325-4661-9d65-f827d98aaf4f.html (accessed 15 August 2007).
"Axel Springer reshil zanovo vypustit' poslednii nomer *Forbes*" [Online Forum] (2006) Grani.ru, 12 Jan. Available online at: http://grani.ru/Society/Media/d.115169.html (accessed 15 February 2008).
Baev, P. (2005) "Moscow Votes for Luzhkov as Rivalry with Putin Intensifies," *Eurasia Daily Monitor* 2, no. 225, 5 Dec. Available online at: www.jamestown.org/publications_ details.php?volume_id=407&issue_id=3547&article_id=2370548 (accessed 10 January 2007).
"Baturina, Elena Nikolaevna" [Online Forum] Nezavisimyi stroitel'nyi portal. Available online at: www.nsp.su/person/a35/ (accessed 20 December 2009).
Borissova, E. and Pyke, N. (2004) "Russia's Wealthiest Collectors Flock to London for Art Sale of the Century," *Independent*, 22 Nov. Available online at: www.independent. co.uk/news/uk/this-britain/russias-wealthiest-collectors-flock-to-london-for-art-sale-of- the-century-534155.html (accessed 10 January 2007).
Boronov, A. and Chistiakova, M. (2007) "Elena Baturina sobiraet delovuiu reputat- siiu po rubliu," *Kommersant*, 15 Feb. Available online at: www.kommersant.ru/doc. aspx?DocsID=742815 (accessed 24 July 2007).
Bushueva, N. (2007) "Kobzon zakatil isteriku v Kremle," FLB.ru, 3 Sept. Available online at: www.flb.ru/info/41601.html (accessed 20 December 2008).
"Dvizhenie 'Moskva bez Luzhkova!'" Luzhkovu, net! Available online at: www.lujkovu. net (accessed 14 February 2008).
Dzhemakulov, S. (2007) "Baturina podala v sud na brata," *Komsomol'skaia Pravda*, 16 Feb. Available online at: www.kp.ru/daily/23856.4/63499 (accessed 24 July 2007).
"Elena Baturina i ee brat podpisali mirovoe soglashenie" (2007) Newsru.com, 15 Feb. Available online at: www.newsru.com/arch/russia/15feb2007/baturiny.html (accessed 24 July 2007).
"Elena Baturina kupila Russkii zemel'nyi bank" (2008) Newsru.com, 6 Jan. Available online at: www.newsru.com/finance/16jan2008/baturina.html (accessed 14 February 2008).
Fomina, O. and Maksimova, T. (2005) "Zvezdy liubiat bit' kopytom," *Komsomol'skaia Pravda*, 31 Oct. Available online at: www.kp.ru/daily/23604.5/46181/ (accessed 14 July 2007).
Forbes Russia (2006) [Cover] December issue.

Gizatulin, R. (2004) "Komu prinadlezhal Transvaal'-Park?" *Nezavisimaia Gazeta*, reprinted in Kompromat.ru, 16 Feb. Available online at: http://compromat.org/main/luzhkov/transvaal.htm (accessed 14 February 2007).

Gledhill, C. (ed.) (1991) *Stardom: Industry of Desire*, New York: Routledge.

Gloria Mundi [Celebrity Photographs] Available online at: www.glomu.ru/photo/20080324/67714330_5.html (accessed 20 December 2008).

Goscilo, H. (2007) "New Regimens: Women's Bodies in Post-Soviet Russian Culture," Keynote Address at AWSS 3rd Biennial Conference, Ohio State Univ., Columbus OH, Apr.

"The Great Fortune of Russia's Only Female Billionaire Grows Still" (2005) *Pravda*, 4 Feb. Available online at: http://english.pravda.ru/main/18/89/355/15217_baturina.html (accessed 10 January 2007).

"Inteko Press Release" Available online at: www.zaointeco.ru/index.php?s=8&sid=15 (accessed 20 December 2009).

"Iurii Luzhkov i Elena Baturina – 1000 mil' po Italii v stile retro," *RIA Novosti*. Available online at: www.rian.ru/video/20080521/108017338.html (accessed 20 December 2008).

Izbrannoe [Web page devoted to Elena Baturina] (2008) 2 Sept. Available online at: www.izbrannoe.ru/44576.html (accessed 20 December 2008).

"Kak meniaet liudei vlast'" [Web page] (no longer accessable online).

Kameneva, O. and Zorina, E. (2008) "Iurii Luzhov i Elena Baturina – 1000 mil' po Italii v stile retro" [Video], *RIA Novosti*, 21 May. Available online at: www.rian.ru/video/20080521/108017338.html (accessed 20 December 2009).

Ledeneva, A. (2000) "Continuity and Change of *Blat* Practices in Soviet and Post-Soviet Eussia," in S. Lovell, A. Ledeneva and A. Rogachevskii (eds) *Bribery and Blat in Russia: Negotiating Reciprocity from the Middle Ages to the 1990s*, New York: St. Martin's Publishers, p.183–205.

— . (2006) *How Russia Really Works*, Ithaca: Cornell University Press.

Liudi.ru [Forum]: "Napisat' pis'mo lichno Baturinoi," Available online at: www.peoples.ru/undertake/building/baturina/forum.shtml (accessed: 20 December 2008).

— . "Photo-gallery: Elena Baturina," Available online at: www.peoples.ru/undertake/building/baturina/photo.html (accessed 20 December 2008).

Lovell, S., Ledeneva A., and Rogachevskii, A. (eds) (2000) *Bribery and Blat in Russia: Negotiating Reciprocity from the Middle Ages to the 1990s*, New York: St. Martin's Press.

Luzhkovu, net! [Website] Available online at: www.lujkovu.net (accessed 15 February 2008).

Maksimov, A. (2008) "Russkii avangard: Elena Baturina rasskazala o novykh proektakh Inteko," *Rossiiskaia Gazeta*, 21 March. Available online at: www.rg.ru/printable/2008/03/21/inteko.html (accessed 20 December 2008).

Mamchur, Y. (2005) "Lawyer Slayings in Russia," *Discovery Institute's Real Russia Project*, 24 Oct. Available online at: www.russiablog.org/2005/10 (accessed 10 January 2007).

Monaco, J. (1978) *Celebrity: The Media as Image Makers*, New York: Delta.

Neate, R. (2008) "London's Biggest Private Home Sells for £50m," *Daily Telegraph*, 21 July. Available online at: www.telegraph.co.uk/news/uknews/2303463/London's-biggest-private-home-sells-for-andpound50m.html (accessed 20 December 2008).

Osborn, A. (2005) "Moscow Stories: Buying a Dream Home? Watch Out for the Wrecking Ball ..." *MAPS*, 10 Apr. Available online at: www.maps-moscow.com/index.php?chapter_id=149&data_id=81&do=view_single (accessed 10 January 2007).

— . (2006) "The Millionaire, the Murder, and the Magazine Having a Little Bad Fortune," *Independent*, 2 Dec. Available online at: www.independent.co.uk/news/europe/

the-millionaire-the-murder-and-the-magazine-having-a-little-bad-fortune-426654.html (accessed 10 January 2007).

Pushkin, A. (1982) "*Exegi Monumentum*" in A. Pushkin, *The Bronze Horseman: Selected Poems of Alexander Pushkin*, trans. D. M. Thomas, New York: Viking Print, p. 92.

Satter, D. (2004) *Darkness at Dawn: The Rise of the Russian Criminal State*. New Haven: Yale University Press.

Schwirtz, M. (2008) "Putin Wants Moscow Mayor to Stay," *New York Times*, 6 June. Available online at: http://query.nytimes.com/gst/fullpage.html?res=9804E4DC1E30F 935A35755C0A9619C8B63 (accessed 14 February 2008).

Skrobot, A. and Ukolov, R. (2004) "Inteki tam ne vidno: glava Gosstroia Rossii Nikolai Koshman poobeshchal proverit' na prochnost' vse sportivno-razvlekatel'nye sooruzheniia strany," *Nezavisimaia Gazeta*, 17 Feb. Available online at: www.ng.ru/events/2004-02-17/9_transval.html (accessed 14 February 2007).

Slepko, N. (2007) *Discovery Institute's Russia* [Blog] 15 March. Available online at: www.russiablog.org/2007/03/the_rooskie_53_of_forbes.php. (accessed 14 Feb 2007).

Tyazhlov, I. (2006) "No Protection Secured: Forbes' German Publishers Give in to the Moscow Mayor's Wife," *Kommersant*, 1 Dec. Available online at: www.kommersant. com/p726454/Forbes_Russia_Baturina_Axel/ (accessed 10 January 2007).

Vainer, N. (2008) "Russian Winter Festival: Russkii Novyi God v Londone," 3 Jan. Available online at: www.fashiontime.ru/news/2750.html (accessed 20 December 2008).

"The World's Billionaires" (2007) Forbes.com, 8 March. Available online at: www.forbes. com/lists/2007/10/07billionaires_The-Worlds-Billionaires_Rank_12.html (accessed 15 July 2007).

Part 2

Prosaic glamour

3 Akunin's secret and Fandorin's luck

Postmodern celebrity in post-Soviet Russia

Brian James Baer and
Nadezhda Korchagina
(Kent State University)

Much like the concept of individualism the use of the term *celebrity* in its contemporary (ambiguous) form developed in the nineteenth century. Studying examples of prior usage, one can see the transformation of its sense from an affinity with piety and religion to some modern sense of false value. The two faces of capitalism – that of defaced values and prized commodity value – are contained within these transforming definitions. The term celebrity has come to embody the ambiguity of the public forms of subjectivity under capitalism.

P. David Marshall (1997: 4)

With the relaxation of censorship restrictions under perestroika, cheap foreign literature – largely, romance novels, detective fiction, and pornography – flooded the Russian market, while the traditional Russian literary field appeared to fragment and Soviet high culture to collapse, leading Karen Stepanian to ask on the pages of the thick journal *Znamia*, "Do we need literature?" (Stepanian 1990: 222).[1] This struck at the very heart of the identity of Russians, "the most readerly people," whose "high" literature had served for almost two centuries as society's moral compass and as a source of enormous cultural capital. Then, in 1998, in the chaotic final years of Boris Yeltsin's presidency, Boris Akunin burst onto the Russian literary scene and very soon his detective fiction was outselling that of the reigning "queen" of the genre, Aleksandra Marinina. Between 1998 and 2004, he sold over eight million copies of his books, and the tenth volume in the Fandorin series, *Almaznaia kolesnitsa* [The Diamond Chariot] (2003), sold out its first printing of 200,000 in a week. The final book in the series, *Nefritovye chetki* [The Jade Rosary] (2006), a collection of short stories about Erast Fandorin's adventures in the nineteenth century, had a print run of 500,000 copies – a record for post-Soviet Russia.

Although working in a popular genre, Akunin was not just another author of detective fiction – a Russian "Conan Doyle" – for his work functioned to repair the fractured Russian literary field, blurring the distinction between high and low culture, hero and celebrity, and authenticity and performance, in the process making him, his pseudonym, and his most famous detective uniquely post-Soviet – and postmodern – celebrities. Set in the decades preceding the October Revolution,

Akunin's most popular novels link post-Soviet Russia not only to its historic but also to its literary past: specifically, the era of two of its most famous novelists, Fyodor Dostoevsky and Lev Tolstoy. On the one hand, the stylization of Akunin's novels and their thick web of intertextual allusions appeared to affect a reconciliation of high and low literature – his were detective novels with a sophisticated literary style. As one critic put it on the pages of *Literaturnoe Obozrenie* (Literary Overview), "Well, finally, a detective writer has appeared in our country whose books aren't embarrassing for an intelligent person to hold in his hands" (Bocharov 2000a: 17).

At the same time, Akunin's consent to the publication of comic-book versions of his novels *Boris Akunin v Komiksakh* [Boris Akunin in Comics] (the series began publishing in 2004 with Azazel) and the fascination with popular culture that imbues his work, in particular his latest series of novels, *Roman-Kino* [Novel-film], which are stylized along the lines of typical silent film plots, indicate that Akunin is not interested in simply reestablishing a traditional notion of high culture. Finally, his first and greatest detective hero, Erast Petrovich Fandorin, with his impeccable British dress, on the one hand, and a thorough knowledge of the Japanese language and culture, on the other, appears as an allegory for Russia itself, situated, both geographically and culturally, between East and West, reminding readers of the world historical role imagined for Russia by Dostoevsky – to "speak the last word to the world."

However, the enormous popularity of Akunin – the pseudonym for Gregorii Shalvovich Chkhartishvili (b. 20 May 1956) – cannot be explained by the content of his novels alone. Chkhartishvili worked very consciously – and self-consciously – to establish his authorial persona, Akunin, and even his detective hero, Fandorin, as *celebrities*, suggesting how quickly Russians in the post-Soviet period learned the value of celebrity and ways to generate and sustain it – an effort made possible by the proliferation in Russia of personal (internet chat) and popular media forms (fan magazines) so important to the "star-making machinery." Or, to use P. David Marshall's terms, the source of Akunin's celebrity is not only "textual" but also "extra-textual" (Marshall 1997). The initial mystery over Akunin's "real" identity, the publicity surrounding the blockbuster films created from his novels, and popular discussion of the author and his characters in Russian chat rooms dedicated to the author and his characters have all worked to make Akunin into that most elusive of creatures in our visual era: the literary celebrity. Akunin, as Bocharov notes, "is condemned and praised, loved and hated, but – that's the main thing – no one just passes him by" (Bocharov 2000a: 17). Indeed, Vanora Bennett went so far as to announce in *The Times Literary Supplement* the "Akuninization" of Russian letters (Bennett 2003: 32).

Analyzing celebrity

Unlike "greatness," which recognizes actual achievements, "celebrity" says more about the masses that bestow it than it does about any qualities inherent in the celebrity individual, a fact lamented by Daniel Boorstin in his classic treatment of celebrity, *The Image: A Guide to Pseudo-Events in America*, "Two centuries ago when a great man appeared, people looked for God's purpose in him; today we look for his press agent" (Boorstin 1961: 72). Or, as Abraham Kaplan succinctly put it, "An idol is constituted neither by its form nor by its substance, but by the idolatry of its worshipers" (Kaplan 1964: 287). Accordingly, scholars in the academic sub-discipline known as celebrity studies focus not on celebrities themselves, but rather on the increasingly elaborate "star-making machinery" that disseminates the celebrity image and on the dialectical, mutually defining relationship between the celebrity and the fan, or, as Marshall puts it, the audience-subject (1997: 62).

This dialectical relationship was first theorized and historicized in two of the foundation texts of the field, Robert Sennett's *The Fall of Public Man* (1997) and Max Weber's discussion of charisma in the lecture "Politics as a Vocation" (Weber 1965). Analyzing the phenomenon of celebrity from the point of view of the society that creates it, these two authors locate the origins of modern celebrity in roughly the same historical period – Weber traces it back to the increasing "rationalization" and bureaucratization of modern societies and Sennett to the nineteenth-century Romantic notion of genius. Moreover, they both focus on the essentially irrational nature of the phenomenon, described by Weber as charisma and by Sennett as artistic genius.

For both Sennett and Weber, the phenomenon of celebrity is produced by the alienation of the modern world. That sense of alienation, or diminished sense of personal agency and individual plenitude, leads the masses – constructed in celebrity culture as "audience" – increasingly to project the fullness of personality onto a select elite, with whom they identify in various, intensely vicarious, ways. In other words, "the celebrity is the epitome of the individual for identification and idealization in society" (Marshall 1997: 19).

The link between the rise of celebrity and the diminution of audiences is represented, for Sennett, in the changing conditions of theater performance in the early nineteenth century. Once the performer is endowed with genius in the Romantic age, the house lights are extinguished (the house had previously remained lit during performances), audiences begin to sit silently through performances (they had interrupted and shaped the performances in the past), and they come to rely more and more on critics to interpret the performance for them (Sennett 1977: 195–218). For Weber, the rationalization of modern society produces a longing for charismatic leadership that could challenge the legitimating structures of an established bureaucracy, with its vested interests (Weber 1965). However, insofar as that longing for charisma reflects the masses' diminished sense of self, it has led in the twentieth century to the rise of charismatic dictators, such as Adolf Hitler.

Although celebrity is predicated on the audience's diminished sense of self, it is the audience that grants celebrity. Moreover, because the source of the celebrity's "essence" is at least partially hidden (any given performance is only a symptom of an essence) and difficult to explain (it is conceived as fundamentally irrational), celebrities – even the most superficial – are typically endowed by their fans with obscure depths (which helps to explain the enormous popularity of celebrity biographies and paparazzi photographs). As Marshall puts it, "Celebrities are the production locale for an elaborate discourse on the individual and individuality that is organized around the will to uncover a hidden truth, or, as Richard Dyer has developed it, to uncover the 'real' person behind the public persona" (Marshall 1997: 4).

Celebrity journalists, photographers, and fans seek to uncover the hidden source of the celebrity's attraction and in doing so present the celebrity as simultaneously ubiquitous and elusive, forever beyond our grasp – as symbolized by the paparazzi's invasive photographs of fleeing celebrities. Scholars in the field of celebrity studies, however, insist on the constructed nature of that elusive celebrity "essence," situating it within a dialectical relationship of celebrity and fans, or individual and audience. It constitutes the *différence* between the individual and the celebrity as "hyperindividual."

If we are to analyze celebrity in this way, then we must look not only at the textual and non-textual factors supporting Akunin's celebrity, but also at what the celebrity status of Akunin says about the Russian public, or the audience-subject. By the time Akunin launched his literary career, the image of the country's leader, Boris Yeltsin, had undergone a complete transformation from that of charismatic hero defending democracy atop a tank during the coup attempt of 1991 to that of ineffective and corrupt bureaucrat, whose drunken behavior had become a source of embarrassment to many Russians. In that context, Akunin's novels can be seen as expressing nostalgia not just for Russia's past, but also for charisma itself, in which case the enormous popularity of Akunin's detective-hero appears in many ways to foreshadow the rise of post-Soviet Russia's arguably greatest celebrity, Vladimir Putin (see Chapter 1).

Postmodern celebrity

It may appear surprising at first glance that an author of detective novels set in the *fin-de-siècle* should be routinely described as "postmodern."[2] However, Chkhartishvili earned the moniker for his highly self-conscious play with intertextuality and historical and cultural allusions. For example, *Almaznaia kolesnitsa* [The Diamond Chariot] (2003) opens with a passage lifted directly – that is, unaltered – from Aleksandr Kuprin's 1905 short story *Shtabs-kapitan Rybnikov* [Staff-Captain Rybnikov]. On the extra-textual level as well, Chkhartishvili appears postmodern for the self-conscious way he has played with contemporary notions of celebrity, most notably by initially concealing his identity and then by projecting an independent existence for his pseudonym, Boris Akunin.

Andrey Kurkov notes that because of Chkhvartishili's decision to hide his identity, "the publication of his first work was shrouded in mystery and gave rise to various legends" (Kurkov 2005). Chkhartishvili, however, maintains that this was not a marketing ploy. His choice to hide his identity as the real author of Akunin's novels was motivated by the idea that it was somehow shameful or embarrassing for a full-fledged member of the intelligentsia – he was the assistant editor of the prestigious journal *Inostrannaia Literatura* [Foreign Literature] and a respected translator of Japanese literature – to work in such a mass genre as the detective novel,

Reluctance to end up in an embarrassing situation – that was the main thing. After all, I was a respectable person – the deputy editor of an important journal, a critic and commentator, a member of this and that, and, well, I was a middle-aged guy with a bald spot and a beard. Then all of a sudden – detective novels. Today attitudes toward our brother the detective novel has softened somewhat among respectable readers, but ten years ago it was the same as writing pornographic novels.

(Chkhartishvili 2007a)

But if his secrecy was not a marketing ploy, it nevertheless succeeded in generating enormous attention from fans and critics of his novels. He appeared on the literary scene with a secret, which immediately lent an extra-textual dimension to his fame, making the writer into a celebrity from the start. The meta-mystery replicated and intensified the textual mysteries. At the same time, the author understood that secrecy alone cannot support the curiosity of fans indefinitely: it requires conscious handling. As he noted of his contemporary Viktor Pelevin, "Everyone was curious to stick his nose into Viktor Pelevin's life ... But he, as they say, didn't enter into contact, and with time the curiosity, starved of new information, died away" (Chkhartishvili 2007a). Although Chkhartishvili goes on to note that this had little impact on the popularity of Pelevin's books, he nonetheless chose a different path, making sure to feed his readers' curiosity.

The pseudonym he invented, B. Akunin, was rather complex, alluding both to the nineteenth-century anarchist Nikolai Bakunin and to the Japanese word *akunin*, meaning "bad guy." And while some referred to the pseudonym as "elegant and transparent" (Prigodich 2000), Chkhartishvili later added to the mystification, "I also invented the surname Akunin, but then I read some musings on the topic: who could be hiding behind this surname, and one theory proposed Irina Khakamada. Imagine my surprise when I later found out that the surname of Khadamada's press secretary was Akunina ..." (Chkhartishvili 2000). The Russian press also played its part. In 1998, with the popularity of Akunin's works growing, Lev Danilkin described a secret meeting with the author. He does not reveal the author's identity, but rather provides clues for the readers, "Actually, any somewhat shrewd person will quickly guess who (or what) B. Akunin is. Well, really, who has such a large and distinctive vocabulary – that's the first thing. What topic is brought up in these texts a little too often – that's the second. And doesn't the author know too many foreign languages – that's the third ... (enough hints!). It's all very simple" (Danilkin 1988). He later adds that the author looks like Umberto Eco.[3]

In keeping with the logic of celebrity culture, a hermeneutics of suspicion, which is the basic mode of reading detective fiction, was directed at the author himself. And the celebrity journalist, in this case Danilkin, helps to keep the secret that had led him to read Akunin's novels in search of clues to the author's identity. "The reading of his books was almost as full of drama as the plot that took place aboard the Leviathan, because I kept searching for possible evidence that would shed some light on the identity of the author of the books" (Danilkin 1998), i.e. guessing the identity of the author was as entertaining as guessing who the criminal was. In other words, the extra-textual life of the author was, one could say, in productive competition with the plot of the novels from the very beginning of this fictional enterprise.

By concealing Akunin's identity, Chkhartishvili *et al.* concretized pop culture's search for the celebrity's "essence" – the reality behind the façade. At the same time, Chkhartishvili was keenly aware that the curiosity he incited with the secret of his identity must be carefully tended, or manipulated, "Incognito only stands in the way of an author's becoming a media figure. You have to show at least a corner of your face from behind the veil. The public is a capricious and fickle child ["ditia kapriznoe i nepostoiannoe"]. It calls out but doesn't wait for an answer and runs to another guy – one it can look at and touch" (Chkhartishvili 2007a). In other ways, too, Chkhartishvili played with his public's desire, often suggesting that he was done with Fandorin, "The list of my addressees has run out. And so, I don't know whom I should write for … Maybe I shouldn't write any more?"

Moreover, Chkhartishvili made Akunin into more than a pseudonym; he became an alternative persona, suggesting a conscious play with the notion of celebrity façade. In 1999, for example, when the true identify of the author was revealed, Chkhartishvili, rather than finally conflating himself and his pseudonym, continued to differentiate Chkhartishvili and Akunin, "Boris Akunin and Grigorii Chkhartishvili are not one and the same person. I'm now wearing Akunin's glasses, but when I'm Chkhartishvili, I wear different glasses" (Chkhartishvili 1999). Eventually, Akunin acquired not only a biography but also a rather well-defined personality, "Akunin was born on 1 May 1998. He is disciplined, loquacious, and elegant. He dresses in late-nineteenth-century style: a bowler hat, a thin moustache à la Lermontov, and a *pince nez*. Even his surname, which is simple to pronounce, testifies to his suitability for high society" (Chkhartishvili 2007b). Akunin even has a human face – his portrait can be found on www.akunin.ru (the portrait, incidentally, bears no resemblance to Chkhartishvili).

The two "authors," Chkhartishvili and Akunin, even collaborated on *Kladbischenskie istorii* [Cemetery Stories] – a unique literary experiment, in which an author co-authors a book with his own pseudonym. The literary trinity of author (Chkhartishvili), semi-fictional authorial persona (Akunin), and fictional hero (Fandorin), far from alienating readers, seemed only to strengthen the aura surrounding the Fandorin novels. As one fan put it, "It must be said that Fandorin has become perhaps an even greater landmark than Akunin. Or maybe not. But the author and EPF [Erast Petrovich Fandorin] complete one another. And it's really wonderful that a world like this has been created where the ruler is on the same level as his subject, and though he rules and directs him, he does so while living peaceably with him. And it's very nice for me to be a mere mortal in that world and to follow the interactions of these two giants" (Dorn 2007). Here we see confirmation of Sennett's theory that the rise of the celebrity ("rulers," "giants") is in direct relationship to the diminution of the audience-subject ("mere mortals").

Chkhvartishili's particular cultivation of the celebrity secret through the use of a pseudonym with its own "reality" became a trend in the post-Soviet publishing world. Zakharov, Akunin's publisher, took this strategy one step further and published "synthetic authors" of the publishing house Zakharov in the series "The

New Russian Novel," "based on the success of B. Akunin: Fedor Mikhailov with his contemporary interpretation of *The Idiot*, Lev Nikolaev with *Anna Karenina*, Ivan Sergeev with the novel *Fathers and Sons*" (Perednii 2005: 853). The authors' names are similar to those of the "original" authors, making the allusion transparent to any Russian reader: Fedor Mikhailov alludes to Fedor Mikhailovich Dostoevsky; Lev Nikolaev, to Lev Nikolaevich Tolstoy; Ivan Sergeev, to Ivan Sergeevich Turgenev. But the pseudonyms also distinguish these contemporary authors from their nineteenth-century predecessors, creating a "hall of mirrors" effect while at the same time commodifying the work – and the personae – of these Russian classics. Overall, the project registers simultaneously the parasitism and the metastasis of celebrity.

A celebrity detective

In his introduction to *The Celebrity Culture Reader*, Marshall maintains, "A useful way to theorize about celebrity is along two axes – surface and depth" (2006: 1). While the modern celebrity is associated with a superficial glamour, s/he is also suspected of harboring a secret core. And while the detective genre, typically categorized as "popular literature," is associated with surface, Chkhartishvili successfully created the illusion of depth both by concealing his identity behind a complex pseudonym (complex in the sense that it was packed with cultural allusions) and by weaving a dense intertextual web of allusions: his detective novels reference works of both "high" and "low" culture.

One can see a similar play with surface and depth in the introduction of his most famous detective, Fandorin. So popular is the character, he is often referred to in the press as a "real" person, and he and Akunin are often conflated, contributing to the blurring of reality and fiction, surface and depth, which Chkhartishvili initiated with his pseudonym.[4] Chkhartishvili makes Akunin into a fictional character while Fandorin appears "real." As the author explains,

> A literary character, if you treat him seriously, to a significant extent acquires an independent life. He doesn't always obey the author, following only the logic of his own actions. And if he doesn't want to do something, you can't force him; if he doesn't want to die, you can't kill him. With my heroes, this happens all the time – with Erast Petrovich especially. For example, I imagined the end of *The Decorator* very differently, and I even tried to make it different, but Fandorin acted just the way he acted (the refined, intellectual court counselor went so far as to take the law into his own hands with the maniac – N.F.) …
> (Chkhartishvili 2000)

Moreover, as Danilkin noted, Chkhartishvili's secret pseudonym extended the hermeneutics of suspicion beyond the plot of the detective narrative itself, as did the complex web of literary and cultural allusions, suggesting hidden depth, or rather depths, behind the textual surface of his works – they were *more* than detective novels. And while on the surface Fandorin appears to belong to the tradition of rational and reserved detectives, à la Sherlock Holmes, he, too, is consciously constructed by Chkhvartishili as enigmatic: there is something elusive about Fandorin. That, combined with his powerful charisma, transforms Fandorin from a detective-hero into a detective-celebrity.

Chkhartishvili achieves this effect, first, by presenting the Fandorin novels as a kind of extended *Bildungsroman*, tracing the maturation of the detective-hero, who is introduced in *Azazel'* (in the English translation, the novel is known as *The Winter Queen*), the first book in the series, as a young man at his first job in the St. Petersburg police department. The idea that Fandorin is as yet "unformed" is underscored by the fact that in the first scene he is wearing a Lord Byron corset for the sake of a shapelier figure. As the series progresses, Fandorin's commitment to physical fitness will render any such "artificial" surface unnecessary. The organization of the Fandorin novels as a *Bildungsroman* sets the detective hero apart from his traditional forebears – Poe's Auguste Dupin, Conan Doyle's Sherlock Holmes, Christie's Miss Marple and Hercule Poirot – who all appear as fully formed, mature individuals from the outset, changing little throughout the respective series. It is precisely the development of Fandorin as a character, Andrei Ranchin argues, that earns Akunin's novels a place in the ranks of "high" literature,

> The hero of nineteenth-century 'high' literature has a character that develops under the influence of circumstances, while the detective in detective novels doesn't change; he's like a mask. Fandorin in Akunin's novels matures, acquires life experience, and changes. How far Erast Petrovich travels in the twenty years of his literary life (his first case is in 1876, and his last in 1900) from the rosy-cheeked youth we meet at the beginning of Azazel'! The series in which the evolution of the main character is represented against the backdrop of scenes from everyday life of the various social classes is an achievement not of a detective novel, but of 'high' literature.
>
> (Ranchin 2003)

At the end of *Azazel'*, the tragic murder of Fandorin's bride leaves him with a premature gray streak at his temples and a pronounced stutter (only when he speaks in Russian). Although he displays a strict British reserve, these outward signs point to an inner trauma, suggesting that Fandorin's elegant surface is concealing great psychological depth. The remaining novels in the series play off Fandorin's elusive core, without ever bringing the reader any closer to uncovering it. That quality of elusiveness is further underscored by the fact that in the three films created from Akunin's novels *Azazel'* [Azazelo] (dir. Aleksandr Adabash'ian, 2002), *Turetskii gambit* [The Turkish Gambit] (dir. Dzhanik Faiziev, 2005), and *Statskii sovetnik* [Councilor of State] (dir. Filipp Iankovskii, 2005), Fandorin is played by three different actors: Il'ia Noskov, Egor Beroev, and Oleg Men'shikov, respectively.

If this elusiveness constitutes part of Fandorin's charismatic appeal, two other qualities feed into it as well: his good looks and his good luck. These qualities set Fandorin apart from the traditional detective, putting him more in line with Fleming's James Bond than with Agatha Christie's Poirot or Miss Marple. Like

Christie's Belgian detective, Poirot, Fandorin is characterized by his sartorial flair. His foppish appearance is one of his trademarks. However, unlike Poirot, who is short, bald, and paunchy, Fandorin is agile and extremely fit physically, thanks to years of training in Japanese martial arts. His physical prowess lends Fandorin a sexiness that is utterly foreign to traditional literary detectives and, for that matter, rare in contemporary detective heroes as well. Consider, for example, the scene from *Koronatsiia* [Coronation], where the narrator, Afanasii Ziukin, gazes at Fandorin, naked from the waist up, as the detective exercises, "I couldn't tear my eyes away from his lean, muscular body" (Akunin 2000: 151).[5] Like James Bond, Fandorin inspires sexual attraction in almost everyone he encounters.[6] Mikhail Topkov describes this sexiness by invoking Lermontov's hero Pechorin, one of Russian literature's most (in)famous lady-killers, "Fandorin is a kind of dream for many of us, a kind of Pechorin-Poirot of our time" (Topkov).

Moreover, Fandorin is not endowed with just heightened powers of observation and intuition, qualities typical if not mandatory in traditional detective heroes; Akunin makes clear that his detective is extraordinarily lucky. In *Almaznaia kolesnitsa*, for example, Fandorin finds himself in a gambling parlor where he must win in a game of chance in order to return Sophia Diogenovna's inheritance. The narrator remarks, "[Fandorin] knew that through some mysterious fate, he always won at all games of chance, even those the rules of which he barely knew" (Akunin 2003: 45). Such scenes appear throughout the series and, as Chkhartishvili himself admits, "I helped my hero in only one thing: I made him inhumanly lucky. Usually, a person of his mold doesn't live long. His set of noble characteristics greatly complicates his survival" (Chkhartishvili 2006).

Fandorin's luck not only sets him apart from classic detective heroes, but also is an important index of his celebrity. As Leo Lowenthal argues in "The Triumph of Mass Idols," luck and circumstance mark the transformation of the hero in twentieth-century society (Lowenthal 1961: 109–40). Success in earlier social systems, Lowenthal asserts, was based on an ethos of hard work, while celebrities make it through luck. Because celebrities now come from the realm of leisure, a rapidly expanding realm in post-Soviet society, they are idols of consumption rather than idols of production (Marshall 1997: 10). "The heroes of popular culture," as P. David Marshall interprets Lowenthal's work, "simultaneously offer hope for everyone's success and the promise of the entire social system to be open to these moments of luck" (Marshall 1997: 10).

Akunin and the post-Soviet audience-subject

The Fandorin novels have generated an enormous and devoted fan base, as evidenced by the chat rooms dedicated to Chvartashvili/Akunin/Fandorin, such as www.fandorin.ru, www.erastomania.narod.ru, the community "Boris Akunin" at www.liveinternet.ru/community/1060161/, the community "Erast P. Fandorin" at www.liveinternet.ru/community/951672/, and others. Here fans share insights and opinions regarding Fandorin's personal affairs and conduct various polls, such as "Do you like Fandorin's marriage?"[7] They even celebrate Fandorin's birthday

– 8 January. Incidentally, this date does not appear in any of Akunin's novels, but is mentioned on the official website in the "Biography" section, making it an extra-textual "fact."

Fandom, however, exists not only on a vertical plane (celebrity–fan) but also on a horizontal one (fan–fan). And while celebrity journalism and fan magazines have been around for decades, advances in technology over the last twenty years have led to a proliferation and intensification of "virtual" fan communities. In the many chat rooms devoted to Akunin/Fandorin, Russian fans often note – and with great respect – the special "community" to which they belong. For example, as one fan put it,

> Hmmm … When you enter a community that's interesting to you, it's nice to ask yourself what the theme of this community means to you (if the community is dedicated to someone in particular). But judging by my user name [FonDorn], you can understand how much this gentleman with gray at the temples who holds monarchist views means to me. I could describe his significance grandly, or sometimes emotionally. But it's also possible to do it briefly though no less informatively. An idol. An ideal. What else? I could give a lot of epithets. They might even cover a part of his spiritual significance, but I don't think it's necessary.
>
> (Dorn 2007)

This fan then proceeds to describe emotionally how his first encounter with one of Akunin's novels resembled entering an alternative world with fundamentally different values,

> But I can't manage without emotion – my life changed radically after I read the first book about EPF. I remember that summer evening well. It was 2003. I had to pass the time before the next match, between the Rangers and TsSKA, at the third qualifying round of the League of Champions. I went to a book store. I bought *Azazel'* in paperback. That the book drew me in goes without saying (excuse the clichés). What soccer?! What are you thinking? After that there was *Gambit, Leviathan* … And later, more profound, more interesting … Nikolas … Pelagiia. It's a new world for me now. A world where I can always bury myself whenever I need to think something over. The author helps me do that. Always in an orderly way and without fail. And I remember the time when my parents heard something somewhere about some author named Akunin, and how ecstatic they were over the first book they read, *Altyn Tolobas*.[8]
>
> (Dorn 2007)

This notion of an alternative world is consciously fostered by Akunin's Fandorin novels, on the covers of which is the line, "In memory of the XIX century, when literature was great, faith in progress was limitless, and crimes were committed and investigated with elegance and taste." The devotion of Akunin's fans suggests just how appealing this notion is to readers in the midst of the chaos, vulgarity, and greed of the post-Soviet years.

Chkhartishvili has mentioned in interviews that he himself visits www.fandorin. ru almost daily and has thanked his fans for pointing out minor discrepancies in his novels, or "goofs" [pliushki], which he then corrects in subsequent editions (Chkhartishvili 2003a). Chkhartishvili also subscribes to the idea that these virtual communities represent an ideal alternative world, where, as he expressed it in an interview he gave to the forum, his fans interact with the same politeness and tolerance as the characters in his novels,

> Previously you said that you enjoy visiting the Forum and reading the discussions on abstract themes. Do you continue to visit the Forum today?

> Yes, almost daily. Essentially, it's my only means of interacting with a reader – you know I don't sign books in stores and I don't participate in various book tours. Of course, I understand that the people who participate in the Forum are well-disposed toward my books. But, honestly, that isn't what pleases me. I like the spirit of tolerance and the general civilized tone of the interaction. In fact, everyone who looks at your Forum notices that. I'm sure that the Hostess is mainly responsible for this, as well as the censor. The Hostess could teach Anna Pavlovna Scherer herself something. Oh, would that everyone in our country treated one another with as much respect and courtesy ["uvazhatel'no i tseremonno"]!

> (Chkhartishvili 2003a)

The alternate universe created by fans is built on an intense identification with Akunin/Fandorin. The author's fans appear to exhibit at least two of the five modalities of identification elaborated by Hans Robert Jauss in his classic work on reader-reception, *Toward an Aesthetic of Reception*, admiring and cathartic identification. In admiring identification, the hero is exemplary for a certain community (Jauss 1982: 166–8). Such identification is obvious in the description of Fandorin by the fan quoted above as "an idol, an ideal." More intense, however, is carthartic identification, which resembles sympathetic identification with the character or suffering personality, but "represents an abstraction or an aestheticized relation to the hero. In this way a moral or judgment can be drawn from the aesthetic experience and the reader feels a sense of emancipation through his or her involvement with the character" (Marshall 1997: 69). Fandorin, in other words, offers access through identification to a better world, a phenomenon that overlaps somewhat unexpectedly with Aristotle's concept of the cathartic function of tragedy.

Carthartic identification with Fandorin is largely facilitated by the tragic personal life of the handsome young detective. As Mikhail Topkov remarks, "Before us passes the life of a unique person; he changes before our eyes, but our perception of this character remains steadfast. Erast Petrovich is successful, almost immortal, noble and attractive, elegant and athletic, in general, a lovely vision, but he is nonetheless unfortunate. The reader involuntarily begins to sympathize with the hero. While reading, the reader merges with him into a single whole" (Topkov). Though handsome and lucky, he is nevertheless "unfortunate," which distinguishes him from the successful but soulless New Russians, and opens him up for cathartic identification from a Russian public, for, as one elderly Russian woman explained to the anthropologist Nancy Ries, "Russians have always had in their hearts a special place for victims" (Ries 1997: 83). Julia Sizikova makes a similar point. Fandorin's tragedy, she suggests, makes him a psychological individual, available to readers for identification, "It's interesting that, unlike the 'mummified' characters of other writers of detective fiction, Fandorin acquires all his traits before our very eyes during his first case. Fandorin is individualized, he changes, and we sincerely sympathize with him and enter into his personal life" (Sizikova 2003).

Akunin, Putin, and post-Soviet celebrity

On internet sites such as Celebrity Mound – www.celebritymound.com/ – one can read biographies of Russian president Vladimir Vladimirovich Putin (Steph 2007). These biographies typically tell us of Putin's career as a spy, his great gifts as a linguist – apparently his command of German is perfect, enabling him to imitate the various regional dialects of Germany – and his ability in Eastern martial arts, not to mention his sartorial flair. (Putin abandoned the ill-fitting gray suits of his Soviet forebears and is often seen in a black blazer with a black turtleneck – mafia chic.) These biographical details, combined with his natural reserve, call to mind post-Soviet Russia's greatest fictional hero: the detective turned secret agent, Erast Petrovich Fandorin. And pictures of a shirtless Putin inspire much the same reaction in Russian citizens as the shirtless Fandorin inspires in Afanasii Ziukin, "a hot piece of muscle meat," as the writer on Celebrity Mound put it (Steph 2007).[9]

These similarities were not lost on Andrey Kurkov, author of *Death and the Penguin*, who noted in a review in the *Guardian Unlimited* on 29 January 2005, "Sometimes, while reading about Fandorin, I found myself thinking that the aim of these stories is to vindicate the secret service and the tough, pragmatic patriotism of today's Russian politics. If we follow this further, the resemblance between Fandorin and Vladimir Putin comes as no surprise: both are dyed-in-the-wool special agents, and the actions of both are aimed exclusively at the benefit of the Russian state" (Kurkov 2005).

Chkhartishvili himself drew a more general parallel in 2006 for a journalist from the *Washington Post*, "'Society was making choices which are pretty much similar to the ones we're having to choose from now,' Akunin said, comparing the assassinated Czar Alexander II to Mikhail Gorbachev and Boris Yeltsin, and the czar's successor, Alexander III, to Vladimir Putin, who succeeded Yeltsin. 'Reactionary, authoritarian, anti-liberal,' he elaborates, 'sporting the round glasses and graying beard of the universal dissident'" (Finn 2006).

This, of course, is not to suggest that Putin has patterned himself after Fandorin or that, with the character of Fandorin, Akunin somehow predicted the rise of Vladimir Vladimirovich. Moreover, it should be noted that Akunin is no fan of Putin, as evidenced in his comments above. Rather, the resemblance of these two post-Soviet figures speaks to a specific construction of celebrity in post-Soviet Russia and of a longing for heroic identification. If Yeltsin was increasingly out of control during the last years of his presidency, Putin and Fandorin are always in control, with perfect command of language(s), their bodies, and their effect. And, like Fandorin, Putin is lucky, having been plucked from obscurity by Yeltsin and named his successor only months before the president's final term ended. But Fandorin's tragic loss of his only love left him with prematurely gray hair and a pronounced stutter – signs of suffering that inspire an intense cathartic identification in the Russian audience. Putin, on the other hand, reveals no signs of suffering, so for his fans, the identification takes the more distant form of admiration. He is closer to the Weberian charismatic leader, while Chkhartishvili, increasingly critical of the president and increasingly harassed by the government, may soon be led to doff his postmodern aura in order to don the persona of a traditional Soviet-era celebrity – that of a moral *intelligent* and political dissident.

Notes

1 All translations from the Russian are by B. J. Baer unless otherwise indicated.
2 See, for example, Bocharov 2000b.
3 Even this seemingly direct "hint" is layered, for while Akunin does indeed bear some physical resemblance to the Italian scholar and novelist, he also followed a similar career trajectory: Eco, the scholar, took to writing fiction and scored his biggest success with the medieval mystery novel, *In the Name of the Rose*.
4 The popular press typically treats Fandorin as a real person, a metonym for Chkhartishvili's novels, as in the headlines, "Fandorin priekhal k Megre" (*Izvestiia*, Sept. 19, 2001: 8) about the first French translations of Akunin's novels, and "Fandorin uzhe blizko" (Abadash'ian A. [2001] "Interview with S. Al'perina," *Rossiiskaia Gazeta*. Available online at: www.rg.ru/Anons/arc_2001/0920/1.shtm [accessed 21 December 2009]), referring to the first serialization of one of Akunin's novels, *Azazel'*.
5 For more on homoeroticism in Akunin's novels, see Baer (2005).
6 Andrey Kurkov, however, refers to Fandorin as an "anti-Bond" for the fact that he never seduces or takes advantage of the women who are attracted to him. This may speak to the traditional Russian ambivalence toward the pursuit of hedonistic pleasure, as represented by Bond. Suffering is in fact what makes the cosmopolitan Fandorin quintessentially Russian.
7 For more on the activities of the forum, see: www.fandorin.ru/forum/poll.php?s= 53fdd30e63eb4a60874503bb19c571b3&action=showresults&pollid=30 (accessed 13 February 2008).
8 It is interesting to note that, despite all the talk of the postmodernism of Akunin's work, the reader here subscribes to the traditional Russian view of the writer as a teacher/guide in everyday life.
9 The homoerotic comments of male fans only underscore the distance between the fan and the celebrity; the adoring male fan is feminized vis-à-vis the hyperindividual and, in this case, the hypermale. The homoerotic gaze of the male fan has its cinematic counterpart in such post-Soviet cinematic works as Aleksandr Sokurov's film *Otets i syn* [Father and son] (2003), in which it expresses a nostalgic desire to restore the "lost" status of the Russian male and the "lost" world of male homosociality.

Bibliography

Akunin, B. (2000) *Koronatsiia*, Moscow: Zakharov.
— . (2003) *Almaznaia kolesnitsa*, Moscow: Zakharov.

Baer, B. J. (2005) "Engendering Suspicion: Homosexual Panic in the Post-Soviet *Detektiv*," *Slavic Review* 64, no.1 (Spring): 24–42.

Bennett, V. (2003) "The Akuninization of Russian Letters," *The Times Literary Supplement*, no. 16 (May): 32.

Bocharov, K. (2000a) "Orkestr v kustakh," *Knizhnoe Obozreniie*, no. 14: 17.

— . (2000b) "Sekretnaia missiia postmodernista", *Knizhnoe Obozreniie*, no 14: 16–17.

Boorstin, D. (1961) *The Image: A Guide to Pseudo-Events in America*, New York: Vintage.

Chkhartishvili, G. (1999) "Boris Akunin: 'Tak veselee mne i interesnee vyskazatel'nomu chitateliu.' Grandioznyi proekt novoi russkoi belletristiki" [Interview with A. Verbieva] *NG Ex Libris*, 23 Dec. Available online at: exlibris.ng.ru/person/1999-12-23/1_akunin. html (accessed 21 December 2009).

— . (2000) "Akunin bez pal'to Dostoevskogo" [Interview] *Samizdat*, 17 May. Available online at: zhurnal.lib.ru/z/zhaklin/akun.shtml (accessed 21 December 2009).

— . (2003a) "Akunin otvechaet na nashi voprosy – pered puteshestviem" [Interview with Aliks] *Forumy Fandorina*, 29 Dec. Available online at: http://fandorin.ru/forum/showthread. php?s=5ac1d321819470fca6c977dffd270f6f&threadid=2986 (accessed 2 January 2010).

— . (2003b) "Almaznaia kolesnitsa pisatel'stva: avtor otpravliaet ego v dekretnyi otpusk" [Interview with Igor Shevelev] *Moskovskie Novosti*, no. 47. Available online at: www. newshevelev.narod.ru/knugol/akunun.htm (accessed 21 December 2009).

— . (2006) "Boris Akunin: Fandorin – intelligent, samurai i dzhentel'men" [Interview with Marina Suranova] *2000 ezhedel'nik* 50, no. 346, Dec. Available online at: www.2000. net.ua/print?a=%2Fpaper%2F10147 (accessed 21 December 2009).

— . (2007a) "Grigorii Chkhartishvili: Novoe imia tozhdestvenno obnovleniiu suti" [Interview with Grigorii Dashevskii] *Kommersant* 69, no. 45, 21 Dec. Available online at: www.kommersant.ru/doc.aspx?DocsID=837630 (accessed 21 December 2009).

— . (2007b) "Prilozhenie k Fandorinu" [Interview with Anna Zhebrovsksaia] *Tema*, 20 Jan. Available online at: www.tema.in.ua/article/1598.html (accessed 21 December 2009).

Danilkin, L. (1998) "Ubit po sobstvennomu zhelaniiu," *Sovremennaia Literatura*, July. Available online at: www.guelman.ru/slava/akunin/danilkin.html (accessed 21 December 2009).

Dorn, S. (2007) "Mmm … Kogda prikhodish' v soobshchestvo" [Blog Posting] 13 July. Available online at: archive.diary.ru/~akunin (accessed 21 December 2009).

Finn, P. (2006) "A Case of Crime and Reward: Mystery Writer a Star in Russia," *Washington Post*, 23 Apr. Available online at: www.washingtonpost.com/wp-dyn/ content/article/2006/04/22/AR2006042201064.html (accessed 21 December 2009).

Jauss, H. R. (1982) *Toward an Aesthetic of Reception*, trans. T. Bahti, Minneapolis: University of Minnesota Press.

Kaplan, A. (1964) *The Conduct of Inquiry: Methodology for Behavioral Science*, Scranton: Chandler Publishing.

Kurkov, A. (2005) "The Tsar's Man," *Guardian Unlimited*, 29 Jan. Available online at: books.guardian.co.uk/news/articles/0,2172276,00.html (accessed 21 December 2009).

Lowenthal, L. (1961) "The Triumph of Mass Idols," in L. Lowenthal *Literature, Popular Culture and Society*, Palo Alto, California: Pacific.

Marshall, P. D. (1997) *Celebrity and Power: Fame in Contemporary Culture*, Minneapolis: University of Minnesota Press.

— . (ed.) (2006) *The Celebrity Culture Reader*, New York and London: Routledge.

Perednii, D. M. (2005) "Reklama: mesto v oformlenii knigi," *Issledovano v Rossii*, 841–60. Available online at: zhurnal.ape.relarn.ru/articles/2005/081.pdf (accessed 21 December 2009).

Prigodich, V. (2000) "Kruche, chem Umberto Eko," *Russkii Pereplet*, 28 Oct. Available online at: www.pereplet.ru/kot/9.html (accessed 21 December 2009).

Ranchin, A. (2003) "Chetyre zametki o 'Prikliucheniiakh Erasta Fandorina' Borisa Akunina," *Russkii Zhurnal*, 14 March. Available online at: old.russ.ru/krug/20030314_ran.html (accessed 2 January 2010).

Ries, N. (1997) *Russian Talk: Culture and Conversation during Perestroika*, Ithaca and London: Cornell University Press.

Sennett, R. (1977) *The Fall of Public Man*, New York: Knopf.

Sizikova, Julia. (2003) "Erast Petrovich Fandorin o Borise Akunine. Literaturnyi portret B. Akunina 'Prikliucheniia Erasta Petrovicha Fandorina,'" 13 July. Available online at: zhurnal.lib.ru/s/sizikowa_j_i/akunin.shtml (accessed 2 January 2010).

Stepanian, K. (1990) "Nuzhna li nam literatura," *Znamia*, no. 12: 222–7.

Steph (2007) "Vladimir Putin Goes Topless for Gay Tolerance?" [Blog Posting] 23 Aug. Available online at: www.celebritymound.com/?cat=1514 (accessed 2 January 2010).

Topkov, M. "Erast Fandorin – geroi liubogo vremeni," *Litra*. Available online at: www.ruslit-ra.narod.ru/nowadays/fandorin.htm (accessed 21 December 2009).

Weber, Max (1965) *Politics as a Vocation*, Philadelphia: Fortress Press.

4   Glamour à la Oksana Robski

*Tatiana Mikhailova (University of
Colorado-Boulder)*

It's interesting – what does a person who can buy a Vertu phone for six grand look
like? Can a woman be that person?

Oksana Robski (2005a: 11)

The first generation of happy girls

Oksana Robski's first novel, *Casual*, published by Rosman Press (which later
published all her other novels), appeared in 2005. It quickly achieved formidable
success as a representation of the private lives of the post-Soviet elite residing in
the glamorous Moscow suburbs Rublevka and Zhukovka. To date, this is the only
novel by Robksi translated into English (2007). Robski built on its success with
further volumes such as *Pro liuboff/on* [About Love off/on] (2005), *Den' schast'ia
– zavtra* [The Day of Happiness Is Tomorrow] (2006), *Ustritsy pod dozhdem*
[Oysters Under the Rain] (2007), a collection of short stories, *Zhizn' zanovo* [Life
Anew] (2006), an ironic handbook, *Zamuzh za millionera* [Marry a Millionaire]
(2007), in co-authorship with Kseniia Sobchak (for further information on Sobchak
see Introduction), and a sequel to her first novel, *Casual 2* (2007). Franchising the
success of her glamour fiction, Robski published two manuals for glam wannabes,
entitled *Rublevskaia kukhnia* [Rublevka Cuisine] (2007) and *Glamurnyi dom* [The
Glamorous House] (2007). (The last two books are published by the Moscow-based
OLMA-Press.) With all her books highly publicized in Russian glossy magazines
and on television as an insider's look at the lifestyles of the *nouveau riche*, Robski
became a symbol of the new consumerist culture of the 2000s.[1] Gaily accepting
the comparison of her writing style to that of a talking purse from Chanel, Robski
presents a gendered view of the *nouveau riche*'s lifestyle, focusing on the lives and
problems of the women in the elitist settlement, mostly the wives and mistresses of
Russian businessmen and politicians. Mediocre in their literary qualities, Robski's
novels nevertheless constitute an illuminating case of the functioning of glamour
culture, in which happiness, as manifested by "status" and "success," is not the
result of certain achievements, but their very foundation. Although in most cases
the characters are already "made" in money and status, the origins of their privilege
are never quite clear.

Analyzing glamour as a system, Stephen Gundle observes, "The glamorous woman was not usually drawn from the upper ranks but from a humble or unidentified milieu. Indeed, two patterns of mobility may be identified as typical: vertical mobility involving ascent from the lower reaches of society by means of talent, luck, or sexual favors, and horizontal mobility or geographical displacement" (Gundle 2008: 11–12). Robski perfectly fits both categories, while characteristically obfuscating the actual circumstances of her ascent. She claims to have grown up in a poor Moscow intelligentsia family, spending her childhood in a *khrushchevka* (a generic five-floor, concrete apartment block quickly built in the late 50s and early 60s as part of Khrushchev's huge residential project), and studying in the Journalism Department at Moscow University. However, according to some sources (Babitskii 2008), there was no such person enrolled the year when she allegedly studied at MGU. According to Robski, she dropped out in the third year (the mystery remains), and some time later completed a degree in film directing, yet failed to establish herself in the film industry. Simultaneously, she married – first a classmate, who turned out to be a drunkard with a zest for debauchery. Then she married a successful businessman who was assassinated at some point: as she observes in an interview with *Moskovskii Komsomolets*, "It was that kind of time, they'd kill everyone back then" (Mel'man 2005). A cloud of mystery surrounds her first two marriages. For instance, Robski never mentions that her first husband was actually killed in a street brawl (Mel'man 2005). Nor is there any certainty about the name of her second husband, whom she sometimes calls Konstantin and sometimes Iakov ("Kak proslavilas'"). In any event, she invested the substantial wealth inherited from her deceased husband in her own business and used his connections to secure her position.

Robski met her third husband-to-be, Michael Robski, at some social event. Typically, in her first interviews Robski called her third husband, whose surname she adopted, a German businessman, while later admitting that he was a Russian Jew who had emigrated to Germany. One of the most beneficial aspects of this marriage was her move to a house on Rublevka, which she was able to keep even after she divorced Michael. This move is a clear example of "horizontal mobility." Although Rublevka is not that far from Verkhniaia Krasnosel'skaia, the street where Robski spent her childhood, the symbolic distance between these two areas is greater than from the Earth to the Moon. Thus Robski effectively raised herself to a new level of financial (hence social) privilege with each remarriage. Robski's obfuscation is not limited to information about her marriages, but extends even to the question of her age. In her first interviews she claimed to be twenty-six years old, while in fact being thirty-six.

Perhaps the nameless autobiographic heroine of Robski's first novel, *Casual*, is the closest reflection of the author. It is she who says to her girlfriends, "We'll be the first generation of happy old ladies, just as we were the first generation of rich girls" (Robski 2005a: 197). The unquestionable equivalence of happiness to wealth in this motto is principal to Robski and is in many ways responsible for what may be called the "Robski effect." However, while commenting on the passage cited above during an interview with BBCRussian.com, Robski said,

I hope that I do not seem so primitive as to give the impression that I equate money and happiness. The heroine [of *Casual*] says that we will be the first old ladies with money ... when a person has no money, money becomes so important, like it's the purpose of life. But when you have money, you don't really think about it, you think about something else.

(Baker 2005)

The attraction of Robski's novels and her persona is based on the fact that she goes beyond the banal "the rich cry too," and presents the quest for happiness by those who already have a lot of money. So, what is happiness for a woman already in possession of a million-dollar cottage in Rublevka, her own business, a luxury car, and a diamond collection? To risk sounding tautological, I argue that this *transcendental happiness* is manifested in the concept of glamour.

As early as the 1930s, Walter Benjamin detected the cultural effects of glamour while describing elegant arcades in which "commodities are suspended and shoved together in such boundless confusion, that [they appear] like images out of the most incoherent dreams" (Benjamin 1999: 254). As Gundle and Clino Castelli point out in their book, *The Glamour System*, the very word "glamour" is etymologically associated with magic, and delusive or alluring charm,

... glamour took shape first in the imaginative realm; however, with the development of commercial culture and the modern city, it rapidly acquired a material dimension. In all instances, it preserved its initial association with illusion and make-believe. To have glamour or to be glamorous was to possess a mysterious aura that attracted attention and aroused emotions.

(Gundle and Castelli 2006: 6)

The magical connotations of glamour may be deduced from its place in consumer society. For instance, Nick Lee argues that "glamour relies for its effects on the denial and refusal of the *normal need to supplement one's material presence*. This glamorous, dignified presence ... places itself beyond the powers of articulate authority and accountability" (Lee 2001: 174) (emphasis added, TM). An illuminating instance illustrating the latter statement may be found in Robski's reaction to a question posed by Maria Baker, a BBC interviewer. When asked whether she was sure that the situation in Russia would guarantee her and her peers lasting happiness, she replied, "What does the situation in this country have to do with my happiness? Are you talking about happiness or about money?" ["A kakoe otnoshenie situatsiia v strane imeet k moemu schast'iu? Vy seichas govorite pro schast'e ili pro den'gi?"] (Baker 2005).

Glamour as a cultural concept emerged as a result of the societal democratization of the mid-nineteenth century, when aristocratic symbolic capital was replaced by the mass consumption of "high culture" signs (see Gundle and Castelli 2006: 43–5). There is an obvious similarity between this process and the rearrangement of social hierarchies in the post-Soviet years, when the Soviet aristocracy of the Party and cultural elite was ousted by the invasion of the *nouveau riche*, whose raspberry-colored [malinovye] jackets and criminal slang within a decade were replaced by Armani suits and Eton English. In this respect, Robski represents a perfect example of a cultural mediator between two epochs: a former member of the intelligentsia (her mother still teaches at one of the Moscow colleges), she grew up in a small *khrushchevka*, and now represents the highest strata of the social elite.

Without a doubt, the very fact of having a house in the prestigious Rublevka neighborhood helped Robski attain the necessary level of immediate credibility in the eyes of her readers. Simultaneously with the publication of *Casual*, it was broadly reported that the author herself belonged to the same – "successful" – social stratum as her characters. Almost immediately after the release of her first book, Robski became a celebrity, a frequent guest and later an anchor of television shows promoting the glamorous lifestyle. Robski's novels gained a broad readership mainly due to the illusion they create of familiarizing us with the world of the rich and powerful, and thus catering to those readers who, by default, do not belong to this world. Her books intend to "humanize" the highly demonized world of the *nouveau riche*, while at the same time exploiting the public mythology of the transgressive and criminal mores typical for this social stratum – evoking the genre of a mystery novel. The fact that a female writer describing the female aspects of this realm performs a "humanizing" function betrays the patriarchal, or rather Victorian, dichotomy in which this discourse is rooted, whereby men = dirty job, women = cozy home. Robski's characters never question their economic dependence on their husbands and lovers; they perceive it quite simply as the route to their self-empowerment in relation to those less "successful" and less happy than they.

The Botox effect

Unlike such Western canonical texts of glam literature as Danielle Steel's and Jackie Collins's bestsellers, Robski's *Casual*, surprisingly, lacks emotion. The botox that eliminates all facial manifestations of emotion becomes an illuminating metaphor in this book: "Wrinkles vanished. Muscles atrophied. The doll-like face of a little girl with blue hair. And when I smile – Phantomas appears from a scary story: forcefully stretched lips and motionless glass eyes" (Robski 2005a: 31). Accordingly, Robski's narrator and heroines are emotionally numb, incapable of being shocked: for them, everything is acceptable, including murder. Indeed, botox appears to be an excellent synecdoche for the entire culture of glamour, since the latter also emphasizes surface and downplays substance; it also stays on a "skin-deep" level, securing the invulnerability of the lucky protagonist from the outside world, and, most importantly, from time, age, and death. Thus, both botox and glamour assign a supernatural, superhuman, or even transcendental status to the glamorous character, while at the same time paralyzing her subjectivity.

Happy glam girls, as depicted by Robski, seem to be incapable of any feeling, except for the excitement of power and envy of those who are more powerful than they. Power and its visible signifiers – wealth, expensive goods, a rich husband – constitute the horizon of happiness in Robski's novel. To achieve this horizon, a woman must mirror a man's attitude to the opposite sex as prey, as another commodity signifying life success. However, the paradox of the Rublevka lifestyle as inadvertently reflected by Robski is based on circular logic: the woman, "masculinized" by the cynical ability to use any means possible to achieve her desires, equates her success with submission to the man whom she "conquers."

Robski's debut novel is colder and more calculating than her later novels, for the markers of "traditional feminine" emotionality are more persistent in such later works as, for instance, *Pro Liuboff/on*, where her protagonist engages in a ritual of "joint sobbing" [sovmestnyi plach] with her girlfriend for a sick unborn child, "I wanted to cry myself. Just as earlier they used to mix blood, so we mixed our tears and became even dearer and closer to one another" ["Mne samoi zakhotelos' plakat'. Kak ran'she smeshivali krov', my smeshivali nashi slezy i stanovilis' eshche rodnee i eshche blizhe drug drugu"] (Robski 2005b: 162). Yet the necessity of acting "masculine" in order to conquer a "proper" man remains. Despite superficial manifestations of emotionality, Robski's heroine typically realizes that she cannot afford to be too emotional, "Men don't show their feelings. I too tried to be a man" ["Muzhchiny ne pokazyvaiut svoi emotsii. Ia tozhe postaralas' byt' muzhchinoi"] (Robski 2005b: 44).

The "feminization" of the cold and power-oriented world of the women belonging to the *nouveaux riches* is performed in these novels by a method borrowed from glamour magazines. Each character's realm is presented through a list of commodities, "things to own": houses, cars, furniture, clothing – frequently with an exact, specified price and brand name; and "places to go": massage and hairdresser salons, "in" restaurants, fashionable entertainment venues, etc. All these details are marked as feminine and thus set the system of standards for a "successful" woman's lifestyle. The heroine possesses things that are quite inaccessible to the majority of Robski's readers, thus placing herself "beyond the powers of articulate authority and accountability" (Lee 2001: 174).

The representation of a character through a list of things s/he owns became a trademark of Robski's literary method and a particularly obvious sign of glamour's "botox effect." Though Robski is far from original in this respect (see, for instance, Martin Amis's *Money* (1984) or Viktor Pelevin's *Generation P* [Homo Sapiens] (1999)), she is probably the first *Russian* writer to assign a neutral or positive meaning to the equation of a human being and her/his possessions. Most of all, this approach resembles a catalog or a fashion magazine. In a sense, a character is equated with a certain kind of fashion magazine. Those characters whose list is the most luxurious are separated from consumers of more affordable things, not only by their economic status, but also by their language and symbolic habitat. For instance, in the novel *Liuboff/on*, the heroine named Dasha does not belong to the circle of the rich and powerful, although her lover tries to introduce her to his friends. These encounters lead to miscommunications, similar to those comically depicted in Bernard Shaw's *Pygmalion*. On the one hand, Dasha corrects lapses in the speech of her beloved, for whom (unlike for Professor Higgins) a good command of Russian has nothing to do with his social status. On the other hand, Dasha finds herself failing to understand even the simplest conversation,

"I can't fit anything into my fridge," complained an unbelievably pudgy girl
... I decided to take advantage of the situation and keep up the conversation;
Rita and I had meditated on the subject of refrigerators for half a year already.

"Bosch is really good," I said.

Several pairs of made-up eyes looked at me with interest. It felt nice.

"Freezes well, beautiful design [...] very conveniently made" – I was enjoying
universal attention – "even a compartment for eggs. Not like other kinds. ..."

My words were drowned out by loud laughter. And the clink of glasses. "To
refrigerators!" everyone toasted in unison. I raised my glass uncertainly.

"But only to refrigerators for fur coats. And not for eggs," specified the girl
in the low-cut dress. And everyone merrily laughed again.

                                                          (Robski 2005b: 35–6)

Continuing the parallel with *Pygmalion*, one might notice that in the world of
Robski's characters, it is not their language that defines their social/cultural status.
Instead, their status and its manifestations through commodities change language
itself. Indeed, words (such as "refrigerator") mean something other than the normal
definition. Furthermore, for the inhabitants of Robski's Rublevka, refrigerators for
food do not belong to the sphere of their discourse (these are objects for common-
ers and the "help"); the only refrigerators that concern them are those specially
designed for the preservation of their furs. Dasha's failure to understand the conversation she invades is especially telling (and painful) because she is a professional
linguist. Language is something she masters, and even her power over her lover
is augmented by her role as his speech trainer. In another episode in the novel,
Dasha revealingly compares a lack of money with the absence of a voice – in other
words, with discursive deficiency: "'Nine thousand, six hundred and forty dollars.'
I had only two thousand, four hundred and eighty. That's probably how the mute
feel. You want to say something, but you can't" (Robski 2005b: 117). The opacity
of glamour language is indicative of the magic aura created by glamour objects.

The magic of sharing

Even within this circle of magic objects, there is an unstated hierarchy between things more and less accessible. The former – such as Mercedes, Toyota,
Mitsubishi, Volkswagen, Makita, Bacardi, Panache – are typically written by
Robski in Cyrillic, while the latter – such as Cayenne, Bentley, Jack Daniel's
Blue Label, Dupont lighters, a fitness center in Rublevka called World Class, and
a Provazi sofa – appear in Latin script. The foreignness of the names corresponds
to the transcendental status of the item, determined by its price. Thus, glamour is
never entirely familiarized by Robski's character: it always preserves some sense

of distance, which is precisely why the possession of a glam object can generate the "magic effect" of happiness.

From this perspective, it is symptomatic that of Robski's four novels, the first has an English title (*Casual*) and the third is based on an international pun (*Про любоff/on*). In *Zamuzh za millionera* (co-authored with Kseniia Sobchak) the first letter of the title, like the syllable "glam" in *Glamurnyi dom*, is written in Latin script. The titles of Robski's first and her latest book (*Casual 2* came out in October 2007) are especially eloquent: what is "casual" for Robski's heroine is foreign and therefore full of glamorous magic for the reader, who may not necessarily move in her sphere.

This effect is self-perpetuating. Characteristically, the "real" wives of Rublevka and Zhukovka sent an angry letter to the NTV channel, which broadcasts her show, accusing Robski's novels of inauthenticity. They were especially enraged by the fact that Robski's heroine receives a monthly allowance of $2,000 from her husband,

> "It's a joke," write the ladies, "– for a whole month? That wouldn't be enough for a day ... After that stupid book our husbands make fun of us: 'Why don't I ask this ... kefir businesswoman for the numbers of those friends of hers who can get by on two thousand a month? ...'" Genuine "Rublevka wives" think that Robski's project is PR for the poor; she just didn't want to scare them with the real price of living in this Moscow suburb. To conclude, the ladies sneered at the writer for underestimating the cost of their lifestyle and devaluing their feminine "services."
>
> ("Proletarskaia pisatel'nitsa")

Ironically, while trying to humiliate Robski, her critics mirror her – or, rather, universal – strategies of glamour self-empowerment. For instance, Alfred Kokh, a businessman and politician (notorious for his participation in the campaign against the "old" NTV), commented in the men's magazine *Medved'* [The bear] on Robski's incompetence at living glamorously with such wrath that he inadvertently appeared comical,

> ... I might not know that much about shopping, but I know that a real "Rublevka wife" (God, what nonsense) avoids Moscow boutiques, where everything is overpriced three times over and the collections are usually from the previous year, and instead goes to Milan and London. No one gets jewelry here; they go to Paris, to Place Vandôme. The best place for men's things is also London, on New Bond Street, or in New York, Bergdorf Goodman on Fifth Avenue or in boutiques on Madison Avenue ... etc. The fact that the amounts are always off is characteristic of Robski's work. For instance, for fifty thousand you can whack not just one, but at least ten people.
>
> ("Kokh protiv")

There is, indeed, something peculiar in Robski's glamour discourse. Through her heroines she readily enjoys and praises cheap products of questionable quality seemingly intended for the poor. She takes pleasure in a Doshirak noodle soup and a *Prichuda* waffle torte (the name of the product means "a whim") (Robski 2005a: 267); she is amazed to learn that a delicious tea that tastes no worse than the one she regularly drinks (at $10 per sip) is actually ordinary Lipton. She is excited by her visit to a simple *khoziaistvennyi magazin* (a small version of the American retailer The Home Depot) and is not afraid of a "dirty job" – although lacking medical training, she nevertheless knows how to give her daughter injections and even immunization shots. Or consider the following statement, "Katya's maid fed us potato casserole. With that Filipino I learned to value simple human food." ["Katina domrabotnitsa nakormila nas kartofel'noi zapekankoi. S filipinkoi ia nauchilas' tsenit' prostuiu chelovecheskuiu edu."] (Robski 2005a: 266).

Such examples are quite frequent in Robski's prose. Hardly any of them can be written off as product placement, and their recurrence reflects Robski's positioning of herself as a mediator between the post-Soviet rich and poor. However, the reason for these intentional lapses in glam taste, I contend, springs from the inextricable link between glamour and happiness.

As Jean Baudrillard points out in *The System of Objects*, everyone in consumer culture "must constantly be ready to actualize all of his potential, all of his capacity for consumption. If he forgets, he will be gently reminded that he has no right not to be happy" (Baudrillard 2005: 51). This universal obligation to be happy is maintained through everyday easy access to solidified happiness as embodied in consumer products, "Everything is appropriated and simplified into the translucence of abstract 'happiness'" (Baudrillard 2005: 37). In other words, every brand, every fashionable symbol of status serves as a signifier of happiness. Though the situation was certainly very similar in late Soviet culture, the list of things manifesting happiness and status in the 1970s–80s was too limited to be the subject of literature: even without authorial guidance, every resident of the USSR knew that a happy person wore a *dublenka* (sheepskin coat) and Finnish boots, drove a Volga, and had a *stenka* (a furniture wall unit) imported from Czechoslovakia or the GDR. The unification and narrow range of these symbols of happiness is reflected by such late-Soviet "cult movies" as *The Irony of Fate* (dir. El'dar Riazanov, 1975). Today's abundance and availability of consumerist symbols of happiness, and especially the speed with which old signifiers of "status" become replaced by new ones, necessitate an entire field of cultural production and consumption represented by glamour magazines, television commercials, product placement, and other cultural outlets, including novels like Robski's.

Yet, I maintain that Robski goes beyond the pragmatics of embedding advice to naïve consumers in her prose. The presence of cheap products like Doshirak or Lipton in the list of happiness-signifiers allows virtually all of her readers to imbibe, in the process of reading, their own dose of glamour happiness, regardless of their income. In fact, the incorporation of cheap products into her "catalogs" of things is a rhetorical device intended to bond her with those readers who can afford nothing more expensive. By this means, Robski truly creates the illusion of sharing, which in turn produces the effect of common values, understanding, and, most importantly, of the reader's belonging to the glamorous world. Even the simple purchase of Robski's book offers the reader an injection of glamour and thus is equivalent to symbolic citizenship in Rublevka or Zhukovka. The creation of this circle of shared happiness is the main reason for the popularity of Robski's books as well as for the transformation of her name into a commercial brand. This rhetorical mechanism is quite typical for the culture of glamour: "… glamour is not the elusive pimpernel attainable through the god of riches … It is easy to attain at least *some* of it, if not all of it, and half a loaf is better than none" (Gundle 2008: 4).

The community of shared happiness is simultaneously open to everyone, on the one hand, and exclusive, on the other. In order to maintain the illusion of exclusivity, the glamorization in Robski's novels functions similarly to the "displacing wow-factor" in Viktor Pelevin's novel *Generation P*. According to Pelevin, the wow-factor suppresses and displaces from an individual's consciousness all feelings and reactions that do not have a monetary value.[2] This mechanism is especially effective in conjunction with those values that a person does not or could not possess. For instance, in *Casual* Robski's heroine feels a pang of jealousy when she sees a "charming girl in blue jeans" making out with a long-haired young man, "I wanted to become that girl, and kiss on the swings. But I couldn't." ["Mne zakhotelos' stat' etoi devushkoi, tselovat'sia na kacheliakh. No ia ne mogla."] (Robski 2005a: 28). However, this frustration – which includes, among other things, the fact that the heroine's husband was recently killed – is easily surmounted,

> My eyes and the girl's met. Her gaze dulled. She wished that she was wearing my clothes and driving to my home. To look out into the world from the windows of my car … In my rearview mirror – the girl's face. Agitated, she was chastising her boyfriend for something. Maybe he checked me out? I smiled at my reflection. The Botox mockingly smiled back.
>
> (Robski 2005a: 29)

Similarly, the false nostalgia for a simple life and feelings concludes with the remark, "And to go to bed, having watched a movie on Channel One. Channel One, because the commercial director of Channel One is my friend, and it means a lot to him that people watch movies on his channel" (Robski 2005a: 30). In these and many other similar moments in Robski's novels, an apparent longing for immaterial values (such as youth, love, simplicity, etc.) is more or less ironically compensated for by statements stipulating the possession and consumption of glamorous things and membership in glamorous circles. This mechanism sustains a stable level of happiness, preserving the heroine from unnecessary frustration.

Yet, Robski's irony is a double-edged sword. On the one hand, she signals that her narrator/heroine does not take these immaterial values seriously. On the other hand, Robski's immediate pang of envy aroused by an innocent bystander suggests the active repression of those very values. Glamour here functions as a self-sustaining ideology that displaces all other value systems, though whether the heroine can live up to its expectations is uncertain. For instance, in *Den' schast'ia – zavtra* [The Day of Happiness Is Tomorrow] (2005) the heroine suffers from a debilitating cocaine addiction, yet Robski presents it as an essential part of her belonging to the world of life in Rublevka, where even transgressions are exclusive to certain circles and thus glamorous. Once again Pelevin's commentary perfectly fits Robski, "People weren't sniffing cocaine, they were sniffing money, and the rolled-up hundred-dollar bill required by the unwritten order of ritual was actually more important than the powder itself" (Pelevin 2002: 54).

Both the inviting and the isolating effects of glamour are visible in the recent franchise of Robski's projects – literary and commercial. On the one hand, she publishes a cookbook, *Rublevskaia kukhnia*, with the clear implication that almost anyone who is willing can cook and eat a "piece of Rublevka" in her own kitchen. Two perfumes co-devised and co-owned by Robski and Kseniia Sobchak rely on consumers' making a kindred connection. One of them bears the name *Zamuzh za millionera* [Marry a Millionaire] and the other is simply but eloquently called *Gold* (in English). Scent is among the oldest "magical tools," and by sharing hers with customers, Robski offers the symbolic essence of glamour at a reasonable price. On the other hand, her book *Glamurnyi dom* [The Glamorous House] (2007) teems with exclusive brands and items whose astronomical price makes them fantastic rather than prosaic objects for the majority of her readers.

To own (f)or to be owned

Robski's characters are reminiscent of Giuseppe Archimboldo's baroque portraits, in which people's faces are composed of fruits, vegetables, fish, and flowers; only Robski's characters consist of fashionable objects, expensive houses and cars, powerful positions, etc. Thus the character itself, and a protagonist female character in particular, appears as an object too, though an expensive, glamorous object that not every buyer can afford. This situation, however, leaves unanswered the ubiquitous question of agency: does Robski's protagonist – or the post-Soviet glam woman – preserve a certain, albeit limited, freedom or does she only enjoy the passive position of a glamorous object?

Robski seems to address the issue of a glam woman's agency quite consistently. Four of her novels begin with a lack or absence typical of fairy tales: a happy family is destroyed, and a heroine has to build her happiness anew. In *Casual*, after the husband's murder, the heroine tries to avenge his death and to find her own place in life. She starts a business that turns sour because of her staff's disloyalty and hires a hitman to kill her husband's murderer; yet, before justice can be served, the heroine administers the murder of an "innocent gangster." As a result of these calamities, however, she finds a new, rich suitor who does business outside of Russia and thus is hierarchically superior to her ex. In *Den' schast'ia – zavtra*, the heroine undergoes a similar crisis. Abandoned by her husband, who tires of her cocaine addiction and her indifference to the family, especially to their son, the heroine overcomes her addiction and creates a successful security firm, even saving her father-in-law's life. As a result, the husband returns to her, and family happiness amidst luxury is restored.

In both novels, Robski's heroine tries to rebuild her life (and happiness) through self-realization in business. This path implies a new (or renewed) model of subjectivity that seemingly invokes the ghosts of the Soviet female overachievers from the 1920s–30s and ostensibly resonates with the feminist ideal of a strong woman breaking through gender stereotypes and proving her worth in a "man's world." However, when asked directly whether she promotes models of women's independence, Robski is aghast at the very idea,

"You wrote a book about a woman who solves difficult 'masculine' problems all alone. Are you a feminist?"

"No! Absolutely not! It's just that they killed her husband, and she has to deal with everything herself. That certainly doesn't mean that I share the theories of feminism."

(Baker 2005)

Her fear of being labeled "feminist" is quite symptomatic of the paradoxical complexes of her heroines. Robski's characters do not find psychological satisfaction by realizing their potential in business or other, similar activities. They sooner resemble the Soviet "strong woman," such as the protagonist of Vladimir Men'shov and Vladimir Chernykh's Oscar-winning *Moscow Does Not Believe in Tears* (1980), who achieved professional self-fulfillment but preferred to sacrifice her independence for "obedient" subordination in the private sphere. Unlike Soviet heroines, however, Robski's protagonists are not interested in "real" men if the latter do not have sufficient income or power. Furthermore, rich men are essential not only to the women's attempts at self-realization through professional endeavors, but also (and preferably) to their "eternal happiness" through a lucrative marriage that provides a passport to glamour and all it entails. Thus, for Robski's heroines what seems like self-fulfillment paradoxically *reinforces* their objectification – or, rather, self-objectification.

The only purpose for the business activities of Robski's heroines is to increase the businesswoman's own price as a commodity. In the world of Rublevka, a single woman with income of her own possesses a higher "market value" than a woman without a business; in other words, the former can have a better, i.e. richer and powerful, husband or lover who will "own" her along with her business. When a man willing and able to "purchase" the heroine appears, she eagerly sacrifices her freedom for marriage and dependence on an affluent, powerful husband. If Aleksandr Ostrovsky's nineteenth-century *Bespridannitsa* [Bride without Dowry] in the play by that title was shocked to learn that she was an "expensive and beautiful thing" auctioned off to the highest bidder, Robski's heroines possess this "market-consciousness" from the outset. In fact, their concept of happiness is derived from it, and they strive to raise their value as objects for conjugal sale. Their acceptance of their own "objecthood" – their desire to become a passive tool awaiting an owner's activating hand – is manifested in the following "words of wisdom":

When you are married, even if you don't do anything, and lie in front of the TV all day, there is still a purpose to it. Because you are not just lying around in front of the TV, but waiting for the evening, which is when your husband comes home from work, and it turns out that you weren't just killing time, but lived another complete day of family life.

(Robski 2005a: 19)

Thus, the agency of a glamorous woman in Robski's novels is inseparable from the concept of commodity. This connection is twofold. First, Robski's heroine herself is a valuable commodity by virtue of the glamour qualifications that make her unattainable to men of modest means. Not just her youth, looks, and desirability, but, more importantly, her lifestyle, clothing, cars, jewelry, etc. are the means that establish her in this role. That these items can be only a simulacrum of actual success is unimportant: as mentioned earlier, glamour is focused in principle on surface rather than substance, and thus the glamorous clan willingly accepts a "member" on appearance alone – dress is indeed the calling card (in Russia, "po odezhke"). This explains why clothes and their brand names are so important for post-Soviet culture – in the realm of glamour, clothes are not just for wearing, but possess an emphatically symbolic function, signifying their owners' social status, which in turn is inseparable from their wealth and power.

Second, upon becoming the valued property of a happy husband (or lover), the Robski woman acquires access to a magic wand (no double entendre intended) that allows her to purchase even more glamorous items and services, thus increasing her own value and enhancing the glamorous enchantment of her being. In other words, Robski's narratives trace female upward mobility. In this upward movement, authentic youthful looks and an aura of desirability are translated into glamour values: expensive clothes, social contacts, and, most importantly, a sense, however false, of exclusivity. Only through these glamorous effects can a woman attain "substance," i.e. actual wealth and power, though almost inevitably through association with a rich and powerful man. Indeed, in Russia as elsewhere, "in the 1990s glamour became a social and cultural lubricant on an unprecedented scale" (Gundle 2008: 352).

The twofold value of the glam woman and her desired marriage to a Rublevka resident are ironically reflected in the book co-authored by Robski and Kseniia Sobchak – the latter widely viewed as the epitome of post-Soviet glamour. Sarcastically titled *Zamuzh za millionera* [Marry a Millionaire] (Robski and Sobchak 2007), the volume teems with hilarious recipes for seduction, which betray the skillful manipulation of patriarchal stereotypes. For instance, one of the chapters begins as follows: "We want to dedicate this chapter to the many women's tricks and deceptions that might help convince your millionaire that you are not a cynical bitch with a calculator, but the winged nymph he has dreamed of his whole life" (Robski and Sobchak 2007: 177). Advice consists of strategies to be employed in "the hunt":

Generally speaking, a girl's handbag should be capacious, since its purpose is to fit at least five interesting books, depending on the presumed tastes of the victim [sic]. A sample collection for almost any situation: Paulo Coelho's *The Devil and Miss Prym*, Viktor Pelevin's *Empire V* and *The Psychological Aspects of Buddhism*, a pocket-book edition of Shakespeare's plays, and *The Newsletter of Condensate Aggregates* in English.

(Robski and Sobchak 2007: 161)

This list of books, however ironic, seems to be all-embracing: it targets any potential "customer" (provided he is a millionaire) – the intellectual with a spiritual drive (the books on Buddhism and Shakespeare), the postmodern hipster (Pelevin), the well-educated technocrat from the oil industry ("*The Newsletter of Condensate Aggregates* in English"), or the simple mind with a touch of pretentiousness (Coelho).

Robski's sarcasm has deeper roots than just the impulse to ridicule unmarried wannabes. Although her heroines' journeys usually end in fairy-tale fashion, with marriage or the prospect of marriage, the heroines cannot sustain family happiness based on their subjugation to a powerful man. Tellingly, Robski's female protagonist in *Casual* cannot relate to the happiness of her girlfriend who reconciles with her husband after he has beaten and raped her, then apologized and showered her with gifts. Female martyrs and obedient wives do not figure among Robski's favorite cultural icons. She prefers Catherine the Great, Scarlett O'Hara, or even the rebellious Princess Tarakanova, "I felt as though I were the Princess Tarakanova, who managed to escape from Count Orlov's boat" ["Ia chuvstvovala sebia kniazhnoi Tarakanovoi, kotoroi udalos' sbezhat' s korablia grafa Orlova"] (Robski 2006: 57).[3] In sync with these preferences, Robski's novels solicit the readers' identification with heroines who have struggled for their happiness. The route to glamour leaves these women too strong and cynical to accept the patriarchal idyll without reservations or inevitable transgressions, ranging from drugs and extramarital affairs to crime (like the murder, with the help of a hitman hired by the heroine, to avenge her husband's death in *Casual*). Tellingly, Robski's protagonists with children are all bad mothers, who rarely remember their children's existence, let alone their needs and interests – which perhaps more than any other trait measures the gap separating Robski's heroines from the patriarchal ideal, even a glamorous one.[4] All these transgressions, in turn, explain why the skillful game of finding, catching, and "Marrying a Millionaire" endlessly repeats itself for Robski's characters.

Conclusion

In conclusion, I return to the issue of the socio-cultural functions of glamour in post-Soviet society and Robski's role in this sphere. Gundle argues that "glamour contained the promise of a mobile and commercial society that anyone could be transformed into a better, more attractive, and wealthier version of themselves [...]. The dreams of consumers included, of course, fantasies of social promotion and of self-aggrandizement" (Gundle 2008: 7). These cultural functions of glamour are indeed similar to the social and economic expectations of the anti-communist revolution of the early nineties, known as perestroika. It is quite ironic that the full-fledged culture of glamour has developed in Russia after the democratic vector of perestroika was replaced by the neo-traditionalist and restoration-oriented tendencies characteristic of the Putin period (with the general rise in living standards exerting an influence on the development of glamour). One may even maintain that the exponential proliferation of glamour in Russian culture of the 2000s appears as a substitute for the decreasing social mobility within Russian society.

In this context, Robski's success not only exemplifies the role of glamour in the culture of the 2000s. A close reading of her novels reveals the simulative character of glamour as a means of social mobility. In other words, if perestroika and the following tumultuous decade offered real, though risky, possibilities for upward movement in the social structure for women and men alike, in the 2000s, the glamour in Robski's novels and elsewhere functions as a simulacrum of this facet – returning to the etymological meaning of the word "glamour" as magical, delusive, or alluring charm. As we can see, glamour in Robski's works imitates democratic values by intertwining cheap products with catalogs of exclusive items and services that, in turn, serve as substitutes for personalities and identities. At the same time, it seemingly encourages women's ambition for upward mobility in the social hierarchy – another liberal value – but only to secure their (self-)objectification and dependence on rich and powerful men. Whether Robski is cynical or sincere in her powerful simulation is a moot point. It is obvious that her writings resonate with mass consumers' *political* appetite of a peculiar kind. She herself formulates the place of glamour (and her own books as a part of this culture), as follows, "If you don't have any other ideology (than the ideology of consumption), then glamour will become your beacon" ("Shalost'").

Notes

1 A collection of reviews of Robski's novels in glamour press is posted on her personal site, www.robski.ru/pressa (accessed 15 September 2008).

2 "A special role is played in this by the displacing impulse. It is like the rumbling of a pneumatic drill, which drowns out all other sounds. [...] In the final analysis the modern individual experiences a profound distrust of practically everything that is not connected with the ingestion or elimination of money" (Pelevin 2002: 87).

3 The Princess Tarakanova was a famous imposter who claimed to be a daughter of Elizabeth I and a competitor of Catherine II in the struggle for the Russian throne. She fled abroad, but was lured back to Russia by Prince Orlov, who became Tarakanova's lover while fulfilling Catherine's order. In Russia, Tarakanova was captured and locked in a convent, where she died in 1810.

4 An "authentic Rublevka husband," Kokh has lashed out at Robski's heroines for their inability to fulfill the maternal function according to patriarchal expectations. "A real 'Rublevka wife' coddles her child incessantly. For her, he is a wonder, and his teachers are dimwits who can't appreciate his talent; his doctors are imbeciles who can't see that the child is very ill; nannies are incompetents who can't teach the child to dress himself, and so on. From birth, the baby is surrounded by such a wall of love and care that it's impossible to imagine him getting a case of advanced appendicitis. This cannot happen, because it could never happen. For the wife, the child is the major outcome of family life, and the main argument for her usefulness to the husband" ("Kokh protiv").

Bibliography

Babitskii, A. (2008) "Oksana Robski-letopisets Rublevki," Available online at: http://luxurynet.ru/bomond/546.html (accessed 21 September 2008).

Baker, M. (2005) "Oksana Robski o schast'e, den'gakh i slave," BBCRussian.com, 12 Sep. Available online at: http://news.bbc.co.uk/hi/russian/entertainment/newsid_4236000/4236360.stm (accessed 21 September 2008).

Baudrillard, J. (2005) *The System of Objects*, London: Verso.

Benjamin, W. (1999) *The Arcades Project*, Cambridge, MA: Harvard University Press.

Gundle, S. (2008) *Glamour: A History*, Oxford: Oxford University Press.

Gundle, S. and Castelli, C. T. (2006) *The Glamour System*, London: Palgrave.

"Kak proslavilas' Oksana Robski," Available online at: www.znaikak.ru/robskio/ (accessed 21 September 2008).

"Kokh protiv 'zhaby' Robski," Available online at: www.skandaly.ru/print/news3971.html (accessed 21 September 2008).

Lee, N. (2001) "Becoming Mass: Glamour, Authority and Human Presence," in N. Lee and R. Munro (eds) *The Consumption of Mass*, Oxford: Blackwell.

Mel'man, A. (2005) "Oksana Robski: Ia davno soshla s uma," *Moskovskii Komsomolets*, 18 Aug. Available online at: http://allrus.info/main.php?ID=237656&arc_new=1 (accessed 21 September 2008).

Pelevin, V. (2002) *Homo Zapiens*, trans. A. Broomfield, New York: Viking.

"Proletarskaia pisatel'nitsa glamurnykh bul'onnykh kubikov," Available online at: www.stringer.ru/publication.mhtml?Part=38&PubID=4556 (accessed 21 September 2008).

Robski, O. (2005a) *Casual*, Moscow: Rosman.

— . (2005b) *Pro liuboff/on*, Moscow: Rosman.

— . (2006) *Zhizn' zanovo*, Moscow: Rosman.

— . (2007) *Casual*, trans. A. W. Bouis, New York: Regan Books.

Robski, O. and Sobchak, K. (2007) *Zamuzh za millionera*, Moscow: Rosman.

"Shalost' – zhizn' mne, imia – shalost'," Available online at: www.robski.ru/pressa/ (accessed 21 September 2008).

Part 3

Mediating glamour

Film, estrada, and new media stars

5 Family, fatherland, and faith

The power of Nikita Mikhalkov's celebrity[1]

Stephen M. Norris (Miami University)

For its 2009 New Year's episode, the Channel One comedy show *Bol'shaia raznitsa* [Big Difference] aired a parody of Nikita Mikhalkov. Billed as a "New Year's address to the Russian people," the short segment mocked the Oscar-winning director's celebrity status. The actor Aleksei Fedotov, who played Mikhalkov, appeared dressed as a medieval tsar complete with the Cap of Monomakh (*Shapka Monomakha*). First wishing "the people" hello and asking God to bless them, "Mikhalkov" commented that the past year had not been a good one for Russian cinema because there were "very few good films, mostly because I took a break." Even worse, the American Academy had failed to award "our Russian film" *12* an Oscar, clearly a blow to Russian national pride and a slight that led "Mikhalkov" to threaten in English, "I will break your smelly asses" if "you don't give me an Oscar." Filmed against a Kremlin backdrop, Mikhalkov's "address" to the people resembled a Soviet-era broadcast despite the director's autocratic costume and shameless promotion of his post-Soviet film to his fans.[2] The parody neatly packages all the contradictions within Mikhalkov's celebrity status.

Mikhalkov is that rarest of Russian celebrities, a colossal cultural icon who gained his status because of his famous family, his talents, and the efforts of numerous intermediaries who bill him as a star. He is, to use Chris Rojek's definitions, an ascribed, achieved, and attributed celebrity all rolled into one. Rojek writes that "ascribed celebrity concerns lineage" and that "status typically follows from bloodline," citing Caroline Kennedy and Prince William as examples. Achieved celebrity, as Rojek sees it, stands in contrast to ascribed, for it "derives from the perceived accomplishments of the individual in open competition." Attributed celebrity "is largely the result of the concentrated representation of an individual as noteworthy or exceptional by cultural intermediaries" (Rojek 2004: 17–18). Mikhalkov's celebrity fuses all three. Under socialism, the Soviet government and media billed heroes such as Yuri Gagarin and Lev Iashin as men of the people, ordinary Ivans who had earned their acclaim because of their talents and hard work (a constructed status that began with Stalinist celebrations of workers such as Aleksei Stakhanov). The heavily censored Soviet media molded the celebrity of Gagarin and others, putting forward their "socialist" or "patriotic" attributes while hiding the unsavory details of their private lives (Jenks 2008).

Mikhalkov grew up and became a celebrity within this cultural world. Soviet journalists and critics presented his status as achieved, yet with an added twist, for his name afforded him recognition similar to that of an ascribed celebrity. Famous on account of his talents as both actor and director, Mikhalkov benefited from being the son of Sergei Mikhalkov, the officially promoted celebrity who authored children's literature and composed the lyrics of the national anthem. Nikita Mikhalkov today presents himself in triple guise: first, as an "aristocrat," a scion of an "ancient family" that connects him to the tsarist past; second, as the son of a Soviet celebrity and therefore a significant personage from the immediate past; and third, as the most famous and influential director of the post-Soviet era.

Mikhalkov regularly claims that his work is service to the Russian nation. His studio – TriTe [Three t's] – created in 1988 and housed in an entire central Moscow apartment block, takes three Soviet-era buzz words – *tovarishchestvo-tvorchestvo-trud* [fellowship-creativity-labor] – as its philosophy. As Birgit Beumers aptly describes, the use of the first "t" (for *tovarishchestvo*) applies to both nineteenth-century management structures and the Soviet-style comradeship that the Bolsheviks introduced with the address "tovarishch" (Beumers 2005: 6). TriTe's use of words that have both tsarist-era and Soviet-era connotations perfectly parallels Mikhalkov's self-promotion. A respected film director before he split from the state-run Mosfilm, Mikhalkov catapulted to superstardom after 1991 largely by managing his celebrity himself. On its website, Studio TriTe describes him as "an elegant man, a conqueror of women's hearts, a nobleman of the new Russia, a famous film director, a distinguished politician, and an ardent apologist for the Russian national idea" ["shikarnyi muzhchina, pokoritel' zhenskikh serdets, barin novoi Rossii, znamenityi kinorezhisser, vidnyi politik, i iaryi apologet natsional'noi russkoi idei"] (Zaitseva I. (2006). It is this self-presentation that the *Bol'shaia raznitsa* parody mocks so well, for it pokes fun at Mikhalkov's aristocratic status derived from his "ancient family," his Soviet celebrity status derived from his father, and his contemporary claims to be a spokesman for all things Russian.

Mama and *father:* Rod Mikhalkovykh

Mikhalkov's celebrity rests first and foremost in his name. His mother, Natal'ia Petrovna Konchalovskaia, is the daughter of the painter Petr Konchalovsky (1876–1956) and the granddaughter of the nineteenth-century painter Vasily Surikov (1848–1916). Her family belonged to the pre-revolutionary artistic aristocracy, albeit one that made its peace with Soviet power. Konchalovsky started out as an artist inspired by Cézanne, joined the avant-garde "Jack of Diamonds" group in Silver Age St. Petersburg, and eventually became a socialist realist painter and winner of a Stalin Prize in 1943. This family background certainly fed Nikita Mikhalkov's stardom, but it was his surname that made him truly famous.

Mikhalkov's father, Sergei Vladimirovich (1913–2009), became one of the Soviet Union's most popular children's authors. Famous for his fictional character Uncle Styopa, Mikhalkov was commissioned by Stalin himself to write the lyrics for a new Soviet state anthem in 1942 because Stalin's daughter, Svetlana, was a fan. The new anthem, finished in 1943 and officially adopted on 1 January 1944, cemented Sergei Mikhalkov's fame. Eventually he served as Secretary of the Soviet Writers' Union, received numerous state prizes (four Orders of Lenin, three Orders of Stalin, Hero of Socialist Labor), and had his works translated into dozens of languages.[3]

The Soviet media had a formula for promoting authors such as Mikhalkov. For example, on 11 June 1980, *Izvestiia* carried a brief report about the "Days of Literature" celebration held in Dagestan to highlight the "important role of North Caucasian literature" (Sergeev 1980). Among the "famous writers" in attendance, *Izvestiia* listed Sergei Mikhalkov first (Sergeev 1980). A May 1982 article in the same paper devoted to the celebration of children's literature at Moscow's House of the Friendship of Peoples read similarly. It commemorated an international conference devoted to "the literary and artistic fight for peace and the happiness of children." The report mentioned the names of three important personages who attended: Mikhalkov, Soviet Educational Minister Mikhail Prokof'ev, and UNESCO representative Henri Isansson (Lobanova 1982). In a sense, loyal Soviet cultural figures such as Sergei Mikhalkov lived a series of what the American scholar Daniel Boorstin called "pseudo-events," or the planted stories usually created by publicists involving celebrities that exist solely to report the presence of a star somewhere (Boorstin 1992: 11–12). Soviet celebrities such as Mikhalkov appeared in the official media countless times to celebrate events such as the ones mentioned above, turning them, much like their American counterparts, into self-fulfilling prophecies. Collectively, these innumerable reports, as Vaclav Havel observed, made socialist life a sort of "pseudo-history" made up of a "calendar of rhythmically occurring anniversaries, congresses, celebrations, and mass gymnastic events" (Havel 1991: 333).

Mikhalkov's celebrity as an ascribed-attributed hybrid is a perfect representation of how the Soviet cultural system conferred significance on its artists. Sergei Mikhalkov first gained fame under Stalin and eventually became a primary player in the innumerable pseudo-events that made up Soviet news stories. His son, Nikita, became famous at a time when a new, post-Stalinist celebrity appeared. Young and glamorous much like their Western counterparts, these late socialist stars began to attract fans who followed their appearances. Gagarin, Iashin, and Tat'iana Samoilova belong to this category, and the way the three women in the 1980 film *Moscow Does Not Believe in Tears* (dir. Vladimir Menshov) swoon over film star Leonid Kharitonov highlights the emergence of a celebrity culture under Soviet socialism. Nikita proved to be a shrewd manipulator of his status, taking advantage of his ascribed and attributed status, packaged as achieved, to draw attention to himself and to his family name.

Mikhalkov has fused his films with his family history. *Neokonchennaia p'esa dlia mekhanicheskogo pianino* [An Unfinished Piece for a Player Piano] (1977, based on a Chekhov play), *Piat' vecherov* [Five Evenings] (1979), and *Neskol'ko dnei iz zhizni I.I. Oblomova* [A Few Days from the Life of I. I. Oblomov] (1980, based on a Goncharov's novel) all focus on family, and the two literary adaptations have a painterly quality drawn from Konchalovsky. Eduard Artem'ev's song "Gde zhe ty, mechta?" [Where are you, dream?] for the film *Raba Liubvi* [A Slave of Love] (1976) is music set to Natal'ia Konchalovskaia's poem of the same title. The film itself is "an extended meditation on the comparative virtues and costs of private and public life" (Neuberger 2002: 261) or an exploration of how to be a Soviet celebrity. His 1981 film, *Rodnia* [Kinfolk] makes family connection explicit as it tells a story of a rural mother who comes to contemporary Moscow to visit her daughter. *Bez svidetelei* [Without Witnesses] (1983) focuses on two people, a man and his former wife, and their tense relationship after it emerges that he wrote a letter of denunciation against her new husband. Mikhalkov's emotions are clear here too, siding with the wife, who has sacrificed everything for her family and who finds happiness in remarriage (it is worth noting that Sergei Mikhalkov was Natalia's second husband).

Mikhalkov's later films also capture the importance of family as the base for his celebrity status and a patriotic Russian superstructure. His Oscar-winning *Utomlennyi solntsem* [Burnt by the Sun] (1994) is essentially a story of how a new Soviet aristocrat deals with his in-laws, a pre-revolutionary Chekhovian family (or, a story of how the Mikhalkovs got on with the Konchalovskys).[4] Viewers who did not understand the allusions to Mikhalkov's family in the overall plot of the film could still grasp how the family story and the personal story intertwine – Mikhalkov played the protagonist, Kotov, and Mikhalkov's daughter Nadia played Kotov's daughter.

From 1980 on, every year Mikhalkov would tape his other daughter, Anna, on her birthday, capturing her responses to questions about the world. The result, *Anna ot 6 do 18* [Anna from Six to Eighteen], is more about Mikhalkov and his famous family than it is about Anna Mikhalkova. Released in 1993, the film reveals that the family changed the stress in their last name to make it sound less aristocratic and more Soviet; features footage from Natal'ia Konchalovskaia's funeral; muses about Vasily Surikov's influence on Anna and the family; and has Nikita explain that he got the idea for the documentary from his work on *Oblomov*. Mikhalkov's movies, in other words, consistently feature the very basis of his celebrity status, focusing on his personal family history. Russian history – whether it is told through a classic literary adaptation like *Oblomov* or a tale of the Stalinist purges as in *Burnt by the Sun* – is essentially one long pseudo-event in the story of the Family Mikhalkov [Rod Mikhalkovykh].

For his 1999 blockbuster, *Sibirskii tsirul'nik* [The Barber of Siberia], Mikhalkov took his family fame and connected it to that of another famous Russian clan, the Romanovs, casting himself as Alexander III. Critics cried foul at this switch of one famous family for another (see Beumers 2000; Norris 2005), seeing it as the latest proof of Mikhalkov's narcissism or a veiled attempt to project himself as a new constitutional monarch for Russia. The director had invited such readings by stating that monarchy might be good for Russia again and that he might consider a run for President. He had won a Duma seat in December 1995 largely because of his famous name and not through any serious campaigning, but declined it when he realized that work would be involved. When *Barber of Siberia* debuted at a lavish Kremlin party, it seemed likely that Mikhalkov could win a Presidential election, taking his celebrity into the political arena and becoming Russia's Ronald Reagan (see Kotkin 1999). Mikhalkov's political aspirations ended with the rise of Vladimir Putin later in 1999, and the director switched his allegiance to the new political superstar.

Mikhalkov has done a great deal to promote his inherited fame by tracing his family tree and publicly presenting it in his films and on television. This Russian family, which is far from typical, yet packaged as timeless as the Russian landscape, appears most clearly in Mikhalkov's two documentaries made in 2003.[5] Entitled *Mama* [Mama] and *Otets* [Father], the two hour-long films are ostensibly about Nikita Mikhalkov's mother and father. Though the two films cover his parents' lives, they are more about the history of the Mikhalkov family and particularly how Nikita grew up among celebrated artists.

It was his work on the two films that led Mikhalkov to research his family tree. He has traced the history of his family back to the first half of the fifteenth century and compares the significance of his "ancient Russian family" [drevnii russkii rod] to Tolstoy's. The Konchalovsky family, which includes the Glebovs, has even deeper roots, stretching back to the foundations of the earliest Russian state – the first Glebov appears in 1022. This side of the family also houses luminaries such as Pushkin and the Romanov dynasty itself. Glebovs served Dmitry Donskoi and Mikhalkovs served princes in Yaroslavl. Both families fought alongside Prince

Figure 5.1 Mikhalkov's aristocratic roots traced on a family tree made for his Moscow office. It includes such luminaries as Petr Konchalovsky and Vasilii Surikov. Photo by Stephen M. Norris.

Pozharskii's army in 1612 and against Napoleon's armies at Austerlitz. "Rod Mikhalkovykh," as the genealogy attests, is as old as Russia and has literally built the nation. No wonder the *Bol'shaia raznitsa* actor wore the costume of a medieval tsar, for in many ways that is how Mikhalkov has presented himself and his family's significance.

In his film *Father*, Mikhalkov makes family connections clear when he talks about his father's near-death experience as a baby. Once, when Sergei Mikhalkov's baby carriage hurtled out of control toward certain death, a peasant stopped it before anything terrible could happen. The apocryphal story serves as an opportunity for Nikita Mikhalkov to make an Ivan Susanin-like claim that "a peasant saved the whole Mikhalkov family, a family so rooted in the Russian land." "Our ancestors," Nikita summarizes, "fought, taught, healed, painted icons, worked the soil of Russia." It is a summary of family life that Mikhalkov has made before. In a 1996 newspaper interview he claimed that "fraternal service, the union of faith, honor, and self-sacrifice on the part of the citizens and the president – this is the ancient tradition of Russian statehood" (qtd. in Moskvina 1999: 97). Seven years later, he made the same claim, this time holding up his own family as exemplars of "personality in its collective symphonic incarnation" and therefore "not a naked individuum, but a complex, hierarchical unity of man, family, society, and state" (Moskvina 1999: 97). In other words, according to Mikhalkov, the Russian nation may best be understood as an extension of the Mikhalkov family and the events in which they have taken part.

Mama consists of Mikhalkov's personal musings about his mother and her family, but focuses on how he grew up within a nest of gentle artists. Shot at Bugry, Konchalovsky's dacha, the film that is ostensibly about his mother gives Mikhalkov the opportunity to talk at length about her father and what it was like for young Nikita to live in such a rarified world. "I haven't been here [Bugry] in forty years," he sighs, "but how many wonderful remembrances are associated with this place." It is a house, Mikhalkov states, "where painters, musicians, and artists" visited over the years, all of them conscious of the proximity of Belkin, one of Pushkin's old haunts. In fact, "Pushkin was an idol in the Konchalovsky house" and when the nearby estate was being torn down in the 1930s, Petr Konchalovsky rushed to save its tiles and place them in his Bugry because "Pushkin might have warmed his hands on them." As for the house itself, it was "inhabited by the spirit of creativity, blessed by the house's idol, Aleksandr Sergeevich Pushkin." This spirit passed down to Mikhalkov's mother, for her poems, for example, *About Autumn* (1935), were about the settlement, much as Konchalovsky's paintings often rendered the landscapes around Bugry. Mikhalkov also stakes his claim for inheriting the spirit of celebrity creativity from the place, "I associate all Russian literature with this place. The boy in *Oblomov* wakes up here [in Bugry]. *Neokonchennaia p'esa dlia mekhanicheskogo pianino* [An Unfinished Piece for a Player Piano], *Ochi chernye* [Dark Eyes], *Burnt by the Sun* – all their sets are modeled on Bugry and all childhoods to me are tied to this house." When the family bought their own house outside Moscow, a house that remains the center of the "rod Mikhalkovykh," "Mama decorated this house like Bugry" and it became "a conscious continuation, a continuity of culture, of tradition, of history." The Russian landscapes that Mikhalkov created in his films, in other words, are personal possessions, memories of a famous family. His mother's main contribution, *Mama* argues, was to give Nikita Mikhalkov a famous family of artists and family memories that he could use to render Russian landscapes, as well as to connect him to the family of believers that make up the Russian faith.

Mikhalkov frames his father's life around that of the Soviet Union's existence and emphasizes Sergei's patriotic service to the state as author of the lyrics for the state anthem. He took "Stalin" out in 1977 and then rewrote the words altogether in 2001 for Putin. Thus Sergei Mikhalkov, as Nikita puts it, "wrote two national anthems for two countries in two centuries," an act of service that Mikhalkov regularly promotes. Sergei Mikhalkov, *Father* acknowledges, was a Soviet celebrity – given state awards, filmed for television, and asked to conspicuously serve his country.

His parents also gave Mikhalkov a famous older brother, Andron (also known as Andrei), born in 1937. The two brothers worked together on many projects in the 1960s and 1970s. Andrei cast his little brother in his films *Dvorianskoe gnezdo* [A Nest of Gentlefolk] (1969) and *Sibiriada* (1978) – Andrei's contribution to the connections drawn between the famous family and the land, and co-wrote the script for *A Slave of Love* (1975). Nonetheless, the two brothers disagreed about the meaning of their celebrity family. Andrei took his mother's name, Konchalovsky, and with it an avowed preference for pre-Soviet culture and a conscious claim to pre-Soviet artistic culture. While he worked in the Soviet Union, he did so under the name Mikhalkov-Konchalovsky. When he immigrated to America in 1979, he left the Soviet aristocratic name in Russia and worked solely under his mother's name. Andrei's immigration did not sit well with Nikita, and the two had a falling out. Moreover, when the Soviet Union collapsed, Nikita not only openly presented himself as a Russian nationalist, but also railed against those who fled the country during the Soviet period. His nationalism, therefore, was intimately tied to a personal, family drama. Nikita was authentically Russian and also was proud of his father's Soviet fame, while Andrei was a rootless cosmopolitan who had turned his back on the family and his country (see Youngblood 2003).

The two brothers reconciled, however, for Nikita's film about their father. In 2003, Sergei Mikhalkov turned 90, the ostensible reason for Nikita to shoot documentaries about his famous family.[6] President Putin bestowed a very Soviet-like award on the venerable Soviet poet (the "Order for Service to the Fatherland, Second Class," which Putin would also award Nikita two years later), an occasion that both brothers celebrated as they finally buried the hatchet. By 2003, Mikhalkov had come to see Anton Denikin, a leader in the anti-Bolshevik White movement, as a patriot forced to leave his homeland, his fate part of the larger tragedy that shaped Russia's twentieth century. After all, Mikhalkov's beloved older brother had also left. Now settled back in Moscow, Andrei could appear in *Father*, whereas he had been notably absent in *Mama*.[7] To sanctify their re-found fellowship (*tovarishchestvo*, one of the t's in TriTe), Konchalovsky and Mikhalkov paid for a statue to commemorate the creativity that lay at the heart of the famous family (*tvorchestvo*, another "t"). Their labor (*trud*, the third in the troika) produced a new statue to Vasily Surikov in the artist's hometown of Krasnoyarsk. Nikita's *Barber* celebrated Siberia as quintessentially Russian and Andrei in his epic *Sibiriada* personalized the same gesture but linked it to national history, both thereby promoting the Mikhalkov name as a brand for Russian itself.

In her recent book about the family, Nelli Goreslavskaia captures what the Mikhalkov genealogy represents:

> It is difficult to find another family in our country that is so well known, one that could be compared with this ancient one, with such a number of gifted personalities .... [For] all the Mikhalkovs and Konchalovskys have talent. But they are all talented in different ways, in different skills and cultures, though all are bright, gifted, and unique. For the people they are idols, for the authorities they are always favorites, even under different rulers and under different social conditions, and this authority always gives them affection, and they are invariably located at the apex of the Russian Parnassus. It goes without saying that in the complex world of creative personalities the position they occupy causes numerous rumors, gossip, and hostility, but ... nevertheless, it is not seriously disputed by anyone. ... Is it possible that the key to this incredible family phenomenon lies in their ancient and deep ancestral roots?[8]
>
> (Goreslavskaia 2008: 1–3)

Figure 5.2 Mikahlkov's celebrity is in part inherited from that of his famous father, the children's author Sergei Mikhalkov. Here Mikhalkov celebrates his father's 90th birthday with Sergei's wife, Iuliia, and his brother, Andrei Konchalovsky; 13 March 2003. Photo by Sergei Velichkin, courtesy of RIA Novosti.

Goreslavskaia conceives of the Mikhalkovs in terms of family, but of a privileged sort – a "nest of elites" that echoes Ivan Turgenev's *A Nest of Gentlefolk*. The idea that "special talent" was passed from generation to generation is precisely how Mikhalkov presented himself in the Soviet era and precisely how he packages himself today. It is all about his family, and his family has it all.

Sentimental Journeys to the Motherland: **Rodina Mikhalkova**

Mikhalkov has managed his celebrity by invoking his family and patriotism. The basis for the latter, as Tat'iana Moskvina has written, is the conflation of the word "Russia" with the name of Mikhalkov, for which she ironically provides the simplistic equation, "its name is Russia, its name is Nikita" (Moskvina 2002: 152–65).[9] Mikhalkov has cultivated this aspect of his fame – a part of "patriotic celebrity culture" – by making use of his Soviet-era attributed status and packaging it with nostalgic Russianness. His popularity rests on this packaging, which manages to present his status as achieved. Mikhalkov's efforts to display his cultural authority are evident when he takes his viewers on familiar excursions into the past. His assumption that most Russians share his patriotism is best articulated in his documentary *Sentimental'noe puteshestvie na rodinu: muzyka russkoi zhivopisi* [Sentimental Journeys to the Motherland: The Music of Russian Painting] (1996). The series examines Mikhalkov's favorite paintings and is addressed as a personal note to his "Dear Friends" from "Nikita," exactly the sort of address parodied by the New Year's address. After an opening wide shot of a Russian landscape, the monologue that follows is an extraordinary encapsulation of Russian identity and Mikhalkov's musings about it that is worth quoting in full:

> About twenty years ago, we came here to film *Unfinished Piece for Mechanical Piano*. [The camera shows an old Russian country home.] This house and this park had been inhabited by Chekhov's characters. They suffered here, loved one another here, said foolish things to one another here. They were sincere with one another and they lied to one another. And all of this in its totality was an attempt to reanimate the world of Chekhov's heroes and the world of that period in general. [The camera then focuses on Mikhalkov sitting on the grass of the park, petting a puppy.] Chekhov said that Russians admire their past, hate their present, and fear their future. Perhaps that's the truth of the Russian character and it would be very sad if it were only that. Though, if we think about it, everything Chekhov said has another side to it, which gives us hope, without which neither a Russian person nor Russian culture could live. For the future that a person is afraid of becomes the present he hates and the past he later admires. Therefore, that endless closed circle of fears, hopes, loves, and nostalgia about the past perhaps was actually the perpetual motion of Russian life. This is a series of twenty vignettes about Russian paintings called *Sentimental Journeys to the Motherland: The Music of Russian Painting*. It's an attempt, through art, to hear and recreate somehow the atmosphere of the Russia that is gone for good. I'm not trying to reestablish or reanimate

it, but instead am trying to remind us and others of what that Russian meant to us – what its uniqueness was, its strengths, its weaknesses. The paintings we've selected were not chosen chronologically or thematically. They're an individual choice, what I love personally, and what I believe expresses the Russian character, the Russian nature. And actually, what constitutes the basis for that mysterious international phrase about the enigma of the Russian soul. We'd like you to hear what the artist might have heard when he was painting a picture. [At the word "you" Mikhalkov points at us.] Because in modern times, with the camera that's filming me now, with your cameras, you can take a picture of a wonderful landscape and you know you have it in your pocket. The next day you can take a picture of the Pyramids and then the Eiffel Tower and, your tourist's egotism satisfied, you think you know the world. But that's not so. You don't know the world because a shepherd who never leaves his locale has seen less, yet knows more. He feels more. An artist sitting for four to five days with his sketchbook and trying to convey a sense of what he sees – this is an artist who perceives life vertically. He's not a tourist. And we're interested in what he hears when he's painting. I want you to hear these paintings, to feel their atmosphere, and through this to try to see and feel the entire panorama of a great country that had been and, let's hope [pause], yes, let's hope will yet be reborn.

(Nikita Mikhalkov. *Sentimental Journeys to the Motherland: The Music of Russian Painting* 1996, Studio TriTe, Leonid Vereshchagin, Nikita Mikhalkov)

The move from "we" to "you," from "us" to "me" is fascinating, for it provides a clue to how Mikhalkov reaches his audience and how he creates his celebrity persona – he is both one of us but also a lot better than us, an art appreciator but also an artist and an art critic. These sentimental journeys to an imagined Russian nation provide a visual menu of those art works produced in the nineteenth century that created the images many Russians have in their heads – an internalized gallery that makes their country unique.[10] Mikhalkov, our guide in this nostalgic journey, lovingly lingers over such paintings as Aleksei Venetsianov's *The Morning of a Country Lady* (1823), Vasily Perov's *Portrait of Fedor Dostoevsky* (1872), Il'ia Repin's *On a Turf Bench* (1876), Vasily Polenov's *Moscow Backyard* (1878), and fifteen others.

The motherland that Mikhalkov films as his personal space is one that he has presented to his fans from the beginning of his career. When he started directing films in the 1970s, he immediately began to equate himself with Russia. From his Russian Federation State Institute of Cinematography (VGIK) diploma film (*Spokoinyi den' v kontse voiny* [A Quiet Day at the End of the War] [1970]) to his breakthrough movies of the 1970s and 1980s such as *Svoi sredi chuzhikh, chuzhoi sredi svoikh* [At Home among Strangers, Stranger at Home] (1974) and *Neskol'ko dnei iz zhizni I. I. Oblomova* [A Few Days from the Life of I. I. Oblomov] (1979), Mikhalkov has consistently filmed Slavophilic visions of Russia. His work presents the countryside as more "Russian" than such "artificial" cities as St. Petersburg; Russian art as a "natural" expression of the soul, whereas Western art is decadent;

and history as something to be resurrected because the past contains values that need to be reclaimed.

Mikhalkov took advantage of the new possibilities afforded by the transition from a socialist economy and his earlier break with Mosfilm and made use of his ascribed celebrity. Studio TriTe, founded in 1988, became the most successful film studio in the 1990s because it carried the name of Mikhalkov. Having successfully branded his name abroad as a "Russian" director, Mikhalkov also enjoyed both the money and the connections necessary to buy the apartment block that still serves as his personal studio. He then cannily negotiated deals with the French company Camera One and allowed TriTe to be used by American film companies, charging foreign companies local rates with no markup. In return, Mikhalkov and his studio gained valuable insight into how Hollywood blockbusters were made and marketed.[11] In addition to his shrewd business techniques, Mikhalkov kept his company together by the sheer force of his persona. George Faraday, who conducted interviews with Mikhalkov's staff in the 1990s, quoted one TriTe employee, who said of the boss:

> He's so powerful. When you're with his organization you feel like there's a wall around you and you're free of the government and the mafia … He'll be famous forever because of his work. He's a genius … And his father was the famous Sergei Mikhalkov. He was never with the government. All the women of Russia love him and he's a model to many of the men of TriTe. He's clean. He's a moral authority." Faraday characterizes his management style as that of a feudal squire or *barin*.
>
> (Faraday 2000: 188–89)

Mikhalkov's status and means enabled him to take advantage of the economic and cultural collapse, but he had long since positioned himself to articulate soothing messages about the past to audiences eager to see something happy in their chaotic world. Mikhalkov's post-Soviet status, a time when he vaulted to the heights of the film world, rested on his ability to sell himself as a new man of the people, ready to make audience-friendly fare by taking audiences on the same kinds of sentimental journeys he had taken throughout his career. In other words, "Nikita Mikhalkov" the Soviet attributed/achieved celebrity became "Nikita Mikhalkov" the post-Soviet ascribed/achieved celebrity, one who openly exploited his famous family name to claim that he understood timeless Russian patriotism better than everyone else.

His first post-communist return to the past and its landscapes came with his complex exploration of Stalinist Russia, *Burnt by the Sun* (1994, co-produced by Studio TriTe and France's Channel One). The film presents history as a pastoral family drama. Alternating between Moscow and the same Kostroma landscapes seen in *Oblomov* and *An Unfinished Piece for a Player Piano*, *Burnt by the Sun* transfers Chekhov's pre-revolutionary world into the Soviet era. Mikhalkov plays the rough and gruff Civil War veteran General Kotov, who is a committed Bolshevik out of love for his country and his family, not love for socialism. Kotov's nemesis is Mitia, a Silver Age intellectual who fought for the Whites in the Civil War and who now works for the Soviet People's Commissariat for Internal Affairs (NKVD). He has arrived back at the same house in which he grew up – the house of Kotov's wife – to take Kotov into custody.

Burnt by the Sun contains many of the impressionistic elements of nationhood Mikhalkov had sprinkled throughout his previous cinematic journeys, but also introduces the idea that the Mitias and the Kotovs of the world both acted out of nostalgic patriotism. Both loved the same land and same landscapes and both loved the same woman. Mikhalkov suggests that Soviet history is best viewed as a long civil war fought between family members who acted out of deep love for their motherland, a fight the Mikhalkov-Konchalovsky brothers also waged. The success of the film in Russia, as many critics suggested, sprang from this redemptive message. Dedicated "to those burnt by the sun of revolution," the film was intended as a means to forgive both the Mitias and the Kotovs by blaming only Stalin for the horrors of the 1930s.[12] Mikhalkov himself stated that "Bolshevism did not bring happiness to our country," but questioned whether "it is morally correct on the basis of this indisputable fact to pass judgment on the life of entire generations only on the grounds that people happened to be born not in the best of times" (Pavliuchik 1995).[13]

This redemptive, patriotic idea formed the basis of Mikhalkov's narration in Elena Chavchavadze's 2003 television series, *Russkie bez Rossii* [Russians without Russia] which rehabilitated former Soviet enemies such as Aleksandr Kolchak and Anton Denikin, White Generals who, like Mitia, fought for a different Russia. His experiences in visiting these pasts led Mikhalkov to campaign for Denikin's remains to be brought back to Russia and buried at the Donskoi Monastery. The campaign worked, for in October 2005 Denikin was reburied, along with the exiled philosopher Ivan Il'in, in a ceremony that included Moscow Mayor Yuri Luzhkov and Patriarch Aleksei II. Mikhalkov used the ceremony as a chance to appeal for Rachmaninov's remains to be repatriated next. After all, in *Oblomov* he had cast the Russian composer as an embodiment of Russian art and Russia itself ("Calls for Rachmaninov's Reburial"). Mikhalkov uses the celebrity status of other figures to promote his own, acting as the primary guardian of all things Russian. He believed that his work in returning these patriots was a spiritual service to the entire nation, conflating his desires with Russia's in a wonderfully irritating way. After the ceremony, he declared that "this [reburial] is the beginning of the end of the Civil War and a spiritual gathering together of the country" ["eto nachalo okonchaniia Grazhdanskoi voiny, eto dukhovnoe sobiranie strany"] (Mikhalkov).

Before helping to rebury former villains turned post-Soviet patriots, Mikhalkov released his epic *Barber of Siberia*. Referred to in the Russian press as "the first blockbuster of the Russian empire" (Gladil'shchikov 1999: 42), Mikhalkov answered his own call for Russian cinema to create new heroes for new times by placing old ones in a new package. The hero in this case is named Tolstoy (Oleg Menshikov), a patriotic cadet during the reign of Alexander III who falls in love with an American woman named Jane (Julia Ormond). Jane represents the crass commercialism of western businessmen of the 1990s (in the film, the 1880s) and Tolstoy, the honor-bound and thus easily-duped Russian.[14] The ubiquitous marketing campaign that saturated 1999 Moscow stated, "He's Russian. That explains a lot." ("On russkii. Eto mnogoe ob"iasniaet ..."). Had American-style marketing campaigns been permissible in the Soviet Union, this slogan could have been used to market all of Mikhalkov's films up to that point, for he had always branded his work and his family name with a heavy dose of patriotism.

The campaign worked, for audiences loved *Barber* even more than most critics hated it. The film's popularity led major Russian film journals like *Iskusstvo Kino* and media outlets like *Itogi* to cover not just the film, but the film's reception and the renewed popularity of its creator, eventually dubbing Mikhalkov "the people's favorite" (Goluboevskii and Dmitr'evskoi 1999: 46). "This is the film of a patriot. We are patriots too," commented one woman after leaving the theater. "I liked the film a lot. I've watched a lot of good films and somehow never considered myself a patriot. I am ashamed to talk about that, but I don't think I love my country [right now]. But I felt how it needs to be loved – with the eyes of Mikhalkov," opined another (Beumers 2005: 120). *The Barber of Siberia* glorified a past that never existed while it reified a value system from that imaginary past that could never work in the present. The film's producers, all employees of TriTe, commodified their best product, Nikita Mikhalkov, and marketed him as a representative of Russian patriotic, masculine values.[15] Mikhalkov played Alexander III in the film and once again offered his famous family as a more Russian one than the Romanovs. It was this performance that led Moskvina to conflate the man and his country, but it also confirmed that Mikhalkov had successfully transferred his Soviet celebrity to new times, explicitly laying claim to his ascribed fame.

When *Sentimental Journeys* appeared in a fancy DVD edition in 2006, it was packaged under Mikhalkov's name in the largest font along with the words "from the creator[16] of the films *Unfinished Piece for Mechanical Piano*, *Several Days in the Life of Oblomov*, *Urga*, and *Burnt by the Sun*." The journeys within, in other words, were the same sort of idiosyncratic, ahistorical, personal journeys into patriotism that Mikhalkov had been taking his entire professional life. He has recently announced that he plans to make an update of *Sentimental Journeys* that focuses on two famous painters omitted from the original: Vasily Surikov and Petr Konchalovsky, his great-grandfather and grandfather (Mikhalkov).

Mikhalkov's family history therefore continues to be at the center of his celebrity status. His use of it points to the patrilinear nature of Soviet society. Mikhalkov became famous because of his name, just as Karen Shakhnazarov, Fedor Bondarchuk, and other famous film celebrities derive their status from equally famous fathers.[17] All, as Helena Goscilo points out in Chapter 10, have parlayed Soviet fame into post-Soviet status. Nikita, for his part, bought extra fame insurance by marrying glamorous celebrities. His first wife, Anastasiia Vertinskaia, was the daughter of the famous Russian cabaret actor Aleksandr Vertinsky, whom he met while acting in Bondarchuk's *War and Peace* (1965–67). His second wife, Tat'iana, was a model turned fashion designer. His name has also conferred ascribed celebrity upon his children, all of whom appear in his films and in the media.

Nikita has offered his own explanations for his celebrity status and has focused on his Russian patriotic values, which, he believes, his fans share. In one interview

(Zaitseva 2006), he defined "patriotism" as "when I say I love this and propose that you love it too" ["patriotizm – eto kogda ia govoriu: ia liubliu eto i vam predlagaiu liubit'"]. In other words, Mikhalkov subscribes to a salesman's notion of influence. He tells you what is patriotic and then you agree to share his feelings, a concept he calls "enlightened patriotism" [prosveshchennyi patriotizm]. As for the "roots of a [patriotic] system," Mikhalkov believes that they consist of "your mom, your family, your grandfather" (Zaitseva 2006). In other words, Russian patriotic culture is essentially the Mikhalkov family tree. His name is Russia, his name is Nikita.

Conclusion: St. Vladimir's hagiography

Celebrities create an aura of sorts that binds their fans to them as part of "the expression of a cultural axis organized around abstract desire" (Rojek 2004: 187). Fans of a famous figure play an active part in the creation of a particular person's celebrity status, often because the celebrity articulates some sort of deeper personal desire. The Mikhalkov aura offers a comfortable culture to its fans, a sense of Russianness that is timeless, connected to the land and to the family, and that defies rational analysis. His celebrity status is one driven by Russian patriotic values, a masculine yet sentimental love for the motherland.

Because Mikhalkov equates himself and his desires with those of Russia, he has become a lifelong Orthodox believer since communism's collapse.[18] His trendy patriotic religiosity helps to explain the close relationship Mikhalkov has with the biggest celebrity of all in post-Soviet Russia, Vladimir Putin (on celebrity bonds, see Chapter 10). The two ski together, laugh together, attend Russian state ceremonies together, and together they believe in Orthodoxy as a Russian institution. Putin has become a political celebrity for many of the same reasons that Mikhalkov has become a cultural one: both articulate a timeless sense of Russianness that evokes religious faith.

On 7 October 2007, Mikhalkov's visual vita, *55*, a living hagiography for Saint Vladimir Vladimirovich, aired on the *Russia* television channel.[19] The short film celebrates Putin's miraculous deeds and presents his presidency as an updated life of an Orthodox saint. Reminding his audience that they need to think about the "atmosphere" of the 1990s, a time when "seven bankers" ruled a chaotic and dispirited country and everyone was "on his knees before them," Mikhalkov intones that "an absolutely new man came" and had "a cross placed on his shoulders." Just eight years later, Mikhalkov claims, the atmosphere has changed completely, for the Russia of 2007 is a prosperous and healthy spiritual nation (on this view of Putin, see Chapter 1). Mikhalkov casts his Saint Vladimir as a latter day Saint George, slaying the dragons of poverty, terrorism, and debt that faced his country. These changes, Mikhalkov states, "did not just happen on their own." They happened because of Putin.

According to Mikhalkov, the President has also performed three miracles. First, he unified the worldwide Russian Orthodox Churches with the Moscow Patriarchate, an act that Mikhalkov openly labels "a miracle." Second, Putin's February 2007 speech at Munich, one where he labeled the USA a rogue state and called for a multi-polar world, is proof of his pious power. Mikhalkov interprets the speech – which most American observers saw as an aggressive attempt to revive Cold War rhetoric – as a sign that the world now thinks Russians are not barbarians after all, but can stand up, fight, and "bridge East and West." Third, Putin has performed a personal miracle for the Mikhalkov family (not covered in 55): when he awarded Sergei Mikhalkov a state medal in 2003, the occasion brought the brothers Mikhalkov-Konchalovsky together and helped them overcome their animosities.

Miracles of faith, fatherland, and family are precisely the patriotic vision created by Mikhalkov and captured in his celebrity status over the years. Mikhalkov's celebrity, according to P. David Marshall's categories, is one associated with a certain kind of power, not quite political but also not just an empty consumer-based construction. His is a celebrity that "structures meaning, crystallizes ideological positions, and works to provide a sense and coherence to a culture" (Marshall 1997: x). That this status appeared as an attributed one in the Soviet era points to the political nature of Mikhalkov's celebrity over the last forty years. As a Soviet celebrity, Mikhalkov enjoyed a status that was an official creation, while his evocations of timeless patriotism packaged as service to the state reinforced his stature. After communism's collapse, Mikhalkov used his family name to articulate the very same mission as the core of his work – he does what he does, in other words, because he serves his motherland regardless of political systems. This version of celebrity culture helps to explain Putin's, for the former Russian president borrowed from Mikhalkov's visions about the motherland, making Putin's Russia a lot like Mikhalkov's sentimental journeys.

Figure 5.3 Mikhalkov promotes himself as an embodiment of Russian patriotic values and as a servant to the state. Here he combines both while hosting Vladimir Putin on the set of his film *Burnt by the Sun 2*; 13 May 2009. Photo by Sergei Subbotin, courtesy of RIA Novosti.

Mikhalkov's most recent film, *12* (2007), can be viewed as an addition to Putin's vita. Based on Sidney Lumet's *12 Angry Men* (1957), the film casts Mikhalkov as an artist named Nikolai, who is placed on a jury with eleven other men. The case they hear involves a Chechen boy accused of murdering his Russian stepfather. Lumet's film reaffirmed the judicial principle of reasonable doubt when Henry Fonda persuades his fellow jurors to acquit a Puerto Rican defendant. Mikhalkov's film casts the other jurors as symbolic representatives of the post-Soviet Russian nation and the director dissects how xenophobes, democrats, rich New Russians, and a neurotic performer, among others, do not know what is right and what is best for Russia. The jury is unconcerned with reasonable doubt; instead, they set out to find the real murderer and discover that a criminal group murders the Russian man because he refused to give up his apartment. The jury then votes to acquit the boy, only for Mikhalkov's character to vote against because he believes that the Chechen will be safer in prison. He asks each of the jurors if they will take the boy in and protect him. All of them say no. Nikolai, by contrast, agrees to take him in, revealing that he is not an artist after all, but a "former officer" of the KGB.

The film is, as the director has claimed, "about Russia and for Russia" (Kichin 2007). The marketing slogan on the film's poster reinforced this claim – "this is a film for everyone and about each of us" [eto fil'm dlia vsekh i pro kazhdogo]. Mikhalkov expanded, "Our film is about the fact that a Russian person cannot live according to the law. It seemed to me that this is a good time to talk about this ... It is important. Why? Because it is boring to live according to the law. The law is without personal relations and a Russian person without personal relations is like a barren flower" (Mikhalkov). Nikolai follows his creator's principles, subverting court justice for his own godlike benevolence, thereby bringing "personal relations" into Russian law. As Tatiana Smorodinskaya has argued, "instead of promoting the law, Mikhalkov promotes 'poniatiia,' which in his view are the particular Russian set of moral values and rules" (2008). In other words, Russia does not need courts and laws; it needs the strong hand of a former KBG agent. Yuri Bogomolov, a critic with *Rossiskaia Gazeta*, clarified the obvious, "Mikhalkov's hero is a broad hint to Putin: Both are former intelligence officers, both speak foreign languages, both have a burning sense of justice, both feel themselves saviors" (qtd. in Rodriguez 2008). Zoia Svetova concurred, "Certainly, Mikhalkov's character is in no way outwardly similar to Putin. But he is similar in his essence." Both claim to be "saviors of the fatherland" [spasiteli Otechestva] (Svetova 2007). Mikhalkov even held a private screening for Putin at the president's residence. Afterwards Putin claimed the film "brought a tear to [his] eye" [vyshibaet slezu] (Isaev 2007).

Nikita Mikhalkov has played the role of attributer to Putin's celebrity, using his own status to cement that of his new leader. Both Mikhalkov and Putin articulate ideas and images meant to combat the supposed spiritual crisis facing Russia today by focusing on a timeless Russianness as the basis of their patriotic platforms. Both men claim to speak for the nation and both equate themselves with Russia, perhaps the primary reason Mikhalkov signed Zurab Tsereteli's October 2007 letter that pleaded with Putin to remain in office.[20] In Mikhalkov's case, his service to Putin is exactly the sort of patriotic work he claims he and his family have performed for centuries. His next work will continue this "service": *Burnt by the Sun 2*, set in World War II and featuring Kotov and Mitia, both resurrected from the dead, premiered on Victory Day 2010.

Notes

1 I wish to thank Helena Goscilo and Vlad Strukov for inviting me to write about Mikhalkov and for their suggestions on an earlier draft. Thanks are also due to Benjamin Sutcliffe and Brigid O'Keeffe for their insightful comments.
2 The video is available online at: http://rutube.ru/tracks/1363136.html?v=49ee278be19 4d1e2061bdfd355a451bf (accessed 1 February 2009), and the parody of *12* is available online at: www.youtube.com/watch?v=YjMvl5xwan0 (accessed 1 February 2009).
3 For a list of Sergei Mikhalkov's work, see the site http://publ.lib.ru/ARCHIVES/M/ MIHALKOV_Sergey_Vladimirovich/_Mikhalkov_S._V.html (accessed 1 February 2009). By 1980, 140 million copies of his books had been published in the languages of the Soviet Union alone.
4 For a discussion of how Mikhalkov's films search for a father figure and therefore a stable fatherland, see Moskvina (1999: 94–7).
5 The family as a model for Russian national identity, a model that Mikhalkov clearly mines, has its roots in the nineteenth-century search for Russianness (see Martin 1998).
6 Sergei Mikhalkov died in 2009.
7 The irony could hardly escape any viewer, given the older brother's adoption of their mother's name and Nikita Mikhalkov's repeated emphasis on the strength of the Mikhalkov clan.
8 You can also visit a website devoted to all things Mikhalkovy, available online at: www. mihalkovy.ru (accessed 18 December 2009).
9 See also Moskvina's "La Grande Illusion," which traces Mikhalkov's Great Life and his quest for an ideal Fatherland. Moskvina sees a change in Mikhalkov's persona and his films in the 1980s, when he turns from the liberal intelligentsia of his youth to a more patriotic, pastor-like sense of himself. The original article appeared in *Iskusstvo Kino*, issue 6, 1997.
10 The literature on national identity is so long that it is somewhat pointless to discuss it here. Clearly the idea of an imagined nation, a visually constructed means of thinking about how a person belongs to a larger entity such as Russia borrows from Benedict Anderson's 1983 classic, *Imagined Communities: Reflections on the Origin and Spread of Nationalism*, London: Verso, and from the work of Anthony D. Smith; see his latest work, (2008) *The Cultural Foundations of Nations: Hierarchy, Covenant, and Republic*, Malden, MA: Blackwell. For Russian nationhood, see Franklin, S. and Widdis, E. (2004) *National Identity in Russian Culture*, Cambridge: Cambridge University Press. Christopher Ely's (2002) excellent work on landscape art and Russian nationhood helps to understand how Nikita Mikhalkov came to imagine his Russian nation, *This Meager Nature: Landscape and National Identity in Imperial Russia*, DeKalb: Northern Illinois University Press.
11 Interview with Sergei Gurevich, Production Manager, Studio TriTe, Moscow, 14 July 2008. Gurevich worked as the Moscow-based producer on Philip Noyce's *The Saint* (1997) and in the interview admitted that "we learned everything about how to market movies, produce movies, and shoot movies in the new conditions" from this experience.
12 Boris Yeltsin appreciated its anti-Stalinist message enough to have the film screened on state television the night before the 1996 elections, when Yeltsin feared he might lose to the Communist Party leader, Gennadii Ziuganov (see Faraday [2000: 190]).
13 For more on the film, see Beumers (2001).

14 For more on the film, see Beumers (2000), Hashamova (2006), Larsen (2003), and Norris (2005).
15 One memorable product tie-in was the cologne, Cadet, which allegedly captured the essence of Mikhalkov's manly mustache.
16 The slogan in Russian reads as *ot sozdatelia*, which is a significant turn of phrase since he is not just a director but a creator of motherland.
17 Georgii Shakhnazarov, later one of Gorbachev's advisors, and Sergei Bondarchuk, one of Mikhalkov's mentors and the winner of the USSR's first Oscar for his *War and Peace*.
18 See the other interviews collected on Studio TriTe's website for examples of how Mikhalkov employs religious sentiments. Available online at: www.trite.ru/mikhalkov_interviews.mhtml (accessed 18 December 2009).
19 The film is also available online for your viewing displeasure on YouTube at: www.youtube.com/watch?v=yl79JkDF-Lc (accessed 18 December 2009).
20 The letter by Tsereteli was allegedly written on behalf of "the entire artistic community of Russia, numbering more than 65,000 painters, sculptors, folk and theater artists," but was signed by only three: Tsereteli, Mikhalkov, and Repin Academy president Albert Charkin. The outcry from the remaining 64,997 artists was swift – over 300 signed a letter on www.stengazeta.net that called for Putin to step down from politics. Tsereteli's letter can be found online at www.rg.ru/2007/10/16/pismo.html (accessed 28 December 2009).

Bibliography

Anderson, B. (1983) *Imagined Communities: Reflections on the Origin and Spread of Nationalism*, London: Verso.
Beumers, B. (2000) "Sibirskii tsiriul'nik (The Barber of Siberia)," in J. Forbes and S. Street (eds) *European Cinema: An Introduction*, Houndmills: Palgrave, pp. 195–206.
— . (2001) *Burnt by the Sun*, London: I. B. Tauris.
— . (2005) *Nikita Mikhalkov: Between Nostalgia and Nationalism*, London: I. B. Tauris.
Boorstin, D. (1992) *The Image: A Guide to Pseudo-Events in America*, New York: Vintage.
Borenstein, E. (2008) *Overkill: Sex and Violence in Contemporary Russian Popular Culture*, Ithaca: Cornell University Press.
"Calls for Rachmaninoff's Reburial in Russia, Lenin's Burial Follow the Ceremony of Moscow Reburial of the Leader of White movement Anton Denikin," Available online at: www.prweb.com/releases/2005/10/prweb293820.htm (accessed 18 December 2009).
Cashmore, E. (2006) *Celebrity Culture*, London: Routledge.
Ely, C. (2002) *This Meager Nature: Landscape and National Identity in Imperial Russia*, DeKalb: Northern Illinois University Press.
Faraday, G. (2000) *Revolt of the Filmmakers: The Struggle for Artistic Autonomy and the Fall of the Soviet Film Industry*, University Park, PA: Penn State Press.
Franklin, S. and Widdis, E. (2004) *National Identity in Russian Culture*, Cambridge: Cambridge University Press.
Gladil'shchikov, I. (1999) "Pervyi blokbaster Rossiiskoi imperii," *Itogi* 145, no. 10: 42–7.
Goluboevskii, A. and Dmitr'evskoi, A. (1999) "Mikhalkov kak narodnyi liubomets," *Itogi* 145, no. 10: 46.
Goreslavskaia, N. (2008) *Mikhalkovy i Konchalovskie: gnezdo elity*, Moscow: Algoritm.
Hashamova, Y. (2006) "Two Visions of a Usable Past in (Op)position to the West: Mikhalkov's *The Barber of Siberia* and Sokurov's *Russian Ark*," *Russian Review* 65, no. 2: 250–66.

Havel, V. (1991) "Stories and Totalitarianism (1987)" in V. Havel *Open Letters: Selected Writings, 1965–1990*, New York: Alfred A. Knopf, pp. 328–50.

Isaev, R. (2007) "V Moskve i Chechne pokazali novyi fil'm Nikity Mikhalkova '12,'" *Prague Watchdog*. Available online at: www.watchdog.cz/?show=000000-000015-000006-000023&lang=2 (accessed 18 December 2009).

Jenks, A. (2008) "In Pursuit of Truthiness: Distortion Zones and the Soviet Cult of Yuri Gagarin," Lecture at Miami University, 10 March.

Kichin, V. (2007) "L'vinaia dolia," *Rossiiskaia Gazeta*, 10 Sept. Available online at: www.rg.ru/2007/09/10/veneciya.html (accessed 18 December 2009).

Kotkin, S. (1999) "A Tsar is Born," *New Republic*, 5 Apr: 6–18.

Larsen, S. (2003) "National Identity, Cultural Authority, and the Post-Soviet Blockbuster: Nikita Mikhalkov and Aleskei Balabanov," *Slavic Review* 62, no. 3 (Fall): 491–511.

Lawton, A. (1992) *Kinoglasnost: Soviet Cinema in Our Time*, Cambridge: Cambridge University Press.

Lobanova, O. (1982) "Za schastlivoe budushchee," *Izvestiia*, 11 May: 3.

Marshall, P. D. (1997) *Celebrity and Power: Fame in Contemporary Culture*, Minneapolis: University of Minnesota Press.

Martin, A. (1998) "The Family Model of Society and Russian National Identity in Sergei N. Glinka's *Russian Messenger*," *Slavic Review* 57, no. 1 (Spring): 28–49.

Mikhalkov, N. [Website] Available online at: www.trite.ru/mikhalkov.mhtml?PubID=117 (accessed 18 December 2009).

Moskvina, T. (1999) "La Grande Illusion," in B. Beumers (ed.) *Russia on Reels: The Russian Idea in Post-Soviet Cinema*, London: I. B. Tauris, pp. 91–104.

—— . (2002) "Ee zovut Rossiia, ee zovut Nikita," in T. Moskvina *Pokhvala plokhomu shokoladu*, Moscow: Limbus, pp. 152–65.

Neuberger, J. (2002) "Between Public and Private: Revolution and Melodrama in Nikita Mikhalkov's *Slave of Love*," in L. McReynolds and J. Neuberger (eds) *Imitations of Life: Two Centuries of Melodrama in Russia*, Durham: Duke University Press, pp. 259–82.

"Nikita Mikhalkov. Interv'iu zhurnalu Time Out Moskva. Sentiabr' 2007" (2007) Available online at: www.timeout.ru/journal/feature/1645/ (accessed 18 December 2009).

Norris, S. M. (2005) "Tsarist Russia, Lubok Style: Nikita Mikhalkov's *Barber of Siberia* (1999) and Post-Soviet National Identity," *Historical Journal of Film, Radio, and Television* 25, no. 1 (March): 99–116.

Pavliuchik, L. (1995) "Nikita Mikhalkov, utomlennyi kinoprokatom," *Izvestiia*, 26 Jan. Available online at: http://dlib.eastview.com.proxy.lib.muohio.edu/browse/doc/3181118 (accessed 28 December 2009).

Prokhorova, E. (2006) "Svoi sredi chuzhikh, chuzhoi sredi svoikh / At Home among Strangers, a Stranger at Home," in B. Beumers (ed.) *The Cinema of Russia and the Former Soviet Union (24 Frames)*, London: Wallflower Press, pp. 171–82.

Ragozin, L. (2008) "Tochka nevozvrata," *Russkii Newsweek* 178, no. 4, Jan. Available online at: www.runewsweek.ru/theme/?tid=150&rid=2326 (accessed 18 December 2009).

Razzakov, F. (2005) *Nikita Mikhalkov: chuzhoi sredi svoikh*, Moscow: Eksmo.

Rodriguez, A. (2008) "Pairing Pop Culture with Propaganda," *Chicago Tribune*, 13 Jan. Available online at: www.chicagotribune.com/news/opinion/chi-corr_russiajan13, 0,7816315.story (accessed 18 December 2009).

Rojek, C. (2004) *Celebrity*. London: Reaktion Books.

Sergeev, V. (1980) "Dni rossiiskoi literatury," *Izvestiia*, 11 June: 6.

Smith, A. D. (2008) *The Cultural Foundations of Nations: Hierarchy, Covenant, and Republic*, Malden, MA: Blackwell.

Smorodinskaya, T. (2008) "Nemesis vs. Mimesis, Rule of Law vs. 'Russian Justice'; Mikhalkov's '12,'" Paper presented at Fortieth National Convention of the American Association for the Advancement of Slavic Studies, Philadelphia, PA.

Svetova, Z. (2007) "'12' kak apologiia Putina," *Ezhednevnyi Zhurnal*, 19 Oct. Available online at: www.ej.ru/?a=note&id=7473 (accessed 18 December 2009).

Turner, G. (2004) *Understanding Celebrity*, London: Sage Publications.

Youngblood, D. (2003) "The Cosmopolitan and the Patriot: The Brothers Mikhalkov-Konchalovsky and Russian Cinema," *Historical Journal of Film, Radio, and Television* 23, no. 1 (March): 27–41.

Zaitseva I. (2006) "Sistema koordinat Nikity Mikhalkova" [Interview with Mikhalkov] Available online at: www.trite.ru/mikhalkov.mhtml?PubID=131 (accessed 22 December 2009).

Mikhalkov's works

Mikhalkov, N. (1970) *Spokoinyi den' v kontse voiny* [A Quiet Day at the End of the War].
— . (1974) *Svoi sredi chuzhikh, chuzhoi sredi svoikh* [At Home Among Strangers, Stranger at Home].
— . (1976) *Raba liubvi* [A Slave of Love].
— . (1977) *Neokonchennaia p'esa dlia mekhanicheskogo pianino* [An Unfinished Piece for a Player Piano].
— . (1979) *Piat' vecherov* [Five Evenings].
— . (1980) *Neskol'ko dnei iz zhizni I.I. Oblomova* [A Few Days from the Life of I. I. Oblomov].
— . (1981) *Rodnia* [Kinfolk].
— . (1983) *Bez svidetelei* [Without Witnesses].
— . (1987) *Ochi chernye* [Dark Eyes].
— . (1993) *Anna ot 6 do 18* [Anna from Six to Eighteen].
— . (1994) *Utomlennyi solntsem* [Burnt by the Sun].
— . (1996) *Sentimental'noe puteshestvie na rodinu: muzyka russkoi zhivopisi* [Sentimental Journeys to the Motherland: The Music of Russian Painting] [Note: 2006 DVD edition is also mentioned].
— . (1999) *Sibirskii tsiriul'nik* [The Barber of Siberia].
— . (2003) *Mama* [Mama].
— . (2003) *Otets* [Father].
— . (2007) *12*.
— . (2007) *55*.

6 "Much ado and nothing"

Mikhail Zadornov as a celebrity of Russian comedy

Oxana Poberejnaia (University of Manchester)

Introduction

This chapter explores Mikhail Zadornov's celebrity as a phenomenon born out of the tension between Soviet and post-Soviet Russian identities and out of the opposition "Russia vis-à-vis the West." I argue that Zadornov is a self-constructed celebrity who has defined his public identity by tapping into Russians' feeling of injured national pride, and who increased his fandom by encouraging his compatriots to share stereotypes of Russianness. I rely on Western theories of public space (Habermas 1999) and celebrity culture (Dyer 1998; Rojek 2006; Turner 2004) as well as studies of Soviet and post-Soviet popular culture (Graham 2003; MacFadyen 2001) to provide a theoretical framework for the investigation of the Zadornov phenomenon. Though my analysis adopts the methodological tools of sociological studies (using such resources as FORM, ROMIR) and political science, it is fundamentally grounded in an interpretative analysis of Zadornov's texts, which encompass different genres and media, including Zadornov's shows, as recorded on audio and video tapes and DVDs, and the short stories they are based on; his official website; and press materials comprising Zadornov's interviews and articles.

Zadornov as author-performer of comedy in post-Soviet Russia: jokes and fans

According to the autobiography he submitted for *Rambler's People of the Year* award 2005 ("Rambler liudi goda"), Zadornov was born in Latvia in 1948 to a mother from an ancient noble Polish family and a father who was a distinguished Soviet author. In 1965 Zadornov moved to Moscow, where he started an engineering degree at the Moscow Aviation Institute. There he became the head of an amateur student theater. The early 1980s found Zadornov working first at the Humor Department of *Iunost'* [Youth] magazine, then as Director of an amateur theater in the KGB club in Moscow. Throughout the 1990s Zadornov toured Russia and abroad, made frequent appearances on television, and published several books. To an extent his friendship with his neighbor Boris Yeltsin accounts for the perception of Zadornov's celebrity status as a part of Russia's post-Soviet democratization.

In the 2000s, and especially the first half of the decade, Zadornov has been a significant presence on the Russian cultural scene. His programs are shown on various television channels (mostly Channel One and Ren-TV) at least once a month, and during the holiday season between December and January they are broadcast as often as once or twice a week. A range of Zadornov's DVDs is readily available in specialized DVD shops selling legal products, on street stalls hawking pirated items, and in online shops such as ozon.ru. At a price of 150 Russian rubles (approximately US$6), these DVDs – typically recordings of Zadornov's television performances – are easily affordable. Standard shops usually carry ten titles of Zadornov's DVD recordings at any one time. His frequent appearances on television, the large sales of his recorded performances, and the huge number of messages people leave on his fan website testify to his popularity.[1]

Zadornov's television career was launched in 1984, when he read his short story *Deviatyi vagon* [Carriage No 9] on the popular Soviet comedy program *Vokrug smekha* [Around Laughter] (*Iumor 585 proby* 2005c).[2] Since then, he has performed his comic stories non-stop in variety and individual programs. His career as an author-performer roughly divides into five periods: During the late Soviet era (1984–6) he produced humorous stories that were basically extended *anekdoty* – an oral genre of Soviet/Russian humor, short jokes on an unlimited range of subjects, concluding with a punch line – about funny incidents in Soviet life. Perestroika (1986–91) saw him poking fun at the drawbacks of Soviet life. Highlighting differences between the wealthy capitalist West and the Soviet Union, he discussed political, economic, and social changes in Soviet life introduced by perestroika. In the early post-Soviet years (1991–6) he continued making fun of the inadequacies of Russian life, while simultaneously making attempts to place post-Soviet Russia in the new political and social context. In the following years (1996–2006), however, he changed his stance, glorifying the post-Soviet lifestyle, which had undergone a significant economic transformation owing to the staggering success of some Russian entrepreneurs who were selling fossil fuels abroad and others who were engaged in various unregulated business practices. At this stage Zadornov began criticizing the West's influence on Russian politics, culture, and language. Since 2006 he has openly embraced the ideology of "Russian Vedism" (a nationalist, neo-pagan "philosophy" of the Russian Right that lends itself to racism and anti-Semitism), which he publicly propagates as the basis for a new post-Soviet Russian national identity, disseminating concepts of "alternative history" and arbitrary linguistic findings to support that ideology. In short, Zadornov has built his celebrity around jokes about Soviet and post-Soviet Russian identity in its relation to the west, in the process moving from a liberal to a conservative position.

The jokes Zadornov has produced throughout his career roughly fall into the following categories.

1 Observational humor: funny situations, phrases, notices, posters, parts of advertisements either observed by Zadornov or reported to him by friends or members of his audience.

2 Practical jokes that Zadornov admits to playing on shop assistants or hotel employees.
3 Word play and jokes about language, with a focus on the influence of English on Russian. This brand of humor has recently devolved into inaccurate reinterpretation of Russian words following the principles of Russian Vedism.
4 Topical humor, centered on new and unfamiliar features of post-Soviet life, such as the nouveau riche, psychics, and the new style of journalism, driven by profit.
5 Anti-Western and anti-American jokes, which criticize Western food as well as its cultural expansion and supposed lack of education and culture.
6 Nationalist jokes, ranging from traditional brief *anekdot*-al characterizations of various nations to political statements about newly independent post-Soviet countries and jokes about Russian émigrés in the West.
7 Jokes about Russian national identity, in which Zadornov satirizes Russians' laziness, drinking problems, lack of organization, but also praises Russian energy, wit, and ingenuity.
8 Jokes about Russian politics and politicians that include general observations about political changes or lack thereof after the collapse of the Soviet Union.

An example of the last is Zadornov's comment that the democrats stripped the Communists of their privileges, which they now enjoy themselves (*Tak zhit' mozhno. Chast' I* 1996c). In a similar vein, Zadornov claims to regret that Egor Gaidar, a representative of the early democrats in Yeltsin's Russia, could not attract an electorate because of his intellectual manner of speaking, whereas Vladimir Zhirinovsky, the infamous leader of the nationalist Liberal Democratic Party of Russia, attracts followers by making outrageous statements and promises. For instance, Zhirinovsky promised to supply all single women with husbands from the ranks of his party, and to turn sexual minorities into a majority (*Mnogo shuma i nichego, Chast' I* 1996c). As for current politics, Zadornov has an entire program dedicated to Putin's era, entitled *Zapiski otmorozka* [Notes of an Outlaw] (2005), where he ridicules the political elite's slavish adoration of Putin (on this topic, see Chapter 1) and also criticizes Putin for not having followed through on his promises.

Zadornov's humor revolves around both mundane and weighty aspects of Russian life, such as the complexities of post-Soviet transition and Russians' inadequacies as well as their resilience and ingenious responses to life's difficulties. Though Zadornov's humorous performances do not explicitly engage the phenomenon of Russian celebrity or glamour, he has expressed his views on the topic, contending that only in Russia can a person of his physical appearance be a comedian, for to qualify as a comedian in the West one must "look funny." Americans, says Zadornov, would immediately recognize the pop singers Filipp Kirkorov and Boris Moiseiev as stars because of their outrageous stage image and costumes (*Ia liubliu Ameriku* 2003), whereas he, Zadornov, has attained celebrity status without having to resort to such strategies. Rather than addressing the issue of celebrity, however, Zadornov as a rule merely mentions his contacts with other celebrities, as in a story about how private planes transported other stars and him to highly-paid gigs (*Mnogo shuma i nichego. Chast' I* 1996a). The types of celebrities that he mingles with and most frequently mentions in his routines and interviews include the nouveau riche (possibly with a criminal past or even present), their supermodel companions, psychics, priests, and KGB and FSB agents (*Iumor 585 proby* 2005c). He also professes to have "star mates" in the Russian army with whom he plays tennis, a sport that became a form of socializing widely accepted in the higher echelons of Russian politicians under Yeltsin (*Mnogo shuma i nichego. Chast' II* 1996b). Zadornov's comments and attitude indicate that he simultaneously adores and despises glamour. On the one hand, it adds luster to his own prominence, but, on the other, it surrounds celebrities to whom he believes himself both morally and intellectually superior. His effort to separate himself consciously – and pretentiously – from the sphere of Russian stars marks his unique status in Russian stardom and its attendant glamour.

While irony fails Zadornov in his social allegiances, it serves as a tool to make people laugh, in the process boosting the self-esteem of those who credit his insistence that only Russians can laugh at their own silliness (*Ia liubliu Ameriku* 2003). In accounting for the inadequacies of Soviet and post-Soviet life, he blames the Soviet regime rather than the Russian "psyche." In doing so he not only offers psychological comfort to his audiences, but also reinforces tradition, for a long-standing habit among Russian commentators distinguishes between the people (narod) and the state, ascribing such features as resilience, wit, and energy to the former, and oppression, bureaucracy, greed, and stupidity to the latter (*Iumor 585 proby* 2005c; *Tak zhit' mozhno. Chast' II* 1996d). Consistency is not Zadornov's strong suit. Though he assesses Russians' lack of organization and efficiency by American standards, he criticizes the West for its material excesses and alleged lack of ethics – a popular tactic during the 2000s. According to his all too familiar argument, Russians are superior to people in the West on account of their supposed indifference to material riches and their ability to preserve spiritual values (*Mnogo shuma i nichego. Chast' II* 1996b). In such routines as *Much Ado and Nothing* [Mnogo shuma i nichego] (1996a; 1996b), Zadornov presents cross-cultural encounters as miscommunication, using the dichotomies of West/Russia and material/spiritual to reassess Russian national values. He presents one culture through the prism of another culture's perceptions, ostensibly aiming to identify cultural stereotypes and the way national identity is constructed. For example, his "representative" German character is a businessman who prizes money and time, pursues an orderly schedule and a mode of operation he considers appropriate to given circumstances. Therefore he experiences shock when offered a heavy meal at a spa, where, moreover, a hospital white coat substitutes for a bathrobe (*Mnogo shuma i nichego. Chast' II* 1996b). Yet while in Russia he falls under the spell of its lifestyle and "becomes human," in Zadornov's words: he learns to appreciate heavy drinking, Russian women, and spending money on cultivating a glamorous life (*Mnogo shuma i nichego. Chast' II* 1996b). In other words, Zadornov points to both attractive and appalling elements of Russian identity and reassures those members of his audience prepared to equate alcoholic excess, sexist behavior, and irresponsible expenditure of funds with "Russianness" that their way of life is valid.

Zadornov belongs to that strand of Russians who since the eighteenth century have advocated a unique Russian sensibility as a reaction to the forced modernization of Russia under Peter the Great. Indeed, on a far from challenging intellectual level Zadornov in his comedy routines adheres to the Slavophile tradition of arguing for a unique Russian identity, also evident in his propagation of "Vedic" ideas, which assign a special messianic role to Russia as a third civilization, destined to balance the differences between West and East.

By offering himself as a role model Zadornov maintains his own celebrity status and, as a nationalist attuned to the political Right, massages the Russian national ego. Fans emulate and interact with him, sharing with their "guru" not only funny occurrences in Russian life but also conservative political views. He encourages their interactive forms of communication at his performances and on his website. The latter has online games, the title of one alluding to the expression "spasitel'nye zadatki" [seeds of salvation] by Alexander Solzhenitsyn, who after his years of dissidence adopted a radically conservative stance. Zadornov's evolution mirrors Solzhenitsyn's trajectory from critic to conservative supporter of Russia's status quo, and, more importantly in the context of celebrity, implies his kinship with the man who during the late Soviet era for many years dominated media reports on the USSR.

Zadornov's website (www.zadornov.net/) provides a refuge for provincial nationalism and exceptionalism. The site offers competitions and quizzes, handing out prizes in the form of Zadornov's books, CDs, and DVDs to winners such as someone called Anna, who posted the naïve comment that only in Russia are hand-made gifts valued more than expensive gifts, whereas in the USA, for example, money alone dictates all of life's preferences. Zadornov responded with the phrase "correct and touching," endorsing his fan's anti-American stance and encouraging others to adopt it. Another online fan, Evgenii, told a story about a lady whose purse was stolen on a bus and how the bus passengers collected money for her. Ignoring the fact that one of the (most likely Russian?) passengers was a thief, he fixed on the collective generosity that he believes possible only in Russia. Thus Zadornov and his website fans cling to a notion of Russian exclusivity and superiority reminiscent of Soviet-era propaganda, which fed Soviet citizens who had never traveled abroad ready-made pronouncements that reassured them and substituted for thoughtful, independent judgments.

In addition to the fandom endorsed by Zadornov on his official website, there exist several independent Zadornov fan outlets online. Moreover, many forums allow internet users to discuss Russian comedy in general and Zadornov in particular, such as *Forumy. Boltalka. Fan klub Mikhaila Zadornova* [Forums. Chat. Fan club of Mikhail Zadornov] (http://forums.playground.ru/talk/humour/133665), whose users admire Zadornov's humor and especially his anti-American jokes. Some post messages there consisting only of his catch phrase, "Nu, oni i tupye!" [How dumb they are!]. The website *MihailZadornov.info* (http://mihailzadornov. info), registered in April 2008, hosts free video and audio files of Zadornov's concerts, full texts of his books, and his biography (available online at: http://forums.

playground.ru/talk/129686). Another fan website, called *Mikhail Zadornov. Iumoristicheskie rasskazy i istorii* [Mikhail Zadornov. Humorous Short Stories and Anecdotes] (available online at: www.zadornov.kiev.ua; the old version was at: http://zadornov.narod.ru), is several years old and is now in its second edition on a different hosting server. Its front page proclaims that the purpose of the project is to open Russians' eyes to the secrets of life [sic]. The website contains a comprehensive collection – 99 titles – of Zadornov's short stories and provides a designated page for fans' observations about the humorous aspects of Russian life, in Zadornov's style; they can also discuss various matters on the website's forum. In addition to remarks about funny labels, typos, and television personalities' slips of the tongue, the fans express political opinions that they feel would be welcome on Zadornov's fan website.

All these websites aim to connect fans with Zadornov's celebrity and offer visitors an opportunity to comment on Zadornov's activities. Most contain free downloadable video, audio, and text files by him. The website *Mikhail Zadornov. Humorous Short Stories and Anecdotes* creates optimal conditions for engaging the audience in creative fandom, as it publishes visitors' observations formatted after Zadornov's example. These websites and the "games" on Zadornov's official website indicate that the consumers of Zadornov's celebrity are excited by sharing the views of such an "outstanding person," by receiving his praise, and by belonging to a community of fans with a similar worldview and aspirations.

Zadornov's celebrity in context: Soviet and post-Soviet influences

Zadornov's celebrity is conditioned by a set of Russian cultural traditions and practices that assign a special status to an author, an *estrada* (varieté) performer, and a comedian. For a large segment of the population, authorship carries extraordinary, almost sacred connotations in Russian culture. The well-known claim "A poet in Russia is more than just a poet" ["Poet v Rossii bol'she, chem poet"] originated by Evgenii Evtushenko (a poet of the post-Stalinist age, thus regarded as one of the symbols of a new freedom in the Soviet Union) opened his *Prayer before a Narrative Poem* [Molitva pered poemoi] (1964), which maps out the poet's mission in Russia in temporal terms: a poet must sum up the past, be an image of the present, and become a model for the future. Zadornov's understanding of his mission is, arguably, similar to that of Evtushenko. Zadornov's short stories and performances discuss Russia's past and present while projecting a plan for the future. While joking, he casts a nostalgic glance back at the Soviet period and presents himself as a successful Russian with the authority to make judgments about the full span of Russian history. For the future, Zadornov advocates a neo-pagan revival under the auspices of "Russian Vedism," which he publicly endorses as a desirable basis for a new Russian identity. His mission is to disseminate Vedist "ideas" (Finiakina 2006b).

In an interview, Zadornov confessed that he nurtures strong feelings about his profession, partially because his father was an author, and also because in Russia an author has always played the role of social conscience. Zadornov urges people to listen to what authors rather than politicians say, as the former speak "from their souls" and not in order to earn money (Tanina 2006). His role models include the following authors, who are also celebrities: Evgenii Evtushenko, Boris Vasil'ev (author and scriptwriter of "cult" Soviet war films), and Leonid Filatov (actor, poet, and author of the satirical *Skazka pro Fedota-strel'tsa, udalogo molodtsa* [Folktale of the Soldier Fedot, a Daring Fellow] (1986) (Tanina 2006). Each of these personalities has been more or less loyal to the Soviet regime, but among a segment of the population they all evoke associations with truthfulness and a rootedness in Russian culture. Elsewhere, Zadornov proudly acknowledges his acquaintance with the émigré novelist Vasily Aksenov (*Neponiatki* 2005d) – scarcely an author beloved by the Soviet state. In other words, his preferences stress his loyalty to cultural authorities, on the one hand, while, on the other, flirting with the dissident tradition. In any event, Zadornov's aspiration is to enjoy the same public esteem as the cultural figures he claims to admire.

In twentieth-century Russian culture a special role is attributed not only to writers, but also to artists working in *estrada*. David MacFadyen's *Red Stars* (2001) traces the history of *estrada* and its relationship to social developments, drawing attention to what he sees as one of its major features: the "direct address of the performer to spectators," of which, according to him, the Futurist Vladimir Maiakovsky (1893–1930) was the master (MacFadyen 2001: 13). If Maiakovsky was a tribune of the new aesthetics and the new social order that he believed inseparable from it, Zadornov adopts a similar stance – that of a popular tribune trying to shape the beliefs and values of audiences. On the basis of his celebrity status, he claims the role of an interpreter of culture, a prophet of the future, and a leader of those who make up his audience. Hardly comparable to Maiakovsky in talent, Zadornov constructs his celebrity on the foundation of post-Soviet Russian national pride.

Under the Soviet regime, two types of comedians prevailed: those who adopted official discourse (stand-up comedians recognized by the state and allowed access to Soviet television and other mass media) and those who favored underground humor, such as unorthodox political *anekdoty* that could be punished by a prison term. As Seth Graham in his work on the Russo-Soviet *anekdot* maintains, the Soviet regime regarded "official" comedy as an ideological tool. For example, in the "reformist" periods of Soviet history the authorities encouraged and used comedy in the hope that it would bring new life to a system in crisis (Graham 2003: 107). Therefore comedians were allowed to criticize the authorities to the extent that doing so would energize the people and reduce their sense of powerlessness. During the Stagnation period, however, comedy was placed under stricter control (Graham 2003: 125). "Underground" comedy, in contrast, opposed official discourse, particularly in the *anekdot*, which was one of its most representative manifestations: "If dissident culture represented a strategic opposition to the institutionalized ideology, the *anekdot* was an instrument for tactical engagement with specific performances of that ideology" (Graham 2003: 118).

Zadornov borrows from Arkadii Raikin (1911–87), a performer who functioned within the official realm of comedy and was arguably the most famous and revered comedian of the Soviet era. At each of his performances Raikin addressed his audience directly with what could be called a Soviet sermon on how one should live. Thus the idea of a comedian as an ideological and political actor is a notion familiar to both Russian performers and audiences.

The peculiarities of Zadornov's position as a comedian in the post-Soviet period may be better understood if we compare him to the outstanding author-performer of the Soviet era, Mikhail Zhvanetskii. Graham suggests that Zhvanetskii's comedy was located on the borderline between official and underground discourse, his social role being that of "both a behavioral exemplar and a source of verbal material; lines from his monologues entered the language, where they were used like proverbs or told like *anekdoty*" (Graham 2003: 131). Hoping to be perceived as Zhvanetskii's successor, Zadornov likes to link his celebrity to that of Zhvanetskii by presenting himself as a personal friend, one privy to Zhvanetskii's profound insights into the role of a satirist in society. According to Graham, Zhaventskii's "thematic repertoire in the Brezhnev years anticipated (and helped to shape) the topical agenda of public discourse during perestroika: shortages, queues, bureaucracy, alcohol, gender relations, and an only semi-ironic appreciation for the value of hardship and struggle to the physical and social development of *Homo sovieticus* (and *Homo post-sovieticus*)" (Graham 2003: 135). During the same era Zadornov's jokes covered the same topics and attempted to define, then as now, what it meant to be Soviet (and post-Soviet). For example, one of Zadornov's short stories, titled *My* [Us], also functions as part of his routines (Zadornov 2003). It lists various features of the post-Soviet character and tries to predict Russia's future based on these characteristics. Among Russians' negative traits he notes their hatred of the West (which they simultaneously emulate) and their tendency to be sentimental about World War II (the key historical event for Soviet and post-Soviet identity) while not caring about veterans. At the same time, Zadornov praises Russians' wit and their ability to dress nicely despite their poverty. His portrait of post-Soviet citizens strives to balance their positive and negative features.

However, Zhvanetskii's and Zadornov's situations differ, for, starting from the perestroika period, there was no need for "underground," "anti-official" discourse in comedy, as censorship and prison terms for political jokes gradually became things of the past – a shift that Zadornov self-consciously discusses in his comedy routines (*Tak zhit' mozhno. Chast' I* 1996a). Recent political changes also have influenced the possibilities of political comedy, for, as Graham points out, "the costumed buffoon of a carnival culture presided over by Yeltsin, Communist Party leader Gennadii Ziuganov, and Zhirinovsky has apparently given way to austere Putinism" (Graham 2003: 214). Under current conditions Zadornov may make jokes about Putin's Soviet-like entourage, whereas Yeltsin's entourage was funnier than any comedian could make it look.

Zadornov's celebrity as a comedy author-performer originated in the late Soviet period and was established in post-Soviet Russia through negotiation between the various roles and political stances of a comedian. Though Zadornov has tried to adopt the public persona of an "anti-official" comedian similar to Zhvanetskii, thus adept at the "underground" discourse that characterized Soviet *anekdoty*, in fact he sooner resembles "official" comedians of the Soviet period.

Zadornov's self-constructed celebrity under Putin: esoteric teaching in a depoliticized public sphere

If the capitalist system uses celebrities to promote individualism and illusions of democracy, what function do celebrities fulfill in Russia, which is a "managed democracy?" The function of Zadornov's celebrity in Putin's Russia, I argue, is to distract people from socio-economic problems and to keep them away from the political process. His celebrity works to preserve the status quo desired by the regime and to negate the population's democratic aspirations.

Jurgen Habermas, in his seminal work *The Structural Transformation of the Public Sphere* (1962), explores the possibility of democracy today by tracing the transformation of both public and private spheres from liberal societies in the early modern period to modern social-welfare states. Though his discussion focuses exclusively on Western liberal and social-welfare societies, some of his insights are pertinent to post-Soviet Russia. Habermas perceives in modern society a situation in which "the public sphere assumes advertising functions. The more it can be deployed as a vehicle for political and economic propaganda, the more it becomes unpolitical as a whole and pseudo-privatized" (Habermas 1999: 175). According to this theory of the depolitization of the public sphere, the contemporary public has no influence over political processes. The mass media and PR institutions fabricate the public sphere so that the public experiences illusory participation in political affairs and relates to the public sphere sentimentally rather than rationally. Celebrity is one way of filling such a depoliticized public sphere with apparent substance, allowing the public to engage it instead of confronting real issues. Zadornov's celebrity provides Russia's depoliticized public sphere with such content: he compensates for the inadequacies of contemporary Russian life by popularizing an "esoteric" teaching from the stage.

Zadornov's celebrity assists Putin's regime in instilling a defensive, conservative worldview in the post-Soviet Russian public. When Putin assumed his duties as president, his challenge was to lead the country that had lost the Cold War and had not even partially recovered its status through any achievements during the Yeltsin regime. No satisfactory or credible system had replaced the economic and social order of the Soviet Union. Soviet identity, intended to give the population a sense of pride in their country and the great mission facing them, had vanished, and national humiliation was rife. Under such conditions, Putin's administration chose not to adopt any particular ideology, preferring instead to play on the public's emotions. One of its techniques for controlling public thought was to divert attention from the immediate social and political problems to a search for scapegoats and the elaboration of the Russian nation's imaginary "great history."

The "worldview" disseminated by state-controlled news media is rife with tendencies that are anti-American (caused by the war in Iraq, the situation in Iran, and the establishment of missile defenses in Europe); anti-Ukrainian (caused by the Russian government's failure to control the election results in Ukraine, followed by the Orange Revolution); anti-Georgian (which are akin to anti-American and anti-Orange sentiments); and anti-Baltic (linked to the oppression of Russians and everything Russian and Soviet in the Baltic states). In his routines and interviews, Zadornov reinforces all these propagandistic trends, paying most attention to the USA.

This strategy is consistent with what Habermas described as the collapse of political ideology:

> The integration culture concocted and propagated by the mass media, although unpolitical in its intention, itself represents a political ideology; a political programme. [...] This false consciousness no longer consists of an internally harmonized nexus of ideas, as did the political ideologies of the nineteenth century, but of a nexus of modes of behaviour" and serves to reinforce the political status quo.
>
> (Habermas 1999: 215–16)

In Putin's Russia, citizens are not required to follow any particular political ideology, but simply to behave in a certain way – specifically, not to oppose the government. Zadornov's celebrity is part of this "unpolitical" culture, which nevertheless represents a political ideology. At its "Russian Vedic" stage, Zadornov's celebrity carries out the role of supporting the status quo in two ways. It provides audiences with an esoteric, anti-scientific worldview that establishes the superiority of Russians and presents the West as an enemy; it also conforms to the state's anti-American, anti-Ukrainian, anti-Georgian, and anti-Baltic official propaganda.

Under the conditions of this depoliticized public sphere, Zadornov constructs his celebrity by carefully constructing a Western-style PR image, producing what one may call a "mythological biography." On the one hand, his journey through time across two home countries (the USSR and the Russian Federation) and several political regimes reflects the experience of an average post-Soviet citizen. On the other, his claimed role as public spokesman for a "philosophy" makes Zadornov "special," a celebrity. He regularly emphasizes not his identity as a celebrity, but his public connections and the public significance and implication of his views, actions, and family life. By doing so, Zadornov attempts to create an image of an exemplary Russian for the twenty-first century, rather than an image of himself as an exceptional post-Soviet Russian. The space for such tactics is prepared by the modern state, with its mass media:

> The public sphere itself becomes privatized in the consciousness of the consuming public; indeed, the public sphere becomes the sphere for the publicizing of private biographies, so that the accidental fate of the so-called man in the street or that of systematically managed stars attain publicity, while publicly relevant developments and decisions are garbed in private dress and through personalization distorted to the point of unrecognizability".
>
> (Habermas 1999: 171)

By connecting to Zadornov's celebrity and his propaganda of a new national identity based on Russian Vedism, the public disconnect themselves from the social and political life as run by Putin's administration. Zadornov's celebrity and his jokes are based on stereotypes that encourage post-Soviet citizens to overlook the intricacies of social life and to abandon sober analysis and conscious political action.

In his routines Zadornov often emphasizes elements of his biography calculated to connect him to his audience. In his early concerts, Zadornov mentioned the "ordinary" facts of his biography, such as his Soviet childhood and youth, as well as his circumstances during the difficult period of the early 1990s. For instance, Zadornov describes how he was nearly banned from school for chewing gum, which, along with wearing jeans and drinking Coca-Cola, was considered an anti-Soviet activity. More unusual, "Soviet romantic" aspects of Zadornov's biography include his part in the Komsomol's "heroic" construction of the BAM railroad (*Ot putcha do Putina* 2005e). Yet Zadornov is happy to note his most glamorous "achievements," such as living in the same block of apartments as the highest authorities of post-Soviet Russia in the early 1990s, having conversations with Yeltsin, and playing tennis with the political elite during Yeltsin's presidency.

As a Russian born in Latvia, Zadornov stood up for Russians in the Baltic states, first by heading a charity intended to help them (1993–5), then, when this effort did not work out, by sponsoring a theater, of which he was artistic director, whose personnel comprised sixteen young Russian-speaking Latvian actors (Mikhail Zadornov's Official Website; Mel'man 2006b). These initiatives contribute to Zadornov's image as a Russian champion combating threats to Russian culture in the territory of the former empire. They spring from his yearning for cultural influence over adjoining territories – a yearning shared by members of his audience. While these endeavors suggest Zadornov cultural influence as a celebrity, at the same time, they highlight his generic Russian or post-Soviet qualities, presenting him as a "super-Russian."

Zadornov's other way of making sense of the current model of social production in Russia, with its oil-dependent economy under the pressures of globalization, is both anti-democratic and racist. This version of reality presents Russia as a proud heir to a great Aryan civilization, and an independent world power. Graeme Turner discusses the primary role of celebrity "in the process through which individual subjects, communities, and nations construct their national identities" (Turner 2004: 102). Zadornov explicitly acknowledges such a role as his and claims that he attempts to help create a new Russian national identity in his interviews and routines (Finiakina 2006b). Since the early post-Soviet period Zadornov has displayed a preachy attitude in his comedy, relying on moral categories in his jokes, explaining the world according to his belief system, and encouraging his audience to take certain actions. The topics covered by his "sermons" include the education of the young generation and Russia's mission on earth, which is to preserve the "life of the soul" (*Ia liubliu Ameriku* 2003).

Russian Vedism, the latest focus of Zadornov's routines, may be preliminarily defined as a synthesis of anti-Western, anti-democratic, anti-scientific, neo-pagan views. Zadornov's conversion to Russian Vedism was similar in some ways to Tom Cruise's joining the Church of Scientology. In both cases, a famous person has embraced an unorthodox religious teaching and made it part of his celebrity. The difference is that Russian Vedism is not a monolithic organization like the Church of Scientology, with a leader, hierarchy, and identifiable ideology. Moreover, Zadornov has never claimed that Russian Vedist beliefs or practices brought him health or other benefits (unlike Cruise's claims of a cure for his dyslexia) ("Cruise Credits" 2005). One similarity, however, links Cruise's and Zadornov's conversions: their militant rejection of established science and alternative views of life's phenomena – in Cruise's case, psychiatry, and in Zadornov's case, linguistics and history. However, while Cruise has been involved in numerous media and political scandals over this issue, Zadornov's anti-academic arguments have prompted no uproar in mainstream media.

During his early career Zadornov was very skeptical about esoteric practices. He made fun of the various esoteric phenomena (UFOs, alternative medicine, spirits, psychics, and horoscopes) that became extremely popular in the early 1990s in post-Soviet Russia (*Tak zhit' mozhno. Chast' II* 1996d; *Lektsiia s iumorom* 2000). But in 2006 he suddenly began speaking freely to his audiences about "energies" and Russian gods, and a year later published a book entitled *Iazychnik epokhi Vodoleia* [A Pagan of the Aquarius Era] (2007). Through the title Zadornov identified himself as a neo-pagan – more precisely, a member of an amorphous anti-Christian xenophobic movement intent on reinterpreting history. Since the Age of Aquarius refers to the astrological notion of a new era following the Age of Pisces, which started with the advent of Christ, Zadornov presents himself as a leader of the new Russian era, one in tune with Russia's astrological sign of Aquarius.

Zadornov incorporated his newly found Vedic wisdom in a show called *Tret'e ukho* [*Third Ear*], broadcast on 13 January 2007 on the television channel Ren-TV. He had declared himself a proponent of Vedism the previous summer in a series of interviews with the popular newspaper *Moskovskii Komsomolets*. The title *Third Ear* plays on the esoteric concept of the "third eye," supposedly possessed by select advanced mystics, and the show appears as a prominent link on the main page of Zadornov's official website. For his stage appearances on *Third Ear* and similar performances, Zadornov dramatically altered his image, replacing the clean-shaven look and designer three-piece suit that he had favored in the 1990s with a beard and moustache, as well as an open-neck shirt that exposed his chest and the cross hanging around his neck, all of which recalled the look of Russian peasants celebrated by nineteenth-century Slavophiles.

Zadornov starts his show *Third Ear* by criticizing the Western reform of education in Russia (*Tret'e ukho* 2007), a topic close to his heart and one that surfaces in his other programs (*Da zdravstvuet* 2005b). The reason for this reform, Zadornov maintains, is the West's conspiracy against Russia: Allan Dulles, the de facto CIA director from 1953–61, allegedly stated that if the West gives the Slavs "wrong ideals, […] they will destroy themselves." Elsewhere Zadornov also mentions Western intentions to destroy the Soviet Union, saying that after World War II the USA government, assisted by the CIA, the Pentagon, and the UN and European

Council, developed plans to this effect (*Ia liubliu Ameriku* 2003; *Mnogo shuma i nichego. Chast' I* 1996a). Thus Zadornov connects the bitterness experienced by many over the loss of the Soviet Empire with suspicions and hostility toward the West.

Third Ear gives Zadornov a platform for publicizing the basics of Vedic "knowledge," which include the idea that the Russian language has preserved divine secrets, manifested in such words as "spasibo" [thank you], which is "spasi Bog" [may God save you], and "zdravstvui" [hello], which stands for "zdorov'ia zhelaiu" [I wish you good health]. If in several cases Zadornov's interpretations of the meanings of words may be justified, the majority of his examples can be easily refuted with the aid of a specialized Russian dictionary, such as his claims that "nebesa" [heaven] is "ne besy" [not demons]; "beskul'turnyi" [uncultured] means a cultured person possessed by a demon [bes]. Though presenting such material in a comedy program, Zadornov is serious about his claims, as are other adherents of Russian Vedism, such as Valerii Chudinov, Konstantin Lipskikh, and Andrei Tiuniaev. In other words, Zadornov attempts to construct an alternative language reality in which he and his colleagues in Russian Vedism assume positions of authority. According to Habermas, such a situation is not unusual, for "modern propaganda" has "the Janus face of enlightenment and control; of information and advertising; of pedagogy and manipulation" (Habermas 1999: 203). Habermas goes on to argue that "to the degree that culture became a commodity not only in form but also in content, it was emptied of elements whose appreciation required a certain amount of training" (1999: 166), but the Russian public lacks the ability to resist such propaganda, which appeals not to training or intelligence, but to emotions.

The level of Zadornov's address emerges clearly in *Third Ear*. There, he refers to "Aryans" [sic], whose priests (volkhvy) authored the sacred books of Vedas, which are older than the Bible, and who came to be known as Brahmans in India. "Vedas" derives from the verb "vedat'" ("znat'," to know). Zadornov "discovers" what he calls "words of light" in the Russian language, which he arrives at by deciphering the stems of words in their ancient forms. For example, he claims that "Ra" originally meant sunshine, and shifts to a reinterpretation of words of modern Russian language containing the syllable "ra," regardless of whether it appears in a stem, suffix, or random combination of the last letter of the stem and the case ending. Accordingly, "rano" [early] is interpreted as "Ra" and "no," meaning that as yet there is no "Ra." Other words treated similarly include "vera" [faith], "era" [era], "raduga" [rainbow], and "rai" [paradise]. On the basis of other supposedly Aryan stems, Zadornov on the show reinterprets a large number of words in this way. Slavs, he argues, cannot be defeated on their territory because of "our native, Slavic 'Ura' [Hurrah]. When we are attacked, 'we' go 'Hurrah,' and you, enemies, had better go away, because StalingRAd is awaiting you" (*Tret'e ukho* 2007).[3] These are the tactics Zadornov employs to define "us" (the Slavs) in opposition to the "enemies" (presumably, the West).

This stance is reminiscent of Aleksandr Blok's in his narrative poem *Skify* [The Scythians] (1918). Blok presents "us" as the Scythians – Asians located between "the Mongols" and Europe. "We" have access to the wisdom of both and are potentially more powerful than they, yet remain incomprehensible to Europeans. Blok's poem claims that "we" refuse the position of Europe's defenders and hereafter will pursue "our" own interests. Zadornov reproduces such claims faithfully. In his identity construction he follows the poet's impreciseness in defining who "we" are. As inhabitants of Russia, "we" are neither entirely Slavs nor Turkic; not everyone is Orthodox, and the Empire embraces ever new nations linked by Russian language and culture.

When questioned about the sources of his supposed Vedic knowledge, Zadornov contends that he acquired it from his travels, from talking to interesting people, and receiving electronic messages from "enthusiasts" (Finiakina 2006a). The last must be Zadornov's fans, who, encouraged by the popularizing of Vedic ideas on television, share with Zadornov their own "discoveries" along the same lines or quote from other Vedic sources.

Conclusion

In constructing his celebrity, Zadornov takes advantage of various cultural and political features of post-Soviet Russia, carefully cultivating his image and his fandom to maximize the size of his audiences. He has influenced the everyday speech, opinions, and practices of post-Soviet citizens, many of whom regularly watch his television concerts and post messages on his internet fan sites. In addition, Zadornov has fitted his celebrity successfully into the political and ideological context of Putin's era by concentrating on jokes about Russian superiority and even embracing an anti-Western, anti-scientific worldview of Russian Vedism. Zadornov's celebrity is attuned to the strategies of Putin's regime, which distract the public from the acute problems of political life and from political participation.

Zadornov's celebrity reflects Russia's troubled path toward democratization. Just as the early fascination with democratic ideals under Yeltsin was followed by disillusionment brought about by economic difficulties and rampant corruption in federal and local governments, so did Zadornov's celebrity persona retreat from democratic principles, to adopt the racist views of Russian Vedism. His celebrity status can be viewed as a pseudo-event filling in the depoliticized public sphere (as described by Habermas) of Russia under Putin. Reinforcing his audiences' emotional attachment to cultural stereotypes, he helps to keep members of the public disengaged from the political process.

Despite his early aspirations to establish himself among Soviet comedians who represented the "underground" opposition, paralleling the position of Zhvanetskii in the Brezhnev era, today Zadornov sooner appears as a compliant supporter of the status quo. During the intervening years, he has hitched his "stardom" to a traditional Slavophile image spiced by the rhetoric of Russian Vedism. In short, Zadornov's celebrity has moved from one pole of the ideological spectrum to the other, and only the future can tell where his final place will be in the development of post-Soviet comedy.

Notes

1 There are data of reputable sociological surveys suggesting that Zadornov's words and opinions have become a significant part of the post-Soviet Russian citizen's life. The Public Opinion Foundation (FOM) [Fond Obshchestvennogo Mneniia] conducted a Russia-wide representative survey "Iumoristicheskie peredachi na televidenii" [Comedy programmes on television] in January 2006. In an open-ended question, respondents were asked to name their favourite stand-up comedians. Evgenii Petrosian (b. 1945) gained 35 percent, Elena Stepanenko (b. 1953) 16 percent, and Zadornov 15 percent. The respondents were also asked to name those stand-up comedians they like the least. Petrosian received 12 percent and Zadornov only 1 percent. Thus, according to FOM, Zadornov's positive popularity features negative popularity, compared with Petrosian. In September 2003 FOM also conducted a survey "Rossiiane ob Amerike i ob ameri-kantsakh. Chto my znaem ob Amerike" [Russians on America and Americans. What we know about America]. There were two cases of respondents using Zadornov's words. On both occasions, the respondents agreed with Zadornov's assessment of Americans. These data suggest that the Russian audience has internalized the message and language transmitted by Zadornov's celebrity.
2 For in-text references for Zadornov's shows I have shown the title in parentheses in italics. For full bibliographical data of these shows please see the "Other Resources Used" section at the end of this chapter.
3 During World War II, the Soviet forces, against all odds and at tremendous loss of lives, withstood the fascists at Stalingrad, which witnessed one of the most brutal battles in modern history and prepared the way for Hitler's defeat.

Bibliography

Dyer, R. (1998) *Stars*, London: British Film Institute.
Evtushenko, E. (1998) "Prayer before a Poem," in L. P. Krementsova (ed.) *Russkaia sovet-skaia poeziia*, Leningrad: Prosveshchenie, p. 15.
Graham, S. B. (2003) *A Cultural Analysis of the Russo-Soviet Anekdot* [PhD Thesis] University of Pittsburgh.
Habermas, J. (1999) *The Structural Transformation of the Public Sphere*, Oxford: Polity Press.
MacFadyen, D. (2001) *Red Stars*, Montreal and Kingston: McGill-Queen's University Press.
Rojek, C. (2006) "The Psychology of Achieved Celebrity," in P. D. Marshall (ed.) *The Celebrity Culture Reader*, New York: Routledge, pp. 609–17.
Turner, G. (2004) *Understanding Celebrity*, London: Sage Publications.
"Cruise Credits Scientology for his Success" (2005) MSNBC, 24 May. Available online at: www.msnbc.msn.com/id/7968809/ (accessed 1 July 2008).

Websites

Mikhail Zadornov's Official Website. Available online at: www.zadornov.net/ (accessed 17 January 2008).

Public opinion surveys

"Rossiiane ob Amerike i ob amerikantsakh. Chto my znaem ob Amerike," Results of a Russia-wide representative survey, 6–7 Sept. 2003, Fond Obshchestevnnogo Mneniia, 10 July 2006. Available online at: http://bd.fom.ru/report/map/ra030903 (accessed 1 July 2008).

"Vspomnim oktiabr' 93-go," Results of a Russia-wide representative survey, 27–28 Sept. 2003, Fond Obshchestevnnogo Mneniia, 10 July 2006. Available online at: http://bd.fom. ru/report/map/d033912 (accessed 1 July 2008).

"Iumoristicheskie peredachi na televidenii," Results of a Russia-wide representative survey, 28–29 Jan. 2006, Fond Obshchestevnnogo Mneniia, 10 July 2006. Available online at: http://bd.fom.ru/report/map/d060530 (accessed 1 July 2008).

"Reiting iumoristov: Rossiia smeetsia vmeste s Petrosianom, Moskva – s Zadornovym," Results of a Russia-wide representative survey, Winter, 2006, ROMIR Monitoring, 23 Aug. 2006. Available online at: www.rmh.ru/news/res_results/256.html (accessed 1 July 2008).

Zadornov's shows

Zadornov, M. (1996a) *Mnogo shuma i nichego. Chast' I* [Audiotape] General Records.
— . (1996b) *Mnogo shuma i nichego. Chast' II'* [Audiotape] General Records.
— . (1996c) *Tak zhit' mozhno. Chast' I* [Audiotape] General Records.
— . (1996d) *Tak zhit' mozhno. Chast' II* [Audiotape] General Records.
— . (2000) *Lektsiia s iumorom* [Audiotape] General records.
— . (2003) *Ia liubliu Ameriku* [Audiotape] Studiia Monolit.
— . (2005a) *Zapiski otmorozka* [Audiotape] Play Music Records.
— . (2005b) *Da zdravstvuet to, blagodaria chemu my, nesmotria ni na chto ...* [DVD] Kamerton.
— . (2005c) *Iumor 585 proby. Tol'ko luchshee* [DVD] Vikkon-Plus.
— . (2005d) *Neponiatki* [DVD] Kamerton.
— . (2005e) *Ot putcha do Putina*. Includes interview with Mikhail Zadornov, 'Tête-*à-tête*' in the Theater "Sodruzhestvo Akterov Taganki" [DVD] Iaros Fil'm.
— . (2007) *Tret'e ukho* [Recording of Television Program] Ren-TV television channel, 13 Jan.

Zadornov's interviews and articles

Finiakina, I. (2006a) "Maiak podkralsia nezametno," *Moskovskii Komsomolets*, 23 Jan. Available online at: www.zadornov.net/interview/20060123 (accessed 1 July 2008).
— . (2006b) "Durak v Rossii bolshe chem durak. Potomu chto on radushnyi i razymnyi," *Moskovskii Komsomolets*, 22 May. Available online at: www.zadornov.net/interview/ 20060522/print.html (accessed 12 July 2008).
— . (2007) "Etot mudryi russkii mat. Poslat' po matushke – oznachaet pozhelat' prodleniia roda," *Moskovskii Komsomolets*, 27 Feb. Available online at: www.zadornov.net/interview/ 20070227/ (accessed 27 April 2007).
Mel'man, D. (2006a) "Ura! i uvy! Mikhail Zadornov: 'Sportsmeny u nas ozhivaiut, chinovniki – nazhivaiut," *Moskovskii Komsomolets*, 3 March. Available online at: www.zadornov. net/interview/20060303/ (accessed 19 July 2006).
— . (2006b) "Mikhail Zadornov stal prodiuserom," *Moskovskii Komsomolets*, 25 March. Available online at: www.zadornov.net/interview/20060325 (accessed 19 July 2006).
Paniukov, M. (2006) "Mikhail Zadornov: 'Bush – glavniuk s samonavodiashcheisia golovkoi!' 'Belorussiia – eto nash partizanskii otriad v tsentre Evropy," *Ekspress Gazeta*, no. 17, 24–30 Apr. Available online at: www.zadornov.net/interview/20060424/ (accessed 18 July 2006).

Tanina, A. (2006) "'Bezumnyi mir' Mikhaila Zadornova," *Vesti Spb*, 14 Jan. Available online at: www.zadornov.net/interview/20060114/ (accessed 21 July 2006).

Zadornov, M. (2006) "Tret'e ukho. 'Razmyshlizmy' Mikhaila Zadornova. Chast' I," *Moskovskii Komsomolets*, 2 June. Available online at: www.mk.ru/newshop/bask. asp?artid=130806 (accessed 10 July 2006).

— . (2006a) "Tret'e ukho. 'Razmyshlizmy' Mikhaila Zadornova. Chast' II," *Moskovskii Komsomolets*, 5 June. Available online at: www.mk.ru/newshop/bask.asp?artid=130897 (accessed 10 July 2006).

Zadornov's books

Zadornov, M. (2003) *Vdrug otkuda ni voz'mis'*, Moskva: Eksmo.

— . (2005) *Etot bezumnyi, bezumnyi, bezumnyi mir*, Moskva: Astrel'.

— . (2007) *Iazychnik ery Vodoleia*, Moskva: Astrel'.

7 Russian internet stars

Gizmos, geeks, and glory

Vlad Strukov (University of Leeds)

> It's so simple, it's so charmingly simple. It takes a few weeks if you don't rush it, and a few days if you try to do it as it should be done. It requires some training, a bit of talent, impudence, and the ability to make use of an opportunity. Joining the elite of Runet is a question of desire.
>
> Linor Goralik *Vkhozhdenie v Runet-elitu: prakticheskoe rukovodstvo*
> [The Practical Guide to Joining the Elite of Runet] (1999)[1]

The internet,[2] like any other form of new media (DVDs, mobile phones, virtual reality, etc.), enjoys all the appeal of "the most recent." The "new" celebrates the avant-garde, a place for unconventional ideas and forward-looking people (both producers and consumers), and an exciting and glamorous lifestyle. People invest in the new media because the new technologies carry a promise of change and development that covers all aspects of social and private life, such as new educational opportunities, increased productivity, more efficient management, new forms of communication and entertainment, and so forth. Of course, the "new" is part of a powerful ideology and a narrative of progress in a modern society that propels infinite consumption of goods and ideas. In the Russian context, the emergence and development of new media have been associated with post-Soviet economic and cultural developments. The new technologies often stand for new entrepreneurial motives and conditions, and for new emulatory values and mores.

On the internet one can become extremely (and often quite suddenly) popular through the word-of-mouth and self-publishing strategies advanced by web technology. Some are short-lived fads, while others remain popular for several years. Popular internet phenomena fall into two groups. The first group includes personalities, artifacts, or communication patterns that initially become popular in the traditional – offline – media and then migrate into the cyberspace thanks to media convergence and the increasing online presence of most media outlets. The second group consists of popular phenomena that emerge on the internet; their notoriety is grounded in the very characteristics of the medium – that is, the internet's multi-user networked environment, immediacy of communication, and performative participation. This chapter is devoted to the latter group and has a twofold purpose. It considers, first, how Russian society glamorizes new media, and, second, how new media serve as a platform for new kinds of communication and create their own celebrities. My focus is on the internet and the computer, which in Russia offer the prime point of access to local and international networks. I analyze how different social groups and actors – business people, politicians, artists, professional media specialists, and amateurs – use the internet to construct discourses of celebrity and glamour.

Digital gadgets

Because the appropriation of cultural products presupposes dispositions and competences which are not distributed universally (although they have the appearance of innateness), these products are subject to exclusive appropriation, material or symbolic, and, functioning as cultural capital (objectified or internalised), they yield a profit in distinction, proportionate to the rarity of the means required to appropriate them, and a profit in legitimacy, the profit par excellence, which consists in the fact of feeling justified in being (what one is), being what it is right to be.

Pierre Bourdieu (1984: 228)

In 2004 the internet in Russia became a bona fide mass medium (Strukov 2008), and since then it has evolved into a new distribution channel for traditional media and industry outlets. Nowadays all major television channels and printed media, as well as companies operating in the financial and manufacture sectors, have a noticeable online presence. For example, Motorola, producer of one of Russia's most popular mobile phones (according to Russian Business Consulting's ratings),

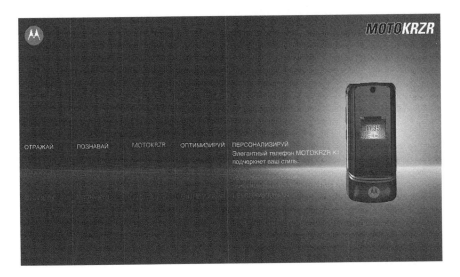

Figure 7.1 Screenshot of Motorola's online promotional campaign of MotoKRZR telephones in the Russian Federation; November 2008. Courtesy of Motorola.

Figure 7.2 Screenshot of Motorola's online promotional campaign of MotoKRZR telephones in the Russian Federation; November 2008. Courtesy of Motorola.

has a regional division on its own main website (www.motorola.com/ru). The company that dominates the global market targets its consumers in their local settings
and spreads among them the notion of inclusion and trust. Conversely, Motorola's
regional division provides a symbolic inclusion of the Russian market in the company's global outreach as well as the contiguity of experience and business and the
instantaneousness of communication facilitated by mobile phone and internet technologies. The company typically utilizes identical online advertising techniques to
promote its new products in Russia and Europe. For example, its advertisement for
the MotoKRZR phone targets young women and promises a sleek design and the
possibility of optimizing and customizing available functions in order to construct
a consumer's personal style ("Motorola"). The ad (see Figures 7.1 and 7.2) displays
an image of an attractive young woman wearing transparent clothes, shown in a
sexually inviting pose against a solid black, mysterious background that seems
to threaten to absorb her; her image combines with a photographic set of three
phones, in light blue, pink, and charcoal. The time displayed on the phones – 11:35
– promises some magical transformation that will probably occur at midnight.
Presented three times, it enhances the miraculous quality of the created atmosphere.
Thus, the advert exploits the alleged ability of new media to introduce changes
into a person's life; it also banks on a mutable string of functions and therefore
glorifies permanent flux as an attribute of a glamorous lifestyle. Finally, the item
may be particularly appealing to a Russian consumer because it is a foreign brand
with a universal appeal. Its display on the internet suggests that its consumer may
immediately enter a global network; the possibility of purchasing the item online

enables the consumer to enjoy instantly an interactivity that defies geographical remoteness.

Russia's current obsession with international brands also includes the consumption of foreign media outlets: for example, Russian internet hubs of such offline journals as *Glamour* magazine (www.glamour.ru) (Figure 7.3). A subdivision of the global publication, it features entries on women's health and beauty, fashion, and the life of celebrities from both Russia and abroad. Unlike its Western counterparts, such as www.glamourmagazine.co.uk, which utilize online competitions, chat rooms, video downloads, mobile phone alerts, and so forth, the Russian journal's interactivity is limited to a forum and drop-down menus that allow users to view the latest fashion items. Russian *Glamour* places more emphasis on the object than do its Western analogues, which may be accounted for by the vigorous restructuring of the material life that has occurred in Russia since perestroika. However, new media and web 2.0 as metaphors for new forms of social cohesion associated with the post-industrial "network society" (Castells 2003) do not feature as a theme for discussion or representation on the website. The debates take place only in the forum section: For its 32,295 registered users (as of May 2007), computers and new media occupy the twentieth position in the rating of most popular topics (politics is twenty-first; fashion, health, and beauty rank second, third, and fourth, respectively). The discussion about mobile phones, for example, focuses on whether it is a simple conduit or an important fashion accessory. Other related topics are ringtones, (online) games, wallpaper and other downloadables, iPods, virtual fashion (digital costumes for avatars), portable DVD players, and so forth ("Glamour" 1).

An analysis of messages and comments on the Glamour forum reveals that the majority of its subscribers view computers and new media technologies as

Figure 7.3 Screenshot of the website of the Russian version of *Glamour* magazine; June 2006.

"an expensive accessory," "a trendy gizmo," and "part of [a] lifestyle" where, predictably, appearance counts more than function ("Glamour" 1). The website moderators also use the forum to promote certain brands and products, and the forum's administration advances its activities as part of a glamorous lifestyle, as evident in the forum's design, sexualized avatars, and constant references to expensive brand names and popular offline activities, such as clubbing and shopping. Forum users seem not to engage in frank and lengthy discussions; instead, they use brief forum postings to express their individuality by means of their online avatars, use of popular expressions, and personalized mottos. For example, on 26 December 2006, a user with the nickname "Maslina" posted a message related to a discussion of beauty products. The actual posting reveals little about Maslina's identity, aside from her preference for Max Factor over Lady Rose. However, her sexually encoded avatar, which shows an area of her body somewhere between the knees and the chest, is quite compelling, as is her motto, "Feelings are like Louis Vuitton, I don't need them if they are fake; Cocaine, like Versace, is not fashionable anymore but some people are addicted to it; Cigarettes, like Valentino, are elegant but they make you look old. Etc."[3] In the Russian original, Maslina spells the names of the international brands using the Latin alphabet, which is not so much a sign of her sophistication as an indication of the proliferation of foreign brands in Russian shops, on computer screens, and in the language itself, facilitated to a large extent by new media technologies that enable the simultaneous use of different scripts. And what about computers and the internet?

Since the internet and new media are quite difficult to commodify and advance, producers find it hard to project consumer fever onto them. In addition, the internet and new media generally do not have an immediate relation to the consumer: one may adorn oneself with jewelry, but one cannot simply wear a chat room. Contrariwise, computers and computer-related devices commonly are presented as consumable glamorous items. My research of online advertising on the Russian market, conducted in May–June 2008 by monitoring 50 online media outlets, indicates that desktops are generally associated with men's culture – they are a technical tool, stationary, related to the work environment – whereas laptops are deemed more suitable for women: they display such features as mobility, flexibility, and enjoyment. This distinction is mainly because, according to online advertisers, portable computers may be used as a glamorous accessory and a personal trademark. They also provide more possibilities for customization (shape, color, etc.) and display instant affinity with their owners. Russian websites propagate the gender-based division between their consumers that reflects Russia's general sex-biased distinctions. For example, on a website dedicated to computer products for women (for example, a women's notebook) users discuss laptops in relation to fashion and describe them as "thin, light, and elegant," which is meant to stress the physical qualities of their owners (equivalents of "slim and glamorous"). On Mjulia community site ("Mjulia") users approve of a laptop as a suitable gift for a woman because its design will complement her appearance. As it appears from Russian online forums, it is the form – shape, color, the glamorous surface – that matters to women, rather than the technical parameters of gizmos – their "inner quality," a characteristic, as imagined by Russian consumers, reserved for men. However, in spite of the presumed gender distinctions, both Russian women and men are engaged in the mediation of surfaces and glamorous attributes through consumption of computer-related merchandise. In fact, as online forums indicate, they often refer to laptops and other gadgets by using vocabulary normally reserved for describing human beings ("sleek," "sexy," and so forth); consumers view them as their own extensions, as their glamorous prosthetic, and the "fabulous" gadgets seem to eclipse the fame of their unremarkable users (Figure 7.4).

While those marketing computers strive to make them into fashion items and signs of prestige, computer devices already enjoy such a function. Different consumer websites present and offer advice about such "glamorous" computer devices as memory cards. For example, according to Phillips and the moderators of the community bulletin www.research.su ("Research" 1) where the celebrated items appear, the memory device is supposed to be used as an accessory. Figure 7.5 demonstrates how it has progressed from an item that one simply carries to an item that one ostensibly wears, and its decorative value far outstrips its technological value. The former challenges miniaturization as a current technological tendency because the large size of the item signals the value and status of its owner. Its other critical objective is to stress the owner's membership in the social elite, since one needs to possess a large sum of money to purchase such a memory card. Proliferation of

Ноутбук для любимой   ноутбуки, компьютеры, розовый гламур

Производители ноутбуков продолжают соревноваться друг с другом - кто придумает более оригинальный дизайн для своей продукции. Компания Ego презентовала специальную партию ноутбуков под названием **Ego Love Edition**, посвященных Дню Святого Валентина! Теперь каждая **продвинутая девушка** поймет, что это именно тот подарок, о котором она мечтала всю жизнь! ☺

Ноутбуки серии Ego Love Edition исполнены в розовом и красном цвете и отделаны кожей. Крышку ноутбука украшает огромное красное сердце, расположенное прямо по центру. По заказу можно выгравировать для любимой девушки любовное послание. Если вашей любимой не нравится ни красный, ни розовый цвета - тогда вы можете подарить ей чёрный вариант.

Всё хорошо, но как таким ноутбуком пользоваться на работе? На совещании директоров такой ноутбук будет совсем не уместен. ☺

Просмотров: 140 Комментарии (3) Автор: mjulia 12 февраля 2007 Прямая ссылка

Компьютеры бывают разные   ноутбуки, компьютеры

Сохраните ссылку на это сообщение. И когда вы будете пребывать в плохом настроении - просто посмотрите на этот компьютерный корпус, самый странный, который я когда-либо видела. И вы поймете, что в общем, в вашей жизни не все так плохо! ☺

Этот, так называемый корпус, имитация героини Leela из мультфильма Futurama (выполненная в человеческий размер). Съемный винчестер вмонтирован ей в руку, а веб камера установлена прямо в огромного размера глаз.

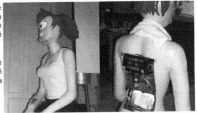

Figure 7.4 Screenshot of an online forum; the members of the forum are debating the qualities of laptops and their appropriateness for women; February 2007.

similar advertisements on the Russian internet indicates that even ordinary users display a strong desire for luxurious items that signify prestige, savvy, or clout. Whether in the realm of real or symbolic consumption, computers, memory cards, and other gizmos exploit the ideals of change and choice propagated by consumer capitalism.

Whereas consumer capitalism was introduced in Russia quite recently, Russia's preoccupation with new technologies has a well-established history (Groys 2006: 5–13). Traditionally, Russians have responded to new technologies in spiritual terms; for example, the technological advancement of the nineteenth century resulted in the emergence of the philosophy of Russian cosmism. At the turn of the century, Russian cosmologists, including the father of aeronautics and space exploration, Konstantin Tsiolkovsky, combined their passion for new technologies with utopian ideas of a new social order (Groys 2006: 5–13). A hundred years later Russians generally tend to see new technologies, especially the computer, as inaugurating a new technologized space of thought that is erotic, poetic, and contemplatively ordered. Some view cyberspace as a metaphysical laboratory, a tool for examining the very structure of reality. For example, in Timur Bekmambetov's 2004 blockbuster *Nochnoi dozor* [Night Watch] cyberspace contains the key to the ongoing battle between the mystical forces of Good and Evil. When the characters of the film attempt to prevent a catastrophe, they enter the cyber world in order to decipher its digital codes as symbols of their individual and collective memory, exploiting the popular imagery of the internet as a depository of all human

Figure 7.5 Screenshot of a Russian website displaying glamorous memory keys; April 2007. Courtesy of www.research.su.

experience. While Bekmambetov's film presents the archival logic of cyberspace as an internal, ephemeral world, structured as a database that grants exclusivity and glamour to its users, Georgii Shengelia's 2006 *Flesh.ka* [Flash.ka] explores the politics of external memory, whereby a digital gizmo functions as a weapon for the destruction of people's identities and lives.

Shengelia's film exemplifies the connotation of the memory device – flash card; in Russian, *flashka* – as an extension of personal memory and lifestyle. In the film, Andrei Ignatov (Il'ia Shakurov) is the subservient husband of a glamorous top bank manager, Viktoriia (Ekaterina Guseva). When Andrei discovers that his wife is unfaithful to him, he abandons her and, as an act of revenge, snatches from her a memory device that contains the data on illegal financial transactions conducted in her bank. Though Andrei soon realizes that the flash card is worth a few hundred million dollars, he does not attempt to sell it; instead, he hides it in the ruins of a church in a remote village in the Volga region, secretly hoping that his wife will follow him. Indeed, Viktoriia pursues her husband to retrieve the card and reestablish her business reputation; however, she soon becomes one of the suspects in the private investigation carried out by the bank administration.

The filmmakers underscore that the flash card as an object – miniature in form – has no value for the characters, but the data it holds, though invisible, functions as a social, and in this case, intimate, connection. Furthermore, similarly to the Motorola advertisement, the flash card is perceived as a magical item that eventually transforms the characters' individualities and coaxes them to confront life-and-death issues, in the process reevaluating their moral principles. In fact, earlier in the film, before Andrei escapes from the bank, he is presented as having access to the bank's cash storage. By having his character choose data over cash, the film director makes a statement regarding the new cash-less economy, where the only value is surplus value, invisible but paramount, and associated with glamour, for it empowers the characters with a sense of chic and prestige. While digital codes replace banknotes, appearances substitute for profound human relations: Viktoriia maintains family relations in order to secure her position at the bank. As Andrei hides the flash card in the ruins of an Orthodox church, the money visually disappears from the film, serving only to expose people's avarice and inability to trust one another.

A bare Russian landscape stresses the characters' spiritual emptiness and makes them recall their past in order to recharge emotionally. Viktoriia, for example, recalls how she and Andrei would spend their summers canoeing in the area and subsequently refutes the investigators' allegations and leaves behind her glamorous city life. Thus, the flash card serves as a narrative tool, as a means of characterization, and as a symbol of the new post-industrial economy. Viktoriia is never able to retrieve the data from the card; instead, she manages to evoke some personal memories and recapture her previous life as a significant ontological experience. Her return to the real self is presented as a journey to the Russian provinces and a gradual de-glamorization of her persona. Her reunion with Andrei – at least in her imagination – involves the reinstallment of the patriarchal order: a subservient husband, Andrei develops into a voluntaristic rebel.

While Shengelia's film presents the glamorous lifestyle and desires of a modern Russian woman as a threat to family values, and chooses the genre of melodrama to achieve the effect of de-technologization of being, Russian internet users attest the glamorous discourse of the new advanced technologies by ironically engaging with Russia's stars and glamorous icons. Web users normally target notorious celebrities or employ the identity of one star to deconstruct the status of others. The example of the first includes numerous travesties of Kseniia Sobchak, a television personality and the infamous embodiment of Russian glamour (see the Introduction for further information on Sobchak). Produced in Photoshop, cynical pictures of Sobchak undermine the foundations of her stardom and accentuate the artificiality of her identity. Web users utilize morphing, collage, and other forms of visual hybridization to transgress Sobchak's essentialist claims to beauty, elegance, and intelligence (Figure 7.6).

As their other strategy, amateurs frequently use digital imagery for deconstructive analysis of popular icons. For example, www.dirty.ru hosts a series of works featuring Mikhail Boiarskii, an *estrada* (varieté)] singer and star of late Soviet cinema, especially after his leading role in Georgii Iungvald-Khilkevich's ultra romantic television adaptation of *Tri mushketera* [The Three Musketeers] (1978).[4] A sex symbol of the early 1980s, Boiarskii has enjoyed a highly recognizable visual identity – thick moustache, sunglasses, and a Fedora hat – which appears seriously dated in the new millennium. The artificiality of his personal artistic

Figure 7.6 Digital artwork demonstrating a caricature of Kseniia Sobchak as a horse. Anonymous, courtesy of www.dirty.ru.

trademark serves as a point of reference in online travesties of contemporary cultural icons and brands such as *Spider-Man* or *The Terminator*. Internet users often employ Boiarskii's looks to question the authenticity of media and film celebrities, affectations of political discourse, and gender stereotypes – the moustache being a Soviet household symbol of masculinity. Boiarskii often appears in the form of a synthesian – a digitally produced character in a feature film, such as Golum in Peter Jackson's *The Lord of the Rings*. Therefore, Boiarskii's synthesian is a powerful commentary on the media-saturated nature of contemporary Russian culture, whereby synthetic creatures help to expose the artificiality of celebrity culture.

The Boiarskii case attests the ability of Russian online communities to decipher and differentiate among various types of glamour politics. Internet users exploit the malleability of the digital environment to contrast and conflate ostentatious imagery borrowed from Western media and cinema and homegrown – but now equally distanced – Socialist Realism. By presenting and circulating images of Boiarskii as a new Che Guevara idol, ironically re-branded as Che Boiara, users endlessly recycle popular imagery as part of their familiarity with legitimate culture (Figure 7.7).

Figure 7.7 Digital artwork demonstrating a caricature of Mikhail Boiarskii as Che Guevara. Anonymous, courtesy of www.dirty.ru.

Internet sensations

> The propensity and ability to raise interests and experiences to the order
> of political discourse, to seek coherence in opinions and to integrate one's
> whole set of attitudes around explicit political principles, in fact depends very
> closely on educational capital and, secondarily, on overall capital composition,
> increasing the relative weight of cultural capital as against economic capital.
>
> Pierre Bourdieu (1984: 417)

As a cross-media multi-user space, the internet displays a strong propensity to
circulate information related to celebrity culture as well as to generate its own
stars and popular phenomena that share more common features and dynamics
with oral discourse and everyday practices than with traditional media outlets. As the history of one such phenomenon, *Preved, Medved!*, indicates, the
mechanisms of fashion regulate not only the use of items, locations, and everyday practices, but also communication. In February 2006, an anonymous user
of the www.dirty.ru blog launched an image (Figure 7.8) that was a caricature
of an original drawing by the American artist John Lurie (b. 1952). Later the
image was posted in *LiveJournal* and through the mechanism of cross-linking
soon became a hit, as hundreds of thousands of users displayed both the original image – and/or their versions of it – on their sites or referred to it in their
postings.

Figure 7.8 Digital artwork *Preved, Medved!* Anonymous.

The original image, executed in neo-primitivist style, shows a couple engaged in sexual activity al fresco; they are taken aback by a bear – *medved*, the misspelled version of the Russian for a bear – who throws his arms in the air and shouts *Preved!*, the misspelled version of Russian *privet*, meaning *hello*. The image stimulated an unprecedented flow of web-based creative activity, resulting in the circulation of numerous visual and linguistic adaptations and parodies of *Preved!* These communications propelled the amusing bear to the status of internet star and helped invent a new language, *la parole*, which connected internet users into an imaginary fan community. The proliferation and adaptation of *Preved!* images exposed the limits of the constructive field of internet communities and offline cultural practices parodically subverting but also inscribing fashion and stardom. *Preved!* images and phrases, which were both critical of and complacent about mimetic representations, propagated themselves and moved through the cultural sociosphere as memes. They immediately became as desirable as designer outfits and as ubiquitous as celebrity images.

As a cultural strategy, *Preved!* was characterized by its transgression of cultural boundaries between online and offline cultures; between the immateriality of the former and the hyperreality of the latter; between the norm of the (Russian) language and its everyday uses aiming to destroy meaning; between official stardom and grassroots instantiations of the new web-based social world. While aiming to reclaim face-to-face communications, *Preved!* focused on the technology of contemporary communication; while producing coherent representations and narratives, through self-referential signs, *Preved!* exposed the digitized reality of contemporary ontology. Initially *Preved!* undermined the stylistic uniformity of Russia's media and cultural institutions, dominated by the demands of state propaganda. Ironically, it was almost instantaneously commodified and appropriated by the world of glamour and fashion. It came to be used as the decorative aspect of glamour style, as the synonym for everything ultra fashionable, as an accessory, an "off-the-peg" option that signified the transition from a subculture to the grand style of surfaces (Figure 7.9). Finally, it was comfortably accommodated by the mainstream media industry, appearing on the promotional poster for the Russian edition of *Newsweek*, with its chief editor, Leonid Parfenov, acting out the skits of *Medved, Preved!*

Preved! had its other moment of glory with the nomination of Dmitry Medvedev as the successor to the Russian presidency. On 6 July 2006 the most popular question at Vladimir Putin's online conference featured *Preved!*, "Preved, Vladimir Vladimirovich, how do you regard Medved?" In this instance *Medved* referred simultaneously both to the political leader and to his internet-animated namesake (medved à Medvedev). Consequently, *medved* has been used on the internet as a transgressing tool: the caricature below shows Russia's political leaders Sergei Ivanov, Medvedev, and Vladimir Putin engaged in a conversation (Figure 7.10). Both Ivanov and Putin prompt the newly elected – and somewhat perplexed – president to make a statement. The now empowered *medved* exclaims *Preved!* The satire produced by an anonymous author symbolically codifies the power relations in the Russian government by explicating Putin's role in the new presidential

Figure 7.9 A photograph of *Preved, Medved!* aficionado wearing a T-shirt with inscriptions in *Preved, Medved!* style. Photograph by Aleksandr Glagolev, courtesy of Aleksandr Glagolev.

office; it also attests the elasticity of the digital environment, which includes shifting connections, temporary encounters, and fluid meanings.

Preved! exemplifies the grassroots, self-organizing, and self-regulating tendencies of the internet that privilege anonymity, creativity, group association, shifting alliances, and networks. The history of Runet (a common name for Russian internet) also testifies to the significant power and pervasive influence of popular personae in web culture. The existence of these gurus confirms that, contrary to popular assumptions, the ideology of the internet relies on the help of linear, authoritarian structures that are inextricably linked to the commercial exploitation of the internet and the commodification of new media technologies through the discourses of stardom and glamour.

Similarly to the logic of the first and second waves of modernization in Russia – those of Peter I and Stalin, respectively – at the outset the processes of *informatizatsiia* relied on the import of new technologies from the West (Saunders 2009). The transmission and transportation of ideas and tools resulted in the emergence of numerous "makers" of the new system of mass communication in Russia. These makers have revealed their hegemony in the construction of a new digital environment; in other words, they have attained authority through authorship. While *Preved!* exemplifies notoriety achieved through citations and affiliation,

Figure 7.10 Caricature of Medvedev as *Privet, Medved!* Anonymous, courtesy of Andrei
    Pochuev.

the popularity of Russian internet gurus is defined by the manner of applying,
showing, and exploiting competence and creativity. If *Preved!* is an assertion
of difference that appears as an admission of the inability to identify, the work
of Runet's "authors" belongs to techno-parvenus legitimizing their status and
eventually attaining the power to recognize or to exclude ideas and tendencies, or
even individuals and networks. While enthusiasts hail the internet's potential for
making connections without regard to race, class, gender or geography, internet
practitioners operate in the digital realms of social networks that – although not
space-oriented – form solidary groups consistent with the present-oriented ethos
of recognizable computer pundits.

Yet, despite this ostensible "democratization," the mechanics of the internet –
interconnected links, page indexing, key-word searches, interactive archives, and
web mapping – paradoxically tend to constitute a web hierarchy as the top ten,
hundred, or thousand most popular websites. For example, the most commonly
used Russian web search engine (www.rambler.ru) lists the most popular websites
on the Russian internet: Russian email service www.mail.ru, the Russian social
media www.odnoklassniki.ru, Russian Business Consulting www.rbc.ru/index.
shtml, and so forth ("Rambler" 1). Rambler determines the popularity of a website by the number of hosts, visits, and hits, thus establishing the central nodes of
Russian cyberspace, which ultimately reflects the distribution of internet activity
among different social groups, geographical areas, and taste associations. However,
the internet is a space not only for the "immaterial labour" (Hardt and Negri 2000)

symbolized by the power of the "mouse click" and "web page hit," but also for immaterial memory, for it harbors knowledge beyond quantifiable parameters and thus gives rise to power endorsement and condemnation, to the celebration of individuals and discrete phenomena. These hierarchies make virtualities become actualities, and vice versa, and they reveal the potential of being realized as processual, constituting moments of cultural, affective, and technical production.

The collective mind of the internet records the present and reconstructs the past in its own meta-language, establishing a cultural perspective on the history of e-spaces. Numerous Russian internet sites dedicated to the history of the medium present their diachronic interpretation of the development of Runet as a modernist celebration of personal achievement, advancement, progress, and innovation. In spite of the de-centered, de-individualized organization of the internet, web history advocates the Romanticist approach to historical processes by asserting the importance of the individual, the unique, and the revolutionary. For example, the acclaimed website www.guelman.ru, dedicated to contemporary art, speaks of the "infocratia" or the web establishment, and lists "the best people" of Runet ("Guelman"); a section of the popular *Ezhe* information service called "The Physiognomies of Russian Internet" collates the major players of Russian cyberspace in an alphabetical order, providing brief biographical notes and listing the most popular e-makers ("Ezhe"); the authoritative portal on the history of Russian internet, www.nethistory.ru, includes a special section on the pioneers of Runet ("Nethistory"), and so forth. In their accounts of the history of Russian internet, these resources celebrate the individual endeavor of web pioneers and position them as individuals who were able to use the internet to express their unique selves as web wanderers, and often on a digital quest.

Appearing in different net histories and coming up as one of the most popular figures of the Russian internet, the public persona of Anton Nosik provides relevant material for the study of internet notoriety, partly because he has been involved in the construction and mediation of Runet through his journalistic activity. Born in 1966 into the family of writer Boris Nosik and Russian literary scholar Viktoriia Mochalova, Nosik trained in Moscow as a doctor and began his journalistic career after emigrating to Israel in 1990. Upon his return to Russia in 1996, he started one of the first blogging projects in Russia *Vechernii Internet* [Evening Internet] (1996–9). In the late 1990s Nosik was involved in the major internet projects that laid the foundation for the emergence of Russia's online media, politics, and economy. In 1999 he joined *Gazeta.ru* (www.gazeta.ru), Russia's main online-only media outlet, with Mikhail Mikhailin as its editor-in-chief, and developed its sister e-news projects, *Vesti.ru* (www.vesti.ru) and *Lenta.ru* (www.lenta.ru).

The development of online news media signified not only the diversification and segmentation of Runet, but also the proliferation of online capitalism, as the brand of *Gazeta.ru* was sold to Yukos, one of Russia's major oil producers. Whereas the oil giant ceased to exist following the arrest of its owner, Mikhail Khodorkovsky, in 2005, the internet conglomerate continued to grow, accumulating new resources and media outlets. According to Russian online media service *Novyi region-2*, in 2000 the daily audience of *Gazeta.ru* was 100,000 visitors, and *TNS Web Index* claims that in 2005 the company owned between 7 and 10 percent of Russia's online advertising market, cashing in over 5 million dollars in 2007 ("nr2"; "Tnsglobal"). While the company's owners, sponsors, and promoters remained low-key, Nosik maintained high visibility as the editor of *Lenta.ru*, which in 2000 was acquired by *Rambler.ru*, Russia's main Russian and English-language-based search engine and a conglomerate of other internet services where Nosik was in charge of the strategy department. His domain steadily expanding, in September 2006 Nosik became the Chief Blogging Officer of a newly established internet media company, *SUP-Fabrik*, a joint venture of the American businessman Andrew Paulson and the Russian oligarch Aleksandr Mamut. Their company includes *LiveJournal*, a blogging and social networking website, *Chempionat.ru*, a leading Russian sports news portal, and two high-profile advertising and recruitment agencies.

Nosik's career exemplifies the success of "the last Soviet generation" (Yurchak 2007), which has been able to translate the knowledge and skills acquired in the privileged circles of the Soviet society into the turbulent environment of 1990s Russia under Yeltsin. Connected to both the Soviet elites and the post-Soviet establishment, Nosik and his contemporaries are capable of maintaining the cultural logic of post-industrial Russia by imposing value on the nature of change and by removing historical development from the sphere of social intentionality and making it seem an objective "natural" process. Nosik's association with the oligarchs ostensibly casts him as a Russian internet magnate (though his capital may be merely symbolic) and illustrates the *sui generis* development of Russian business in the past decade: from oil-based enterprises it has moved to a post-industrial, e-based economy, with Mamut as a brilliant example of an aggressive player in the stock, insurance, print and electronic media, and mobile technology markets (for example, in September 2008 Mamut purchased Russia's largest mobile phone trading company, *Evroset'*) (Trefilov 2008).

Nosik's authority derives from his command of the language[5] of the medium, not only in terms of his techno-savvy background and attitude, but also in terms of the virtual environment's social aspects. Whereas in the West, to become an internet super star one needs to "crawl over broken glass, walk on hot coals, and swim through shark-infested waters to be at [...] Internet Super Stars [...] it's that important" ("Internet Super Stars"), in Russia one merely has to be proficient in one of the two main registers of Runet: either "intelligentsia talk," or "iazyk padonkov," meaning "the language of scum." These styles account for the social profile of internet users in Russia – predominantly 20–35-year-old urban males (Strukov 2008). Though occasionally Nosik flirts with the *Preved, Medved!* kind of vocabulary and spelling (for example, his online identity is coded as *dolboeb*, which in Russian means something similar to *fuckhead*), he normally communicates as a representative of a different social milieu. However, his verbal virtuosity both explains and affirms his power because, when required, he can transgress grammatical or pragmatic rules, making optional liaisons between linguistic units and coining new tropes. These opposing strategies are not mutually exclusive; rather, they are the two forms of conspicuous freedom – unconventional constraint and deliberate transgression – granted by the medium, which positions Nosik as an arbiter of taste and a star. In addition, Nosik's avocation highlights the tension between the intellectual/artistic and common uses of the medium, with the former striving for purity, authenticity, and distinction, while the latter relies on the medium's efficacy, anonymity, and negligibility.

Through his internet journalistic and managerial activities, Nosik achieves a self-representation normally associated with the position of a social leader, in the Russian context traditionally symbolized by the intelligentsia. An internet aristocrat, Nosik has become the man of "image," endlessly occupied with appearing in a good light in order to inspire confidence and respect as a guarantee of the product/information he offers. Through presentations at numerous academic, media industry, and e-technology conferences in real life (for example, at the University of Oxford in May 2006 and Columbia University in October 2008), Nosik has built up his authority in the virtual realm – one that carries a definition of excellence and gives him an aura of distinction that accounts for his celebrity status.

Nosik sometimes utilizes scandal as a technique to maintain his authority in the industry and notoriety in online communities. In December 2007, *SUP-Fabrik* acquired *LiveJournal*, owned by *Six Apart*, a San Francisco software developer. While in America the acquisition came as a big surprise because it was the largest-ever takeover of a USA net outfit by a Russian company, in Russia it caused uproar among online communities because Russians perceived the deal as a threat to their online freedoms. *LiveJournal* – or *ZhivoiZhurnal* as it is known in Russian, commonly abbreviated as *Zhe-Zhe* – is one of Russia's top websites and the leading provider of blogging space, with eight million unique visitors monthly. It has over fifteen million accounts worldwide and continues to add over 200,000 every month ("Sup" 1). *Zhe-Zhe* users had always perceived the blog as a safe haven for their online activities primarily because it was located in the USA. Once ownership and hosting moved to Russia, many bloggers became vocal about being exposed to the control of the Russian government, which many perceived as intent on censoring political malcontents ahead of the presidential elections in March 2008 (Strukov 2009). Many subscribers left the service in protest ("Web Planeta"). The other area of discontent has been the increasing commercialization of *LiveJournal*, with *SUP-Fabrik* defining the service as one of the oldest and most popular "internet brands" ["*LiveJournal* – odin is stareishikh i naibolee izvestnykh mirovikh internet-brendov"] ("Sup" 2). Many common users see Nosik as having betrayed his established persona by abandoning the ideals of early Russian internet, perceived as the utopian – artistic/intellectual – world of freedom and democracy, in contrast to the greed of the Yeltsin era and the stifling tendencies of Putin's regime. Yet for many bloggers he has epitomized the success of a media entrepreneur who rose to the highest ranks of new media management and who continues to project the flair of an independent intellectual and industry guru – a status that Nosik confirmed when he announced his resignation from the corporate *SUP-Fabrik* in his own blog in August 2008 ("Novaya Gazeta"), and eventually returned to his own enterprise of independent online journalism. While migrating from one internet company, media outlet, or business association to another, Nosik has maintained his integrity and popularity in online communities and offline circles by engaging with the configuration and distribution of the Russian blogosphere. In fact, his personal blog is one of the oldest in the space of Russian-speaking internet, and it has become Nosik's habitus, with its inherited asset structures, developed social trajectories, and acquired lifestyle properties.

Blog-busters

> When it is a matter of selling goods and services which, like cultural goods or material 'comfort' goods – household equipment, buildings or furniture, clothing or leisure goods – are more or less successful materializations of the dominant life-style, the acquisition of which implies a recognition of the dominant ethical or aesthetic values, nothing succeeds better than the disposition to sell one's own virtues, one's own certainties, one's own values, in a word, the certainty of one's own value, in a sort of *ethical snobbery*, an assertion of exemplary singularity which implies condemnation of all other types of being and doing.
>
> Pierre Bourdieu (1984: 456)

A blog is a form of online diary in which entries are displayed in an anti-chronological manner, with the most recent comments appearing first. Blogs are similar to the traditional genre of diaries or journals, established in the eighteenth century. In Russia, prominent nineteenth-century authors produced professional diaries that entered the public domain. For example, Feodor Dostoevsky's *Diary of a Writer* was published monthly, and comprised a memoir, political pamphlet, literary analyses, literary and historical anecdotes, and commentary on everyday life and literary and political developments in Russian society. However, blogs – and their precursors (online diaries and personal web pages) – differ significantly from the traditional literary diary due to the speed of production and distribution, as well as their interactivity. A reader of a blog may post comments in the blog environment and engage in a discussion of a posted item with other blog readers. As a result, the distinction between writer and reader is blurred in the blogosphere.

The quality of the published material is, of course, largely what accounts for the popularity of a traditional literary diary or blog. A blog is always identified with an individual, whether s/he be a celebrity or a well-known journalist. In the current digital age, when time and space seem to have collapsed, speed and regularity of updates bear equal weight in the propagation of a specific blog, with some authors updating their blogs many times a day. Their frantic activity creates a sense of their permanent online presence and invites communication, which in turn guarantees a blogger's omnipresence, a condition required for celebrity status. As a rule, a blog that is not updated on a regular basis soon falls out of fashion because of the frustration of the unsatisfied blog readers. Bloggers value acceleration and interactivity in blog communication, which relies on the technical parameters of the very environment they work in. Most blogging software enables users to post their own responses – normally called "comments" – to the author's content, allowing them to engage in discussions and debates prompted by certain postings. Such a form of interactivity creates a sense of belonging, of a community in which members share certain values. Over time, users form an association of fans who perpetuate the popularity of a given blog and its author through links, cross-references, and mail lists. To post comments, users may need to register and reveal – or fabricate – their identity. Or, on the contrary, they may remain anonymous, which suggests that any section of the blogosphere is a voluntary organization of individuals who form temporary groupings according to their preferences and lifestyle. The popularity of a blog – and, therefore, of a specific community – is equally grounded in its subject matter and its author's presentational skills. Therefore, the blogosphere is an ideal medium for the proliferation of taste communities and fan associations.

Most bloggers assemble their content by collecting information from an array of other sites, thereby situating a given news event within a larger context, and illuminating the multiple dimensions of its elements. As individual blogs are linked into ever larger blogging communities, users are able to migrate freely from one blog to another – a process akin to web surfing – and a returning user displays a strong interest in the blog and ultimately maintains its popularity. Some users refrain from posting comments on blogs and so their function is that of a "passive" reader – or a "lurker" – who does not engage directly with the blog community. In general, however, users are keen to express their opinions or even to initiate their own blogs, and thus the distinction between producers and consumers becomes blurred. Therefore, blogs function according to the contradictory principles of maintaining common values and interests, while concurrently celebrating distinctions.

Brian McNair distinguishes three features of blogs: subjectivity, interactivity, and connectivity (2006: 122–3). By connectivity, he means the ability of a blog to connect users to any other relevant resource on the internet. It is worth adding a few other distinguishing characteristics to his definition: multiparty communication, decentralization, unfixed identity, mutability, proximity to events, inter-media competition, and an emotional feel for life on the ground.

Russian blogs generally contain large amounts of textual information because broadband internet connection, necessary for downloading high-bandwidth content (graphics, sound, video, etc.), is not always available. However, most popular blogs combine various media and representation techniques, and typically appeal to an international audience, particularly the Russian diaspora. Blogs in Russia really kicked off in 2001. Between 2004 and 2006 blogging became one of the most popular activities on Runet, with many blog writers subsequently migrating into mainstream media (Strukov 2007). According to Jenkins, some bloggers are driven by a form of repetition compulsion, others – by epistemophilia, "not simply a pleasure in reading and knowing but a pleasure in exchanging knowledge" (Jenkins 2006: 139). A large proportion of Russian blogs create an environment where one can find active, critically engaged, and creative consumers of information. The novelty effect accounting for the popularity of blogging and the emergence of blog "stars" lies in their offering users the ability to archive, annotate, appropriate, and circulate media content and media forms. The types of messages that bloggers provide to their audiences typically relate to various forms of individual identification, social difference, and distinction. Bloggers present subject positions that audiences can adopt and adapt in their formation of social identities. The authors actively (de)construct meaning as they form temporary tactical alliances with other bloggers and/or with media producers to ensure that important messages are more widely circulated. These bloggers have become important grassroots intermediaries – facilitators, not jammers – of the signal flow.

Figure 7.11 provides information on Russia's most popular blogs. *Yandex.ru*, a popular Russian search engine (www.yandex.ru), identifies the most popular blogs by collating about 5.5 million units of information worldwide. It also measures the *avtoritetnost'* of blogs – that is, their status and authority in the blog community – by analyzing the number of readers, comments, cross-links, and other data. Though the data fluctuate from month to month, Nosik's blog has occupied the leading position in the Russian blogosphere; for example, in 2008–9 it was one of the top five most popular blogs of Runet ("Yandex"). As the figure demonstrates, the distribution of leading blogs signifies a hierarchal pyramid structure (Strukov 2007). At the top of the pyramid is a small coterie of websites (between five and seven in 2007) that regularly register more than 10,000 viewers per month. At the next level of usage are some 50 sites that regularly register more than 1,000 page viewers per month. In the next tier, there are millions of personal diary-type sites, recording monthly hits of up to about 250. Russian is the largest non-English domain of *LiveJournal*, with almost 200,000 accounts. The Russian section of the *LiveJournal* domain is distinct from its non-Russian sections; since its inception in 2001 it has attracted a disproportionably high number of the Russian media and culture elite, including journalists, writers, publishers, politicians, and so forth.

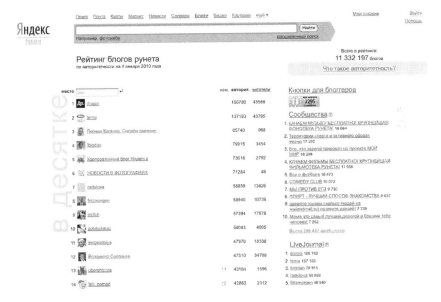

Figure 7.11 Screenshot of Yandex.ru web page listing most popular Russian blogs; 4 January 2010.

Nosik's online diary, located at http://dolboeb.livejournal.com, is one of the oldest and most popular blogs on Runet, which includes readership in the Russian Federation as well as diasporic Russians and Russophones outside of Russia. He regularly updates his blog (on average, once or twice a day) with news bites, hyper-links, pithy statements, and extended postings often exceeding 150 words, as well as photographic and/or computer-generated images. He replies to users' comments – sometimes as many as 200 – with methodical regularity and enthusiastically moderates discussions on various topics. Similarly to fan associations, Nosik's blog creates an interminable circuit of inter-legitimation – that is, the practice of legitimizing the authority of discourse agents. The popularity of Nosik's blog has provided him with business and societal opportunities as well as having catapulted him into the realm of celebrities – a fact noted in the authoritative online publication *Gazeta.ru* (www.gazeta.ru). For example, on 24 July 2009, the newspaper published Nosik's article entitled "Zhizn' – eto ulitsa s odnostoronnim dvizheniem" [Life is a one-way street] (Nosik 2009). As the screenshot of the newspaper's website demonstrates (Figure 7.12), the publication exploits Nosik's status of star blogger by filling the space of the web page with his multiple images and also running a slogan that reads in Russian as "Prisoediniaites' k izbrannym" [Join the elect]. Both of these devices symbolically attest an important feature of Nosik's lifestyle and celebrity status, which is mobility, manifested in the qualities of the medium, and symbolic of the social changes of the past decade.

Mobility means not only the opportunity to travel – generally unthinkable in the USSR – but also new forms of social and cultural negotiation. In contemporary Russia, mobility is generally perceived as a celebration of freedom gained by individuals in the post-Soviet period. The opportunity to cross state borders and to transcend social and cultural boundaries is a desirable commodity that guarantees its owner a special status in society. While literal mobility is not necessarily

Figure 7.12 Screenshot of Gazeta.ru web page with an article by Anton Nosik; 24 July 2009.

unattainable for the majority of Nosik's blog readers, it also stands for the symbolic mobility empowered by the transmittable and extra-territorial qualities of cyberspace. As a mark of distinction, in his travelogue Nosik has a special section – *ideia nakhozhusia*, which is the mispronounced *where I am* (the subtitle records the colloquial way of pronouncing *gde ia nakhozhus'*) – that identifies his location in the actual space at the time the message is being posted ("Nosik"). For example, in March 2008, Nosik traveled in the USA and visited ten cities in ten days. In his postings he was quite specific about his geographical location – Cadogan Square in London, the Venetian hotel in Las Vegas, or the Domodedovo Express in Moscow ("Nosik"). In other instances, he remained quite vague, thus allowing his choices to identify different systems of properties and dispositions. Such systems involve travel experiences, observations, and cross-cultural encounters; they all divide the actual space into familiar and strange, ordinary and glamorous. Whereas the first type of space is normally associated with Moscow, Russia (and the offline world), the other evokes various foreign cities and countries (and the virtual world). Such duality of experience – also manifested in the use of different registers of the Russian language discussed above – signifies recognition and deciphering, accumulation and interpretation of experience, and its mediation on the internet. Nosik converts his private adventures into public experiences, the mundane into the aesthetically-charged, necessity into luxury. In the process, his blog becomes an exhibition, a consumable display of symbols of excellence, and it reaffirms the celebrity status of its author.

While always on the move in the real world, Nosik creates a virtual home through his blog, which serves as a fixed point of reference and an intersection of dispersed social links. In technical terms, the internet is an ever-expanding, constantly evolving medium; in symbolic terms it is a place of stasis, it is a home for the displaced, de-territorialized subjects seeking confidence in the connectivity provided by the internet. Furthermore, blogs invert the dichotomy of private and public: similarly to reality shows, bloggers use their public online space as their private domain, celebrating the gaze of the others. As I argue, blogs serve as a space that enables subjects to construct their authority through the manipulation of the private in the realm of the public.

Nosik's authority rests primarily in his wide access to new technologies and devices. For example, on 14 March 2008, in his blog Nosik posted a photograph displaying the contents of his carry-on luggage during his return journey from the USA; they include the latest models of iPods, mobile phones, digital cameras, laptops, and other technologies ("Nosik"). These objects and Nosik's predilection for moving them across political and geographical borders, as well as across different media, evince both the commonality and exclusivity of his experiences. The former is grounded in the post-Soviet *chelnok* economy, when after the collapse of the old Soviet distribution networks in the early 1990s, the *chelnoks* – the Russian for *shuttles* – would travel outside the country, normally to the neighboring states of Poland, China, or Turkey, and return with goods for sale, thus contributing to Russia's growing black market economy. By importing into Russia the technological devices unavailable inside the country, Nosik speaks to the common *chelnok* experience, and establishes a link of neutrality and commonality with his fans. However, by bringing in these devices for his personal consumption, he distances himself from the crowd, and makes himself even more desirable and exclusive to his blog readers. On one level, the possession of these gadgets signals Nosik's keen interest in new technological advancements, but on another, it elevates his status to that of a celebrity, since he owns desirable objects unattainable by the majority of his fans (on the use of objects and celebrity, see Chapter 4). Therefore, the function of these items is similar to that of designer clothes in the world of pop stars and television celebrities, in which the social profile of an individual depends on material manifestations of the person's status. Technological paraphernalia help Nosik create his own individual style, a recognized social trademark, and a recognizable brand. In general these gadgets serve as a promise of happiness since they satisfy the desire for commodified innovation characteristic of Western modernity.

Nosik demonstrates his status not only by displaying valuable objects but also by utilizing new technologies in his professional life and commenting on them in his blog. In fact, he constantly augments his authority by providing extensive first-person commentary on new gadgets and technologies. The language he uses – a hybrid form of technical Russian, internet slang, and a Russified form of global English – signals his worldwide awareness (whereby technological diversity serves as a substitute for cultural cosmopolitanism) and exceptionality, as in the post in his blog on 16 March 2008, "'Teper' suschestvuet odna na vse versii utilita, kotoraia v odno kasaniie vam i razlochit operatora ..." [there is now only one version of the utility which in one go will let you unlock the operator ...] ("Nosik").[6] Though in real terms excluded from communication by the use of such highly specialized vocabulary, in symbolic terms, users feel that they belong to a select community of professionals who exchange valuable information for free. Nosik gains prestige and maintains his status of – technical – celebrity in a community of like-minded fans. Finally, his ability to invent a new language guarantees his preeminence.

Whether operating via a linguistic phenomenon, intriguing personality, or constructed environment, cyberspace has the propensity to create its own stars, who, like their offline analogues, may have a short life span or enjoy perennial popularity. The difference between the online and offline celebrities lies in the immateriality of the digital celebrity discourse, the speed of production and circulation, and that the grassroots basics of the digital media provide an illusion of the accessibility and transparency of web structures. In fact, Russian internet stars like Nosik enjoy their popularity and authority thanks to their role in the very construction of the medium. As a result, they are highly aware of the logic of the new medium and are capable of manipulating the discourses of power and popularity. The Nosik phenomenon illustrates an important feature of Russian web culture: namely, the tendency toward the establishment of hierarchies, figures of authority, and realms of resistance. Nosik has maintained his celebrity status because he has been able to migrate from one medium to another; in other words, his celebrity status is not specific to one cross-section of the internet, but functions as a cross-medium phenomenon. As the star of the "knowledge" class, Nosik has utilized the broader phenomenon of glamour – in his case, primarily exhibited in the values associated with traveling and gadgetry – which disavows the immaterial nature of the medium by providing phenomena in an objectified form. Technological objects, "the gadgets," defy established technical and personal conventions, as they reveal the status of their owners, "the geeks." New media and the internet enable consumers to archive, annotate, appropriate, and circulate media content and forms, constructing a space for the propagation of glamour, albeit in an altered, techno-centric form unrecognizable to those outside the milieu. In the information economy of the internet, knowledge and status equate prestige, authority, and power. Individuals negotiate their personal ambitions via corporate interests as the diversity of media culture increases, making commodity culture more responsive to consumers, and establishing their status as internet celebrities.

Notes

1 "Eto tak prosto, eto zavorazhivaiusche prosto. Eto zanimaet neskol'ko nedel', esli ne toropit'sia, i neskol'ko dnei – esli postarat'sia kak sleduet. Eto trebuet podgotovki, nekotoroi doli talanta, naglosti i umeniia ispol'zovat' situatsiiu. Vkhozhdenie v elitu Runeta – eto vopros zhelaniia."

2 By the internet I mean the collection of networks that link computers and servers together to create either a local or a global network. The internet is not a single media form; it involves many traditional media and serves as a point of connection for many new media.

3 "Chuvstva – kak Louis Vuitton – ili nastoiaschie, ili ne nado; Ponty – kak shuby Roberto Cavalli – idut tol'ko Filippu Kirkorovu; Seks – kak Gucci – mnogo ne byvaet; Kokain – kak Versace – uzhe ne modno, no mnogie privykli. Sigarety – kak Valentino – elegantno, no starit; Kluby – kak Richmond – uzhe prosto smeshno; Alkogol' – kak Dolce & Gabbana – tol'ko v meru; Zamuzh – kak Chanel – traditsionno, vse khotiat; Skromnost' – kak Cartier – ukrashaet" ("Glamour" 2).

4 In February 2009 Georgii Iungval'd-Khil'kevich released a remake of the film entitled *The Return of the Musketeers* starring Mikhail Boiarskii.

5 I use the term "language" here to refer to the actual forms of the Russian language as well as to the medium-specific culture of the internet as presented in Lev Manovich's influential *The Language of New Media* (2001).

6 The sentence includes the Russian verb "razlochit'" – a coinage derived from the English "to unlock," with a mutation of the consonants kàch and substitution of the English prefix with its Russian equivalent.

Bibliography

Bourdieu, P. (1984) *Distinction: A Social Critique of the Judgment of Taste*, trans. R. Nice, Cambridge, MA: Harvard University Press.

Castells, M. (2003) *The Internet Galaxy: Reflections on the Internet, Business, and Society*, Oxford: Oxford University Press.

Hardt, M. and Negri, A. (2000) *Empire*, Cambridge, MA and London: Harvard University Press.

Goralik, L. (1999) "Vkhozhdenie v Runet-elitu: prakticheskoe rukovodstvo," Available online at: http://old.russ.ru/netcult/19990802_goralik.html (accessed 12 December 2008).

Groys, B. (2006) *Ilya Kabakov: The Man Who Flew into Space from his Apartment*, London: Afterall Books.

Jenkins, H. (2006) *Fans, Bloggers, and Gamers: Exploring Participatory Culture*, New York, London: New York University Press.

McNair, B. (2006) *Cultural Chaos: Journalism, News and Power in a Globalised World*, London, New York: Routledge.

Manovich, L. (2001) *The Language of New Media*, Cambridge, MA and London: MIT Press.

Nosik, A. [Blog] Available online at: http://dolboeb.livejournal.com (accessed 25 April 2008).

—. (2009) "Zhizn' – eto ulitsa s odnostoronnim dvizheniem," Gazeta.ru, 24 July. Available online at: www.gazeta.ru/dewars/3226984.shtml (accessed 28 July 2009).

Saunders, R. (2009) "Wiring the Second World: The Geopolitics of Information and Communications Technology in Post-Totalitarian Eurasia," *Russian Cyberspace*, no. 1, Oct. Available online at: www.russian-cyberspace.org (accessed 25 January 2009).

Strukov, V. (2007) "The Stars of Russian Blogosphere. Considering Issues of Internet Authorship and Fandom," Paper presented at Centre for Research in the Arts, Social Sciences, and Humanities of the University of Cambridge, Cambridge, 24 Oct.

—. (2008) "The Performativity of Fear: Andrei Bakhurin's Scary Dolls," *Static*, no. 1, Oct. Available online at: http://static.londonconsortium.com/issue01/strukov_performativity.html (accessed 12 October 2008).

—. (2009) "Russia's Internet Media Policies: Open Space and Ideological Closure," in B. Beumers, S. Hutchings, and N. Rulyova (eds) *The Post-Soviet Russian Media: Conflicting Signals*, London: Routledge, p. 208–23.

Trefilov, I. (2008) "Aleksandr Mamut kupil Evsroset' vmeste s dolgami," Available at: www.svobodanews.ru/Article/2008/09/22/20080922175616403.html (accessed 12 October 2008).

Yurchak, A. (2007) *Everything Was Forever, Until It Was No More: The Last Soviet Generation*, Princeton: Princeton University Press.

Websites

Ezhe. Available online at: http://ezhe.ru/fri (accessed 7 October 2008).

Feelovblog. Available online at: http://feelovblog.ru/wp-content/uploads/2007/12/medvedev_preved.jpg (accessed 19 May 2007).

Fotograpiya. Available online at: www.fotografiya.ru/other/preved.htm (accessed 19 May 2007).

Glagolev. Available online at: www.glagolev.ru/photo/pict0108.jpg (accessed 19 May 2007).

Glamour (1). [Forum] Available online at: www.glamour.ru/forum/index.php?showforum=27 (accessed 19 May 2007).

Glamour (2). [Forum] Available online at: < www.glamour.ru/forum/index.php?showtopic =7167 (accessed 19 May 2007).

Guelman. Available online at: www.guelman.ru/obzory/nosik.htm (accessed 7 October 2008).

Internet Super Stars. Available online at: www.Internetsuperstarsconference.com (accessed 7 October 2008).

Mjulia. Available online at: http://mjulia.org.ua/index.php?do=cat&category=notebook (accessed 18 May 2007).

Motorola. Available online at: www.motorola.com/ru (accessed 19 May 2007).

Nethistory. Available online at: www.nethistory.ru/biblio?topic=1046983764 (accessed 7 October 2008).

Novaya Gazeta. Available online at: www.novayagazeta.ru/news/319459.html (accessed 5 October 2008).

nr2. Available online at: www.nr2.ru/technology/45039.html (accessed 2 October 2008).

Rambler. Available online at: http://top100.rambler.ru/top100/All/07/10/08 (accessed 7 October 2008).

Research (1). Available online at: www.research.su (accessed 18 May 2007).

Research (2). Available online at: http://research.sputtv.com/image.php?id=2281&PHPSE SSID=549291a59f9f20cdd0204f6884f76c78 (accessed 18 May 2007).

Russian Business Consulting ratings. Available online at: http://rating.rbc.ru/article. shtml?2007/03/27/31417469 (accessed 19 May 2007).

Sup (1). Available online at: www.sup.com/en (accessed 2 October 2008).

Sup (2). Available online at: www.sup.com/index.html (accessed 2 October 2008).

Tnsglobal. Available online at: www.tnsglobal.com (accessed 2 October 2008).

Web Planeta. Available online at: http://webplanet.ru/news/business/2007/02/05/vegan-sup. html (accessed 2 October 2008).

Woman Notebook. Available online at: www.womannotebook.ru (accessed 18 May 2007).

Yandex. Available online at: http://blogs.yandex.ru/top (accessed 9 October 2008).

Part 4

Gendered sounds and screams of stardom

8   Feminism à la russe?

Pugacheva–Orbakaite's celebrity construction through family bonds

Olga Partan (College of the Holy Cross)

"And how many have you kissed,
Grandma, my little dove?"
"I paid my tribute with songs,
I received a tribute of rings."
> Marina Tsvetaeva, "Grandmother" (1965)[1]

The 60-year-old pop star Alla Pugacheva and her 38-year-old daughter, the singer and actress Kristina Orbakaite, enjoy royal celebrity status in contemporary Russian popular culture. In recent years, post-Soviet media and internet sources dedicated to the glamorous lives of the rich and famous frequently refer to Pugacheva as "the empress," "her Excellency," and even "Alla the Great." In turn, Pugacheva's daughter, the westernized, stylish Orbakaite, is not only often called the princess of Russian pop music, but was actually introduced with this title to Prince Albert Grimaldi of Monaco (Razzakov 2003: 663). While during the Soviet era the state-run media often broadcast Pugacheva's concerts at Easter to distract people from attending religious services, nowadays, comfortable in her royal celebrity status, Pugacheva gives Russian Orthodox blessings to crowds of fans during her concerts. In fact, Chris Rojek argues that the decline in organized religion is one of the main reasons for the emergence of the celebrity industry in the West, with the others being the democratization of society and the commodification of everyday life (Rojek 2001: 13). Following in her mother's footsteps, Orbakaite sends best wishes to her younger-generation fans from "our family," screaming, "We love you; we live and perform only for you!" (The observations are based on the author's attendance at Pugacheva and Orbakaite's concerts such as Pugacheva's on 23 February 2000 at the Orpheum Theater, and Orbakaite on 13 October 2006 at the John Hancock Hall, both in Boston, USA.) Completing the picture of a royal celebrity family, the media often call Pugacheva's former male partners/protégés her "ex-favorites," resuscitating the term historically used to denote former lovers of Russian empresses (Kostina 2006).[2]

Pugacheva's three-decade-long position on the throne of pop culture is unsinkable in Russia and unthinkable in the West. The turbulence that has shaken her homeland and her private life has not affected her stardom. Her worldwide record sales are comparable to those of The Beatles and Elvis Presley, and her voice is recognized in any Russian household, though she remains virtually unknown to Western audiences.[3] Pugacheva's appearance, hefty body, and performing style do not fit with the aesthetics of a Western pop-diva image. Nevertheless, the post-Soviet media glorify her precisely for her distinctive Russian originality, which is incomprehensible to Western logic.

For decades, Pugacheva has remained one of the most famous Russian celebrities. In 2007, the *Russian Forbes* list of the top fifty most popular and wealthy Russian celebrities ranked her second only to the internationally famous, svelte young tennis player Maria Sharapova ("Russian Forbes"), whose reported 2007 income of $23 million far exceeds Pugacheva's, of $2.7 million.[4] Orbakaite also made the list, with an official income of $1.2 million a year and placing twentieth in popularity. This rating certifies Orbakaite's celebrity status, placing her financially ahead of the filmmaker Nikita Mikhalkov (twenty-first) (Mikhalkov's celebrity status is discussed in detail in Chapter 5), the supermodel Natalia Vodianova (thirty-second), the bestselling writer Boris Akunin (thirty-eighth) (Akunin's celebrity status is discussed in detail in Chapter 3), and the baritone Dmitry Khvorostovsky (forty-sixth). Furthermore, in December 2007, Pugacheva once again was ranked second in the annual *Kommersant* opinion poll listing the most popular and influential members of the Russian elite (Alekseev 2007). In this list she came in second only to President Vladimir Putin, and ahead of then Prime Minister Dmitry Medvedev, later elected President. Pugacheva left behind not only actors, writers, and athletes, but also leading representatives of the sizable Russian political and business elite.

What, then, is the significance of the Pugacheva–Orbakaite family bond in contemporary Russian pop culture? Richard Dyer suggests that "stars represent typical ways of behaving, feeling and thinking in contemporary society" and "must always be examined in relation to historical, cultural and socio-economic contexts …" (Dyer 1986: 17). I contend that there is a specifically Russian twist to the celebrity image-making of the Pugacheva–Orbakaite dynasty that can provide insight into their fame – namely, its feminist slant. Despite the fact that feminism continues to carry negative associations in Russian culture, the Pugacheva–Orbakaite dynamic represents a certain "feminism à la Russe": both mother and daughter pursue individual achievement and control over their personal and professional lives, find male partners disillusioning, and rely heavily on each other's support. Agency is their forte.

According to the definition of feminism by the political theorist Susanne Okin in her controversial, yet influential, book, *Is Multiculturalism Bad for Women?* (Okin 1999), both Pugacheva and Orbakaite qualify as feminists. Okin writes:

> By *feminism*, I mean the belief that women should not be disadvantaged by their sex, that they should be recognized as having human dignity equal to that of men, and that they should have the opportunity to live as fulfilling and as freely chosen lives as men can.
>
> (Okin 1999: 10)

As I argue below, mother and daughter are not disadvantaged by their sex and they both freely choose not only their lives but also their male partners, consigning men to a position of secondary importance.

Today, the majority of Russians misperceive feminism as the masculinization of women. During the Soviet era, the term suggested bourgeois values, while within the post-Soviet cultural landscape it is considered a Western women's movement, neither relevant nor appropriate for Russians (Goscilo 1999: 10). While contemporary Russian women complain about their male partners' failure to perform their functions as husbands, fathers, or sexual partners, the majority "not only sh[y] away from feminism but violently denounce it" (Goscilo 1999: 11).

The first part of this chapter traces how, within the Soviet and post-Soviet cultural context, Pugacheva's gender construction as a loving mother/grandmother who is openly involved with younger men sends a powerful message to the Russian age-discriminated female audience. Pugacheva's paradoxical behavior expands the frame of femininity and sexuality through grandmotherhood, challenging the traditional image of an asexual Russian "babushka" wholeheartedly dedicated to her offspring. Pugacheva's observance of Russian family traditions and devotion to her children and grandchildren, however, are interwoven with sexual promiscuity and business acumen – a rebellion against conventional gender roles that enhances her celebrity image.

The second part of this chapter focuses on Pugacheva and Orbakaite as two different types of musical celebrities representing different generations. Adopting P. David Marshall's definitions of musical celebrities (1997), I maintain that Pugacheva belongs to an early popular type of celebrity who relied on vocal skills and emotionality. In contrast, Orbakaite represents the contemporary type, who rely not only on technical developments within the music industry that add texture to a voice, but also on excellent dancing skills. The performing styles, repertoire, and onstage personae of the two singers have been shaped by notions of glamour in post-Soviet society.

A Russian feminist twist: promiscuous (grand) motherhood as a mechanism of celebrity construction

A celebrity's motherhood or relationships with her children do not interest fans as much as do problems in her erotic life (Dyer 1986: 45). The relationship between a star and her offspring, who inherit celebrity status by birth, tends to be rather sour and stormy. Henry Fonda's comment about his daughter, Jane, is a vivid example, "Daughter? I don't have a daughter" (Dyer 1986: 69). In a country where public rhetoric pronounces maternity sacred, Pugacheva has cultivated her public image as Kristina's loving mother, despite the fact that she played little role in raising her daughter due to her turbulent personal life and busy schedule.

Whatever the nature of Orbakaite's private relationship with Pugacheva may be, publicly, at least, Pugacheva's maternal side and the mother–daughter bonding have been methodically staged and projected on television screens from the start of her career. Discussing the staging of celebrity, Chris Rojek writes,

Figure 8.1 Icon pop singer Alla Pugacheva attending a gala for "The Glamour Woman of the Year Award"; 12 June 2007. Photo by Ekaterina Chesnokova, courtesy of RIA Novosti.

Figure 8.2 Pop singer Kristina Orbakaite performing at a concert dedicated to the 50th anniversary of Moscow's Sheremetievo airport at the Khodynka Arena ice palace; 23 September 2009. Photo by Marina Liseva, courtesy of RIA Novosti.

Staged celebrity refers to the calculated technologies and strategies of performance and self projection designed to achieve a status of monumentality in
public culture. In cases where these technologies and strategies are successful,
the achieved celebrity may acquire enduring iconic significance

(Rojek 2001: 121).

When Pugacheva burst onto the Soviet pop-culture scene in 1975 with her song
about a tragicomic clown Arlekino (Harlequin), she was already the mother of a
three-year-old daughter, Kristina, and had a rather chaotic love life. One of her
image-makers during the Soviet era, her second husband, the filmmaker Aleksandr
Stefanovich, defined her image as that of a "prima donna with a child" (Beliakov
1997: 167). This image as a mother was important even for a singer as emancipated
and rebellious as Pugacheva. As Helena Goscilo puts it, "From time immemorial
the dominant Russian iconography has projected nationhood as female, its ethos
and moral identity metaphorized as maternity" (1999: 32). Linguistically, Russia
is feminine in gender – Mother Russia (Matushka-rus' and rodina-mat') – and the
metaphor of Mother Russia was decisive for the country's sense of nationhood,
despite the cult of masculinity imposed by state officials (Goscilo and Lanoux
2006: 9). Rosalind Marsh observes that in the 1970s and 1980s, diversity in
women's lives was not widely accepted in Soviet society: "In both Russian culture
and the media, the childless or infertile woman is generally seen in negative terms"
(1998: 16).[5]

In the 1970s and 1980s, without having the option of constructing a Western-
style celebrity profile, Pugacheva sang many songs targeting children – an
approach that rarely figured in the repertoires of other Soviet pop stars, whose
songs were dedicated either to romantic love or to the Soviet homeland. Children's
songs were traditionally performed by youth choruses, and few performers found
a way to attract both children and parents as Pugacheva did. In addition to her gift
for parody, flamboyant theatricality on stage, and preoccupation with love themes,
she was also a star-parent familiar with problems in the Soviet educational system –
which brought her close to many segments of her audience. Performing children's
songs as miniature plays with catchy tunes and comic lyrics, Pugacheva would
transform her voice and body language to impersonate a child, thereby appealing
to fans from many generations.[6]

In 1983, at the age of eleven, Orbakaite became a celebrity in her own right
after playing a leading role in Rolan Bykov's film *Chuchelo* [The Scarecrow].
Moviegoers – curious to see what Pugacheva's daughter looked like – were not
disappointed. Orbakaite had inherited her mother's gift for acting and gave a
touching, convincing performance as an orphan who lives with her grandfather
and faces the cruelty of her classmates, who refuse to accept her independence
and otherness. Given cinema's powerful role in shaping celebrity image (Dyer
1998: 61), the public developed a perception of Orbakaite as both a lonely orphan
on screen and the popular diva's daughter in real life. Pugacheva had "achieved"
celebrity status, which derives "from the perceived accomplishments of the individual in open competition," while her daughter had a combination of ascribed and

achieved celebrity, based both on "biological descent" and a successful cinematic debut (Rojek 2001: 17–18).

Shortly after her daughter's cinematic success, Pugacheva brought her on stage and started to appear on television singing together with her. The demonstration of maternal love and protection – the eccentric red-haired singer and her fragile blonde daughter – projected a powerful public image. Their popular 1983 duet "A znaesh' vse eshche budet" [You know, everything's ahead of you] (by Mark Minkov and Veronika Tushnova) was staged as a conversation between mother and daughter in which the former is proud of sharing her life experience with the latter, who in return sends her admiring, loving looks. The song was first shown on television on 8 March – International Women's Day – and the visual image of a harmonious, close relationship between the two conveyed a sense of stability and strong family bonding, helping Pugacheva establish solidarity with her largely female audience (Razzakov 2003: 281). As P. David Marshall observes, a performer's "communication of solidarity with an audience" is an important part of the mechanism for constructing popular music celebrity (1997: 164).

While developing her public image of a prima donna/single mother with a child, Pugacheva was also the object of constant rumors about her scandalous behavior and numerous love affairs. Since glossy magazines and the yellow press did not exist in the Soviet Union, Pugacheva's private life was not openly discussed in the mass media. In fact, the Soviet mass media were powerful tools of state propaganda, in which published interviews were sanitized and not very informative, for government bureaucrats controlled all aspects of the mass media's image-making. Nevertheless, rumors as a form of popular discourse circulated among Pugacheva's fans and served as a powerful, effective means of shaping her celebrity status. Cultivating gossip about herself – some of it of her own fabrication – Pugacheva would let slip false rumors about her activities, then wait to see how soon they would make a full circle, reported back to her (*Neizvestnaia Pugacheva*).

While relying on her motherhood as a critical part of her life and public image, Pugacheva nonetheless rebelled against traditional gender roles in patriarchal Soviet society, suggestively flirting with younger singers in front of the television cameras and staging scandalous relationships with her composers and singing partners in her performances. Such sexualized behavior, which was not permitted on Soviet television, intrigued the public, and she clearly benefited from the ability of scandals to enhance a celebrity's image. Discussing the images of Western stars, Dyer notes that "scandals can harm a career ... or temporarily give it a new lease on life" (1998: 61). Expanding the definition of femininity and sending a powerful liberating message to her female compatriots, Pugacheva's public image challenged the well-established canons of the Russian and Soviet cultural "phallocentric tradition" (Marsh 1998: 22), where a female "is not allowed to be both a sexual being and a mother" (Marsh 1998: 5).

Rumors and gossip about Pugacheva's love life blossomed every time she sang a duet with a new male performer or composer. During the period of her collaboration with the enigmatic and handsome Latvian composer Raymond Pauls, she addressed him as "My maestro" in her songs and dramatically changed her appearance: she lost weight, replaced her trademark shapeless tunics with elegant black dresses, and briefly changed her hairdo. Even if the chemistry between Pugacheva and Pauls on stage was part of her performance, millions of Pugacheva's fans were mesmerized by the artistic union of the singer and her maestro.

During the early 1980s, one of Pugacheva's hit songs, "Million alykh roz" [A Million Scarlet Roses] (by Raimond Pauls, lyrics by Andrei Voznesensky), which tells of a painter who falls in love with an actress and sells all his canvases and belongings to buy roses so he can transform the square in front of her window into a sea of scarlet roses, became a hymn for millions of Pugacheva's female fans who were yearning for romantic love.[7]

> A million, a million, a million scarlet roses
> From your window, from your window, from your window you see.
> One who is in love, one who is in love, one who is in love and seriously so
> Will transform his whole life for you into flowers.[8]
>   (Radio Alla Songs)

Ironically, the romantic refrain of this song was immediately transformed into a widely circulated (yet untranslatable) pun about the reality of Soviet women's views from their windows. Instead of seeing a million scarlet roses, they could only see a million drunk faces, "Million, million, million p'ianykh rozh / Iz okna vidish ty." [A million, a million, a million drunk mugs / From your window, from your window, from your window you see.] This mock refrain vividly illustrated the dramatic contrast between the dreamworld of Soviet women and the harsh reality of millions of Soviet men suffering from alcoholism.

While Pugacheva denied any romantic involvement with Pauls during their collaboration in the early 1980s, she did not deny her extramarital affairs with others, such as the rock musician and composer Vladimir Kuzmin during her third marriage in the mid-1980s. Pugacheva's infatuation with Kuzmin transformed her into a voluptuous rock star wrapped in leather miniskirts. Jumping and clapping rhythmically, she sang to Kuzmin, her young lover, "How could it happen, How could it happen? / How could I fall in love like that?" (Pugacheva and Kuzmin 1987). She looked energized and was sharing her passion with the audience.

The Russian rock historian and music critic Artemii Troitskii recalls that on numerous occasions he tried to convince Pugacheva to change her musical style and consider seriously collaborating with rock musicians such as Boris Grebenshchikov and his group, *Aquarium*. Pugacheva's rejection of such ideas suggests how aware she was of her position as a pop star for the millions and that such changes would violate the expectations of her audience. Troitskii reports that she repeatedly said that "she was a singer for the people" ("Ia narodnaia pevitsa") and "sang for the grannies on the street" ("ia poiu dlia babushek"), not for western-ized intellectuals (Troitskii 2007).

Aware that her position on the throne of pop culture should be based on cul-tural tradition, as far back as 1982 Pugacheva prepared her audience for a future transition to her role as a grandmother in poetic fashion with the song "When I'll

Be a Grandmother," based on the 1919 poem by Marina Tsvetaeva. The stylized folk tune for this song was written by Pugacheva herself, with a rhythmic pattern of dashing Russian folk music that makes Tsvetaeva's poetry more accessible to mass audiences and illustrates a connection between Russian folk traditions and Pugacheva's art. The poem depicts a poetic persona imagining herself in the future role of a flamboyant and loving grandmother (Pugacheva 1996),

> When I'll be a grandmother –
> In a decade or so –
> I'll be whimsical and entertaining,
> A whirlwind from head to toe![9]
> > (Tsvetaeva 1965: 148)

Responding to her granddaughter's queries about her past, the grandmother avoids giving a direct answer, saying only that her lovers inspired her to write songs cherishing her métier as a creative artist,

> "And how many have you kissed,
> Grandma, my little dove?"
> "I paid my tribute with songs
> I received a tribute of rings ..."[10]
> > (Tsvetaeva 1965: 149)

Tsvetaeva's poem reflects a traditional Russian relationship between several generations of women, where grandmothers play an important role in the upbringing of the younger generation. The multiple lovers implied in the text have no tangible presence. Reversing the age-old conventions of male poetry, which casts the female beloved as Muse, Tsvetaeva assigns male lovers the function of inspiring the female artist's creativity. The poem presents a matriarchal family structure, focused on the transmission of female experience and "wisdom" from one generation to another, and the grandmother's inextinguishable passion for life. The song had prophetic significance for Pugacheva's public persona, presaging the future celebrity status of the empress of Russian pop culture and her daughter, the princess of Russian pop. While the lives of grandchildren, a daughter, and a grandmother intertwine, men are completely erased from this family picture, recalled only via memories that inspire women's art.

Many of the post-Soviet interviews by Pugacheva and Orbakaite contain the clear message that their mother-daughter love and support have outlasted their many marriages and love affairs. While Pugacheva's partners far outnumber Orbakaite's, Orbakaite has been linked romantically with several men, and has children by two of them. Male partners play temporary, secondary roles in the lives of the two women, whose bond is primary and permanent. This reversal of traditional Russian gender stereotypes is particularly striking in the context of typical post-Soviet media depictions of successful businesswomen as often unhappy and lonely individuals, while casting housewives and, paradoxically, models in a positive light, for they serve the needs of successful businessmen (Azhgikhina 1997).

The prominent Russian journalist Nadezhda Azhgikhina has noted that winners of Russian beauty contests have the unique opportunity to become businessmen's model-girlfriends and, subsequently, their (house)wives. Since a woman's chief image is that of a sex object, even when she becomes a successful entrepreneur, the press often emphasizes that business is just her hobby; otherwise, she is "just a normal woman." Moreover, women themselves internalize this imposed image, "the vast majority of articles dealing with 'women's issues' (including those that present women as caricatures, sex objects, or simply complete idiots) are written by female authors" (Azhgikhina 1997).

The post-Soviet media continue to depict the strong Pugacheva–Orbakaite bond, having thoroughly covered Pugacheva's divorce from her fourth husband, Filipp Kirkorov, nineteen years younger than she, and Orbakaite's recent marriage to the Russian-American businessman Mikhail Zemtsov. Flouting conventional gender expectations, the 60-year-old grandmother Pugacheva frequently appears in public with her 33-year-old partner, Maksim Galkin, while Orbakaite recently fired Vasilii Rutka, her younger lover/dancer of several years, stating that she did not want rumors of their romantic involvement to undermine her new marriage ("Kristina Orbakaite"). Kept constantly in the limelight, these publicized amours offer readers and viewers the illusion of intimate knowledge about the two women's private lives – a titillating glance into a world inaccessible to the average fan.

Understanding all too well the market value of publicizing the private, Pugacheva often makes provocative public comments about her personal life. In a 2006 interview, she laughingly replied to a journalist who criticized her taste for handsome young singers, such as Filipp Kirkorov and Maksim Galkin, "Well, yes, I like young, good-looking men …. they give me … an aesthetic and intellectual pleasure. I'll let myself have a sweaty older man with a cigar when I'm seventy … Maybe … Okay?" (Polupanov 2006a). The interview conveys a message simultaneously provocative and comforting, as it conceives of men not as aggressors, but as objects of a mature woman's desire. Such interviews challenge gender stereotypes, confirming Goscilo's observations about "hormoned heroines" openly exploring their sexuality and pleasure, who emerged in fictional narratives of the 1980s and 1990s authored by women writers such as Liudmila Ulitskaia, Tatyana Tolstaya, and Marina Palei (Goscilo 1999: 105). Deconstructing traditional male roles, Russian women artists now transform men from desiring agents into objects of female sexual desire. They challenge the male perspective equated with Russian culture, whereby experiencing pleasure is restricted "to young women in tragic cases (to older women in comic ones)" (Goscilo 1999: 105). Perhaps unexpectedly, an advocate of such a metamorphosis is Irina Khakamada, one of the few prominent female politicians of the post-Soviet era, who at the very end of her book *Sex v bol'shoi politike* [Sex in Big Politics] (2006) addresses her middle-aged fellow countrywomen,

> All of you are wonderful women; just be more decisive. Do not be afraid of yourselves, do not be afraid of the world, do not deprive yourselves of anything that would give back to the world its colors and shape. If not for yourselves,

do it for your children. Because nothing good can happen in a country where the largest group is deprived of the taste for life (and there are about 60 million women in their forties and older in Russia).

(Khakamada 2006: 229–30)

One of the few middle-aged women to have anticipated Khakamada, Pugacheva indeed seems free of fear and far from inclined to self-deprivation.

While good taste may not be Pugacheva's strong suit, boldness certainly is. In December 2007, she again co-hosted the *Dve zvezdy* [Two Stars] musical show on Russian television, this time with her current young partner, Galkin. Dressed in a bridal-white miniskirt tunic, she managed simultaneously to sing and flirt with Galkin while promoting her daughter via Galkin's numerous exclamations, "Here is the princess of Russian popular music!" or "Next, the two megastars: mother and daughter, Alla Pugacheva and Kristina Orbakaite will sing for us together!" (*Two Stars* 2007).

On 2 March 2008, the day of the Russian presidential election, the media heavily publicized the Pugacheva–Orbakaite dynasty's arrival at a polling station. True to herself, the 59-year-old diva appeared in front of journalists in the roles of a mistress, mother, and grandmother, having come to the polling station with her young partner, Galkin, her daughter, Kristina, and her youngest grandson, Danny. When a journalist solicited her position on the elections, instead of endorsing any

Figure 8.3 Showman Maksim Galkin and singer Alla Pugacheva at the 45th birthday party of fashion designer Valentin Yudashkin in Moscow's Manezh; 14 October 2008. Photo by Ekaterina Chesnokova, courtesy of RIA Novosti.

politician, Pugacheva pointed to her grandson and replied, "This is my position," thus emphasizing her grandmotherly role and suggesting that, while politicians may change, the primacy of family bonds remains stable ("Alla Pugacheva. The Election …").

Two generations and two types of stardom

Though Pugacheva and Orbakaite strive to create a public image of artistic unity and the continuity of family traditions, the two singers not only belong to two different generations, but also represent two dissimilar types of musical stars, with diverse performing styles. Examining historical and theoretical perspectives on celebrity within music, Marshall notes that in the early twentieth century, celebrity status was defined by "the power of voice – its depth and range," when, like "the opera singer, the popular singer was able to project his or her voice to the very back of the concert hall" (1997: 155). Technological progress in the popular music industry, such as the invention of the microphone and voice amplification, drastically changed expectations of musical stars (Marshall 1997: 155–6). Today, Marshall observes, the technological capabilities of recording studios allow some stars not to sing at all during their concerts, "Instead they lip-synch and dance to the reproduced sounds of their records in front of the audience" (1997: 154). This time-dependent difference marks Pugacheva's and her daughter's performing styles. Pugacheva's emotionality and vocal power enable her to reach the back rows of the concert hall in live concerts that demonstrate her now diminished but still considerable vocal strengths. Her popularity stems from her rather old-fashioned performing style, based on her voice, originality, and the intensity of her performances. Juggling various genres and moods, she mines her fabled stage charisma. In contrast, Orbakaite's enthusiastic adoption of more recent trends in musical performance means a heavy reliance on her dancing and lip-syncing skills, as well as her pre-recorded vocals, which, of course, can amplify a modest voice almost beyond recognition.

Marshall contends that, unlike classical music celebrities, who tend to distance themselves from the audience, popular music performers usually establish direct and emotionally intimate contact with the audience in a ritualized dialogue, "The personal sentiments expressed in the song's lyrics are freely exposed in action and voice. Audience participation and response are encouraged in the concert setting during the performance of most songs. In this way, a ritualized dialogue is maintained between performer and audience" (Marshall 1997: 158). Therefore, according to Marshall, concerts are "not an introduction to the music for the fans, but a form of ritualized authentication of pleasure and meaning of the records and the pop star. The fan is demonstrating his or her solidarity with the artist's message and with the rest of the audience" (Marshall 1997: 158). Both Pugacheva and Orbakaite engage in this kind of ritualized dialogue with fans. Pugacheva addresses shared cultural memories, always intermingling songs from the past with new songs in her concerts. In turn, Orbakaite frequently conducts a double ritualized dialogue, with both her audience and her mother's art. While constantly reminding the public whose daughter she is, she claims an independent identity as a talented, original performer in her own right, not her mother's imitator or clone.

The Western industry of popular music celebrities is driven by non-stop innovation and vitality, as well as the constant appearance and disappearance of teen idols (Marshall 1997: 181–3). While contemporary Russian popular music shares these features, Pugacheva's stardom is based on something more: namely, audiences' collective cultural memory and a performing style that evokes and satisfies nostalgia for the Soviet era. Projecting the image of a woman with an indomitable spirit, she emanates an aura of immortality, partly because her fans include representatives of many generations. When naïve teenage fans ask her what kinds of songs she sang during World War II, the diva, who sometimes wears clothes more suitable for a teenager, does not point out that if she had enjoyed a singing career during World War II, she now would have to be over eighty years old (Komatoza.net).

Dyer states that in any media construction a "star image" should include "a complex configuration of visual, verbal and aural signs" (1998: 34). The performing style of a musical celebrity engages such elements as a "musical code, new form of dance, or an altered way of dress" when "the new style is invariably drawn from a particular audience group or subculture and is then rearticulated by the popular music performer" (Dyer 1998: 34). Orbakaite's style and signs differ radically from her mother's, both women capitalizing on their individual assets.

Pugacheva relies heavily on her vocal and emotional intensity, tends to be somewhat static, and when she jumps and walks her movements emphasize her clumsiness. Instead of hiding her physical imperfections, she ridicules herself on and off stage for her struggles to keep her weight down and suggests to her audiences that it is perfectly acceptable not to look glamorous. In her performances she invariably projects a mature confidence in herself and her uniqueness.

Lacking her mother's vocal and emotive talent, Orbakaite uses various audio-effects to amplify her singing. In fact, during her solo concerts she frequently has a female singer who, standing in the background, sings along with her as a part of the chorus, so as to augment the sound of Orbakaite's voice, which was particularly obvious during her concert in Boston in October 2006. Moreover, in her performances Orbakaite showcases her skills as a professional dancer, demonstrating her flexibility. Her glamorous appearance, impeccable taste in clothing, and stylishness contrast with Pugacheva's clownish extravagance in clothing and her improvised interaction with the public.

Though both mother and daughter select their repertoires with meticulous care so as to point up their respective skills, those repertoires fundamentally diverge. Rich in experimentation based on the intermingling of various musical genres and moods, Pugacheva's repertoire comprises songs written on folkloric, gypsy, jazz, and disco tunes, with lyrics either of her own composition or borrowed from various classical poets. Furthermore, the alternation of comic and dramatic moods is a trademark of her performing style. Orbakaite's repertoire favors the rhythmic patterns of dance – tango, foxtrot, Charleston, or disco – that enable her to supplement her singing with dance movements. Elements of Pugacheva's famous eccentricity find expression in Orbakaite's dancing, which shifts from dramatic to clownish, to acrobatic, depending on the content of her songs. Whatever the parallels between the two female celebrities, they unquestionably represent different eras, aesthetics, and modes of self-fashioning and communication.

Image and self-presentation

The attention paid by glossy magazines to the mother-daughter duo offers living proof of the extent to which Western-style approaches to celebrity culture have affected post-Soviet media. The Russian editions of *In Style, Cosmopolitan, Bazaar* and other glossy magazines publish titillating interviews and articles about scandals and provide intimate details about the New Russian rich and famous, interweaving these items with news about western celebrities, and thereby creating an eclectic panoramic picture of "internationalized glamour." Russian celebrities overshadow their western counterparts by virtue of their priceless diamonds and expensive designer outfits, as if to proclaim that "Russian glamour is the most glamorous in the world!" Coverage of that reassuring national one-upmanship undoubtedly reaches the post-Soviet glamour-conscious readership, since, as Goscilo wittily observes, "In the new post-Soviet aesthetics, beauty and conventionalized signs of wealth became as inseparable as Marx and Engels in the pre-market era" (Goscilo 2000b: 17).[11] In 2007, the word "glamour" – and its endless variations, such as the adjective "glamurnyi" (glamorous), the verb "oglamurit'" (to make glamorous), and even a new concept of "Glamuria" (land of glamour) as a new name for Russia (Epstein 2007) – was proclaimed the word of the year. Russian intellectuals interpret the ubiquity of this vocabulary as the replacement of "truth" by a glossy golden appearance, but for fans of glamour and celebrities, "truth" is a throwback to the illusions of an earlier era discredited by post-Soviet developments.

While Kristina Orbakaite follows Western fashions and celebrity culture styles, Pugacheva insists that as Alla Pugacheva she elaborated her own style and image and ignores changing fashions. Asked about her attitude to fashion, Pugacheva laughs, "I never tried to follow fashion. Fashion follows me, but just can't catch up" ("O, Alla!" 2008). When a journalist queried whether she ever wanted to change her image or herself, or at least to experiment with her hair color, Pugacheva replied:

> Change my image by coloring my hair differently? God forbid! Image isn't just hair color. I've never changed my image. As for my hairdo … of course I was experimenting a lot! But I came to the realization that my hairdo looks good on me. While I still have hair I'll wear this hairdo … Why change it! Alla Pugacheva – what better image can I invent for myself! And it's kind of too late now to change …
>
> (Vinogradova 2007)

Pugacheva admits that her legendary tunic (becoming shorter and shorter over time) was originally designed during the Soviet era by Viacheslav Zaitsev and brings her luck, which is why she has asked the designers Valentin Iudashkin and Andrei Sharov to modify it, but stay faithful to her image. "'My designers, who work and socialize with me, have a difficult time,' she admits, 'my body's not ideal, and all the extravagant ideas that I frequently come up with plunge them into a state of total shock'" ("O, Alla!" 2008). Clearly, Pugacheva is fully aware that her image has an iconic significance within Russian culture and has achieved monumental status, so should not be subject to radical change.

While many post-Soviet stars follow the Western celebrity culture obsession with wealth, beauty, and youth, Pugacheva has chosen a different path, emphasizing her own quirky personal style and seeking to demonstrate solidarity with her fans. As she approached sixty, Pugacheva openly discussed her age-related health problems (such as her heart surgery) ("Govoriat, chto" 2008; Polupanov 2006b) and her flaw-riddled, aging body (*Pesnia goda 2006* 2007), while also insisting that her outfits are an *artistic* statement that reflects her unique style (Polupanov 2006b). This apparent rejection of a standardized glamour seems to be a logical continuation of Pugacheva's notorious rebellion during the Soviet era against an established etiquette that dictated the norm for renowned performers: a modest, neat appearance; proper public behavior; and respect for high government officials.

Unlike stars who often brag to the media about their post-Soviet wealth and proudly admit to owning expensive property abroad, Pugacheva downplays her wealth, perhaps so that her fans can more easily identify with her. Appealing to her fans' nostalgia for the stability of the Soviet era, she seeks to build solidarity with middle-aged women of her generation:

> During the Soviet era the financial situation was much more predictable – I knew that I would receive my salary on the 15th of every month – no matter what. I knew how much sour cream cost – now I have no idea – prices for sour cream are different everywhere. That's why I address my audiences during concerts by saying, 'Thank you, my bread providers'.
>
> (Polupanov 2006a)

It is common knowledge that Pugacheva employs bodyguards and housekeepers, certainly does not shop for her own groceries, and consumes foods infinitely more expensive than bread and sour cream. Yet during interviews she purports to share the experiences of her fans' everyday lives, thereby boosting her popularity as a singer "for the people."[12] She is, nonetheless, one of the wealthiest stars in Russia, and the post-Soviet media constantly speculate about her wealth and possessions. According to some sources, after her divorce from Kirkorov, Pugacheva has been living in the luxurious Hotel Baltschug, where she pays for two large rooms. Providing a detailed description of her lifestyle, menu, and fitness routine, an anonymous author concludes that the prima donna's suite is rather modest compared to those enjoyed by Richard Gere and Luciano Pavarotti in the past ("Kak zhivet Alla Pugacheva?"), but even a day at the Baltschug costs sums unimaginable to the average Russian. Against all expectations, Pugacheva claims that she owns just one apartment and one suburban house near Moscow, where she spends the summer, which is always supplied with food and open to her friends.

Markers of "fabulous wealth" usually include not only residences but also servants, cars, designer clothes, and the like. Post-Soviet fascination with luxury cars is reflected in the media's regular reports on celebrities and their cars as well as the honoraria paid for their appearances at corporate parties for mega-companies. *Komsomol'skaia Pravda* (a leading newspaper for Soviet-era communist youth, but now more interested in scandals) and *Izvestiia* (the major source of Soviet propaganda for the masses) regularly dedicate space to celebrity gossip. Accordingly, *Komsomol'skaia Pravda* claims that Pugacheva owns a Rolls-Royce and Orbakaite has a Mercedes-Benz 500 (Bakhtiiarova and Remizova 2008), and *Izvestiia* in its list of fees paid to celebrities for performing at various corporate events cites Pugacheva as charging from $160,000 up, Galkin only $90,000 and higher, while Orbakaite did not make the list of the most expensive performers ("Plati 100 tysiach evro …"). Pugacheva also has started several business ventures in the post-Soviet period, including her own perfume, her own glossy magazine titled *Alla*, her shoe collection, and, in 2007, her radio station – *Radio Alla*. Though it is difficult to take seriously Pugacheva's claims of worry about her finances and ability to retire, some sources report that Pugacheva is impractical and has suffered monetary losses owing to actions by her managers and financial advisers – another demonstration of what Russians proudly believe is their quintessentially Russian impractical nature (Troitskii 2007).

Unlike her mother, Orbakaite enthusiastically embraces Western-style fashion and glamour. Tellingly, the December 2006 Russian edition of *In Style* featured a photo of Orbakaite as a fairy-tale princess on its front cover, and inside, photos of her showing off her shapely body in outfits by Valentino, Gianfranco Ferre, and Roberto Cavali and jewelry by Dior and Bvlgari. The stylist Ol'ga Mikhailovskaia and the internationally renowned star photographer Carole Bellaiche created a romantic, feminine, and vulnerable image of Orbakaite, who in the text accompanying the photos is gushingly characterized not only as "her Highness, the crown princess of show business," but also as "a famous daughter of a famous mother, who achieved her own fame at the age of eleven, a star of *estrada* (varieté, pop music), a successful movie actress who occasionally performs on stage as well, a businesswoman who manages her own band, a woman who is loved, and the mother of two sons. All the details of her private life unavoidably become known to the public" (Zhiliaeva 2006: 338).

The interviewer responsible for the text of the article notes that Orbakaite's attire and manners are "quiet, tactful" – something one could never claim about Pugacheva. "It is difficult," the interviewer maintains, "to imagine her being angry or involved in any sort of inappropriate behavior" (Zhiliaeva 2006: 338). In short, Orbakaite's public image is the antithesis of Pugacheva's, which is synonymous with shock value, aggressiveness, and mockery. When Orbakaite talks about her career and her role as the mother of two sons from different fathers, she presents herself as an emancipated businesswoman capable of resolving any financial and family problems that may arise.

Orbakaite's emphasis on the cosmopolitan nature of her family background reinforces her image as a westernized star: her paternal ancestry is Catholic, her maternal is Russian Orthodox, and her younger son's father is Muslim. Limning herself as multi-cultural and respectful of all religions in the era of globalization, she contends, "We are a multi-national family – we start the New Year celebration together with the Catholic world and celebrate up to the Russian Orthodox Christmas" (Zhiliaeva 2006: 345). These assertions are doubtless intended to convey her worldly sophistication, a desirable trait in slick magazines' agenda of "internationalized glamour."

In a March 2007 interview with *Ona* [She] magazine, a glossy publication that discusses women's issues in fairly down-to-earth detail, offering readers practical legal and medical advice, Orbakaite appears in a somewhat different light. Promoting her new film *Liubov'-Morkov'* [Lovey-Dovey] (dir. Aleksandr Strizhenov, 2007), a romantic comedy about troubled spouses who magically switch bodies and learn to better understand each other's needs, Orbakaite gave an interview advocating married life. She confirmed rumors of her long-distance marriage to a Russian-American businessman, saying that she was at peace with herself and the world around her (Rakhlina 2007). In other words, she adjusts her self-presentation whenever the occasion calls for it, while consistently projecting moneyed glamour.

That the mother-daughter relationship packaged for public consumption is complex may be inferred from Pugacheva's strategy of both promoting Orbakaite and using her as an extension of her own personality for self-serving ends. Whereas over a decade ago she expressed the hope that her daughter would succeed in becoming a star in her own right, nowadays she publicly proclaims Orbakaite a major pop star of her generation. When asked by a journalist who inspires her optimism about the future of Russian pop, she replied, "My own daughter, Kristina, who may not be singing some sort of super hits, but is producing very high quality pop music" (Polupanov 2006b). Hitching Orbakaite's professionalism and success to her own, Pugacheva states that her daughter continues the family tradition of never betraying audience expectations, "Even if the public comes to her concerts out of curiosity – just to look at Pugacheva's daughter – Kristina proves to them all that she is a star in her own right" (Polupanov 2006b). Needless to say, curiosity need not necessarily be about "Pugacheva's daughter," but about Orbakaite as an independent artist – a possibility that Pugacheva apparently finds inconceivable.

Pugacheva's star status and consequently her influence exceed her daughter's. It is Pugacheva, after all, who produces and hosts the annual *Pesnia goda* [Song of the Year] concert that is televised early every year, often as a showcase for the Pugacheva–Orbakaite dynasty. The concert dates from the Soviet era, when it was an enormously popular entertainment show attracting huge television audiences. Today the show not only testifies to Pugacheva's staying power, but also enables her to influence other singers' visibility. In 2007 she invited contemporary pop music celebrities, including the rock group Banderos and the internationally known female duo T.A.T.U., as well as long-established figures in Soviet pop music, such as Edita Piekha and Lev Leshchenko. Allowing Pugacheva to play the role of a "cultural mother," the show unwittingly dramatized the discrepancies in professional values between the two eras, revealing the lack of vocal and performing skills among female singers of the new generation even as it vividly displayed their glamorous façade. The long-legged, barely-dressed singers, better equipped to participate in a Victoria's Secret parade than a popular musical extravaganza, uncannily illustrated Vasily Aksenov's view of post-Soviet young Russian women,

> The dominant female type today is a gigantic, tall young woman with very long legs who expends all her efforts on maintaining her image. This young woman worries so much about looking sexy that she has no time left for sex itself. She's not talkative because she has nothing to say. As with almost everything else in Russia – she's trying to become a consumer product.
>
> (Aksenov 2006: 54)

Visually, Pugacheva, the overweight grandmother, appeared to straddle two different eras: her black outfit combined her Soviet-era tunic with a post-Soviet-era miniskirt; her mane of fire-engine red hair was as outré and uncontrollable as ever, and her jokes targeted her interest in twenty-something-year-old men. While exposing her body's many imperfections may have gone against conventional norms of glamour, it also sent the message to millions of her age-discriminated female fans across Russia that middle-aged women need not be enslaved to ever-changing fashion, but should stay true to themselves and not fear showing their physical flaws. Pugacheva admits her body's flaws and says that she does not strive to achieve physical perfection but is comfortable with her looks:

> I'm not trying to lose weight drastically, and nowadays I simply don't need anything like that anymore. My figure was never my forte. I lost weight twice in my life, and nearly died because of it. My God, from being sick. It's better to be healthy and plump than sick! I was able to lose weight only when I was ill. Why the hell do I need that! I can't constrain myself! I love to enjoy everything in life. And tasty food also!
>
> (Vinogradova 2007).

Conclusion

Released in the same year, the Pugacheva–Orbakaite music video "I'm Inviting You to the Sunset" ["Priglashenie na zakat"] (Pugacheva 2007) showcases not only Pugacheva's repeatedly proclaimed identity as mother and the lynchpin in a close family (strategies ritually deployed to promote her adopted image), but also the two women's star status and the reversal of gender roles in their amorous relationships. For this public confession of an aging diva about her love life and stardom, Pugacheva wrote the lyrics herself, but though the song recalls Pugacheva's many lyrical love numbers, the visual narrative makes clear that the video is dedicated to everlasting maternal love instead of fleeting romance. The opening sequence shows a midwife in a delivery room announcing that the patient has just given birth to a baby girl. In the next shot, a young girl returns from school to a hotel room, only to have one of her mother's young lovers open the door and gesture for the girl to leave. Thereupon the camera shifts to a close-up of Pugacheva as the mother, dressed in a peignoir, with an unmade bed in the background. She ridicules the lover, making faces at him as she dismisses him and welcomes her daughter, thus establishing her priorities. Mother and daughter gradually become inseparable and even look stunningly alike – two parts of a single whole. In a transparently symbolic scene, the mother gives her daughter a large toy star as inspiration for the pursuit of her own "stardom."

In the following segment, clever makeup and skillful visual effects enable mother and daughter as performing artists to gaze at each other through a dressing-room mirror as mutual reflections, thereby stressing their indissoluble unity, symbiosis, and artistic interconnectedness. In several short shots Pugacheva improbably appears as a golden-age diva virtually flying above the earth against the background of a golden sky and a sunset. Like Mother Earth, she nourishes the world around her before transferring her stardom to her daughter and, at video's end, being absorbed into a shining sphere full of light. This public act of flagrant self-aggrandizement by Pugacheva stages celebrity via motherhood, relegates younger male partners to insignificance, and tropes her final, grandiose apotheosis as a "force of nature" in cosmic, transcendent terms. In the refrain Pugacheva sings,

> Gradually, the celestial light is growing dim,
> Gradually, the celebration will decline …
> I was late to meet the sunrise with you,
> Perhaps, I'll be in time to meet the sunset with you.[13]
> (Pugacheva 2007)

Figure 8.4 Kristina Orbakaite and Alla Pugacheva attending a concert in the Grand Kremlin Palace in Moscow (with Orbakaite's husband, the Russian-American businessman Mikhail Zemtsov, in the background); 29 October 2007. Photo by Aleksei Nikolsyi, courtesy of RIA Novosti.

The successful staging of celebrity as "a family affair" by Pugacheva and Orbakaite represents a unique manifestation of female power in patriarchal contemporary Russian society. Highlighting methodically staged mother-daughter symbiosis, Pugacheva reverses gender roles, reducing her young male partners to fleeting episodes in her life that inspire her artistic creativity, while emphasizing the primacy of her motherhood. After all, family and maternity remain key categories among all strata of Russian society. Through their public reliance on each other and a constant insistence on their stable, permanent relationship, the two singers send a powerful "feminist" message to millions of gender- and age-discriminated female fans. The Pugacheva–Orbakaite dynasty has created a distinctive familial "feminism à la Russe" that has acquired iconic significance, fuels their popularity, and enjoys unprecedented public approval.

Notes

1 All literary translations of lyrical excerpts and Russian sources are mine.
2 Alla Pugacheva's artistic achievements and her 30-year-long stardom represent a complex and multifaceted phenomenon. This chapter focuses exclusively on the mechanism of the Pugacheva–Orbakaite celebrity construction and the various aspects of their stardom, not aiming to provide a detailed artistic evaluation of Pugacheva's whole career. For a more detailed chronological analysis of her artistic development from Soviet to the post-soviet era see my article "Alla: The Jester-Queen of Russian Pop Culture" (Partan 2007), and for a description of her role in Soviet pop culture, see MacFadyen (2001) and MacFadyen (2002).
3 According to various internet sources, including the Encyclopedia Britannica website, Pugacheva's record sales can be compared to those of ABBA, Elton John, and Madonna, as over 200 million Pugacheva records have been sold ("List of Best-Selling"; "Rossia Velikaya: Pugacheva").
4 Pugacheva took an honorable second place in this celebrity list, despite the fact that her international celebrity status does not compete with that of Maria Sharapova, Natalia Vodianova, Nikita Mikhalkov, or Dmitry Khvorostovsky, whose names are ubiquitous in the western media. In terms of annual income, Maksim Kasulinsky, the editor-in-chief of *Forbes Russia*, admits that as Russian pop stars are paid in cash, it is very difficult to accurately calculate their annual income ("Russian Forbes" 2007).
5 It is worth noting that in *The Basics of Marketing*, a 2006 Russian textbook targeting students of the young but rapidly developing field of advertising, public relations and marketing, the authors emphasize the importance of reliance on Russian cultural norms and ideals for successful marketing of products. The authors argue that a Russian system of the cultural values and ideals is a part of the Eastern, not Western cultural cannon (Kostina *et al.* 2006: 103). Therefore, motherhood is proclaimed the leading Eastern cultural ideal, while individualism is the Western cultural ideal. Throughout her career, Pugacheva's celebrity construction intuitively and masterfully relied on both – individualism and motherhood – throughout her more than thirty-year career.
6 Pugacheva's children's songs both ridiculed the Soviet educational system as being overly controlling and unimaginative, and encouraged experimentation and freedom even if the results are disastrous. For example, in her 1977 "Volshebnik-nedouchka" [The Half-Educated Magician] (by Aleksandr Zatsepin and Leonid Derbenev), Pugacheva took on the stage persona of a child learning magic and rejecting authorities in a Harry Potter-style institution where the teachers are wise magicians. The half-educated magician mocks his own failure but enjoys the process of trying – a highly original message in the context of the Soviet children's music industry.

7   Andrei Voznesensky's lyrics were based on a legendary love story between the Georgian painter Niko Pirosmani [Pirosmanishvili] (1862–1918) and the mysterious actress-dancer depicted in one of his paintings as Margarita. Pirosmani transformed the square beneath her windows with flowers.

8   "Million, million, million alykh roz / Iz okna, iz okna, iz okna vidish ty. / Kto vliublen, kto vliublen, kto vliublen i vser'ez / Svoiu zhizn' dlia tebia prevratit v tsvety."

9   "Kogda ia budu babushkoi–/ Godov cherez desiatochek–/ Prichudnitsei, zabavnitsei,–/ Vikhr' s golovy do piatochek!"

10   "A tselovalas', babushka, / Golubushka, so skol'kimi?" / – "Ia dan' platila pesniami, / Ia dan' vzimala kol'tsami ..."

11   Nowadays, the Russian celebrity Kseniia Sobchak plays the role of a social butterfly akin to Paris Hilton, while photographs of Russian décolleté and miniskirted pop singers are placed next to pictures of Mariah Carey and Britney Spears, and the French movie star Emmanuelle Béart is captured by Russian paparazzi while attending the opening of a fashionable designer boutique in the "Barvikha Luxury Village" on the outskirts of Moscow (Zhiliaeva 2006: 339). This is the luxury shopping mall where flabbergasted Western jewelers sold out of diamonds within days of opening the stores. Post-Soviet readers should now be proud of Mother Russia, for the presentation of new fashion collections in the Oktiabr' movie theater in the center of Moscow is no less glamorous than the fashion shows in Paris.

12   Pugacheva's 2005 popularity rating, based on national polls in Russia, suggests that the singer attracts middle-aged fans: 56 percent of those polled whose ages ranged from 36 to 54 reported liking Pugacheva (Shmerlina). Overall, 56 percent of the women polled expressed a positive view of her, and 54 percent of the respondents said that they listen to her songs when they are played on the radio.

13   "Malo-pomalu merknet nebesnyi svet, / Malo-pomalu prazdnik poidet na spad ... / Ia opozdala vstretit' s toboi rassvet, / Mozhet uspeiu vstretit' s toboi zakat."

Bibliography

Aksenov, V. (2006) "Rossiia i seks sovmestimy" [Interview with Dmitrii Bykov] *Ogonek*, no. 5 (30 Oct–30 Nov): 54–5.

Alekseev, A. (2007) "VIP-parad 2007," *Kommersant*, 28 Dec. Available online at: www. kommersant.ru/doc.aspx?DocsID=840552 (accessed 15 January 2008).

Alla Pugacheva and Vladimir Kuzmin (1987) "Nado zhe" [Video] Available online at: http:www.youtube.com/watch?v=0TaTzHQ3A3s (accessed 28 December 2009).

"Alla Pugacheva. The Election of the President of the Russian Federation" [Video] Available online at: www.youtube.com/watch?v=alH5lQqeG7w (accessed 28 December 2009).

Azhgikhina, N. (1997) "'Zheleznaia ledi'" ili Baba Iaga? 'Zhenskaia tema' v sovremennoi rossiiskoi presse," in Conference proceedings of the First Russian Summer School on Women's and Gender Studies, Moscow: MTsGI, pp. 43–6. Available online at: www.a-z. ru/women/texts/azhgir (accessed 22 December 2009).

Bakhtiiarova, M. and Remizova, M. (2008) "Tigran Keosaian teper' goniaet na 'Rolls-Royse' kak u Pugachevoi," *Komsomol'skaia Pravda*, 20 Feb. Available online at: www. kp.ru/daily/24052/103995 (accessed 1 March 2008).

Beliakov, A. (1997) *Alka, Allochka, Alla Borisovna Pugacheva*, Moscow: Vagrius.

Dyer, R. (1986) *Heavenly Bodies: Film Stars and Society*, London: Routledge.

— . (1998) *Stars*, London: British Film Institute Publishing.

Epstein, M. (2007) "Kul'tura Pis'mennoi Rechi," Available online at: www.gramma.ru/ RUS/?id=1.39 (accessed 30 December 2007).

Gorov, A. (2006) "Kristina Orbakaite: Ia – odna iz samykh prodavaemikh pevits Rossii," Available online at: www.galya.ru/cat_page.php?id=8982 (accessed 22 January 2007).

Goscilo, H. (1999) *Dehexing Sex: Russian Womanhood During and After Glasnost*, Ann Arbor: University of Michigan Press.

— . (2000a) "Introduction: Centrifuge and Fragmentation," *Studies in Twentieth Century Literature: Russian Culture of the 1990s*, 1, no. 24 (Winter): 3–14.

— . (2000b) "Style and S(t)imulation: Popular Magazines, or the Aestheticization of Postsoviet Russia," *Studies in Twentieth Century Literature: Russian Culture of the 1990s* 1, no. 24 (Winter): 15–50.

Goscilo, H. and Lanoux, A. (2006) "Lost in the Myths," in H. Goscilo and A. Lanoux (eds) *Gender and National Identity in Twentieth-Century Russian Culture*, DeKalb: Northern Illinois University Press, pp. 3–29.

"Govoriat, chto …" *Argumenty i Fakty*, no. 42 (17–23 Oct 2008): 32.

"Kak zhivet Alla Pugacheva?" Available online at: www.NEWSmusic.ru/news_3_579.htm (accessed 12 May 2008).

Khakamada, I. (2006) *Seks v bol'shoi politike*, Moscow: Novaia Gazeta.

Komatoza.net. "Poklonniki Ally Pugachevoi sprosili pevitsu, kakie pesni ona pela vo vremia Velikoi Otechestvennoi Voiny," available online at: http://komatoza.net/modules.php?name=News&file=view&news_id=1570 (accessed 12 December 2007).

Kostina, M. (2006) "Eta pesnia khorosha, nachinai snachala," *Trud*, no. 230, 12 Dec. Available online at: www.trud.ru/article/12-12-2006/110628_eta_pesnja_xorosha_nachimaj_snachala (accessed 22 December 2006).

Kostina, A. V., Makarevich, E. F., and Karpukhin, O. I. (2006) *Osnovy reklamy*, Moscow: Knorus.

"Kristina Orbakaite uvolila liubovnika" Available online at: www.newsmusic.ru/news_3_5371.htm (accessed 5 January 2008).

"List of Best-Selling Music Artists" [Entry in Wikipedia] Available online at: http://en.wikipedia.org/wiki/Best_selling_music_artists (accessed 5 January 2008).

MacFadyen, D. (2001) *Red Stars: Personality and the Soviet Popular Song, 1955–1991*, Montreal: McGill-Queen's University Press.

— . (2002) *Estrada?! Grand Narratives and the Philosophy of the Russian Popular Song since Perestroika*, Montreal: McGill-Queen's University Press.

Marsh, R. (1998) "An Image of Their Own?: Feminism, Revisionism and Russian Culture," in R. Marsh (ed.) *Women and Russian Culture: Projections and Self-Perception*, New York: Berghahn Books, p. 2–41.

Marshall, P. D. (1997) *Celebrity and Power: Fame in Contemporary Culture*, Minneapolis: University of Minnesota Press.

Neizvestnaia Pugacheva [Documentary Film; Part of *Russkie sensatsii* Series] NTV. Available online at: http://Filmzdemon.nnm.ru/russkie_sensacii_neizvestnaya_pugachjova (accessed 16 April 2007).

"O, Alla!," (2008) *Stil'nye pricheski*, no. 2 (Feb): 72–5. Available online at: www.radioalla.ru/?an=alla_media_page&uid=2783 (accessed 18 April 2008).

Okin, S. with respondents (1999) *Is Multiculturalism Bad for Women?* eds J. Cohen, M. Howard, and M. Nussbaum, Princeton, NJ: Princeton University Press, pp. 7–26.

Partan, O. (2007) "Alla: The Jester-Queen of Russian Pop Culture," *Russian Review*, no. 66 (July): 483–500.

Pesnia Goda 2006 (2007) [DVD] ARS Records.

"Plati 100 tysiach evro – i v Novyi god obkhokhochesh'sia" (2007) *Izvestiia*, 24 March. Available online at: www.izvestiia.ru/prival/article3111296 (accessed 29 March 2008).

Poiurovskii, B. M. (1997) *Alla Pugacheva glazami druzei i nedrugov*, 2 Vols, Moscow: Izd. Tsentrpoligraf.

Polupanov, V. (2006a) "A. Pugacheva: O Filippe, azarte i piratakh," *Argumenty i Fakty*, no. 44. Available online at: www.gazeta.aif.ru/online/aif/1357/03_01 (accessed 15 February 2008).

— . (2006b) "A. Pugacheva: Stilist? Iumorist? Vot i poite!," *Argumentiy i Fakty*, no. 45. Available online at: www.gazeta.aif.ru/online/aif/1358/56_01 (accessed 15 February 2008).

Pugacheva, A. (1996) *Pesni na bis* [Audiocassette in *Alla Pugacheva: Kollektsiia*, collection of recordings, Volume 13] General Records.

— . (2007) "Priglashenie na zakat" [Music video: Composed by I. Krutoi, Lyrics by A. Pugacheva, Directed by A. Badaev] Available online at: www.youtube.com/watch?v=Ebz_W6oeH1l (accessed 5 May 2008).

Radio Alla Songs "Million Alykh roz," available online at: www.radioalla.ru/?an=alla_songs_page&uid=515 (accessed 5 May 2008).

Rakhlina, A. (2007) "Po-domashnemu: Nakanune prem'ery kartiny *Liubov'-morkov'*," *Glamour* [Russian edition] (3 March): 42–5.

Razzakov, F. (2003) *Alla Pugacheva: Po stupeniam slavy*, Moscow: Iauza.

Rojek, C. (2001) *Celebrity*, London: Reaktion Books.

"Rossia Velikaia: Pugacheva" [Website] Available online at: www.Russia.rin.ru/guides/10848.html (accessed 5 January 2008).

"Russian Forbes Publishes Top 50 Celebrities List" (2007) Available online at: www.russiatoday.ru/entertainment/news/11524 (accessed 6 January 2008).

Shmerlina, I. "Singer and Public Figure Alla Pugacheva," Available online at: www.bd.english.fom.ru/report/cat/az/A/pugacheva/ed054925/printable (accessed 5 January 2008).

Troitskii, A. (2007) Author's interview. Boston, 13 Apr.

Tsvetaeva, M. (1965) "Grandmother," in M. Tsvetaeva *Izbrannye proizvedeniia*, Moskva: Sovetskii pisatel'.

Turner, G. (2004) *Understanding Celebrity*, London: Sage Publications.

Two Stars (2007) [Television broadcast] Channel One, 23 Dec. Available online at: www.1tv.ru/stars (accessed 22 December 2009).

Vinogradova, M. (2007) "Alla Pugacheva," *Domashnii ochag* [Russian version of *Good Housekeeping*], Nov. Available online at: www.radioalla.ru/vardata/modules/lenta/images/2042_1_1200667923 (accessed 8 January 2008).

Zhiliaeva, I. (2006) "Siiatel'naia osoba," *In Style*, no. 014 (Dec): 336–45.

9 Elevating Verka Serdiuchka

A star-study in excess performativity

Jeremy Morris (University of Birmingham)

"I'm like Ukraine: self-reliant, free, and independent."
"Whether you're a star or not, life is such nowadays that everyone needs a vegetable plot close at hand."

Verka Serdiuchka

How did Serdiuchka become a star?

Verka Serdiuchka is a Ukrainian Cinderella, a Ukrainian dream. Of the most humble social beginnings, she worked as a train guard before taking part in amateur talent contests and then setting up her own talk show, where she invited famous people, including singers. Later, Verka Serdiuchka wanted to become a singer herself and was successful. She won over her native country, Ukraine, and neighboring Russia. In Moscow, Serdiuchka performed to twenty thousand people at two Luzhniki Sports Palace concerts. The star's records sell millions of copies. Verka Serdiuchka has become popular in all CIS and Baltic countries. In addition, her songs are covered [performed] in Poland, Germany, Israel, and even India ... What's next? Eurovision, of course, for Verka Serdiuchka is a dove of peace; her main task is to amuse and elicit only positive emotions in those around her.

Introductory material on Verka Serdiuchka's homepage[1]

Verka Serdiuchka is the stage persona of the mainly Russian-speaking Ukrainian[2] performer Andrei Danilko (b. 2 October 1973). Until Danilko appeared as himself alongside a (pre-recorded) Verka on Channel One Russia in 2006, he had much less chance than his creation of being recognized – either on stage or in public. In the twenty years since inventing the Verka act, Danilko has achieved wealth and popularity, and in this chapter I plan to show that while he has been unable to avoid the probes into his private life that inevitably accompany a spot in the limelight, he has managed to use Verka as something of a distancing device, achieving celebrity elevation through performance (both on and off stage Danilko maintains media interest through the scandalous behavior of his foil), while his act comments ironically on the very process of celebrification itself. The Verka phenomenon illustrates a number of related issues in post-Soviet popular culture: the rapid process of the rise to celebrity status that is often accompanied by the conscious masking of modest social origins; the importance of maintaining media interest through "scandal";

and the difficulty on the part of audiences, media, and performers alike of resisting a constructed version of the media "personality."

For achieved celebrities[3] the Verka act illustrated that self-promotion is of paramount importance. Danilko, following the typical route of an achieved celebrity described by Rojek (2001: 121), uses strategies of "performance and self-projection" in order to achieve a high degree of visibility in public culture. As both Verka and himself, he has been available on demand to journalists and broadcasters for comment on his act and the controversy that it continues to arouse. While he gained initial popularity by virtue of his comedic talents and the provocative image of Verka – the first act approximating "drag" on mainstream television in Ukraine and Russia – this chapter argues that it is through the manipulation of all kinds of "scandal," both in Danilko's private life and on stage as he performed Verka, that he succeeded in maintaining celebrity status.

Ultimately any "entertainment" act, even one with satiric intent, illustrates the necessary complicity of a performer-operator with modes of media construction and distancing. In utilizing scandal so effectively, Danilko began to achieve celebrity status for himself as a media personality distinct from that of his comic creation. The use of Verka as a foil had limitations, and scandal eventually came to be associated with Danilko, which drew increased attention to his performances and persona. Whether he liked it or not, the value of his creation's continuing media currency involved his putting his "own" (mediated) personality on show.

Figure 9.1 The Verka act during Eurovision 2007. Photo by Indrek Galetin, courtesy of Indrek Galetin.

The evolution of Verka: from Poltava to Moscow, from 1+1 to Channel One

Verka Serdiuchka began life in a short sketch as part of an amateur dramatics performance at Danilko's high school in Poltava in the late 1980s (Shablinskaia and Grachev 2004). Danilko developed a number of similar characters for the comedy stage – satirical representatives of Soviet lower-class life. Once Verka gained her own television show in 1997, he retired the other characters. Stints in the local theater led to Danilko's touring provincial cities in Ukraine with a small group of variety artists. In the mid-1990s the part of the act featuring Verka made the transition to television, where Danilko orchestrated a parody of the celebrity interview format – not unlike Barry Humphries' show *An Audience with ...* featuring the Dame Edna Everage character.[4] By the late 1990s the program was being shown in Russia and in 2000 Verka was voted the fifth most popular television presenter in *Komsomolskaia Pravda*'s phone-in poll, establishing "her" as a television celebrity if not yet a music "star." Since the early 2000s Danilko's act has existed as a hybrid, featuring theatrical sketches, some of which readily transfer to television, but increasingly relying on comedic musical cameos with established stars and a modicum of semi-rehearsed verbal sparring with presenters and co-performers. Pop songs and music videos featuring Verka enabled Danilko to reach a much wider CIS audience, culminating in the Ukraine entry for Eurovision 2007.

The original Verka was a Ukrainian train attendant, a readily identifiable representative of the intermediary group of slightly crooked, self-seeking public servants with whom it paid Soviet citizens to be on good terms to smooth their progress in a highly bureaucratized society. In one sketch Verka offers her services as an (unsuccessful) stripper, reflecting the economic pressures of perestroika, when various women turned to "sexual service" so as to make a living; shown to be obsessed with spandex, she attempts to teach her protégées a massage called "a thousand fingers" that she learned from a women's magazine. These and other "gags" explain why a reading of the act as misogynistic – a charge routinely leveled at drag – seems justified. This is indeed a problematic part of the act: in the first television program, *SV Show*, that I discuss in detail below, Verka's associate Gelia, played by Radmila Shchegoleva, was routinely abused and humiliated for comic effect, functioning as an almost mute, unloved stepdaughter-*cum*-sister and idiot assistant – a representative of vulgar mass taste. Gelia was a classic comic foil, against which Verka sought to appear ostensibly superior in matters intellectual and aesthetic. However, her behavior toward the unfortunate Gelia clearly revealed her own uncouth, boorish nature and chronic lack of self-confidence to the audience. Since the act developed from the stable format of interview show to encompass a wider variety of settings from music videos and guest television performances, a somewhat similar role to that of Gelia was reserved for Verka's mother, played by Inna Belokon'. Both roles were similar to that of the character Madge Allsop in Barry Humphries' Everage performance.

Verka's act, like those in the West that arguably inspired it, concentrated on the contingencies of female life, for both its pathos and comedy. Nina Tsyrkun, writing in the premier Russian journal of film criticism, *Iskusstvo Kino* [Art of Film], took the interesting view that the act relied for comedy on the routinely jealous and difficult relationships between women typical of female-only workplaces (2004: 63–5). In such a reading, the Verka act would be seen to derive much of its popularity from its careful replication of some of the unpleasant myths of Soviet and post-Soviet women's lives that might well be seen as truisms by its audience. Yet Verka is a character continually stressing her self-reliance and independence, even if her understanding of taste and talent is a permanent part of Danilko's joke. While this could be seen as a reflection of the stereotypical working woman's necessary toughness in late-Soviet times, it can also be interpreted as another stereotype that is of interest to Danilko, especially in the context of the act's later parody of the female star: that of the post-Soviet achieved celebrity, albeit one that does not take enough account of the hidden work of media producers, agents, and the like.[5] Verka believes that obtaining the veneer of a "star" – a glamorous image and a permanent performance spot on Channel One – means that she has made it as a celebrity, has been "elevated" (Rojek 2006: 611), and is now on first-name terms with other stars. Danilko seeks to make visible the packaging of self and the star's suppression of her idiosyncrasies and normality. Such a mediation is unsuccessful in Verka's case. Her failure to hide her origins and uncouthness is a primary source of comedy, but it is precisely this inability that, ironically, adds to her genuine popularity with audiences.

Just as the media forms new to post-Soviet reality (for example, popular magazine television shows, glossy lifestyle weeklies) attempt to teach the naïve audience to emulate the required poses, affectations, and preferences that are supposed prerequisites for the constructed "good taste" of a new star, Verka, half-understanding these lessons, attempts to enlighten her own female entourage by introducing them into a world of conspicuous consumption and paraded wealth. Their often unfazed, cynical village mentality offers a more grounded view of Verka's talents and achievements. Her frequent fits of rage, caused by their stubborn refusal to treat her any differently from when she was just like them, reveal the mismatch between her manipulated aspirations and her meager talent. Danilko's nasal, rather squeaky voice also works well to reveal the discrepancy: it is ironic that Verka is described as a "pop diva" in the press when the act, through exaggeration, draws attention to the weak singing of so many popular performers who have quickly risen to Russian stardom. According to Danilko's parody, Verka's elevation is transparent, the kind of representation of celebrity dreaded by stars. She has completely bought into the myth of manipulation of the self: Danilko makes Verka comically unable to suppress her "veridical self" and at every turn betray her crude origins. For example, in conversation with a leading jazz musician during which she has tried to downplay her love of pop music, she suddenly exclaims, "I love to eat sunflower seeds from a paper cone, it's much more cultured" (Tsyrkun 2004: 64). The Tango song from the television film *Pervyi skoryi* [The First Express] (Gusev, 2006, Channel One, Russia) sees Verka incredulous that the pale, insipid Danilko can claim credit for her success as he appears alongside her, playing "himself":

[ANDREI:] We've both known for a long time
    Who leads and who's led.
[VERKA:] Oh, so that's what you think, pal?
    You've lost touch.
    Without me you're a bore,
    What, without my smart clothes and songs.[6]

Danilko shows Verka to be completely spellbound by her celebrity aura, to the extent that she believes herself a celebrity through proximity to "real" celebrities, with whom she has contact thanks to her role as the chat-show hostess. The act reveals that one of the main functions of the ongoing female rivalry between Verka and her relatives is to comment on the increasingly mediated sense of taste and glamour, and the enculturation of the celebrity as role model in women's lives. The revue sketches might seem removed from the glitzy musical numbers of this later incarnation of Verka, but the focus on the disparity between aspirations and reality – the comic gap between the staging of self according to media models and the more prosaic nature of life – prevails.

Even in the very early stages of the evolution of the stage act, accompanied by a concern for the specific difficulties of women's lives during economic transition, Danilko showed an interest in the relationship between media projections of idealized femininity and their reception by ordinary people. While Danilko portrayed male characters too, it was Verka's forthright manner and pronouncements on relations between the sexes that were the most original and striking aspects of her act. Scathing in her general attitude toward men, Verka specifically stressed that during the comprehensive economic chaos of Ukraine in the 1990s, women had to provide for the family. The sketches featured the harsh economic realities of that period and showed how in such a context "success" meant survival. Against a backdrop of barter, sexual exploitation, petty bureaucracy, corruption, mass unemployment, and Ukraine's general political stagnation – explicitly foregrounded in the sketches – ordinary women's obsession with celebrity and glamour are both a grotesque expression of fantasy (ironic and ripe for comic exploitation) and an understandable symptom of desperation. Thus Danilko's act reflected the absurdities of everyday life. Although Danilko's stage performances of the mid-to-late 1990s featured a number of similar working-class female characters (cafeteria workers, prostitutes, collective farm workers), it was Verka, the garish consumer of lifestyle magazines, who came to dominate the act and its perspective on gender. To a degree, the women working in these occupations represent working-class dead-end lives, and it is often assumed, not least by popular tabloids, that they find a special attraction in the discourse of achieved celebrity. That assumption explains why the act repeatedly revisits the gulf between Verka's achievements and her humble beginnings.

As the act grew in popularity, Danilko landed a late-night celebrity-interview slot, *SV show* ("SV" standing for "sleeping car"), on the Ukrainian television channel 1+1 (1997–2002). This format, where Verka only initially appeared as a train guard, involved a small audience presence and some audience participation.

It guaranteed proximity to old and new celebrities, especially once the show was quickly adopted by Russia's TV6 (1998–2001) and subsequently by STS (2002), where it became vastly popular. Danilko could not have chosen a profession for his character demanding more cunning, obtuseness, self-reliance, and resilience than the universally loved and feared female train attendant of Soviet cultural mythology. Guests (mainly singers and actors) were invited into the sleeping car of a long-distance train by Verka, who was simultaneously obsequious, brusque, charming, and overbearing. The celebrities proved easy game in this entertainingly provocative version of the tired one-to-one interview format as train passengers, won over by the combination of controlled aggression, guile, and charm.

Unusually for a mainly female profession, the train guard wields absolute power within her domain, a fact used for comic effect in the film *Prikliucheniia Verki Serdiuchki* [*The Adventures of Verka Serdiuchka*] (Gorov 2005). The guard can choose to accept a bribe from passengers without tickets or deny them passage, her decision dictated solely by whim. She can enforce the strict anti-drinking rules on the train, turn a blind eye to them, or herself join the drinkers. She is one of the few Soviet women in uniform, but there is nothing and no one to prevent her from adding "feminine" touches to her appearance (taken to a comic extreme by Danilko's trademark pink beret) or dispensing with the uniform altogether on later editions of *SV Show*. She is both permanently in public space – the long-distance sleeper carriage, which is her main responsibility on the job – but is also afforded a private inner sanctum – her own personal compartment.

It was perhaps inevitable that train attendants would become some of the most successful shuttle traders [chelnoki] after the breakdown of distribution networks for goods in the late 1980s and 1990s, for their personal compartments in every carriage functioned as a safe repository for tradable wares, while their working relationships with border guards protected them from customs duty and interference (for analysis of "chelnoki" practices in relation to new media see Chapter 7). Danilko captures this social development when Verka offers her talk-show guests various poor-quality items of clothing for sale. Such scenes likewise reflect the disparity between "origins" and aspirations, as well as providing comedy, which derives from Verka's repeated *faux pas* in relation to social status.[7]

The job of train guard also entails playing multiple roles and being on show – features that work both for and against accepted notions of femininity. Perhaps these qualities are just coincidentally those likely to be shared by the achieved celebrity. If so, they are a happy accident, making the new Verka – the superstar of the stage and music-channel – so much more believable as a "rough diamond" in the constellation of celebrities, refracting the continual effort needed by such a celebrity to mediate between the past and present, to channel the representation of the journey from humble beginnings, maintaining distance and yet professing closeness to roots.

As soon as duets with guest musicians became a permanent aspect of the show, the commercial exploitation of Verka's vocal talents in the hope of a comic one-hit wonder became unavoidable. Less predictable – surely to Danilko and his Ukrainian management as much as to anyone else – was the fact that a comic routine parodying pop-music celebrities would succeed so dramatically in selling pop music and achieving proxy stardom for Danilko. Verka quickly cast off her uniform and started living the high life she had only read about previously in glossy magazines. A series of fast-tempo, unashamedly strident dance songs were released in 2002, accompanied by lavish music videos produced by Inter.[8] These videos established the highly successful extant image of Verka that most Russians and Ukrainians identify with her. Though she is dressed to shock, her songs feature upbeat lyrics about how "everything will be fine," the title of her best-known hit from 2003. The songs, like Verka's comic personality, are in turn crude, grating, loud, and very energetic, mixing folk and dance-oriented pop.

From 2002–5 episodes of *SV Show* ran as repeats on Muz-TV (a channel similar to MTV), to be subsequently replaced by Verka's songs on video, marked by high-quality production and a large budget and cast.[9] That Verka as star had "arrived" may be deduced from the significant roles she has played in the New Year televisions films, particularly on Channel One Russia, watched by huge audiences throughout the country in 2004–6. Yet en route to glamorous success Verka did not leave her extended Ukrainian family behind – a useful way of contrasting folksy yet authentic life with the smoke and mirrors of stardom. In each video that family provides more than its fair share of the comedy and is treated with disapproval yet indulgence by Verka, the matriarch who, after all, partially helped them enter the Russian "high life," the sphere she now inhabits. As in the stage act, the jokes tend either to be on the male buffoons who could not find a place in the new social order, or to wryly reflect the gap between lived (often touchingly naïve) Soviet experience and the hard realities of the present. Danilko continues to explore issues of femininity and the extended family. Since the character has become a "pop diva," Danilko is careful to perpetuate the image of a sympathetic though overbearing single mother (depending on the iteration, Verka's ward is her own mother, brother, or, in various film musicals, her own child). This image exploits the stereotype of the sentimental but bullying "mama," fond of a drop of vodka, wide of girth, and capable of knocking an opponent down with her ample bust. More important, however, are the act's incorporation of the standard milestones in the rapid attainment of celebrity favored by tabloid journalists: social disorientation and relentless *faux pas*; a discomfort with one's own status, which leads the "new" celebrity to seek out more established stars; addiction to status-clothing regardless of taste; public inebriation, and so forth.

Self-splitting promotion, scandal, and Eurovision

It was Verka, not Danilko, who through ubiquitous presence in musical film and video performance achieved stardom of a peculiar sort, for the media often wrote about Serdiuchka as if she had a life of her own beyond the act. Indeed, while often this move was part of playing along with the joke of a caricature's popularity exceeding its creator's, it also reflected the distancing effect of television performance, where Verka as an act was not framed in any way by the performer and was presented as a self-sufficient personality. Since she appeared alongside sometimes grotesque-looking pop idols, it was easy and profitable for the media to treat Verka as another larger-than-life pop personality. After all, she provided excellent material for scandalous headlines and salacious exposés of the lives of other celebrities with whom Danilko (or was it Verka?) had close relations, such as Alla Pugacheva, Filipp Kirkorov, and Maksim Galkin. The print media, always ready to publish rumors and gossip about these performers, found Danilko willing to provide them with comments on both his and, bizarrely, Verka's relationships with Russian stars.[10] While occasionally pausing to remind the reader of Verka's true identity, many articles wrote about Serdiuchka as a celebrity subject in her own right,[11] sometimes conflating the biographies of performer and character.[12] The high-circulating weekly newspaper *Argumenty i Fakty* managed to cover all bases at once, providing no small number of articles with such tempting titles as "Which Gender Is Serdiuchka?" and "Verka Serdiuchka Bares Her Chest," in which Danilko gave more or less candid interviews about his life, while the journalist analyzed the irony of a stage character's acquisition of an independent celebrity status. For example, one article in the newspaper reported that Danilko, thanks to his double celebrity status, receives twice as much fan-mail as other "telestars." While discussing audiences' confusion of performance with reality (male fans offer heterosexual fantasies about Verka), the article also quizzed Danilko about his sexual orientation, allegations of a relationship with his female co-performer, and the charge that he brought disrepute to the Ukrainian language through his constant use of Surzhik – a hybrid of Russian and Ukrainian (Kostenko-Popova 2000). Andrei Arkhangel'skii (2007) argued that the debate over Serdiuchka was a question not so much of her representing a Russo-centric cultural and linguistic identity as of her reinforcing a division between the intelligentsia and ordinary Ukrainians, with the latter likely to support her regardless of any political and ethnolinguistic identity.[13] While Arkhangel'skii's view itself needs to be acknowledged as coming from a Russo-centric position on culture, it coincides with that of many observers in Ukraine, who see Verka's use of more vernacular cultural and linguistic currency as a moderating, conciliatory influence in the debates on national identity.[14] Indeed, in the most extensive and scholarly analysis available thus far of Surzhik and Danilko's use of it, Laada Bilaniuk (2005) argues that Danilko's usage of the language-mix and his sophisticated shifts between Ukrainian and Russian result in a complexity that suggests a fundamental lack of linguistic purity.[15]

The most recent and well-publicized scandal involving Verka was Danilko's linguistically "mongrel" song (including words in German, English, Russian, Ukrainian and, allegedly, Mongolian) for Ukraine's entry in the 2007 Eurovision contest. This event, described below in some detail, for the first time led to widespread exposure on national television, in both news programs and talk-shows, of Danilko, not Verka, as a "personality." The moment indicated the consummation of Danilko's rise to celebrity status in Russia through notoriety, and marked the high point of a career based on relentless exposure on Channel One mainly through musical shows – the mainstay of prime-time programming for a channel increasingly eschewing analytical broadcasting.[16]

Though Danilo was established as a permanent television presenter prior to

Figure 9.2 A shot from a post-Eurovision photo shoot for a French glamour magazine. Photo by Aleksei Kolpakov, courtesy of Aleksei Kolpakov.

2000, first in Ukraine, then in Russia, the importance of musical variety performance on Russia's central television channels is what made him one of the most sought-after acts in both countries. Because of the feedback loop between press and television concerning celebrities, without popular musical success newspapers would have had little interest in either Verka or Danilko. Moreover, without a stream of salacious articles linking Verka/Danilko with more established stars, television offers extended to him might not have been so lucrative. In 2004 *Argumenty i Fakty* ("Zastol'e 'pod Serdiuchku'" 2002: 48) identified Danilko as the second-highest-paid television personality to take part in both the live and pre-recorded segments of the most prestigious Russian broadcast event of the year: the New Year holiday shows carried simultaneously by several national channels.[17] By 2005, in an acerbic listing by the well-known music journalist Artemii Troitskii of the most successfully self-promoting people in contemporary Russia (Troistkii 2005: 5), Verka occupied fourth place, just ahead of then Prime Minister Fradkov and Konstantin Khabensky, star of the film *Nochnoi Dozor* [Night Watch] (dir. Timur Bekmambetov, 2004), and behind Vladimir Putin, Kseniia Sobchak (daughter of the St. Petersburg ex-mayor), and Mikhail Leont'iev (popularist television journalist). The point of this listing was not only to acknowledge Danilko's celebrity status as Verka, but also to highlight ironically the extent to which Russian culture had become dominated, in Troitskii's view, by facile celebrity. Media exposure and performance in large-scale shows depended now on the key factor of *vostrebovannost'* [being in demand] in the sense of having front-page and terrestrial channel media currency. This list of the visible glitterati of Russian media culture supports Rojek's view of the importance of "self-staging" and the successful projection of the status of achieved celebrity[18] over other factors in the success and popularity of celebrities (Rojek 2001: 121).[19] According to Troitskii, in today's Russia popular performers and politicians alike had become "successful" not by dint of talent, but by the ability to successfully mediate their visibility and manipulate their image, such as President Putin's image of a tough, incorruptible leader (see Chapter 1). Without intending to dismiss Danilko's talents as a performer, the Troitskii list nonetheless illustrates the importance of self-promotion – both for public figures and celebrities. The latter – with Kseniia Sobchak and Verka as prime examples – were able to hitch their provocative public image to the endless narrative of scandal, often media-manufactured, on which many newspapers and internet sites rely.[20] Interestingly, these two popular cultural figures were also linked, albeit in sometimes perfunctory fashion, to power politics. In Verka's case, Danilko responded to domestic criticism in Ukraine by fronting a state-sponsored campaign for linguistic standards, flirting with Left-Green politics, and publicly supporting Ukrainian identity in Russia. Sobchak, as might be expected of a politician's daughter, has similarly dabbled in party politics, attempting to create her own youth movement, called "Everyone Is Free" (Klin 2006: 4). These actions can be seen not as an attempt to recast one's image as a more serious operator, but merely as an extension of the field of celebrification into the equally scandal-prone zone of politics.

Just as Verka's popularity and celebrity status was reaching its height, evidenced by speculation that representatives of Ukraine, and, more importantly, of Russia, had approached the star about performing in the Eurovision Song Contest (Kononenko 2005: 15), Troitskii placed Danilko's seemingly innocuous if trashy act alongside the politically conservative and the reactionary in the media. Of course, Eurovision is hardly a politically neutral affair; the controversy about Verka as a choice for both Ukraine and Russia (in the former some felt that the act ridiculed Ukraine; in the latter some considered a Ukrainian drag artist a thoroughly unsuitable entrant) highlighted the importance of popular culture in representing continuity and change in the political and social life of Eastern European countries in transition. More importantly, it underscored the continual recourse by Danilko to scandal as a promotional technique. Danilko's lyrics, despite his protestations, were unambiguously interpreted by the Russian media as an attack on Russia, the "Mongolian" line "lasha tumbai" understood to be "Russia, goodbye." Verka finally got her chance to represent Ukraine, winning both the jury and the SMS national vote on 9 March 2007 (Tomak *et al.* 2007). In the final Eurovision competition in Helsinki, a toned-down but lyrically unchanged performance of the song "Danzing Lasha Tumbai," with largely nonsensical lyrics, came in second, behind Serbia but ahead of Russia. The predictable result of the media-fuelled debate in Russia and Ukraine was enormous media coverage of Danilko's song outside those countries, and worldwide exposure for the Verka act, as the story was carried by international broadcasters such as the BBC (Fawkes 2007). His widely advertised success allowed Danilko to continue parodying the aspirational myth of the star's rags-to-riches journey in his post-competition interviews with the Western media. Remaining in character as Verka, Danilko suggested that the whole point of her performance was to show that anyone, even a poor Ukrainian housewife living on fried potatoes, could become a star.[21]

At the same time, Eurovision was a big risk for Danilko, for it could potentially have closed off Russian television, an important source of income, to the performer.[22] Interpretations varied as to the innocence of the song's lyrics. The already buzzing web forums and feedback on articles about Verka became even more sharply split between her supporters and detractors.[23] It is reasonable to assume that Danilko calculated that the international publicity surrounding the Eurovision scandal would compensate for the Russian public backlash, though there is little evidence that the backlash itself was much more than a media-manipulated event.[24]

Post-Soviet Ukraine is a drag

British and American observers have compared the Verka phenomenon to "drag," or, more accurately, to "cross-dressing" Anglophone performers such as Barry Humphries and Paul O'Grady. As in the case of these stage characters from

Figure 9.3 Another shot from the post-Eurovision glamour shoot. Photo by Aleksei Kolpakov, courtesy of Aleksei Kolpakov.

British television, the comic effect of Verka is said to derive from the grotesquely exaggerated nature of cross-dressing. While drag is a phenomenon historically associated with gay communities, especially in the UK and USA, cross-dressing has a long history in the mainstream popular culture of many countries, including Russia, where "Mavrikievna and Nikitichna" – a pair of mismatched gossiping old women played by Vadim Tonkov and Boris Vladimirov – delighted USSR television audiences in variety shows that aired from 1970–82. Arguably there is the most distant of genetic links between this act and Verka in that part of the comedy of the Mavrikievna and Nikitichna routine stemmed from the disparity in the two characters' social and educational background (in Verka's act it is the audience that plays the role of intellectual superior), and a willingness to touch on political issues, using buffoonery as a defense for sometimes outright politically provocative content. In the earlier stage acts, Danilko's characters all reflected social collapse, corruption, and chaos, and therefore any comic act relating to reality was by definition satirically political. Some sense of activism and political sensitivity certainly survive in the music-video-based performance of Danilko's career post-2000. A good example is the lyrics of the songs "Gulianka" (Night Out) and "Gop Gop," both of which address the issue of hybrid cultural and national identity. In the former, a song performed in a film[25] created mainly for Russian consumption, Verka sings (in Ukrainian), "Ukraine has not yet perished if we make merry in this way"[26] – a celebratory, affirmative expression of Ukrainian identity, parodying the opening line of the Ukrainian national anthem. In the latter song, the cast of the music video are dressed in Ukrainian folk costumes and sing in unison with Verka in Surzhik, "If they don't like us, beautiful and fine [people]. If they don't like us, they can go … ."[27] These lines can be interpreted unambiguously as a reply to Ukrainian criticisms of the damage Verka does to the national reputation of her country of origin.

In terms of overall effect, however, the Verka act is much closer to the British tradition of bawdy humor and camp than to any Russian or Soviet antecedents. In the former, some of the humor derives from the otherness of the character's speech: just as Verka often speaks a hybrid of Russian and Ukrainian (Surzhik) when playing to a Ukrainian audience, and accented Russian when performing in Russia, O'Grady's character has a strong Scouse (Liverpudlian) accent, and Humphries' character is Australian. For the British audience of both acts these accents may connote substandard cultural values. Verka fits the classic analysis of the cross-dressing stage comedian: the masculinity of the actor (unlike that of the drag performer, traditionally associated with homosexuality)[28] is "on show" beneath the veneer of prosthetics and female clothing; the voice is also both masculine and feminine; the behavior of the persona is aggressive, sexually provocative, and scandalous; musical numbers are performed for comic effect. However, the Verka act is unusual for a cross-dressing routine, inasmuch as it has gradually metamorphosed into a comic and musical performance that is much more than the sum of its parts. Verka is the nearest to a transnational popular cultural icon as the post-Soviet space can muster. With as much ease as the performer changes costumes, the performance crosses over from sketch-based comedy into dance-pop, film, television musical, chat show (also familiar territory for Humphries and O'Grady), and even advertising.[29]

Danilko's act comments on celebrity and popular culture while simultaneously promoting his claim to celebrity status by recourse to overly theatrical parody, commonly described as camp. After Bergman (1994),[30] and Ross (1999), I employ camp as a particular set of stylistic tactics, "extreme," "theatrical," "artificial" – bordering on the grotesque in this case – whereby a performer creates dissonance with the media-hyped high life in which he avowedly seeks membership. Camp in this sense appropriates the self-publicist, the self-stylization of celebrity culture, to then turn it back on itself, revealing the constructed nature of media identity. Three aspects of this process stand out in terms of their relevance to Verka. Camp is "[d]eterminedly facile [...]. Mock luxurious [...]. Mock glamorous" (Booth 1999: 73–4). The analysis in this chapter of the Verka act within the Russian cultural context no doubt supports the argument of observers such as Moe Mayer about the mainstream appropriation of camp and the resulting diffusion of its political radicalism and roots in queer culture (Mayer 1994).[31] Erasure of the homosexual origin of camp performance is necessarily carried out for it to survive in a hostile environment.[32]

One could conceivably maintain that the ambiguous nature of the act allowed for a measure of resistance to the political and sexual conformity and conservatism that typified televisual popular culture in Russia in the Putin era: a variety performance that sends up itself and other celebrated variety performers; the lack of adherence to a single cultural, national, or linguistic "paradigm," the rapid maneuver between popular cultural forms such as stand-up comedy, quasi-comic chat show, variety song, narrative music video, and film-length musical. Such "polysemy" was both popular with audiences and, at the very least, troubling for guardians of cultural capital (the perceived dilution and ridicule of Ukrainian linguistic identity criticized by intellectuals and journalists alike).[33] Finally, as strongly argued by Sontag (1999) in her seminal work on the subject, camp is about enjoyment. Nothing could be more true of Danilko's Verka: despite the awareness that celebrity is strongly mediated, representing conservative and patriarchal values, the performance, in its "tender"[34] fascination with stars like Pugacheva, seeks to foreground the celebrity as subject, rather than object, and in particular the subaltern subject, in terms of class, peripheral origin, and gender. In that respect, camp as a radical dehierachical category in the Russian context can be said to have the potential for a critical, deconstructive (albeit limited) response from within. Similarly, the complex interplay of cultural signifiers in Verka's performances makes for an "excess" performativity – a complexity and ambiguity that avoid reductive readings of the cultural formations they present, whether the discourse of achieved celebrity or, more generally, the consumption and enjoyment of popular culture.

Pugacheva's crooked mirror

The metamorphosis of the Verka performance did not just entail a generalized camp satire on the nature of celebrity and stardom, which tended to erase the personality of the subject, entailing a loss of what Rojek calls the veridical self (2001: 11). It was also a parody of a particular Soviet and post-Soviet celebrity *type* – the highly self-publicizing, "achieved" popular music celebrity – most recognizable in the persona of Pugacheva. Pugacheva is not a completely "achieved" celebrity. From a musical performance background she rose to fame through her emotional performances, which connected with audiences, and her equally powerful virtuoso singing. She also wrote some of her own songs. Something of a gay icon in her later years, she became so ubiquitous (especially on television after the collapse of the Soviet Union) that she came to be synonymous with *epatazh* – overblown, over-the-top music performance, something almost tasteless, a kitsch victim of its insistent emotionalism.[35] Olga Partan ably captures the idiosyncratic nature of Pugacheva's performance: at once emotionally intense, but also "clownish," "improvised" (see Chapter 8 in this volume). In attempting emotional connection with a voracious audience, hungry not for "a staging of intimacy," but for the signs of fame, wealth, and glamour, at times Pugacheva appears grotesque and self-indulgent, a celebrity who has truly come to be consumed by her public self, despite her success in creating an atmosphere of closeness with her fans, as described by Partan.

Danilko can perhaps be forgiven for aiming at an easy target in the persona of "Alla," the celebrity who sells the most front-pages of tabloid newspapers by a long margin. Just as Pugacheva gains attention by associating herself with younger performers such as Galkin, relatively new stars also benefit from the link with her. In the recent film *Za dvumia zaitsami* [Going after Two Hares] (Papernik 2003),[36] where, approaching the age of sixty, Pugacheva plays a young singer and the production crew is forced to resort to a thick layer of makeup, Danilko's Verka also has a leading role as the Pugacheva character's aunt. In a duet, she calls the latter a "typical Serdiuchka" and asks her when she last "looked in her own passport." While these statements have their own logic within the plot that the song moves forward, Danilko's lyrics have a double meaning, implying a likeness between Serdiuchka and Pugacheva.[37] The successful positing of likeness creates a mutually supportive discourse related to celebrity. The audience associates Pugacheva with Verka, a younger, more "up-to-date" star, whose media image epitomizes the myth of self-elevation to stardom. Equally, Verka benefits from association with Pugacheva's image, for in the less hierarchical post-Soviet league of stars, Pugacheva's undeniable super-celebrity status comes closer to Verka's orbit.

The "tender" parody of Pugacheva is continued in *The Adventures of Verka Serdiuchka*. This 75-minute musical film follows Verka from her birth under a Ukrainian haystack to a Moscow television dressing-room.[38] Starting out as an irrepressible and bright young child, in the final scenes Verka-the-star is a careworn veteran of the stage and screen, commenting to her faithful mother, "Mass art is such a venal thing." This biopic is not a parody of Pugacheva's life, though Verka's setbacks, victories, and general trajectory are similar to the older pop star's. Pugacheva is a constant presence in the pop-culture references that frame the film and is the in-joke of choice. For example, Verka's selected song for her entrance examination to Circus school is Pugacheva's breakthrough song, "Harlequin." As Verka performs the song, Pugacheva's face – shown in posters in the background of several scenes – looms large and sends a subliminal visual message that Verka and Pugacheva are inextricably linked in terms of origin and pathway to fame.

It should be noted that the Verka of *The Adventures* film, though changed by her "elevation," remains close to her moral anchor – her simple rural family. A review representative of responses to the film within Ukraine defended Danilko's creation against charges of cultural slander against the country, defining the film as the apotheosis of the act's carnivalesque impulse. It observed that those intellectuals weaned on Bakhtin and critical of Verka should be less discriminating in their application of his most famous theory. Verka is a "geyser of the people's laughter," both penetrating and acerbic, but also "laughingly kind" (Rezanova 2007). If not so much her music, then Verka's entire persona, her dress, and to a degree her on- and Danilko's off-stage coterie (Pugacheva's ex-husband Kirkorov and Galkin, favorite candidate for Pugacheva's off-and-on lover according to the tabloids) can be said to form a grotesque but sympathetic double of the media-filtered Pugacheva personality.[39] Danilko's Verka merely exaggerates everything a little, and the result is camp, commonly defined as theatricality taken to such an extreme that the constructed nature of the original, parodied object is revealed.

The unbearable weight of a moral anchor

The music video for a major song release, "Tuk, tuk, tuk" from the album *Chita Drita* (Mamamusic 2003), illustrates how important to Danilko's parody is the discourse of the celebrity's often uncomfortable "elevation." The lyrics, like those of many songs by Verka, are a seemingly lighter-than-air mixture of couplets modeled on traditional folk-song lexis ("I read my palm yesterday/ my heart was torn, torn from my chest"), repetitive declarations of love and loneliness ("Oh, I don't know why, but I like you/ I don't know why myself, but I like you"), and onomatopoeic or nonsense words used in a strikingly rhythmic way ("tuk, tuk, tuk, went my heart/ tuk, tuk, tuk, it beats and sobs"). Most negative commentary in the media has focused solely on the music and lyrics, while ignoring the performative context as a whole, especially within the music video. An important part of the music video – often divorced from the musical and lyric content – is the consistent (and ongoing) narrative of the performer's social mobility and Verka's rise to stardom. The following paragraph describes one of many videos devoted to these themes.

Verka and her extended family, identifiable from other musical videos and performances, enter a high-class restaurant (for dining at chic restaurants as an exercise in performativity, see Chapter 11). It becomes clear that Verka is treating her country-bumpkin relatives, who are dressed in a mixture of traditional Ukrainian dress and clothing typical of rural workers and market traders. The disparity between their dress and behavior and Verka's is a source of embarrassment and some agitation to her, but characteristically steeling herself – as the waiter seats them – Verka attempts to manage the unruly horde and impress upon them the privilege this visit represents. They, too, are far from relaxed in the midst of this new experience, showing confusion and bewilderment. Despite the vast gulf in status and behavior between Verka and her family, the message of loyalty and staying true to one's roots comes across visually and structurally in the use of a prologue and epilogue consisting of dialogue and non-musical action that precede and follow the song proper, a framing device typical for these carefully produced and choreographed music videos. The party is loud and unruly, the other patrons unimpressed by the interlopers. Initially cringing, Verka is gradually won over by the uninhibited atmosphere, joining in their raucous behavior. To the offer of some under-the-table vodka smuggled into the restaurant in a plastic bag by one of her party (so as to avoid the traditional restrictions on the amount of hard liquor served, and the high prices), her response is to order cocktails for all – her idea of the height of taste in beverages. However, this generosity backfires, as Verka is left with a huge bill, and she itemizes its contents in an attempt to find out which member of her party has consumed so many cocktails to wash down oysters. Discovering that the culprit is her own mother, Verka remarks ironically, "You, Mother, I begrudge nothing," while an impatient restaurant manager and admiring policeman look on.

These videos serve as an effective bridge between the stage sketches and the often satiric content of the music and lyrics themselves in Verka's pop performances. Other video performances highlight the construction of the celebrity by framing the video itself with a sketch between Verka and her coterie, in which the latter subjects the celebrity product of the latest "promotional" video to critical comment or indifference. These "stories" within the musical performance are not merely bookends or sketches. They are often of significant length, beginning, ending, and interrupting the narrative of the song itself. While most songs feature at least some satirical commentary on Verka's rise to stardom, in particular the songs "Ia popala na liubov' (I came upon love)" (2003), "A ia smeius'" (2005 – part of the film *The Adventures of Verka Serdiuchka*), and "Trali vali" (2006) unambiguously exploit and parody the discourse of roots that provide a "moral anchor" for the star (Rojek 2006: 610). Taking at face value the notion that stars' success may be traced to their roots and the communities from which they emerged, Danilko's Verka enlists her extended family in the execution of these videos. Their narrative reflects Verka's not altogether successful attempt to balance the management of her career and her relatives. Much is made of her punishing schedule and the constant attention demanded of her (by the technicians of her mediation, such as make-up artists and managers) because of her new status. Incongruously, her mother – who never removes her headscarf, a marker of her peasant status – is ever at her side, bewildered and dazzled by the glamour of the music industry, and she provides an ironical stand-back point. Even one of the first music videos, for "Ia popala na liubov'," is particularly revealing of the reflexivity of Danilko's performance and its continuing interest in celebrity identity formation. The narrative takes place in the family flat where Verka has come back for a visit during New Year celebrations. Over dinner, Verka seeks their approval of her new "vid," showing it on their video player. Their approval is rather mixed, one troublemaking relative noting that the song is "a bit dreary, though." The comic effect of a family's jealous rivalries continuing despite the difference in status between its "star" and its other members is heightened when Verka's mother attempts to distract her daughter from such comments by asking her whom she intends to represent at the Eurovision contest. While Verka glowers in silence, relatives on either side of her report the rumors they have read in the media regarding her choice. With a tired shrug she finally states that she will represent Kazakhstan.

The play with the self-authoring myth of the achieved celebrity is coupled with the act's focus on Verka's obsession with "taste" and fashion, illustrated by her choice of cocktails and exotic "European" foods in the restaurant scene, not to mention her ever-present penchant for clashing colors and outlandish costumes. True to her roots, she has mistaken over-dressing for glamour and chic – an error resulting in a vivid camp image of tacky excess. Typically, she sports huge colorful hats, furs, and sequins. Danilko, cast as himself in the 2006 performance, is pained by her failure to realize that she is anything but glamorous. The earlier scene at the railway station between Moscow and St. Petersburg reveals Verka in her final form, that of pop-star diva. To Verka's assertion that it is her glamour and songs that make for a popular act, Danilko retorts,

[ANDREI:] It's you who brought up the songs.
           Who writes them, have you forgotten?
[VERKA:] From Moscow to Khanty-Mansiisk
           People love these here forms.
[ANDREI:] These forms, Vera,
           Are merely lightweight foam.
           Chorus:
[ANDREI:] Do you remember how I met you
           In a stupid pink beret?
           You were walking through the carriage bringing someone tea,
           And I forgot about everything in the world.
[VERKA:] You were young, I wasn't really,
           You were no one, I was a star.
           In broad daylight you captivated me,
           And I'm a captive forevermore.[40]

As they sing of their inseparability the song plays out and the couple is joined on the dance floor by a group of dance partners – each of the women represented by men in drag (costumes similar to Verka's), including, of course, prosthetic bosoms. Verka, ever the self-publicist with an unwavering sense of her own importance and her status of beloved icon, is given a dressing down by her creator. The punch lines in the song are reserved for her (for example, the name of the Siberian town, Khanty-Mansiisk, rhymes with the Russian colloquialism for "breasts") but Danilko's part tells the true story of a celebrity's "cultural fabrication" and manipulation by others (Danilko standing in for the machinery of publicity and promotion) (Rojek 2001: 9). In Verka's case, not only is her talent illusory – the songs are written by another person – but her very body is artificial, her origins lowly, her taste abominable. Verka is simultaneously victor and victim. The audience laughs at her delusions, for as a subject she is an empty shell, just as her greatest assets are similarly empty, made of foam. The extreme nature of Verka – her over-the-top, histrionic delivery of her lines, her dress, and her clumsy, jerky movements on the dance floor – is a sum of the parts of every performer's nightmare. At the same time, however, if taken individually, they are only an exaggeration of the very behavior required of the celebrity performer: petulance, arrogance, delusions of grandeur, alcohol-induced indiscretions, an obsession with fashion quickly segueing into tastelessness, and borderline performance, especially in the vocal department. These qualities make for the ongoing mediation of the celebrity image within the public domain and ensure an endless source of gossip and scandal. Verka's star turn is excessive and extreme in that it takes the celebrity construction machine to its most grotesque conclusion. It poses the rhetorical question of what parts make up the sum of the elevated star who comes from humble beginnings. The more risible, even pathetic, of these parts are made more visible by the camp effect, for more is revealed through its excess than through "straight" stylistics. However, in the achieved celebrity stakes, where self-publicity and manipulation of origin and self are prerequisites, the boorishness, lack of talent, and unprepossessing origin are usually masked by the process of mediation within the performance space. Verka is mediation gone wrong, but she is nonetheless witness to the unenviable process of the suppression of the veridical self that every achieved celebrity undergoes.

At the same time Verka is clearly the victor, for indeed it is "she" who has achieved tangible popularity; Danilko's performances out of drag have attracted less interest (Remizova and Sokolovskii 2004). In short, the Verka act is a comic act relying on parody, of which celebrity, satirically treated, is an important theme (among others). While Verka's presence and appearance are an ever-visible joke – the drag act's constant – she is equally the joker, her greatest joke being that her presence forces others to play it straight. The joke of her stardom, maintained by other celebrities in their duets and performances with her, is also a joke on them – Danilko in drag makes transparent that his act is a fiction – and a fiction with a fairly incisive parody on the star personality and celebrity mores. Yet, while treating Verka as an "equal," they must sustain their public mask. Finally, Verka is the victor because, at the same time as rendering transparent the celebrity's world of posture and posing, she is allowed to make visible the constituent parts of the celebrity usually kept under wraps: the disparity between humble roots and the pretentious etiquette of the show business world is a source of rich comedy, too. In a single line about smallholder's allotments or eating sunflower seeds from a paper cone, Verka exposes the multi-layered category of the subaltern in post-Soviet life – female, peripheral, working-class, and non-Russian – while simultaneously deflating the achieved celebrity's self-importance and self-distancing from roots.

Ironically, Danilko's focus on exaggerating the glamour part of celebrity (Rojek 2001) has resulted in Verka and Danilko's attainment of actual celebrity status as regards the other aspect of stardom: notoriety. Serious reviewers and popular artists rail against what they see as the vacuousness and vulgarity of Danilko's Verka. They hate the kitschy lyrics, "I was born to love, with fire in my heart and a mimosa in my hands. But where are you, my peony?" ("Ia rozhdena dlia liubvi," from the album *KHA-RA-SHO*, Mamamusic, 2003) without getting the joke: such a kitschy, affirmative, and emotive song is very much a part of the public/private fracturing of the stage celebrity personality, nowhere better represented than in the ongoing saga of Pugacheva's public performances and not-so-private life. Such lyrics and music are, in any case, merely an exaggeration of the over-symbolic yet content-less, high-tempo yet folk-influenced fare of popular music today in post-Soviet Russia. By exaggerating key elements of popular music performance, such as glamour, luxury, and facile content, Danilko's Verka problematizes the construction of post-Soviet popular taste by the *estrada* (varieté) elite. Verka's "festival of the heart," whereby the rags-to-riches little Poltava girl who leaves no member of her hapless family behind on the road to Moscow's starlight, is a deconstructive narrative of the achieved and elevated media performer. Yet, its complex metonymical trajectory around the Pugacheva-like personality displays a fondness for the original in its theatrical parody. This play on the popular *epatazh* is a warmly comic camp, reveling in the well-established kitsch of Soviet and Russian culture. It is clearly a winning formula; the majority of viewers and listeners clearly "get" the affectionate yet revealing joke Verka provides, and join her in celebrating the old and the new, the high and the low, through the prism of camp (excess performativity), privileging neither the one nor the other.

Susan Sontag's vision of camp posited a complex sensibility: comic, involved yet ironic, and sincerely artificial in that it recognizes that sincere seriousness (politically motivated concern for the purity of the Ukrainian language, for example) is a denial of the complexity and enjoyment of mass culture, where judgment is overcome by a generosity of aesthetic enjoyment. Similarly, the ambiguous parody of Pugacheva's celebrity persona, the largest larger-than-life star in the former Soviet Union, is part of the campy, deconstructing sensibility embraced by the Verka Serdiuchka act in relation to celebrity culture.

Verka's parody of celebrity likewise turns attention to the subaltern category of the geographically peripheral working-class woman, and to the tactics of achieved celebrities of distancing themselves from their lower-status roots and audiences. Verka breaks the rules of the achieved celebrity, for while her *faux pas* are comic, her refusal to disavow her kin makes for a valorization of the ordinary against the vapid culture of wealth and beauty to which the "simple" Verka is elevated.

Danilko's parodic performance takes place within a centralized media space – national Russian television – characterized by relative homogeneity, conservatism, and informal but rigid vertical control, ensuring that a clique of core variety performers appear frequently in rotation. However, it is this very sameness that makes Danilko's parody, and particularly that of the glamorous pop performer, resonate. The Verka act derives much of its comedy and popularity from making transparent the highly mediagenic nature of Russian popular culture – in particular the domination by television, with its tendency to frame performance in terms of the "celebrification process," and the ongoing ability of performers to maintain status through scandal. Serdiuchka's scandals illustrate the manufactured nature of much celebrity gossip. Danilko himself has been unable to escape the orbit of his creation and inevitably attention turned to him too, especially after the Eurovision scandal of 2007. It is perhaps indicative of the political priorities of popular cultural production in Russia that Danilko's notoriety was firmly established not by interest in his sexual orientation, but by the question of loyalty to the host nation of Russia.

Notes

1 The page is maintained by the performer's agent and record company and is available online at: www.mamamusic.ua/~serduchka (last accessed 18 December 2009); all translations, unless otherwise indicated, are my own.
2 A variety of Ukrainian music acts, such as Natasha Koroleva and more recently Okean El'zy feature quite respectably in the Russian music media. Unlike Verka, these acts utilize standard Russian or Ukrainian language only.
3 The use of the term "achieved celebrity" in this chapter follows Rojek's (2001) definition of celebrity status achieved through self-staging.
4 Everage, like Verka, is a satirical creation initially targeting what Humphries saw as the cultural shortcomings of his homeland (Australia). There are a number of other similarities, including both characters' "awareness" of their creators' existence for comic effect, and the acts' evolution into satires on stardom.
5 A private communication (May 2006) with an executive at Channel One Russia revealed that, in his opinion, Danilko was one of a new breed of largely "self-elevated" stars, who, while having significant support from agencies, and in Verka's case, Channel One, had worked hard early in their career, without significant industry connections, to achieve star status. This hard work included a large amount of touring in the provinces for little monetary reward.
6 "Znaem oba, s toboi davno my, / Kto vedushchii, a kto vedomyi. / Akh, vot tak ty, zagovoril druzhok, / Bez menya ty – ne interesen, / Bez nariadov moikh i pesen."
7 Verka's mobile domain was given extended treatment in *The Adventures of Verka Serdiuchka*, a film-length musical shown in Russian on Ukrainian television (Gorov 2005). A stereotypical figure in the popular imagination of the late-Soviet and early post-Soviet periods, the female train guard remains an important site of ambiguous female power. The guard is like a man: her role is to enforce rules and wear a uniform, but at the same time she has the "feminine" role of caretaker: she is expected (though this expectation is often confounded) to bring tea on demand to the passengers from the permanently piping-hot boiler at the end of the carriage. It is also her role to keep that boiler at the requisite temperature. She represents a particular type of toughness and thick-skinned self-reliance in women.
8 Inter is a popular television channel and production company in Ukraine. Director Maxim Papernik has played a significant role in the look and feel of the Verka act on television.
9 Yuri Nikitin, owner of Verka's record company, Mamamusic, produced many of these videos, which Semen Gorov directed.
10 In an overview of the pop world, Danilko's comments on the scandalous behavior of Filipp Kirkorov are exclusively given in character as Verka and reported as such. No mention is made at all of Danilko (Khoroshilova 2004).
11 This extended even to some of the more serious articles in high-brow publications: for example, Kononenko (2005).
12 In a typical "confessional" interview, Danilko revealed that he had committed theft as a young man due to straitened circumstances. While Danilko's speech is in the first person, he is introduced by the author using the feminine form of a past tense Russian verb (Bekicheva 2005).
13 Joe Crescente's article on Serdiuchka's act provides much insightful analysis of issues

of cultural and linguistic identity (Crescente 2007).

14 Two key articles published in Ukraine on Verka and cultural-linguistic identity were Paramoshko (2006) and, in response, Rezanova (2007).

15 See Bilaniuk (2005: 165–72).

16 Interestingly, Danilko continues to appear on television, even on interview slots, mainly as Verka, indicating perhaps that the elevation process is never wholly complete or, since Eurovision, a comfortable position for him.

17 Television viewing during this holiday period is a traditional way of passing the time in family company at home and the most popular performers can appear on more than one channel, their performances being pre-recorded. Danilko reportedly demands up to thirty-five thousand Euros for such appearances ("Zastol'e 'pod Serdiuchku'" 2002).

18 As opposed to "ascribed" status. For example, Kseniia Sobchak is famous largely due to the social status of her family in Russia and the connections this brings – a kind of Soviet-era version of "old money." See Introduction for further analysis of the Sobchak phenomenon and Chapter 8 on Pugacheva's "ascribed" origins.

19 See also Rojek (2006: 608–17).

20 A typical example is the September 2007 internet news story about an alleged pornographic video of Sobchak, which ironically confirms that the video in question does not feature her at all (http://novostey.com/society/news21415.html, accessed 18 December 2009). The leaking by celebrities themselves of DIY sex tapes to maintain media interest is often alleged: see, for example, http://gawker.com/5003214/how-gene-simmons-sex-tape-is-the-fairytale-romance-of-our-time (accessed 18 December 2009).

21 The entire post-competition interview is available at www.youtube.com/watch?v=Q-dc-t8d8Uk (accessed 18 December 2009).

22 For some time it appeared that this controversy had resulted in an unofficial partial ban on Verka, but not on Danilko (!), on Channel One Russia and Channel Rossiia. However, Verka has begun appearing again on these channels, but not in order to perform musically. Since Eurovision 2007 Verka has performed only on the Russian national channel NTV, and focused mainly on Ukrainian projects. In addition, see Polupanov (2007).

23 Without having the space to comment in detail on online reaction to Verka, I can briefly state that internet postings about Danilko/Verka fall into four categories: violently homophobic; warmly supportive of the "heartfelt, festive" atmosphere of the performance; critical of the image of Ukraine that the act is felt to promote; and highly critical on the basis of the perceived vacuousness of the pop performance and lyrics. Some representative feedback relating to the *Argumenty i Fakty* article can be found online at: http://gazeta.aif.ru/online/dochki/287/10_01?comment (accessed 18 December 2009). Entertainment internet portals and sites also reveal the appeal of Verka's act to a much wider post-Soviet audience than just Ukraine and Russia. For example, one of the most prominent multi-lingual forums on popular musical culture in Azerbaijan contained (as of spring 2008) over three pages (44 posts) of user posts on Verka under the category of "znamenitosti" (famous people). By comparison, Justin Timberlake had 12 pages, Alla Pugacheva three pages, and Kseniia Sobchak 21 pages of posts. Sobchak was very much in the public eye when this resource was accessed in March 2008 (www.az-maz.com/forum/index.php?showforum=11).

24 On 29 March 2007 Danilko and Kirkorov appeared on a debate-type talk show "Pust' govoriat" (Let Them Talk) on Channel One to defend the song (available online at: www.youtube.com/watch?v=73oOuUnJmBA, accessed 18 December 2009).

25 *Za dvumia zaitsami*. This film is discussed in some detail later in this chapter.

26 "Shche ne vmerla Ukraina, esli mi guliaem tak!"

27 "Yakshcho ne liubliat nas, krasivikh i prekrasnykh. Yakshcho ne liubliat nas, to khai idut' v …"

28 The question of Danilko's sexuality is beyond the scope of the present study. It is clearly an issue with some of the television audience, as Danilko is very frequently subjected

to homophobic comments in online forums. Some newspaper articles have discussed the issue, one rather earnestly stressing that Danilko's act does not reflect his sexuality.

29 Danilko has advertised washing powder in Russia as Verka, as well as participating in social advertising in Ukraine to promote the Ukrainian language, a reaction against the harsh criticism of the hybrid Russian-Ukrainian speech his character employs. Verka-branded butter and *kvas* have also been promoted, and Danilko, again in character as Verka, has been involved in supporting the Ukrainian Green Party and at one point discussed the possibility of forming his own political party.

30 Bergman's introduction summarizes well the key movements and positions in the theoretical debate about the meaning and uses of camp in popular culture.

31 Analysis of the act in terms of sexual identity lies outside the focus of this chapter.

32 As is, arguably, the performer's sexuality itself.

33 The key terms "polysemy" and the (lack of an) "authoritative paradigm" are discussed at length in relation to the linguistic meaning of Danilko's act by Bilaniuk (2005). The usage of these terms adopted here parallels their application to the cultural-linguistic milieu examined by Bilaniuk.

34 Sontag's keyword in her description of camp's relishing relation to the object parodied.

35 David MacFadyen in *Èstrada?!* (2001: 35), sees Pugacheva, who began her career in the 1960s and rapidly became the biggest-selling non-Anglophone popular music performer in the world, as projecting an "affect" of displayed emotion that worked to undermine any purely social or civic content in her performance and its content. However, after the end of the Soviet Union this type of performance was ripe for parody.

36 Another breakthrough for Danilko, this film, for which he wrote most of the music, saw him share performances with Pugacheva and Galkin. The director also shot most of the music videos for Verka. The title of the film (a remake of a nostalgic Soviet film version of a nineteenth-century Ukrainian comedy by the playwright Mikhail Staritskii) is part of the saying "to run after two hares" (and consequently catch neither).

37 It is a commonly unkind, but not unjustified, observation that many pop divas as they age come more and more to resemble men in drag. In a recent review of her television work with Verka, Pugacheva was described as undergoing a process of transforming herself from a Russian version of Barbra Streisand into a bad copy of Cher, and even the most detached observer of the present Verka's dress and performance cannot help but be reminded of a younger Pugacheva (Gasparian 2007).

38 *The Adventures of Verka Serdiuchka* (Gorov 2005). This film, commissioned by Channel One, was never shown on terrestrial Russian television. It was shown on Ukrainian terrestrial television as part of the 2005 New Year's programming.

39 Pugacheva was one of the few (together with Kirkorov) to publicly defend Danilko from criticism about his allegedly anti-Russian Eurovision song lyrics (Gasparian 2007: 18). Pugacheva is never one to shy away from giving expression to the problem of person-ality for the celebrity, and does so in songs and comments to the press. A recent duet with Galkin saw the performers comment on each other's public personae. Galkin calls Pugacheva both "ice" and "flight." In Verka's parody of the song – a duet with none other than Kirkorov – the latter calls her "splendour" and "style" in the corresponding part of the song. The song quickly degenerates into a self-congratulatory duel of celeb-rity status indicators, Verka dedicating her pop videos to Kirkorov, and he, his CDs to Verka.

40 "Ty pro pesni zagovorila, / Kto ikh pishet, ty ne zabyla? / Ot Moskvy do Kanty-Mansiiska / Liudi liubiat vot eti formy. / Eti formy, Vera, / Vsego lish' porolon. / PRIPEV Pomnish' kak tebia ia vstretil, / V duratskom rozovom berete. / Ty po vagonu shla, komu-to chai nesla, / I ia zabyl pro vse na svete. / Ty byl iun, a ia ne ochen', / Ty byl nikto, a ia zvezda. / Sredi bela dnia, ty nashel menia, / I v tom plenu ia navsegda."

Bibliography

Arkhangel'skii, A. (2007) "Serdiuchno tseluem," *Ogonek*, 23 Apr. Available online at: www.ogoniok.com/4993/28/ (accessed 18 December 2009).

Bekicheva, I. (2005) "Greshna ukrainskaia 'doch'" Verka Serdiuchka, okazyvaetsia, v detstve podvorovyvala," *Tribuna RT*, 4 Feb: 28.

Bergman, D. (1994) "Introduction," in D. Bergman (ed.) *Camp Grounds: Style and Homosexuality*, Amherst: Massachusetts University Press, pp. 4–5.

Bilaniuk, L. (2005) *Contested Tongues: Language Politics and Cultural Correction in Ukraine*, Ithaca and London: Cornell University Press.

Booth, M. (1999) "*Campe-toi!* On the Origins and Definitions of Camp," in F. Cleto (ed.) *Camp: Queer Aesthetics and the Performing Subject*, Edinburgh: Edinburgh University Press, pp. 67–79.

Crescente, J. (2007) "Performing Post-Sovietness: Verka Serduchka and the Hybridization of Post-Soviet Identity in Ukraine," *Ab Imperio*, no. 2.

Fawkes, H. (2007) "Eurovision Angers Ukrainians," BBC News Online, 2 Apr. Available online at: http://news.bbc.co.uk/1/hi/entertainment/6516927.stm (accessed 18 December 2009).

Gasparian, A. (2007) "Pugacheva zastupilas' za Danilko," *Moskovskii Komsomolets*, 18 May: 18.

Gasparian, A. and Legostaev, I. (2004) "Zvukovaia dorozhka. Kogo nazvali sukoi?," *Moskovskii Komsomolets*, 9 Jan: 12.

Gorov, S. (2005) *The Adventures of Verka Serdiuchka* [Musical] Ukrainian television.

Gusev, O. (2006) *Pervyi skoryi*, Channel One, Russia.

Khoroshilova, T. (2004) "Sobytiia. Publichnoe priznanie," *Rossiiskaia Gazeta*, 17 Dec: 7.

Klin, B. (2006) "'Vse svobodny!' Kseniia Sobchak stroit novoe molodezhnoe dvizhenie," *Izvestiia*, 26 May: 4.

Kononenko, M. (2005) "Geopolitika. Serdiuchka emigriruet v Rossiiu?" *Gazeta*, 2 Feb: 15.

Kostenko-Popova, O. (2000) "Litsa. Kakogo pola Serdiuchka?" *Argumenty i Fakty*, 20 Dec. Available online at: http://gazeta.aif.ru/online/aif/1052/14_02 (accessed 18 December 2009).

Mayer, M. (1994) "Reclaiming the Discourse of Camp," in M. Mayer (ed.) *The Politics and Poetics of Camp*, London and New York: Routledge, pp. 1–22.

Papernik, M. (2003) *Za dvumia zaitsami*, Inter, Russia and Ukraine.

Paramoshko, D. (2006) "Verka Serdiuchka: shcho na spodi?" *Telekritika*, 28 Dec. Available online at: http://telekritika.ua/view/2006-12-28/8038 (accessed 18 December 2009).

Polupanov, V. (2007) "Serdiuchka, gud-bai!" *Argumenty i Fakty*, 18 July. Available online at: http://gazeta.aif.ru/online/aif/1394/44_01 (accessed 18 December 2009).

Remizova, M. and Sokolovskii, A. (2004) "Andrei Danilko otkazalsia ot Verki Serdiuchki," *Komsomol'skaia Pravda*, 5 Nov: 15.

Rezanova, N. (2007) "Plutovskoi roman s Verkoi Serdiuchkoi," *Telekritika*, 3 Jan. Available online at: www.telekritika.ua/media-suspilstvo/view/2007-01-03/8063 (accessed 18 December 2009).

Rojek, C. (2001) *Celebrity*, London: Reaktion Books.

— . (2006) "The Psychology of Achieved Celebrity," in P. D. Marshall (ed.) *The Celebrity Culture Reader*, London and New York: Routledge, p. 608–17.

Ross, A. (1999) "Uses of Camp," in F. Cleto (ed.) *Camp: Queer Aesthetics and the Performing Subject*, Edinburgh: Edinburgh University Press, pp. 308–29.

Shablinskaia, N. and Grachev, S. (2004) "Ukrainskaia zhenshchina Verka Serdiuchka," *Dochki-materi*, 26 Oct. Available online at: http://gazeta.aif.ru/online/dochki/287/10_01 (accessed 18 December 2009).

Sontag, S. (1999) "Notes on 'Camp'," in F. Cleto (ed.) *Camp: Queer Aesthetics and the Performing Subject*, Edinburgh: Edinburgh University Press, pp. 53–65.

"Telereiting. Vybiraem luchshego televedushchego goda" (2002) *Komsomol'skaia Pravda*, 22 May.

Tomak, M., Bilokon', K., and Kononenko, I. (2007) "Saliut, Vera! 'Ne mozhna karikaturistiv vvazhati za portretistiv," *Den'*, 13 March. Available online at: www.day.kiev.ua/178549/ (accessed 18 December 2009).

Troitskii, A. (2005) "Period otstoia. A kak tam otchestvo Fradkova?" *Novaia Gazeta*, 13 Jan: 5.

Tsyrkun, N. (2004) "Kommentarii. Landshaft rodnykh osin. Devichii perepolokh," *Iskusstvo Kino*, no. 8: 63–5.

"Zastol'e 'pod Serdiuchku" (2002) *Argumenty i Fakty*, 29 Dec: 48.

Part 5

Moscow snobbery

From "high" art to haute cuisine

10 Zurab Tsereteli's exegi monumentum, Luzhkov's largesse, and the collateral rewards of animosity[1]

Helena Goscilo (Ohio State University)

Bol'shoe viditsia na rasstoianie.

Sergei Esenin, "Pis'mo k zhenshchine"

Timeo Danaos et dona ferentis.

Virgil, Aeneid

La gloire et le repos sont choses qui ne peuvent loger en même gîte.

Montaigne, *Essais*[2]

Celebrity as media production-*cum*-political savvy

Chris Rojek summarizes a consensus among analysts of celebrity culture when he maintains that "[c]elebrity must be understood as a modern phenomenon, a phenomenon of mass-circulation newspapers, television, radio and film" (2001: 16),[3] as well as the internet. If unremitting multi-media attention constitutes both the primary requisite for celebrity construction and the cardinal earmark of celebrity status (Rojek 2001: 13), then Vladimir Putin indisputably reigns as post-Soviet Russia's premier celebrity (see Chapter 1). Tirelessly featured on television, on internet blogs, in newspapers, magazines, and a formidable array of cultural genres, Putin's perceived persona of a strong, disciplined leader who restored both national pride and the country's economy (touted as his achievement though enabled by petrodollars) won unprecedented popular support at home while sparking a revival of Cold War suspicions abroad. The media blitzkrieg also facilitated his metamorphosis into Russia's cultural icon or what he himself called "a brand" (*Putinki* 2004: 71).

Keen awareness of the media's decisive role in sustaining Putin's publicized image as the people's Kremlin hero prompted his administration to silence dissenting opinion in tried and true Soviet fashion: by closing down newspapers, magazines, television channels, and radio stations with independent views.[4] Negative press, as Richard Nixon and Edward Kennedy painfully learned decades ago, erodes politicians' reputations. In an age of scandal-hungry audiences, however, it can enhance the celebrity status of figures in sport, the arts, and the entertainment industry – a truism amply demonstrated in the USA by the likes of Woody Allen, Michael Jackson, O. J. Simpson, Paris Hilton, Winona Ryder, Britney Spears, and an entire stable of unruly rappers, not to mention Martha Stewart.[5] That dynamic of "fame through felony or defamation" is exemplified in Russia by the unusually controversial case of Zurab Tsereteli (b. 4 January 1934). "Controversial," in fact, invariably attaches to his name as a fixed epithet. Probably the only post-Soviet sculptor/painter to enjoy broad international recognition,[6] Tsereteli is "the man people love to hate" (Rodriguez 2005), and the reasons for that singular public status illuminate the paradoxes of celebrity.

The notoriety that critics theorizing celebrity acknowledge as a potential component of celebrification tends to spotlight behavior generally deemed illegal, scandalous, or destructive. In today's world, that behavior regularly results in arrests and court cases adjudicating such legal infractions as bodily violence, theft, "perverse" sexual practices, drunken driving, drug use, and even homicide. Though earlier eras resorted to social ostracism as an additional punitive measure, notably in the case of Byron (incest) and Oscar Wilde (sodomy), public opprobrium no longer assumes such forms. As Rojek rightly contends, "Transgression [...] is a tried and tested route in the acquisition of notoriety" (2001: 169), perhaps most visibly in bohemian culture. He echoes Erving Goffman's insight that though "unfavourable celebrity is usually stigmatized, [...] that deviation can be developed as a positive life strategy geared to the acquisition of status" (2001: 172). Reasons for actively pursuing notoriety are self-evident: the media's extended focus on such activities sets individuals apart from the "ordinary" masses, keeping them in the spotlight, generating speculation and gossip, and preparing the way for interviews, appearances on talk shows, or the publication of ghost-written confessional volumes. Yet, as Rojek notes, "The pressure is on the individual to produce one outrage after the other, so that the effect of diminishing returns sets in" (2001: 177). Of course, not all notorious celebrities court scandalous attention, many striving to keep their illicit actions secret, thereby rendering revelations of their transgressions all the more piquant.

Within such a framework, Tsereteli's notoriety constitutes an anomaly, for he has neither actively sought negative celebrity nor engaged publicly in criminal activities. How has he transgressed? What outrages has he perpetrated? The answer, I contend, resides in the unusual trajectory of his career, particularly though not exclusively during the post-Soviet era.

In demeanor and style the short, stocky Tsereteli distractingly evokes the cartoonish media image of the New Russian – a moneyed vulgarian in thrall to acquisition and flashy display.[7] Indeed, Tsereteli's black Rolls-Royce, gilt-rimmed cell phone, gold fountain pen, gold watch, outsized gold cufflinks, gold bracelets, huge ring, chain nestling against a bared chest, and custom-made suits, plus his several residences, advertise his wealth and betray the taste characteristic of the 1990s' "rough diamond" entrepreneurs, tirelessly satirized in *anekdoty* (jokes), the press, film, and conversations among the intelligentsia.

Neither new nor Russian, however, Tsereteli is a seventy-five-year-old Georgian from Tbilisi[8] who during the Soviet era inherited a sizable fortune from his

Figure 10.1 Multiplication: Tsereteli posing in his studio in Moscow, gilt-rimmed cell phone and mega-ring on display, with one of his numerous paintings of flowers and a photograph of him surrounded by smiling beneficiaries of his largesse in the background; 2008. Photo by Vladimir Fedorenko, courtesy of RIA Novosti.

aristocratic wife's relative in France (Grant 2001: 340)[9] and vaulted to international fame with dazzling speed. That Tsereteli was permitted to travel to France in 1964 bespoke his ideological reliability as a Soviet citizen. Whereas practitioners of Sots-Art and *sui generis* artists like Sergei Paradzhanov encountered the authorities' implacable hostility, Tsereteli sweepingly disclaims even a hint of censorship's shadow over his thriving Soviet-era career, "I don't consider it a problem. We create problems for ourselves, don't we?" (Malpas 2004). In short, Tsereteli from the outset was a genuinely Soviet artist in tune with the regime, which rewarded him accordingly, thereby rendering him a questionable figure among those Russian intellectuals who were at odds with the powers that be.

Less than a decade after graduating from the Academy of Arts in Tbilisi (1958), Tsereteli was entrusted with the design of a recreational complex in Pitsunda, a resort town now in the breakaway Georgian republic of Abkhazia (1966). His efficient supervision of the team and his own contribution of a huge, colorful, mosaic-decorated structure reminiscent of a runaway bagel (*Solntse i luna* [Sun and moon]) not only set the pattern for his future activities as an architectural monumentalist, but also earned him the title of Honored Artist of the Georgian SSR (1967). Other projects, both in the USSR and abroad, followed in quick succession, so that by 1990 a modest sampling of Tsereteli's commissions, posts, and awards included the following:[10]

1968–73

Lenin memorial complex in Ul'ianovsk (awarded the State Prize); mosaic in the swimming pool of the Venets Hotel complex, mosaic display window in the Tbilisi Professional Unions' Palace of Culture, mosaic designs for Aragva restaurant, Iveriia Hotel, and Victory Park; sculpture *Coral* at a resort town in Adler on the Black Sea

1974–9

design of Soviet Embassy in Brasilia, the capital of Brazil (1974), interiors of the Soviet Embassy in Portugal (1975) and Tokyo (1975); two hefty monuments in Brockport, New York: *Happiness to All Children of the World* and *Science and Education to the World, or Prometheus* (both in 1979); Professor of Fine Arts at SUNY University in Brockport (1979); BS in the International Academy of Alternative Sciences (1979); Lenin Prize (1976); People's Artist of Georgia (1978); USSR State Prize (1978); People's Artist of the USSR (1979)

1980–4

monumental composition at the Izmailov Hotel complex (1980); *The Tree of Life* in the courtyard of Gruziia-fil'm studio (1980); interior of Georgia's official center in Moscow (1981); *Friendship of Nations* in Moscow; several monuments for the military in Moscow (1984); chief artist in the Organizing Committee of the XXII Olympics in Moscow (1980); Professor of Georgia's Academy of Arts (1981); USSR State Prize (1983)

1985–90

two enormous monuments for the Soviet Embassy in the USA (1987); *Tear Down the Wall of Distrust* in London (1989); *Good Conquers Evil* at the UN Crowne Plaza in New York (1990); Full Member of the Russian Academy of Arts (1989); Ambassador Extraordinary and Plenipotentiary of the Russian Federation (1989).

Tsereteli's intimate ties with officialdom may be inferred not only from the frequency with which he decorated Soviet embassies and produced monuments commemorating the Soviet armed forces, but also from the political pragmatism of foreign governments and organizations that were intent on demonstrating their receptivity to art approved by the Soviet state.

With the dissolution of the USSR, Tsereteli's career, instead of petering out, increasingly resembled a Homeric catalogue of media-glamorized appointments and coveted awards: recipient of the decorations Hero of Labor (1991), Friendship of Nations (1994), and For Service to the Fatherland, 3rd category (1996), he won the Picasso Prize (1994), the Russian State Prize (1996), three medals from France in recognition of his contribution to high culture (1998, 2000, 2002),[11] and was named Man of the Year by the American Biographical Institute (1996) and Man of the Decade by the Russian Biographical Institute (2000). Moreover, he became President of the resuscitated Russian Academy of Arts (1997), Vice President of the Russian Academy of Informatics (1998), Fellow of the Academy of Fine Arts in Kyrgyzstan (1998), Corresponding Member of both the Spanish and the French Academy of Fine Arts (1998, 2002), Member of the Public Chamber of the Russian Federation (2006 and 2008) and of the European Academy of Sciences and Arts (2009), and Fellow of the Academy of the World Elite (1997).[12] While accruing these honors and the influence they automatically carry, Tsereteli produced portraits and statues of the rich and famous, including Marc Chagall, Charlie Chaplin, Liza Minnelli, Mother Teresa, Margaret Thatcher, Princess Diana, the Swedish King and Queen, and the like.[13]

Countless photographs of Tsereteli inevitably captured him hobnobbing with presidents and premiers and frequenting photo-op events – or, as one American journalist put it, "For decades, no visiting head of state or celebrity has been safe from Tsereteli's attentions" (Finnegan 2007). (Figure 10.2) Consequently, any reader of Yuri Olesha's 1920s' novel *Zavist'* [Envy] could probably explain the broad-based hostility to Tsereteli among lesser mortals with access to print, for, as the film director Pavel Lungin noted during a discussion of his film *Oligarkh* [Tycoon] (2002), unlike the French, "we [Russians] cannot tolerate somebody else's success."[14] One could conceivably ascribe envy not only to Tsereteli's outspoken critics, but also to those Muscovites who withhold negative comments on his works only so as not to extend the circulation of his name in the media (Glasser 2004) – a restraint showing awareness of how negative press can enhance the fabrication of celebrity. What accounts for this groundswell of antagonism is the extreme, excessive nature of Tsereteli's modus operandi and success: his ever-increasing wealth, his highly-placed connections, his epic productivity, his seemingly limitless power in the sphere of art, and his unfailing optimism, which (however reductively and misleadingly) projects his life as a seamless sequence of stunning, accolade-greeted achievements. He exceeds accepted excess. Part of Tsereteli's transgression, in other words, consists of the excessive distance separating his life from that of the Russian population at large.

"Social distance," Rojek contends, "is the precondition of both celebrity and notoriety" (2001: 12). Yet the complex nature of the relationship between glamorous celebrities and their "aspiring" fans necessitates the illusion that the distance may be surmounted, if only partially and sporadically, thereby allaying the thirst for intimacy and identification with one's icon. As Rojek admits, "the illusion of intimacy, the sense of being an exalted confrère [...] is part of celebrity status in the age of mass-media" (2001: 19). Fantasies woven by fans around their celebrity idols feed off that illusion. Tsereteli's public persona of impervious omnipotence, however, leaves no room for the average Russian to identify with him or to exercise Russians' fabled sympathy for the underdog. In interviews, he undeviatingly articulates a sanguine perspective on the world that verges on Leibnitzian optimism (all is for the best in the best of all possible worlds). Unlike Alla Pugacheva, who has struggled with weight and aging (see Chapter 8), he appears immune to any and all adversities even as he exceeds the prerequisites for celebrity success. Yet such an explanation of Tsereteli's notoriety, though probably accurate, is insufficient, for his detractors, who transcend Russia's borders, offer other, less visceral reasons for their animosity, and on wholly different grounds.

Figure 10.2 Among the countless photo-op events that maintain Tsereteli in the spotlight, the ceremonious induction of fashion designer Pierre Cardin into the Russian Academy of Arts, Moscow, as an honorary fellow; 27 November 2008. Photo by Anton Denisov, courtesy of RIA Novosti.

Burdensome munificence as troublesome titans

An exuberant politico-cultural imperialist determined to conquer the maximum possible space susceptible to artistic colonization in Russia and abroad, Tsereteli not only aggressively pursues contracts for massive monuments and sculptures in open public venues, but also engages in "immodest proposals." Intent on seeing his mega-monuments overrun the world's surface, he is not content with commissions alone, but repeatedly presses his works as gifts upon unsuspecting governments and organizations, assuring them of his readiness to defray costs out of his own pocket if necessary. Given the dimensions of his leviathans, those sums are formidable. On at least two occasions this strategy misfired, eliciting sardonic commentary by American journalists. In 1991, as a purported gesture of goodwill, Tsereteli offered the United States his *Birth of the New World*, an unassembled 350-foot, 660-ton statue of Christopher Columbus, to mark the 500th anniversary of the explorer's voyage. After at least five USA cities, including New York, refused the gift (faulted for anachronisms, pomposity, and excessive size), Puerto Rico consented to have the mammoth assembled in the town of Cataño. At the final hour, however, it had to abandon the project because of insufficient funding and public support; just the transport of thousands of pieces cost the taxpayers approximately $30 million (Dixon 2003). Like many "free gifts," this one proved inordinately expensive.

According to Marcel Mauss's concept of exchange in his classic study of *The Gift* [*L'essai sur le don*] (1923–4), the recipient of such 'generous gifts' typically feels obliged to reciprocate – in Tsereteli's case, by issuing a subsequent invitation, conferring a title, or at the very least ensuring the media's reports of the donor's largesse. "Free gifts," in other words, can garner laudatory attention – a *sine qua non* of celebrification.

A slightly less ignominious fate awaited Tsereteli's next artistic overture to the USA. In December 2002, when his name did not appear on the list of seven finalists selected to memorialize the World Trade Center site, determined and undeterred, he crossed over to New Jersey to "make a deal" with Jersey City. Efforts to donate what would become his 9/11 memorial, "a 100-foot-tall, 175-ton, bronze clad [sic] tower enclosing a 40-foot glass teardrop" called *To the Struggle against World Terrorism: Tear of Grief*, failed. Residents of Jersey City reportedly balked at installing it on the pier downtown, for "[u]nfortunate descriptions of the project and views of Mr. Tsereteli's work were proliferating," and the City Council rejected the colossus (Applebome 2005). Members of the "resistance" protested that the work was a "monstrosity" conceived on an "overwhelming scale," had an "outsized presence," and was "simplistic" in design (Figure 10.3). Daniel Levin, the group's organizer, remarked, "Everyone was aghast" (Glasser 2004). Finally, through connections, Tsereteli negotiated to have the structure – which one wag called "another XXL, in-a-class-of-its-own monument" resembling "a giant tea biscuit" – installed in the two-acre Harbor View Park, at the end of the long, man-made peninsula in Bayonne, New Jersey (Finnegan 2007). Its construction widely reported to have cost $12 million in materials and shipping, the monument carries the inscription "Gift from the People of Russia – President Vladimir Putin," though Tsereteli contradictorily has claimed to be its donor, thereby yoking his name to Putin's and presenting himself as a spokesman for the entire Russian population. Bill Clinton, Michael Chertoff, the United States Secretary of Homeland Security, speaker of the Federation Council Sergei Mironov, and a raft of lesser dignitaries attended the formal dedication ceremony on 11 September 2006, at which Clinton delivered an address. Putin had flown in for the ground-breaking installation the previous year. Both rituals, of course, were accompanied by the customary fanfare: press releases, photos, and television coverage.

American reactions to the monument ranged from admiration to consternation and ridicule. A Jersey City artists' organization allegedly blasted it as "an insensitive, self-aggrandizing piece of pompousness by one of the world's blatant promoters" (Finnegan 2007). Leon Yost, an artist and critic of the Jersey City site, straight-facedly pointed out the welcome remoteness of its final location: "It's further out in the harbor there. Maybe from a distance it's not as, if I can use a negative word, ostentatious, not as in your face" (Applebome 2005). Various bloggers on Wired New York Forum volunteered less polite opinions: "Even that creepy statue in spain [sic] is better than this ugly thing" ("Johnnyboy"); "It looks like a vagina with a drop of sperm" ("twinhk"); "Horrible design" ("JCMAN320"); "IT SUCKS!" ("Jake"); "Zurab Tsereteli is a megalomaniacal quack. he [sic] defaced Moscow with his sculptures, and now Bayonne" ("injcsince81"); "This

Figure 10.3 Perceived by some detractors as "indecent" in its realization, the *Tear of Grief*, a monument, commemorating the victims of 11 September 2001, installed in Bayonne, USA, exactly five years later. Photo by Aleksandr Chumychev, courtesy of RIA Novosti.

'artist,' Zurab Tsereteli (google him if you wish), is well known for putting up humongous, kitschy monstrosities of 'sculptures' around the world, particularly in Moscow. I have no idea how the guy gets away with this, but I am happy that at least this piece of sad kitsch will be in Bayonne instead of Jersey City, at the tip of [the] 2-mile long Marine Ocean Terminal, where it will hopefully blend in with the port cranes. National Monument my a$$" ("injcsince81"); "Don't blame this on Russia as a whole. Tsereteli is a hack, and Russians know this much better than the Americans, making his monument the butt of numerous jokes" ("LeCom").[15] In short, not only Tsereteli's incessant, publicized drive for acclaim – a "syndrome" captured in luridly disturbing specifics by Bret Easton Ellis's *Glamorama* (1998) – but also his aesthetics may account for the hostility that dogs his celebrity status.

The online reception of what some apparently view as his crocodile *Tear of Grief* converged with many Russians', and particularly Muscovites', sentiments about Tsereteli's mega-monuments during the last fifteen-odd years, some of them also directed at the statue in Bayonne. Kseniia Larina, a host on the Moscow radio station Ekho Moskvy, deplored the *Tear of Grief* as a "horror" that "looks extremely indecent," and found reprehensible the report that among the names of those who purportedly perished in the attack carved into the monument's base,

43 actually belong to survivors (Khokhlova 2006)![16] Such an error could stem from the Stakhanovite speed with which Tsereteli typically works to generate the utmost possible within a short span of time, each new creation resulting in media coverage.

More recently (2009), Tsereteli produced a ten-foot-tall copper sculpture of the famous miniature silver hare by Fabergé, installed in the Fabergé Museum's courtyard in Baden-Baden, close to the city's central square of Leopoldplatz. Predictably, the donated replica is now the largest monument in the city ("Zurab to Fabergé" 2009; "Giant Hare ..." 2009). And who can doubt that Ethiopia's long-planned Tsereteli monument of its "native son," Pushkin, slated for installation in 2009, will dominate the local landscape? In light of his devotion to outsized structures, Tsereteli's 154-foot *Colossus of Olympia* (2008) in Beijing – one of two Colossal sculptures he submitted to the Olympic Games in Beijing – seems a perfect reification of his aesthetic credo.

Figure 10.4 Quintessentially Tseretelian in its title, the *Colossus of Olympia*, a monument erected in China, intended as a symbol of the 2008 Summer Olympics in Beijing; 2008. Photo by Sergei Piatakov, courtesy of RIA Novosti.

As Russia's principal producer of official, large-scale art, Tsereteli predictably has both sycophantic supporters and derisive critics – with both parties ensuring his perennial spot in the limelight. Lengthy passages in a recent hagiographical monograph on Tsereteli by Lev Kolodnyi, bathetically titled *Serdtse na palitre: Khudozhnik Zurab Tsereteli* [Heart on the Palette: The Artist Zurab Tsereteli] (2002),[17] read like a polemical apologia aimed at Russian art critics' sometimes hilarious and often annihilating appraisals of Tsereteli's oeuvre, such as comparisons of his monuments to *kolbasa* and *shashlyk*. An item in the Latvian monthly *Rigas Laiks* in 2006 joined the chorus of Russian negators, along political lines, "Ideological symbolism, corporate links, and southern temperament have combined to create an atrocious cultural phenomenon which has assumed the role of a substitute for art in the public sphere. Nevertheless, the simulacrum of totalitarian art has given rise to numerous outbursts of social consciousness" (*Rigas Laiks* 2006). In fact, Tsereteli inadvertently has stimulated considerable social debate and protest. No one denies that he is boundlessly prolific. Impassioned disagreement concerns only the desirability of such fecundity, which detractors impute to adroitness – the Pyrrhic triumph of quantity over quality. And the polemic, as well as Tsereteli's indefatigable, publicized activity, regularly makes headlines, buttressing his celebrity status. As Kolodnyi, who without even a hint of irony repeatedly calls Tsereteli "my/our hero" [moi/ nash geroi], points out, "The more they [protesters and critics] fabricated myths about [the statue of] Peter, the more they attracted attention to its creator's name" (2002: 262).[18] Indeed, in the world of celebrity, cynosure is the name of the game.

Moscow as "moi" Mecca

Russians' animosity toward Tsereteli peaked after 1993, the year marking the beginning of his friendship with Moscow Mayor Yuri Luzhkov, which launched his vertiginous ascent to the position of the capital's "court artist." Tsereteli proved an ideal collaborator for Luzhkov's project of transforming the city into a gaudy showcase of New Moscow architecture – which *World Architecture* magazine decried as "an abysmal rhetoric of traditional architectural elements, recreated Disney-style in poor-quality materials and with no attention to detail" (Dixon 2003).[19] The imposition of this "flamboyantly ornate style" (Dixon 2003) has entailed the destruction of unique, centuries-old buildings to make room for huge, profit-making architectural complexes calculated to stun, while violating both stylistic integrity and aesthetic sensibilities. As one American journalist summed up this process, "In architectural terms few cities have endured more abuse than Moscow [...] during the last decade or so, from the demolition of major historical landmarks to the boom in garish faux-historical reproductions" (Ourousoff 2007). The Luzhkov–Tsereteli "partnership" seemed inevitable, given the two men's similarities, down to their physical features: short, thickset, and Soviet-proletarian in appearance even in formal wear, they belong to the same generation (Luzhkov – b. 1936; Tsereteli – b. 1934), have inexhaustible energy, ruthless ambition, the habit of oversize, cynosural gesture, skill at self-advertising, and a determination to leave their indelible signatures on the nation's capital (see Chapter 2).

During the 1990s the "free-spending, opportunistic" Luzhkov (Bennett 1997) was the supreme New Russian writ large, with all of Moscow as his oyster.[20] A crowd-pleaser who carried the 1996 mayoral election with a sweeping 95 percent vote, he dexterously juggled contradictory images so as to garner support from the broadest possible constituency. In a 1998 poll Russians voted him their country's most trusted politician (*"Kuranty"* No.1, 1998). On the five-year anniversary of his mayorship, the magazine *Delovye liudi* [Business People] complimented Luzhkov on having improved the circumstances of Moscow's less well-to-do, even as it applauded the impetus he had given to the creation of a new middle class (No. 79, July 1997). The Russian media, in short, hailed him as the avatar of positive change.

While New Russians proudly displayed their luxuriously remodeled "Euro" bathrooms and apartments to visitors,[21] the enterprising Luzhkov showcased the dramatic upgrading of *his* domain – the entire city of Moscow. The greatest coup of his exhibition-career transpired on 5–7 September 1997, which he arbitrarily declared Moscow's 850th anniversary, featuring the theme "Moscow: Yesterday, Today, and Tomorrow" – a shrewd choice, calculated to appeal to all age groups, from teenagers to pensioners. That profligate display required three years of preparation, necessitated one of the most elaborate urban facelifts in history, and temporarily turned the world's attention to what formerly had depressed and impressed visitors as a provincial, moribund capital. Although the sums invested in Moscow's stunning visual metamorphosis remain a closely guarded secret, the estimated cost of the internationally media-hyped three-day extravaganza totaled somewhere between $50 and $60 million.[22]

Amid copious flags, bunting, balloons, fountains, gardens, spruced-up famous landmarks, and hastily assembled structures – such as the Manezh Plaza shopping mall, the immense Cathedral of Christ the Savior, Moscow's largest railway station, Kazanskii Vokzal, and statues of Dostoevsky,[23] Peter the Great, and Prince Daniel of Moscow – the pseudo-populist "Moscow Mussolini" (vanden Heuvel and Cohen 1997) treated the madding crowds of Russians and foreign visitors to parades, picnics, concerts, dances, fireworks, a fire-breathing dragon in a drama titled *Our Ancient Moscow*, produced by the film director Andrei Konchalovsky (Gordon 1997) (see the Introduction for more information on Konchalovsky), star performances by the likes of Luciano Pavarotti, a cornucopia of tricks by the illusionist David Copperfield, and a laser-technology sound-and-light demonstration by Jean-Michel Jarre, culminating in a projected mammoth image of the Virgin Mary in the sky and the eye-popping spectacle of Luzhkov himself inside a gigantic champagne glass.[24] An ex-KGB cabdriver sourly summed up the relentlessly promoted bash as "Luzhkov's little party" (Durden-Smith 1997)[25] – one that ended in near-calamity, as access to streets was blocked, the subways closed down, and a railroad bridge almost collapsed when tides of weary revelers struggled to return home from the city center.

While Luzhkov trumpeted, "The jubilee is a wonderful, glorious date for us all," inasmuch as "the history of Moscow is the history of Russia" – a revealing predicate – Westerners largely concurred that self-promotion and the desire to attract investment in the city motivated the grandiose extravaganza.[26] In short, power politics. Some journalists and spectators discerned two sets of festivities, "one for the inner circle and another for the masses" (Gordon 1997), deploring "the omission of average Russians from the main events" (Williams 1997). Luzhkov's mode of refurbishing the capital, in fact, wholeheartedly embraced the twinned New Russian principles of "the best for the most moneyed" and maximum visibility liberally seasoned with vulgarity. As one journalist, tabulating the city's deluge of plastic plants, huge, garish animals, and over-decorated exteriors, lamented, "For sheer bad taste [...] five years of capitalism have outdone three-quarters of a century of communism" (Martin 1997b). Some owners of establishments complained of pressure from the city's officials, at the risk of otherwise incurring a fine, to "beautify" the entrance to their emporia with tacky plastic greenery to the tune of several hundred dollars as cosmetic touch-ups for the anniversary jamboree. Rather than confirming Moscow's role as representative of the whole country, the event underscored its status as a highly privileged exception.[27] Whatever the nationalist tenor of the pageantry, it ultimately advertised Moscow as a dynamic international metropolis, wired to a modern technology, yet blessed with an ancient pedigree, boasting both the mad money to splurge on a Disneyland Walpurgis Night and a Magician who wielded absolute control over his kingdom.[28]

Though he overreached in his intention to run for the presidency in the 2000 elections,[29] Luzhkov was appointed mayor by Yeltsin in 1992 and subsequently won three mayoral elections by a landslide.[30] Putin's reappointment of him for a fifth term, despite Luzhkov's announced intention to step down in 2007, further consolidated his status as the Master of Moscow and its sizable budget.[31] A dictatorial, combative practitioner of hands-on governance, Luzhkov has exercised his vast power to guarantee lucrative contracts for his intimates (above all, his billionaire wife, Elena Baturina, who holds a virtual monopoly on the cement industry and luxury-apartment construction),[32] to ban what he deems undesirable elements – dark-skinned residents, gay parades ("satanic"), and performances by irreverent groups such as Leningrad – and to bully the city's residents into compliance with his radical building agenda, which has encountered some ineffectual local opposition.[33] According to preservationists, from 1992 to 1994, more than 400 buildings dating back to the seventeenth century were bulldozed to accommodate either architectural imitations or generic mammoths of cement, glass, and steel (Bransten 2004). Lukhkov's signature passion for architectural "power verticals" – "buildings topped with triangular turrets, popularly called Luzhkov turrets," and his plan for the tallest skyscraper in Europe (Levy 2008) – attests to his epic ambitions.[34] Thus, for someone with Luzhkov's addiction to massive structures and ostentatious gesture, Tsereteli the arch-monumentalist was a dream come true.[35]

Accordingly, from the beginning of his tenure Luzhkov openly singled out Tsereteli for special favors of a legally dubious nature that eventually elevated him to the position of most powerful artist-entrepreneur in Moscow. Under terms that remain murky, Luzhkov allotted Tsereteli a palatial apartment-*cum*-studio at 17 Bol'shaia Gruzinskaia – the former residence of the West German Embassy, no less. Second, Tsereteli became the director of "his" Museum of Contemporary Art in the restored eighteenth-century building at 25 Petrovka (1999), the courtyard of which teems with his monuments of the ultra-famous (Brodsky, Okudzhava, Shostakovich, Shukshin, Vysotsky), most of them reproduced in various sizes elsewhere. The following year the chic, ultra-modern Zurab Tsereteli Art Gallery – the renowned eighteenth-century residence of the Dolgorukov dynasty – opened at 19 Prechistenka as a temple glorifying its director. Steeped in rich history, these imposing, sumptuously appointed architectural landmarks are located in the very heart of what for a while was the most expensive city in Europe and therefore boasts incalculable "symbolic capital."[36]

While the process whereby Tsereteli acquired these stately tsarist-era buildings remained questionable (and questioned by some), what most incensed Muscovites was Luzhkov's arbitrariness in entrusting Tsereteli, in rapid succession, with a series of major lucrative projects that would definitively reconfigure Moscow's landscape: the construction of the gigantic complex at Victory Park [Park Pobedy] to commemorate World War II (1992–5); the supervision of rebuilding the colossal Church of Christ the Savior [Khram Khrista Spasitelia] (1995), for which Tsereteli also cast the crosses and bronze doors; the design of Manezh Plaza and "Okhotnyi riad" – the underground trade and shopping mall (1996); the decoration of the entrance to the children's playgrounds of the Moscow Zoo and the sculpture *Tree of Fairy Tales* inside the Zoo (1996); the notorious statue of Peter the Great marking the tercentennial of the Russian navy (1997); and Wonder Park [Park chudes], the projected children's fantasy playground on the outskirts of Moscow.[37]

From interviews one may deduce that Tsereteli, who presents himself as a future-oriented, modern/ist artist and his critics effectively as myopic, uncomprehending philistines, views Luzhkov's largesse as his due. Implicitly comparing himself to such universally acclaimed figures as Picasso, he argues, "To work out the value of an artist or a work you need time. There have been plenty of artists, but time passed and what's left is Leonardo da Vinci, Michelangelo, Velázquez and Goya" (Malpas 2004). Elsewhere Tsereteli has asserted, "I'm one of those artists who gives birth to ideas and sees them through to the end. I want my works to live for a long time, and I really wish my works to be appreciated by everyone." Then, doubtless recalling those who have panned those creations, he added, "But if everyone likes your works, it's a tragedy" (Dixon 2003).

Tsereteli has succeeded in circumventing that tragedy. David Sarkisian, director of the Shchusev State Museum of Architecture, has openly accused Tsereteli of "do[ing] more harm to Moscow's appearance than anybody else has ever done. [...] Tsereteli is a genius of kitsch. He is the personification of kitsch.[38] It is only his limitless energy and push that have helped him to get his ugly sculptures put up all over the world. In that sense, Zurab Tsereteli is a world champion in terms of the number of ugly works he has managed to palm off to different countries. It is simply beyond comprehension how he manages to be so successful" (Dixon 2003). In a similar vein, Grigorii Revzin, a respected art critic for the newspaper *Kommersant*, after cautioning that all criticism is subjective, confessed, "I personally do not like anything about Tsereteli's sculptures. Indeed quite a few people in Russia don't much like Tsereteli and his works" (Dixon 2003). Regarding the final resting place of the anti-terrorism monument in New Jersey, Revzin pointed out, "We should congratulate ourselves … that it isn't being done here" (Glasser 2004). Almost immediately after news spread of the intention to honor Joseph Brodsky's memory with a monument by Tsereteli, a website sprang up on which people pleaded, "We are REALLY, REALLY fed up with your bronze monsters. Please, save our city [St. Petersburg] from them. You are the only person who can" (Rodriguez 2005). The protesters won the day. Igor' Markin, private collector and owner of a small museum of contemporary art in Moscow called Art4.ru, placed a box offering visitors the chance to make donations toward the cost of destroying all of Tsereteli's monuments in the city ("I hate his work") (FitzGerald 2007). Though he removed the box at the request of Tsereteli's grandson Vasily,[39] he claimed to have "already received enough money to tear all the monuments down" (FitzGerald 2007). Indeed, Crimean Tartars in Yalta "announced their intention to blow up not only the bronze Stalin but also the sculptor himself" if he realized his projected homage to the 1944 Yalta conference in an ensemble piece featuring Stalin, Churchill, and Roosevelt (*Rigas Laiks* 2006). In early July of 1997, some extremists actually tried to destroy Tsereteli's statue of Peter the Great (Kolodnyi 2002: 265–6), which more than any of his other monuments aroused outraged protests. Since that failed attempt, which drew widespread media attention – according to Kolodnyi, all of the city's newspapers on 7 July covered the event (Kolodnyi 2002: 265) – many have reconciled themselves to the gigantic bronze excrescence towering over the Moscow River. In the meantime, Tsereteli continues to expand his domain: in 2008 alone, his works were exhibited in thirty provincial areas [regiony] (Nikolaeva 2009).

Ever buoyant[40] and seemingly immune to all forms of criticism, Tsereteli calls the statue of Peter "a city favorite" (Dixon 2003), declaring that people who initially experienced fear (?) upon seeing it "are apologizing, saying, 'It's a sin [sic] that I criticized such a great [sic] work of art'" (Glasser 2004). Ol'ga Kabanova, a writer for *Rossiiskaia Gazeta* who expressed condolences to New Jersey over the Christopher Columbus "gift," phrased it somewhat less flatteringly in terms coined by a criminologist/psychiatrist referencing victims and abusers:

> Every year it's harder and harder to speak about Tsereteli. He's become not a sculptor but rather some kind of natural phenomenon, as if it were raining for a month and you criticize the weather, but if the rain continues for an entire year, you consider it just to be the climate. You can call it Stockholm syndrome, and we are in the state of a hostage who starts to like his captor.
>
> (Glasser 2004)

However immodest, some of Tsereteli's boasts are, in fact, valid. As his defenders and even detractors acknowledge, he abounds in irrepressible energy and generates an endless stream of ideas for new projects. Moreover, he can manipulate any material, from bronze to enamel and stained glass, possesses technical expertise in all conceivable genres, and finishes all his commissions by the stipulated deadlines

– an indisputable sign of professionalism. In popular parlance, like his patron Luzhkov, he "gets things done." According to reports, he also extends encouragement and generosity to younger artists,[41] whose works he exhibits in the Tsereteli Art Gallery. Furthermore, as anyone who spends time in the gallery cannot fail to notice, his own smaller-scale paintings and intricate mosaics are fine examples of the Georgian tradition in art, some recalling the primitivism of Niko Pirosmani (1862–1918) and, to an extent, the decorative collage and assemblage techniques of the Armenian Sergei Paradzhanov (1924–90) – a long-time resident of Tbilisi more renowned as a film director. Yet almost all commentators tend to overlook these genres within Tsereteli's oeuvre, instead lambasting or justifying his mega-monuments. Why? A glance at his most controversial works in Moscow suggests several related reasons, which likewise illuminate the animus against Tsereteli that inflects his celebrity status with notoriety.

Ubiquitous gigantism and faux eclecticism

Disparagement of Tsereteli's major statues in Moscow and elsewhere iterates the same set of epithets: "ugly," "pompous," "monstrous," "kitschy," and "flamboyant." Whether a work of art is judged ugly depends, of course, on a viewer's aesthetic criteria, and, as Revzin has been careful to acknowledge, subjectivity unavoidably suffuses such value judgments (Glasser 2004). Yet it is perhaps all too easy to understand what prompts not only Russian but also Anglophone critics' accusations of pomposity and kitschiness – not Barcelona's Gaudí, but Moscow's gaudy. The common denominators of Tsereteli's structures are, first, their monumental syncretism – one is tempted to say *bricolage* – whereby proportion alone facilitates the automatic solemnization of derivative eclecticism, and, second, their prestigious, politico-historically saturated locations, which guarantee maximal visibility: the Moscow Zoo, the Manezh Plaza,[42] Poklonnaia gora/Victory Park, the Moscow River, and the space of the vast Church of Christ the Savior, rebuilt for a reported $250 million (Grant 2001: 342) amid melodramatic conflict and unremitting media coverage. Quite simply, in downtown Moscow one cannot avoid being "tseretelied." Exposure to his obtrusive creations is involuntary and unavoidable, for they are inseparable from the urban environment that they dominate and sometimes eclipse.

For anyone with an awareness of history, monumentalism and the exploitation of the symbolic vertical – associated above all with the famous "vysotki" [high-rises] and architectural grandiosity that reified totalitarian aspirations under Stalin – evoke the spirit of imperial power. Gargantuan in both dimensions and pretensions, Tsereteli's monuments are aggressive, calculated to rivet the eye and stop traffic. One of the many satirical jabs aimed especially at the bronze Peter looming over the small, artificial island in the Moscow River targets the incapacitating shock of drivers encountering such a titanic composition,

> [...] it's said that traffic accidents on the Crimean Bridge have become more frequent. Upon seeing from the bridge the somber giant that's as tall as the

church [of Christ the Savior], drivers lose the power of speech and control of their cars. The question on the tip of everyone's tongue is: how did Mayor Luzhkov permit the erection across from his favorite offspring of this massive hulk, whose volume kills one's view of the church? The unanimous opinion is that the mayor's drivers simply don't take the Crimean Bridge – so that he won't have a heart attack....

(Kolodnyi 2002: 240)

Tsereteli's penchant for excess – a major hallmark of his monuments – results not only in gargantuanism but also in incoherence, or, to borrow a term formalized by studies of postmodernist style and invoked by his critics, kitsch.[43] For instance, the 300-foot sculpture of Peter the Great disrupting Moscow's "lovely, low-slung cityscape" (Gambrell 1997) showcases Peter in his historically attested role of sea-faring tsar steering the ship of acceleratedly expanding state (Figure 10.5). It recalls Stalinist iconography of the Nation's Father at the Helm, as in Boris Efimov's famous poster *Kapitan strany Sovetov vedet nas ot pobedy k pobede* [The Captain of the Land of the Soviets Leads us from Victory to Victory] (1933). Just as the tiller in the Christopher Columbus sculpture provoked ridicule as an anachronism, so here does Peter's puzzling garb – that of a Roman legionnaire. Does the monu-ment evoke both Stalin and Rome so as to emphasize the concept of state power – symbolic capital as reification of political absolutism? Given Tsereteli's passion for indiscriminate inclusion, he possibly also wished to exploit other traditional associations by reworking Palekh renditions of Sadko, the folkloric Novgorod merchant, or the prize-winning celluloid version of *Sadko* by Aleksandr Ptushko (1952),[44] or even illustrations of Robert Louis Stevenson's *Treasure Island* and the adventurous search for gold – a quest inseparable from Russia's risky eco-nomic ventures of the 1990s, thus *à propos* for Russia's post-Soviet identity.[45] Whatever the intention, the mixture of naturalistic and symbolic representation makes for disjointedness, exacerbated by distracting and puzzling elements, such as the superfluous scroll brandished in Peter's raised right hand (a rolled-up map? an edict? a laundry bill?).[46]

Not only the scale of the "overbearing construction [...], likened to a big toy soldier stuck atop a bunch of broken model ships" (Gambrell 1997) and chris-tened "Moscow's Godzilla" (*Rigas Laiks* 2006), but also the inexplicability of its installation in a city loathed by St. Petersburg's founder propelled Muscovites to agitate for its removal. Tsereteli's stranglehold on contracts for prestigious offi-cial "artworks"[47] throughout the capital led artists to sign a petition and *Itogi* to publish an article expressing consternation at the lack of transparency in the use of municipal funds. After all, the $17 million estimated as the monument's cost could have rescued many of Moscow's disenfranchised and poor from the parlous conditions in which they were subsisting during the 1990s. In response, Moscow – a channel owned and controlled by the city – quickly arranged interviews with Tsereteli, during which he asserted that the anti-monument campaign was a plot against him (Gambrell 1997).[48] Subsequent action, spearheaded by the gallery owner Marat Guelman, who called for a public referendum to decide Peter's future,

Figure 10.5 Tsereteli's contentious monument of Peter the Great on the spit of the Bolotnaia and Iakimansaia embankments in the center of Moscow (May 1997), with the Cathedral of Christ the Savior, likewise his contribution to the cityscape, in the background; 2007. Photo by Valerii Shustov, courtesy of RIA Novosti.

lost momentum after Luzhkov cannily negotiated with Guelman to settle the issue via a committee, reportedly handpicked by the mayor. The predictable outcome was a vote in favor of keeping the statue in place, especially since a poll of citizens' opinions showed only 14 percent of Muscovites in favor of dismantling the work. Foreseeably, the protracted disputes, the poll, and the artist's appearances on television only further consolidated Tsereteli's image as a celebrity whose every work arouses passions and merits public discussion. Ultimately, his televised self-justification served as an advertisement, not unlike the avidly watched confessions of wrongdoing by "personalities" on American talk shows. And in 2006 Tsereteli's immoderately sized statue of Peter the Great was mounted in front of St. Petersburg's elite hotel, the Pribaltiiskaia.

Civic (though not always civil) protest, accompanied by media fanfare, proved marginally more effective in the case of Park Pobedy (1995), the vast complex dedicated to World War II. First conceived in 1957, it was completed under Luzhkov's personal oversight almost forty years later.[49] Sited, with political resonance, close

Figure 10.6 Another big Peter during installation in front of the Pribaltiiskaia Hotel on Vasil'evskii Island in the city he founded; 19 September 2006. Photo by Aleksei Danichev, courtesy of RIA Novosti.

to the Triumphal Arch symbolizing Russian victory over Napolean (Forest and Johnson 2001), the Park encompasses a museum refurbished by Tsereteli (1993), in addition to three major structures he designed and executed: the Orthodox Cathedral of St. George (1995); a dizzyingly tall obelisk, for which Luzhkov drew the original sketch,[50] with a sculpture of St. George at its base; and a composition in bronze titled *Tragedy of Nations* (1996), all conceived within radically different aesthetic systems. As the centerpiece, the statue of St. George, which essentially replicates the earlier *Good Defeats Evil* (1990) at the New York UN Headquarters, recasts the popular image depicted in medieval Byzantine and Russian icons of St. George killing a dragon, allegorizing the victory of Orthodoxy over heathenism.[51] Once again, public dismay at the monument was voiced in far from flattering terms: one detractor lamented Tsereteli's ignorance of the historical provenance of the image he had imitated; others compared the vanquished dragon to cheap deli-style sausage (Kolodnyi 2002: 269, 243), "The dragon defeated by St. George is like chopped-up Doctor-brand *kolbasa*, with a swastika and Masonic signs drawn all over it" (Kolodnyi 2002: 212). One humorist fancifully likened the obelisk to a gas pipe (Kolodnyi 2002: 213).

Derogatory remarks of a kindred sort greeted the ensemble *Tragedy of Nations*, executed in a markedly contrasting style from the other Park components. At odds with the presiding theme of victory, this grim reminder of war and suffering – *memento mori* writ large (Tsereteli-large) – comprises emaciated, naked bronze figures with stricken faces grouped together as if lined up for the gas chamber, victims helplessly succumbing to their doom. Many took exception to the gloominess of the work, some to its "ugliness." General Aleksandr Lebed', then aspiring to the presidency and therefore unburdened by objectivity regarding any of Luzhkov's projects, stated, "Since Tsereteli sculpted [these] monstrosities, prices for apartments in this region have fallen twofold. You get up in the morning, look out of the window, and your mood for the whole day is ruined" (Kolodnyi 2002: 222). A less primitive remonstrance raised the perennial question of "Why Tsereteli?", "It's a strange sculpture, gloomy, and, what's most important, not contemporary. There are a lot of artists in Moscow. And there are talented ones. This isn't envy, but I don't understand why this particular person has made a second monument of this sort. Why is he, rather than someone else, defining the look of our city[?]" (Kolodnyi 2002: 222). Others cast their objections in a more sardonic mode, "*Tragedy of Nations*," according to one newspaper, "has become the tragedy of Moscow" (Kolodnyi 2002: 269). In response to the public outcry, this part of Tsereteli's design finally was transferred, at prohibitive cost, from the central space of the complex to a location by the park-promenade behind the museum.[52]

Somewhat unexpectedly, reservations and disdain did not focus explicitly on the kitschiness, fast becoming Tsereteli's trademark and instanced here in "cute bunnies" – presumably, as a metonymy for executed children – scattered at the feet of the condemned in his otherwise chilling *Tragedy of Nations*. The incongruity is not unlike Beatrice Potter's suddenly popping up in Auschwitz. *Bricolage* likewise characterizes the obelisk. Topped by Nike (the Greek goddess of victory) proffering laurels, and two plump cherubs blowing trumpets, with St. George at its base, the obelisk is imprinted top to bottom with abstract designs as well as the names of Soviet cities and naturalistically rendered miniature scenes of battle that could have come straight from World War II posters. The disconcerting impression is of haphazardly assembled bits and pieces in conflicting styles that disperse the viewer's focus.

Like his other creations, the obelisk and *Tragedy of Nations* left few doubts that, in his omnivorousness, Tsereteli recognizes no aesthetic limitations. Like the New Russian festooned in gold chains and clashing colors, Tsereteli valorizes plenitude and magnitude. Since for him "most is more," minimalists or proponents of a less inclusive aesthetic perceive him as the exemplification of sheer bad taste. Yet ultimately, the issue may be one of sophistication and class. Specialists trained in art, as well as a minority of "discriminating" viewers, respond less benignly to Tsereteli's works than the "average man or woman on the street" for whom aesthetic considerations may be secondary. When all is said and done, Russian families enjoy outings to Victory Park, where they can recall the momentous defeat of the Axis forces, stroll around the grounds, and gaze at works created by someone constantly featured on television and in the press. Moreover, the historical and psychological importance of World War II for Russians predisposes them to revere Victory Park as an affirmative symbol of their nation's extraordinary capacity to triumph over adversity.[53] Outsized dimensions in tandem with traditional and familiar elements stimulate both pride and reassurance in a population eager to forget the ignominious chaos and deprivations of the 1990s. The optimistic affirmation and size-as-power institutionalized in socialist realism inform Tsereteli's oeuvre and likely comfort those who yearn for the familiar visual markers of Soviet empire. His aesthetic of vertically oriented monumentalism extends the exhibitionism of the 850th anniversary of Moscow (1997) masterminded by Luzhkov, as befits the sweeping claims and procedures of imperial power – a self-image shared by Moscow's glitterati.

Moscow's glamorous elite

An official member of the Academy of the World Elite, Tsereteli also belongs to Moscow's unofficial elite – an "in" circle of artists and entertainers known for their wealth, cornucopia of awards, and intimate connections with the Kremlin or the mayor's office. Tsereteli's desire to ingratiate himself with Putin and his government may be deduced from his instant response to Putin's declaration of the year 2008 as The Year of the Family. In record time he created *Zheny dekabristov. Vrata sud'by* [The Decembrists' Wives. The Gates of Fate], now housed in the Tsereteli Art Gallery (Figure 10.7). As Irina Kulik remarked in a review, "It's as if Zurab Tsereteli with almost parodic, naïve diligence tried to respond to all the demands of the time – to address the family and Russian history" (Kulik 2008).[54] Here, too, Tsereteli made inexplicable choices, for the Decembrist wives, as Kulik notes, are elaborately coiffed and wear décolleté dresses (Kulik 2008), though in execution and stance they recall the victims in Tsereteli's *Tragedy of Nations*. True to his policy of endorsing Russian culture, Putin generally attends installations of Tsereteli's monuments, thereby guaranteeing substantial media coverage and authenticating Tsereteli's status as one of Moscow's elite.

Reports via TV, magazines, and newspapers of this *privilegentsiia*'s presence in the most expensive restaurants, at film premieres, concerts for the select "by invitation only," prestigious receptions, and kindred photo-op events provide an opportunity to show off chauffeured luxury cars, invaluable jewelry, and designer formal wear, as well as to delectate the celebrity-seeking public. These are the pseudo-events, Daniel Boorstin declares, that constitute celebrity culture, with the celebrity as "the human pseudo-event" "known for his well-knownness" (1992: 57). The older generation of this cohort, mainly but not solely the *shestidesiatniki* who established careers during the Soviet era, includes *estrada* (varieté) performer Alla Pugacheva (b. 1949), actress/singer Liudmila Gurchenko (b. 1935), film directors Nikita Mikhalkov (b. 1945) and El'dar Riazanov (b. 1927), poet Andrei Voznesenky (1933–2010), fashion designer Slava Zaitsev (b. 1938), crooner Iosif Kobzon (b. 1937), and painters Aleksandr Shilov (b. 1943) and Il'ia Glazunov (b. 1930). In the elite rating annually reported by *Kommersant*, based on 1,600 Russians' votes, most of the above made the top hundred in 2007: Pugacheva once again came in second (following Putin), Gurchenko seventy-ninth,

Figure 10.7 Group composition in bronze of the Decembrist wives and a child at the prison gates, carrying an icon and verses by Pushkin dedicated to the Decembrists, Moscow; 17 March 2008. Photo by Mikhail Fomichev, courtesy of RIA Novosti.

Mikhalkov (rank unspecified), Riazanov tenth, Kobzon eighth, with Glazunov trailing in one hundred and fourth position. Moreover, Pugacheva was voted best female singer, Luzhkov best mayor, Kobzon best male singer, Mikhalkov best film director, and Zaitsev best fashion designer. With an ironic reference to Tsereteli as master of the epistolary genre, *Kommersant* noted his absence from the list (Alekseev 2007), thereby implying that his exclusion confounded expectations. The very assemblage of such a list, of course, is a hardy convention of celebrity culture.

Personal alliances within this echelon have fostered professional advancement and its concomitant perks. For instance, Shilov and Glazunov, who, like Tsereteli, paint(ed) portraits of foreign dignitaries, presidents, and monarchs, have benefited from Tsereteli's endorsement. In his capacity as President of the Academy of the Arts, he could simply ensure their membership. Tellingly, Tsereteli attends his friend Kobzon's concerts with his friend Luzhkov (Kolodnyi 2002: 374), and has "immortalized" the latter in two sculptures, both prominently displayed in the Tsereteli Art Gallery: one strikingly captures the mayor playing tennis (Figure 10.8), the other symbolically depicts him as a *Dvornik* (Groundskeeper), sporting a "proletarian" cap à la Lenin, broom in hand, "cleaning up" the city – an image that paradoxically forges links with the Soviet poster of Lenin sweeping the newly formed USSR free of bourgeois elements (Figure 10.9). The publications prominently displayed in Luzhkov's large pocket – the newspaper *Moskovskie Vedomosti* [Moscow News], established in 1756, and *Putevoditel' po Moskve* [Guide to Moscow] – certify his status as Moscow's overseer. They evoke, respectively, the city's purported historical continuity over centuries and Luzhkov's codification of a visually transformed, New Moscow. Somewhat less flattering but similarly larger-than-life statues of Kobzon, Riazanov, and Voznesensky – as well as a bronze Putin in judo garb – may be found at the Tsereteli Art Gallery.

It is no coincidence that representatives of this coterie figure in Ekaterina Rozhdestvenskaia's celebrity-driven photography project, *Chastnaia kollektsiia* [Private Collection], first exhibited in 2002 at the House of Photography and more recently at the Manezh (July–August 2008). Riding the 2000s wave of nostalgia, Rozhdestvenskaia began photographing current celebrities mimicking the appearance and posture of individuals in classic portraits, with all details of costume, setting, etc. meticulously replicated.[55] Among the essential effects anticipated by Rozhdestvenskaia was viewers' pleasure at a double recognition – not only of the original "old masterpieces" (reproduced and identified below the larger new versions), but also of the contemporary celebrities assuming the subjects' roles and stances. Obviously, average unknowns posing as the personae of universally

Figure 10.8 Statue of an idealized Mayor Luzhkov, the ardent tennis player, located in the Zurab Tsereteli Art Gallery, Moscow. Photo by Shakko, courtesy of Creative Commons.

Figure 10.9 Luzhkov doubling as cicerone and groundskeeper [dvornik] on his "estate" – the city of Moscow; 2000. Photo by Andrei Sdobnikov, courtesy of Creative Commons.

acclaimed portraits would not stimulate the curiosity and "delight in detection" occasioned by the partially defamiliarized but familiar faces of celebrities. The impact of the photographs hinges on the comparison of the paired visages, "now" and "then," "represented" and "re-represented" – the lynchpin of the project. Among the most convincing recreations in Rozhdestvenskaia's series are Kobzon as Aleksandr Golovin's *Ispanets* [Spaniard] (1910s), Riazanov as Sergei Ivanov's *Benois* (1944), and above all Gurchenko as Gustav Klimt's *Judith II* (1909) and Pablo Picasso's *Absinthe Drinker* (1901–4), Luzhkov as *Lomonosov*, and Tsereteli as the pope in Raphael's *Pope Leo X with the Cardinals Giulio de' Medici and Luigi de' Rossi* (1517–19). Comments by the milling crowds at the exhibit in August 2008 confirmed the enormous satisfaction afforded by double recognition – of celebrities incarnating celebrated art works.[56] Luzhkov as Lomonosov attracted special attention, more than the nude Lada Dens as Edouard Manet's *Olympia* (1863) and the unclothed Irina Alferova as John Collier's *Circe* (1885).

Loyalists whose values reflect or serve the state, members of the aging contingent of the art-and-entertainment elite adhere to national traditions in their professional spheres, eschewing genuinely modernist aesthetics and reaping the rewards of having parlayed their Soviet popularity into a post-Soviet establishment-clique. Thoroughly Soviet, they nonetheless share with countless government functionaries a yearning to resuscitate aspects of the aristocratic past, including what one journalist ironically dubbed the imperial "power vertical" manifested in the reintroduction of a Table of Ranks to formalize a hierarchy not only within the administrative bureaucracy, but also within other professional areas (Zubchenko 2008). These ranks and the concomitant monetary perquisites co-exist with the Soviet-era honorary titles of People's Artist, Honored Artist, etc., and under tsardom mandated a strictly observed form of address. Hence the monarchist Mikhalkov's anachronistic, pretentious use of "Vashe Vysokoprevoskhoditel'stvo" (Your Supreme Excellency) at a Kremlin reception in 2000 when speaking to Putin after the latter's victory in the presidential election (Zubchenko 2008).[57] Titles vouchsafe entitlement, and as the most "(en)titled artist" in Russia, Kobzon, with 294 awards and titles, has entered the Guinness Book of Records (Zubchenko 2008). This group is the moneyed, privileged circle in which Tsereteli moves.

If an eloquent measure of celebrity status, apart from power, influence, and the ceaseless circulation of the public persona's name in the media, is a range of cultural genres devoted to that persona's instantly recognizable image, Tsereteli indisputably qualifies as a super-celebrity, having inspired a series of *anekdoty* (jokes) and a satirical short story by a best-selling author. In singling out the artist's oblivious passion for Luzhkov-approved gigantism, the aggressive imperialism of the sculptor's modus operandi, and the public's hostility to his works, the *anekdoty* reproduce almost verbatim the sardonic barbs of Tsereteli's sharpest critics in the media:

Tsereteli comes to Luzhkov and says:
"Iur Mikhailych, give me the Tsar Bell"
Luzhkov: "Whad'ya want it for?"
"I'm making a small sculpture here. It's called *Troika*. And I'm one bell short."

Zurab Tsereteli asks Yuri Luzhkov:
"Yuri Mikhailovich, did you like *Brother-2*?"
"Yeah."
"And *Aliens-2*?"
"Yeah, not bad."
"And *Omen-2*?"
"Also good."
"That means we can consider *Peter-2* a done deal?"

An eye for an eye, a tooth for a tooth: the descendants of Peter I have erected a monument to Zurab Tsereteli.

Pskova: "Tell me, does this road lead to the church?"

"No, all roads lead to Tsereteli."
[referencing the closing scene of Tengiz Abuladze's glasnost film *Pokaianie* {Repentance} {1984, released 1986}, about the horrors of Stalinist repressions]

A monumental statue by Zurab Tsereteli will be erected on the site where the World Trade Center buildings were demolished. In the New York mayor's opinion, "It's the only thing capable of frightening off Arab air terrorists from new attacks."

("Anekdoty ...": 2008)

Were Mr. X substituted for Tsereteli's name in these quips and mini-dialogues, no Russian would puzzle over the identity of the sculptor. And a quirky story by Boris Akunin bearing no resemblance whatever to the Fandorin mysteries that catapulted him to fame (analyzed in Chapter 3) similarly assumes readers' intimate familiarity with Tsereteli's persona and oeuvre – his celebrity status – on which the effect of the narrative pivots.

Akunin's whimsical miniature volume *Skazki dlia Idiotov* [Fairy Tales for Idiots] (2000) contains the nine-page illustrated "Tefal', ty dumaesh' o nas" [Tefal', You Think of Us], an allegorical *conte à clef* masquerading as science fiction, with Tsereteli as protagonist. The story opens with a meeting between the general-governor of Moscow (whose "Eto ty chë?" "sliapat'," and so forth evoke Luzhkov's crude prole-speech) and its main sculptor [glavnyi stolichnyi vaiatel'] (Akunin 2000: 31). The latter is an extraterrestrial from Vufer (Woofer!) called Iagkfi Eyukueudsh / Ягкфи еыукуеудш – a name whose Cyrillic characters correspond to "Zurab Tsereteli" typed out on the Latin QWERTY keyboard. By command of the Interstellar Committee, the alien has pursued the secret mission of installing special structures in Moscow that will facilitate an invasion by his own kind but that he "hypnotizes" the ignorant general-governor into accepting as life-affirming works of art. Saved by his bodyguards from an attack by a knife-wielding assassin who accuses him of hating Moscow (a charge often leveled ironically at Tsereteli), Iagkfi retires to his temporary residence, where he removes his human mask and contemplates both his own greatness and the impending Apocalypse, from which the population will be rescued by transportation to the planet Vufer.

Akunin's simple device for revealing Iagkfi as Tsereteli is to ascribe the latter's work to the former: the Triumphal Arch commemorating the 55th anniversary of The Great Victory (Poklonnaia gora), "gigantskaia belaia zagogulina, i sverkhu – urod-Osvoboditel' tychushchii v nebo falloobraznym avtomatom PPSh" [a giant white curlicue, and on top the freak-Liberator thrusting into the sky like a phallus-shaped World War II submachine gun {PPSh}] (2000: 32) (Park Pobedy); "pamiatnik Ottsu Russkogo Flota" [monument of the Father of the Russian Navy] (2000: 32) (the monument of Peter the Great); "on ponastavil na Moskve nemalo otvratitel'nykh chudishch. Snachala – bronzovyi bestiarii u sviashchennoi krem-levskoi steny" [he installed quite a few repulsive monsters all over Moscow. First was the bronze bestiary at the sacred Kremlin wall] (the Manezh Plaza);

"narezannogo lomtikami, da eshche i pronzennogo rogatinoi zmeenysha na Napoleonskoi gore" [the huge dragon on Napoleon Hill, cut into slices and if that weren't enough, pierced by a javelin] (St. George at Park Pobedy); "koshmarn[yi] istukan nad s"ezhivsheisia Moskvoi-rekoi" [the nightmarish idol above the braced Moscow River] (2000: 35) (Peter the Great), etc. President of the Academy of Fine Arts, Iagkfi is hated by Muscovites (2000: 34), who "know not what they do" ("Ne vedaiut, chto tvoriat" 2000: 34) in loathing him and trying to dynamite the statue of Peter the Great (Akunin 2000: 35). These far from subtle echoes of persistent Tsereteli-bashing, his defensive rebuttals, and the caricature of his condescend-ing self-satisfaction ally the story and, presumably, Akunin's attitude with the intelligentsia's outspoken aversion to Tsereteli's aesthetic and its reified forms.[58] Mildly amusing in its presiding conceit of an alien "secret agent" – alluding to the immeasurable distance separating Tsereteli as celebrity from average Muscovites and possibly his fans – the story testifies to Tsereteli's standing in a city not overly given to inscribing its artists in prose fiction.[59] Clearly, he is a case apart. And in lambasting his celebrity status and especially the means whereby he gained such prominence, the *anekdoty* and the Akunin text parallel internet users' exposure of "the artificiality of celebrity culture" (discussed in Chapter 7). Indeed, one could argue that the virtual "synthetic creatures" produced by skeptical internet patrons bear a resemblance to Tsereteli's syncretic monuments.

Whatever reaction his mammoths elicit, they indubitably contribute to Tsereteli's extraordinary celebrity status, which results not only from the omnipresent and obtrusive visibility of his controversial structures, his remunerative friendship with Luzhkov, and his personal wealth, but also from his comprehensive voracity, which declares itself in multiple ways: he is a sculptor, painter, architect, graphic illustrator, ambassador, academician, and museum owner, who, moreover, works with every conceivable material; he has outfitted embassies, engineered Olympic Games, contributed the metal work for and overseen the design of Moscow's most publicized church, etc., etc. Convinced that most is more, though never enough, Tsereteli wishes to do and be everything for everyone, to leave his ineradicable mark on the metropolis administered by his convenient ally Luzhkov, who himself nurtures identical aspirations to immortality, as evidenced above all in his decision to build sixty American-style skyscrapers in Moscow that will exceed the Stalinist Seven Sisters in height.[60] For both, scale is all.

Whether Tsereteli's admirers number in the hundreds or the thousands hardly matters, for his most significant achievement is not popularity, but the attainment of notoriety-inflected celebrity status on an international scale. Loathed or loved, he cannot be ignored, avoided, or overlooked. In 1999 a journalist in *Izvestiia* averred, "[I]f you ask any chance passerby which artist he knows, then hereafter he'll name Zurab Tsereteli. If this isn't recognition, then at least it's nationwide fame" (Kolodnyi 2002: 270). During the intervening years that fame (or notori-ety) has metastasized into an international reputation that keeps Tsereteli's name constantly in the limelight, along with those of Hollywood stars, sports idols, and Harry Potter. Tellingly, the first exhibit at the Tretyakov Gallery under the auspices of its new director, Irina Lebedeva, which ran from 27 May to 26 July 2009, was

Zurab Tsereteli: 100 Works from Paris. Marat Guelman, the owner of a subversive Moscow gallery that features postmodernist works, interpreted the choice as "a bad sign" (IZO 2009). Guelman's view, however, hardly coincides with that of the average Russian. As the indefatigable architect of symbolic capital in Russia's capital, Tsereteli will thrive and remain a celebrity as long as the New Moscow remains indentured to cynosural novelty in a faux-traditional vein.

Notes

1 My gratitude to Serguei Oushakine for dozens of useful items and exchanges over the years; to Susan Corbesero for acquainting me with Bruce Grant's article on Zurab Tsereteli and for sharing my first, breathlessly speedy visit in August 2003 to the Tsereteli Art Gallery (Galereia iskusstv Zuraba Tsereteli) at Prechistenka 19, Moscow; and to sundry friends in Moscow who shared with me their views on Tsereteli and his monuments in the capital.

2 "What's big is visible from a distance" (Esenin); "I fear the Greeks, especially when they bring gifts" (Virgil); "Fame and tranquility cannot be bedfellows" (Montaigne).

3 Celebrity, of course, existed earlier, but Rojek has in mind the magnified scale of the phenomenon made possible by contemporary technology.

4 For one of the latest reports on censorship of television programming that potentially allows for criticism of Putin, see Clifford J. Levy, "It Isn't Magic: Putin Opponents Vanish from TV," *New York Times* (June 3, 2008). Available online at: www.nytimes. com/2008/06/03/world/europe/03russia.html (accessed 11 July 2008). See also the closure of the American publication *The Exile* (June 2008), the Russian newspapers *Moskovskii Korrespondent* (April 2008) and *Segodnia* (Spring 2001), the takeover of the independent NTV by Gazprom (2001), the liquidation of TV6 (2002), all intended to silence any opposition or unflattering items about Putin.

5 For the role of notoriety – or, as he puts it, transgression – in celebrity culture, see Rojek (2001: 148–80).

6 Grigorii Revzin, a leading architectural critic who writes for the newspaper *Kommersant*, has observed, "It's an amazing phenomenon that the only internationally well-known artist we have is Tsereteli" (Glasser 2004).

7 For a discussion of the New Russians, see *The New Russians* in *Russian Review* 62, no. 1 (Jan 2003): 1–90.

8 Born 4 January 1934, in 1958 Tsereteli graduated from the Academy of Arts in Tbilisi. For information about his early years, see Kolodnyi (2002).

9 In 1957 Tsereteli married Inessa Andronikashvili, allegedly a Georgian princess who could trace her roots to ancient royalty.

10 *Dekorativnoe iskusstvo* (2002) contains a chronological list of Tsereteli's accomplishments, encompassing his fulfilled commissions, prizes, and so forth.

11 In 1994 his *Birth of the New Man* appeared in Paris, soon followed by another version of the construction in Seville (1995).

12 For a fuller list of Tsereteli's professional "assignments," see *Dekorativnoe iskusstvo* (2002), Grant (2001: 340), Kolodnyi (2002), *passim*.

13 Tsereteli's museum houses these and numerous other portraits, as well as monuments of Princess Diana and other Big Names, plus intricate works in enamel. The bright, spacious, enclosed courtyard contains Tsereteli's utopian "religious" and "philosophical" installations, in which the apple and the egg figure centrally as symbols of birth, fall, and resurrection.

14 "Chuzhoi uspekh u nas voobshche neterpim. A vo Frantsii pochemu-to vyzyvaet simpatiiu i interes" ("Konets ..." 2002: 17).

15 Blog punctuation adjusted to conform to grammatical correctness. Online. Available

online at: http://wirednewyork.com/forum/showthread.php?t=4349&page=2 (accessed 3 October 2007).

16 A Russian blogger on LiveJournal, using the nick name *larinax*, called the tear "soplia" [snot] (Khokhlova 2006).

17 Translated into several foreign languages, the volume is prominently displayed in the shop at the Tsereteli Art Gallery.

18 "Chem bol'she fabrikovalos' mifov o Petre, tem sil'nee vnimanie naroda privlekalos' k imeni avtora."

19 Tsereteli, in fact, does pay attention to detail in the sense that he "decorates" his works with small-scale flourishes, but insofar as these are invisible from a distance, they tend to go unnoticed, especially in grandiose monuments intended to be see from afar. In August 2008, a TV news show titled *Nash gorod* [Our town] carried Muscovites' protest against the destruction of the city's architectural treasures and the proliferation of what one individual called "awful imitations" [strashnye podrazheniia].

20 Gareth Jones accurately characterized the dome-headed mayor as "an intriguing blend of old-style Soviet apparatchik and entrepreneurial New Russian" (1997). In addition to maintaining a dictatorial control over the city's finances, politics, and business interests, Luzhkov also exerted power over the media (running his own television channel) and enjoyed the distinction of having a "macho" male cologne, "Mer" [Mayor], named after him (see Lowe [1999]). The image of the mafia boss Denisov in several of Aleksandra Marinina's murder mysteries bears an uncanny resemblance to Luzhkov: above all, both "protect" and rule an entire city.

21 Psychologists, doubtless, would have some fascinating explanation for the widespread focus on specifically the bathroom as the New Russians' "jewel in the crown." Intriguingly, Michael Specter (or his photographer, Lisa Sarfati), seems to have imitated or collaborated in this curious tendency when he interviewed the spectacularly successful real-estate developer Chalva Tchigirinsky, who rented a Moscow apartment for $10,000 per month (Specter 1997: 51).

22 Almost a third of the funds, Luzhkov claimed, came from private sponsorship (Jones 1997) – chiefly banks, businesses, and Western aid organizations (Gordon 1997). The approximate sum underwriting the gala has been variously hypothesized as $30 million to more than $60 million. According to one Western journalist, the city's Hydro-Meteorological Service spent $500,000 to operate six cloud-dispersing airplanes and helicopters in a technique of controlling nature inherited from the Soviet era ("it shan't rain on our parade"). A parallel attempt to curb a different form of nature entailed the relocation of the city's prostitutes for the duration of the festivities (Gordon 1997).

23 The statue, by the sculptor Mikhail Posokhin, measuring approximately 3.7 meters and costing $1.4 million, was erected outside Moscow's Lenin Library, as a companion piece to the one unveiled in St. Petersburg earlier that year.

24 For a list of the events associated with the festivities, which were implemented as early as 25 December 1996 (see "Calendar of Events for Moscow," in the *Official Site of the Russian National Tourist Office*. Available online at: www.geographia.com/russia/moscow_850.htm [accessed 13 December 1997]).

25 Durden-Smith accurately noted Luzhkov's ubiquitous presence throughout the city, concretized in the reconstructed Cathedral of Christ the Savior ($176 million), the renovated stadium at Luzhniki, and the World War II memorial park on Kutuzovsky Prospect, boasting a huge obelisk topped by a five-ton Goddess of Victory. Massive construction and renovation throughout Moscow altered the most trafficked parts of the city, especially the area around Red Plaza and along Tverskaia Street. Vanden Heuvel justly argued that the city's facelift "has less to do with municipal services [...] than the national political ambitions" of the mayor (vanden Heuvel and Cohen 1997). For a brief but eloquent glance at Luzhkov's prerogatives and achievements, see Durden-Smith (1997). For ironic, useful coverage of the 850th anniversary festivities, see Jones

(1997), Koshkareva (1997), Martin (1997b).

26 See Gordon (1997), Lowe (1997), Taibbi (1997), vanden Heuvel and Cohen (1997), Williams (1997). It is difficult to imagine how medical personnel, miners, teachers, and other professionals in the provinces who had not received wages for months could identify with this supremely Muscovite brand of civic and national fervor. In general, Luzhkov persistently confuses his fiefdom, Moscow, with the entire country. In an interview he asserted, "If we omitted this event [the 850th anniversary], it would be a loss for all of Russia. By celebrating the birthday of the capital, Russia is saying that we're sure that we're building a better life" (*Nezavisimaia Gazeta* 2 September 1997).

27 For Luzhkov's self-contradictory and bragging viewpoint on the event, see the interview in *Trud* (5 September 1997). For a trenchant analysis of Luzhkov's control over Moscow and the city's unique status, see Fossato (1997).

28 Several Russian and especially Western commentators wondered whether some of the funds might have been more sensibly (but less flamboyantly) invested in paying off wage arrears, funding education, medicine, and science, and salvaging the city's transportation system. Work on extending one of Moscow's metro branches was halted "for lack of funds" in late summer of 1997; the number of trams operating in the city had diminished by approximately 35 percent since the 1980s, and half of those remaining showed signs of obsolescence; the city's trolleys were not expected to last much longer (see *Russian Life*, Oct 1997: 4).

29 His plan to run in the 2000 presidential election as the head of his party, *Otechestvo* [Fatherland], was thwarted by strong public support for Putin as Yeltsin's appointment. Ever a pragmatist, Luzhkov joined forces with United Russia and favored Putin as the presidential candidate.

30 Initially appointed as a replacement for Gavril Popov, who resigned as mayor in 1992, Luzhkov won 95 percent of the vote in 1996, approximately 70 percent in 1999, and 75 percent in 2003.

31 That budget accounts for 72 percent of the money circulating in Russia, at the disposal of a city with 9 percent of the population (Zhdanowa 2008: 2).

32 For instance, Fossato cited a *New York Times* report that Inteko, a thriving plastic-manufacturing company run by Luzhkov's wife, Elena Baturina, "won a million-dollar contract to manufacture plastic seats for the huge Luzhniki stadium" (1997). Other contracts, involving huge sums, followed.

33 On the failed attempts to curb Luzhkov's mania for razing ancient buildings so as to build maximally profit-yielding banks, elite apartment houses, etc., see Arnold (2007). See also Klimenko (2008: 15–16).

34 As Clifford Levy notes, while officially a municipal functionary, Luzhkov has spent millions of dollars from Moscow's huge budget on building projects abroad. In South Ossetia, the town of Tskhinvali has named a street after him (Levy 2008).

35 As Kolodnyi formulates it in a spirit of approval, "Vlast' goroda nashla pod stat' sebe khudozhnika" / "The city's government found an artist befitting it" (2002: 215). Given the opaqueness of Russia's financial arrangements and its wholesale system of bribery, it is impossible to ascertain whether money exchanged hands at the early stages of that relationship.

36 On the struggle over symbolic capital in the nation's capital, see the Bourdieu-inspired studies by Grant (2001) and by Forest and Johnson (2001).

37 Plans for the playground, which occupy an entire room in the Tsereteli Art Gallery, remain unrealized for lack of adequate funds.

38 For the conceptualization of glamour and kitsch – *poshlost'* – see the Introduction to this volume.

39 Tsereteli's grandson is the executive director of the Moscow Museum of Modern Art, an appointment indicating that the artist shares the mayor's preference for keeping business in the family.

40 In a 2009 interview Tsereteli volunteered the information that sometimes he wonders

250   H. Goscilo

whether he is overly joyful [ne slishkom ia radostnyi], only to conclude that the heart should dictate one's attitude and behavior [Nado {vesti sebia} kak serdtse diktuet] (Nikolaeva 2009).

41 As reported in private conversation by Natal'ia Kamenetskaia, a member of the Moscow artistic community.

42 Though estimates as to cost vary, this 82,000-foot Plaza subterranean business complex just outside Red Plaza exceeded $100 million.

43 Grant refers to the "motley character" of Tsereteli's Park Pobedy ensemble (2001: 341).

44 The seventh most popular film of 1952, Ptushko's *Sadko* won a prize at Venice the following year.

45 The adolescent note sounded here accords with Russia's (admittedly obstacle-studded) maturation into a new identity – that of a modern European nation.

46 Kolodnyi explains the object in both symbolic and realistic terms – as a *plan* [map] guiding Russia through the sea of international relations, i.e., westernization, which literally required travel by sea. Evgenii Lansere's paintings in the early twentieth century celebrated the Petrine spirit of bold venturesomeness, troped as ships, often in the open sea. See Goscilo (2008).

47 The poet Timur Kibirov noted, "To speak about it as about an aesthetic object, in my opinion, is beneath human dignity." The painter Tat'iana Nakarenko stated, "Everything in it is bad," while a sculptor declared, "Not a single artist [in the past] has come close to such vulgar cynicism" (Kolodnyi 2002: 246, 240).

48 Kolodnyi's biography denounces all such efforts as vicious conspiracies against his resentment-free "hero," irrationally paralleling them to the Soviet administration's hounding of such writers as Boris Pasternak. See Kolodnyi (2002), especially the passage, "What were they writing about Tsereteli, when they were persecuting hounding him as they had Rostropovich?" ["A chto pisali o Tsereteli, kogda ego travili, kak Rostropovicha?"] (Kolodnyi 2002: 269).

49 For the history behind Victory Park, see Forest and Johnson (2001: 15–25).

50 Its height of 141.8 meters (approximately 465 feet) represents the 1,418 days of the war, though, of course, the significance is lost on the viewer, who has no means of gauging the height. As with all monuments by Tsereteli, however, the looming monolith may be seen from afar.

51 The heraldic emblem has been not only Moscow's but also Russia's coat of arms since the sixteenth century.

52 For details on the brouhaha leading to this transfer, see Grant (2001) and Kolodnyi (2002).

53 According to a recent survey, 78 percent of Russians consider World War II the most important event in Russian history. See *Russian Life* (Sept/Oct 2008): 8.

54 "To est', vrode by Zurab Tsereteli s pochti parodiinoi naivnoi staratel'nost'iu popytalsia otvetit' na vse trebovaniia vremeni – chtoby bylo pro sem'iu i pro russkuiu istoriiu."

55 Not all of Rozhdestvenskaia's photographs target portraits, for several reproduce paintings, as, for example, Kuz'ma Petrov-Vodkin's *Kupanie krasnogo konia* [Bathing the red horse] (1912), while others engage sculptures, notably Michelangelo's *David*. For an excellent analysis of Rozhdestvenskaia's project in the context of 2000s' nostalgia, see Oushakine (2007).

56 Overheard during the two hours I spent at the exhibit (8 August 2008), where visitors were allowed to photograph the photographs.

57 Mikhalkov, whose romance with tsardom and macho leadership feeds into his films and who parallels Tsereteli in his power within the film industry, his knee-jerk attraction to hyperbole, sentimental rhetoric, and the grand gesture, similarly provokes resentment among his peers and professional critics, as best illustrated by the reception of his embarrassing film *The Barber of Siberia* (1999). See Chapter 5.

58 See comments by artist Tat'iana Narazenko, composer Gennadii Gladkov, and writers Bulat Okudzhava and Timur Kibirov (indignantly cited in Kolodnyi 2002: 246).

Liudmila Ulitskaia expressed similar sentiments in a personal conversation in Moscow, 9 August 2008.

59 The bloody conflict in 2008 between Georgia and Russia over Ossetia provided a new, unsettling context for Tsereteli's status as an alien in Moscow, but had no perceptible effect on his professional life.

60 Addiction to size is not confined to Moscow and Tsereteli, for the 80-year-old Texas sculptor David Adickes produces gigantic concrete statues of historical figures such as Stephen F. Austin and The Beatles that have become tourist attractions in South Dakota, Texas, and Virginia, while St. Louis sculptor Robert Cassilly is known for huge statues of animals. As in the case of Tsereteli, serious art critics lambaste Adickes's efforts, which corroborate his confession, "I'm into overkill." Bigger, he concedes, is not better, but it *is* more visible. Tsereteli could only endorse that insight. See Warren (2006: A1).

Bibliography

Abdullaev, N. (2002) "Notes from Moscow: The Bronze Chekist," *Transitions Online*. Available online at: www.tol.cz (accessed 2 February 2004).

Akunin, B. (2000) *Skazki dlia Idiotov*, Moscow: GIF.

Alekseev, A. (2007) "VIP-parad 2007," *Kommersant* 241, no. 3817, 28 Dec. Available online at: www.kommersant.ru/doc.aspx?DocsID=840552 (accessed 5 May 2008).

"Anekdoty o Zurab Tsereteli" (2008) Available online at: www.peoples.ru/anekdot/6453. shtml (accessed 7 May 2008).

Applebome, P. (2005) "Disputed 9/11 Monument, at Sea for a Bit, Gets a Home Nearby," *New York Times*, 3 March.

Arnold, C. (2007) "Russia: Moscow Mayor's Power on the Wane as He Enters Fifth Term," Radio Free Europe/Radio Liberty, 24 July. Available online at: http://rfe.rferl.org/featuresarticleprint/2007/07/4602e891-a325-4661-9d65-f827d98aaf4f.html (accessed 8 January 2008).

Bennett, V. (1997) "Capitalist Revolution Makes Moscow a Work in Progress," *Los Angeles Times*, 4 Aug. Available online at: http://articles.latimes.com/1997/aug/04/news/mn-19271 (accessed 2 December 1997).

Boorstin, D. (1961; 2nd edn., 1992) *The Image: A Guide to Pseudo-Events in America*, New York: Vintage Books.

Bransten, J. (2004) "Russia: Moscow Is Becoming a Developer's Dream, Historian's Nightmare," Radio Free Europe/Radio Liberty, 25 March. Available online at: www.rferl.org/articleprintview/1052041.html (accessed 18 November 2004).

Cashmore, E. (2006) *Celebrity/Culture*, Abingdon, UK: Routledge.

Cecil, C. (2003) "Moscow Mayor has High Hopes for Third Term," *The Times*, 24 Sept.

Dekorativnoe Iskusstvo (*DI*) (2002) Moscow: Moskovskii muzei sovremennogo iskusstva.

— . (*DI*) (2003) 5–6. Moscow: Moskovskii muzei sovremennogo iskusstva.

— . (*DI*) (2003) 7–8. Moscow: Moskovskii muzei sovremennogo iskusstva.

Dixon, R. (2003) "'Genius of Kitsch' Has His Say on Meaning of 9/11," *Los Angeles Times*, 14 Oct.

Durden-Smith, J. (1997) "Moscow Dynamo," *Electronic Telegraph*, 6 Dec.

Finnegan, W. (2007) "On the Waterfront: Monument," *New Yorker*, 25 June.

FitzGerald, N. (2007) "In Moscow, a Little Museum Thumbs Its Nose at Tradition," *Washington Post*, 10 Oct.

Forest, B. and Johnson, J. (2001) "Unraveling the Threads of History: Soviet-Era Monuments and Post-Soviet National Identity in Moscow," *The Annals of the Association of American*

Geographers. Available online at: www.dartmouth.edu/~crn/crn_papers/Forest-Johnson. pdf (accessed 2 March 2007).

Fossato, F. (1997) "Why Is Moscow the Exception to the Privatization Rule–An Analysis," *RFE/RL*, 12 Sept.

Foucault, M. (1984) *The Foucault Reader*, ed. P. Rabinow, New York: Pantheon Books.

Gambrell, J. (1997) "Moscow's Monumental Woes: Controversy over Peter the Great Sculpture in Moscow, Russia," *Art in America*, July. Available online at: http://find articles.com/p/articles/mi_m1248/is_n7_v85/ai_19628872/print?tag=artBody (accessed 23 July 2002).

"Giant Hare Found in Germany," (2009) *Russia Today*, 18 May. Available online at: www. russiatoday.com/Art_and_Fun/2009-05-18/Giant_hare_found_in_G (Accessed 3 July 2009).

Glasser, S. (2004) "Controversial From Moscow to Hudson: Provocative Sculptor to Unveil 9/11 Work," *Washington Post*, 10 June.

Golomstock, I. (1990) *Totalitarian Art*, trans. R. Chandler, London: Collins Harvill.

Gordon, M. R. (1997) "Journal: Moscow Throws Gala 850th Anniversary Celebration," *New York Times*, 6 Sept.

Goscilo, H. (2008) "Unsaintly St. Petersburg? Visions and Visuals," in H. Goscilo and S. M. Norris (eds) *Preserving Petersburg: History, Memory, Nostalgia*, Bloomington and Indianapolis: Indiana University Press, pp. 57–87.

Grant, B. (2001) "New Moscow Monuments, or, States of Innocence," *American Ethnologist* 28, no. 2: 332–62.

IZO [Blog by Matthew Cullerne Bown] (2009) Available online at: www.izo.com/2009/06/ according-to-marat-guelman-the-first-show-at-the …. (accessed 3 July 2009).

Jones, G. (1997) "Moscow Throws Big 850th Birthday Bash," *Reuter*, 4 Sept.

Khokhlova, V. (2006) "Russia: Tear of Grief," *Global Voices Online*. Available online at: www.globalvoicesonline.org/2006/09/13/russia-tear-of-grief-intr (accessed 29 October 2006).

Klimenko, A. (2008) "'The Battle for Moscow': On the Conservation of Architectural Heritage and the Cityscape," in D. Zhdanowa (ed.) *The New Moscow: Between Neo-Classicism and High Tech*, *Kultura*, 3 July. Available online at: www.kultura-rus.de/ kultura-dokumente/ausgaben/englisch/kultura-3-2008-EN.pdf (accessed 3 July 2008).

Kolodnyi, L. (2002) *Serdtse na palitre. Khudozhnik Zurab Tsereteli*, Moscow: Golos-Press.

Komissarov, D. (2003) "Zurab Tsereteli uvekovechit generala de Gollia" Available online at: www.stog.ru/article.asp?oid=EB41EE60-8AA0-4E11-A62F-01BA595 FCACA&rubric=5FA264B4-06D5-4F0B-B40F-2C8DA313C8DF (accessed 5 January 2004).

"Konets dinozavrov" [Conversation among Pavel Lungin, Aleksandr Timofeevskii, and coordinator Lev Karakhan] (2002) *Iskusstvo Kino*, no. 5: 5–17.

Koshkareva, T. (1997) "Moscow Marks Its 850th Anniversary," *Nezavisimaia Gazeta*, 5 Sept.

Kulik, I. (2008) "Iz glubiny sibirskikh prud dobyli bronzu: 'zheny dekabristov' Zuraba Tsereteli," *Komersant* 44, no. 3861, 19 March. Available online at: www.kommersant. ru/doc.aspx?DocsID=868472&print=true (accessed 19 March 2008).

Kurilko-Ryumin, M. and Drobitsky, E. (2004) "Recognizing Russian Art," Letters to the Editor, *Washington Post*, 26 June.

Levy, C. J. (2008) "Kremlin Rules: Moscow's Mayor Exports Russia's New Nationalism," *New York Times*, 26 Oct. Available online at: www.nytimes.com/2008/10/26/world/ europe/26mayor.html?pagewanted=print (accessed 5 November 2008).

Lowe, C. (1997) "Tsar of Moscow Launches Bid for Yeltsin's Crown," *Sunday Times*, 7 Sept.

Malpas, A. (2004) "Highest Laurels," *Moscow Times*, 27 Feb–2 March.

Marshall, P. D. (1997) *Celebrity and Power: Fame in Contemporary Culture*, Minneapolis: University of Minnesota Press.

Martin, S. (1997a) "Floating the Virgin. Energetic Overspending on Kitsch is the Prime Feature of Moscow's 850th Anniversary Party," *Irish Times*, 6 Sept.

— . (1997b) "Capitalist Bad Taste Outdoes Communism," *Irish Times*, 6 Nov.

Ndalianis, A. and Henry, C. (2002) *Stars in Our Eyes: The Star Phenomenon in the Contemporary Era*, Westport, CT: Praeger.

Nikolaeva, E. (2009) "Zurab Tsereteli" [Interview] Ekho Moskvy, 3 Jan. Available online at: www.echo.msk.ru/programs/features/562954-echo.phtml (accessed 4 January 2009).

O'Flynn, K. (2001) "Tsereteli Tires for a Statue Fit for a Princess," *Moscow Times*, 6 July.

Ourousoff, N. (2007) "The Malling of Moscow: Imperial in Size and a View of the Kremlin," *New York* Times, 15 March. Available online at: www.nytimes.com/2007/03/15/arts/design/15fost.html?ei=507 (accessed 15 March 2007).

Oushakine, S. A. (2007) "'We're Nostalgic, But We're Not Crazy': Retrofitting the Past in Russia," *Russian Review*, July: 451–82.

"Persons Involved in Arts Receive the Russian National Olympus Prize" (2008) *Russian Culture Navigator*. Available online at: www.vor.ru/culture/cultarch274_eng.html (accessed 5 July 2008).

Ponce de Leon, C. L. (2002) *Self-Exposure: Human-Interest Journalism and the Emergence of Celebrity in America, 1890–1940*, Chapel Hill; London: University of North Carolina Press.

Prikhodko, V. (2002) "Fifth Anniversary of Tsereteli's Monument to Peter the Great in Moscow," *RIA Novosti*, 5 Sept. Available online at: http://english.pravda.ru/culture/2002/09/05/36065.html (accessed 5 September 2002).

Putinki: Kratkii sbornik izrechenii prezidenta (pervyi srok) (2004) with illustrations by A. Merinov, Moscow: Ekho Buk.

Rigas Laiks [Riga time] (2006) *Eurozine Review*, no. 5. Available online at: www.eurozine.com/articles/2006-05-23-eurozinerev-en-html (accessed 5 January 2008).

Rodriguez, A. (2005) "Sculptor is the Artist Russians Love to Hate (Zurab Tsereteli)," *Chicago Tribune*, 29 Aug.

Rojek, C. (2001) *Celebrity*, London: Reaktion Books.

Romer, F. (2008) "EROTIKA. Grafika Zuraba Tsereteli," *Moskovskii Muzei Sovremennogo Iskusstva*, June. Available online at: www.mmoma.ru/index.php?path[]=home_container&path[]=exhibition-2008-05-27-23-23- (accessed 26 June 2008).

Rozhin, A. (ed.) (2000) *Contemporary Russian Artists*, (ed. of English text, Galina Tchemakova) Moscow: Mikhail Afanasyev & Helen Lavrinenko.

Specter, M. (1997) "Moscow on the Make," *New York Times*, 1 June.

Stanley, A. (2004) "At 850, Moscow Takes a Bow," *New York Times*, 17 Aug. Available online at: http://query.nytimes.com/gst/fullpage.html?res=9C02E6D8113CF934A2575BC0A961958260&sec=&spon (accessed 5 May 2004).

Taibbi, M. (1997) "Baldfellas: An eXile Guide to Russia's Hot Autumn," *eXile*, 16 Sept.

"Tsereteli dobralsia do Afriki" (2007) *Moia Sem'ia*, no. 42.

"Tsereteli Zurab Konstantinovich," *Art Gallery Shenco*. Available online at: http://gm.iatp.org.ge/caucasusculture/1.8htm (accessed 3 September 2003).

Tykulov, D. (2005) "V Moskve poiavitsia svoi tsentr Pompidu," *Vzgliad*, 12 Aug. Available online at: www.vzglyad.ru/print.html?id=4331 (accessed 2 December 2005).

vanden Heuvel, K. and Cohen, S. F. (1997) "The Other Russia," *Nation*, 11–18 Aug.

Warren, S. (2006) "Texan David Adickes Renders Presidents, The Beatles; Now Aiming for 280 Feet," *Wall Street Journal*, 18 Jan: A1.

Williams, C. J. (1997) "Moscow's 850th Birthday Party Has Select Guest List," *Los Angeles Times*, 6 Sept.

Wired New York [Forum] Available online at: http://host.wirednewyork.com/~edward/forum/search.php?searchid= 331741 (accessed 13 April 2007).

Zhdanowa, D. (ed.) (2008) "The New Moscow: Between Neo-Classicism and High Tech," *Kultura*, 3 July. Available online at: www.kultura-rus.de/kultura-dokumente/ausgaben/englisch/kultura-3-2008-EN.pdf (accessed 3 July 2008).

Zubchenko, E. (2008) "Generaly shtatskikh kar'er: Sovremennaia tabel' o rangakh navela sredi chinovnikov pochti armeiskii poriadok," *Novye Izvestiia*, 18 July. Available online at: www.newizv.ru/print/94205 (accessed 18 July 2008).

'Zurab to Fabergé' (2009) *Russian Life*, July/August: 17.

"Zurab Tsereteli" [UNESCO] Available online at: http://portal.unesco.org/en/ev.php@URL_ID=8331&URL_DO=DO_TOPIC&URL_SECTION=201.html (accessed 13 September 2003).

11 Hot *prospekt*s

Dining in the new Moscow

Darra Goldstein (William College)

When in 1999 the late Warner LeRoy reopened New York's famous Russian Tea Room, the city's sophisticates complained that "his taste for rococo shimmer and dazzle was just noisy kitsch, that his pursuit of the fantastic sometimes crossed the line from exuberance to wretched excess" (Asimov 2001: A11). *New York Times* restaurant critic William Grimes confirmed the "appalling" result,

> … upstairs, Mr. LeRoy has pulled out the stops, and he has proceeded with the confidence, and the taste, of a newly minted Moscow billionaire.
>
> It's a room that makes your jaw drop, a long banquet hall with mirrored walls, gold candelabra extending from the walls and a balcony on which a small orchestra plays "Lara's Theme" from *Doctor Zhivago*, "Moscow Nights" and the theme from *The Godfather*. By now, the giant acrylic bear that dominates the room has entered into legend, although the sturgeons within its revolving form were not up to the job and have been replaced by red clown fish. A convoluted gold tree with enormous decorated eggs hanging from its branches contributes to an odd synthesis. The room is meant to conjure up the glittering halls of the Peterhof Palace and the magic world of Afanasyev's fairy tales. It feels more like a pinball machine.
>
> (Grimes 1999: F1).

Grimes got it just right – as did Warner LeRoy, whose only error was that he opened his fanciful restaurant in New York City, not Moscow. For the New York crowd, after all, food is foremost, and the city's adulation of celebrity chefs knows no bounds. "Foodies" follow like lemmings as the chefs' empires grow, and when an auteur-driven restaurant receives a favorable nod from the *Times*, it becomes nearly impossible to reserve a table. Even after the first buzz has died down, the most sought-after restaurants maintain a stringent system of reservations to ensure their exclusivity, forcing anxious would-be patrons to resort to elaborate schemes to secure a coveted table. On that score things are much easier in Moscow, where reservations are not difficult to obtain. The real problem occurs when one arrives at the restaurant. To enter many of the city's hottest dining spots one must first pass "feis kontrol'" [face control] – about which more below.

New Yorkers quickly dismissed the revived Russian Tea Room as a tourist trap.

But, in fact, Warner LeRoy's ode to excess epitomized a very Russian spirit of dining, one that is visible in Moscow's new gastronomic landscape. Food there is not yet the real draw; eighteen years into the post-Soviet era, the play's the thing. The city's most talked-about restaurants aim to stage a meal, not just serve one, and it is in these public spaces that the Russian propensity for lavish spending and love of illusion are acted out. If hyperbole is a negative value in New York, it is, arguably, the most desirable feature of the Moscow dining scene today. To visit a trendy restaurant means to enter a fantasyland and leave reality behind; the performance of the meal trumps the meal itself, turning each venue into a literal "theater of consumption" (Firat and Nikhilesh 1998: 135).

Restaurateur Andrei Dellos, whose Café Pushkin and restaurant Turandot are two of the most glamorous and fantastic (in a literal sense) spots in Moscow, has claimed that after seventy-odd years of Soviet rule, "Russians are tired of ideology and my goal is to give people somewhere to which they can come, enjoy themselves and dream" (qtd. in Robinson 2005). In fact, dining in Russia has long been preoccupied with illusion, and the current restaurant scene in Moscow is more than simply a reaction to decades of grim "stolovye" [canteens]: patrons wish to experience a waking dream. Contemporary diners are drawn to the trendiest restaurants in order to live out a fantasy, if only for the duration of an evening's meal. It is partly for this reason that genuine connoisseurship of food has yet to develop in Russia, though it is beginning to do so. The restaurant scene is part of a new Russian world, and a new vocabulary, that embraces the concepts of "effektnost'" [glamour] and "znamenitost'" [celebrity], and uses for its descriptors such borrowed catchwords as "glamurnyi" [glamorous] and "elitnyi" [elite].[1] In turn, the English cognate "lakshari" [luxury] makes objects seem more desirable than does its Slavonic counterpart, "roskosh'."

Such iconic words are repeated throughout central Moscow in storefronts beckoning with all that money can buy. Western brand-name [brend] stores are everywhere; the shoppers are consciously stylized and chic. Powerbrokers and beautiful people announce themselves like royalty and expect to be taken seriously. A visitor to Moscow in 2009 might be forgiven for concluding that beyond the ubiquitous onion domes and *matryoshka* dolls, distinctive Russian culture has been lost. But the apparent lack of traditional markers actually reveals a good deal about the current state of Russian culture, in which certain deeply engrained traits have simply reemerged in new form. How great a leap is it from the jaded restaurant-goers in Chekhov's poignant short story *Ustritsy* [Oysters] (1884) to the restaurant-goers of today, who similarly seek entertainment to quell their ennui?

Today's street scene replaces the top-hatted gentlemen of yesteryear with overfed men sporting slicked-back hair, gold sparkling on their fingers and around their necks. Versace-draped beauties displaying prominent cleavage, long blonde hair, and even longer legs are inevitably in tow, their diamond-studded cell phones clasped in perfectly manicured hands. The appearance of such couples brings pedestrian traffic to a halt, and they stop for an instant to revel in their glory before sweeping through restaurant doors that have magically opened to admit them. Like a chimera, they disappear, though the Lamborghinis left blocking the sidewalk remind passersby of their existence.

A look back into Russia's past can reveal a rich layer of meaning underlying the slick surface of this new money and the behavior it engenders. First, however, we must consider our approach to such cultural signs. Is it fair to judge as tacky, kitschy, or just plain ostentatious all that the New Russians perceive as glamorous, especially when the judgments come from Americans, who carry their own ugly national stereotypes? Taste is, after all, relative, *chacun à son goût*. And yet, over the centuries foreign travelers have repeatedly commented on the excess they encountered in Russia. One of the earliest, Richard Chancellor, described a mid-sixteenth-century wedding feast in which the bride and groom "fall then to drinking, till they be all drunk; they perchance have a minstrel or two. And two naked men, who led [the bride] from the church, dance naked a long time before all the company" (Hakluyt). Fast-forward to early-twentieth-century Moscow, when a visitor noted, "It is clear to the most superficial observer that this is essentially a city of commerce and trade; every one if its inhabitants only thinks of making money, but strains every nerve that he may succeed in doing so" (Meakin 1906: 101). Was I, then, just another in a long line of visitors who, blind to Russia's essence, was ready to declare it "excessive and vulgar," a place that fills even "the most courageous stomachs … with horror"? (de Segur 1865: 41). Despite my personal ambivalence, I believe that the current excesses of fashionable Muscovite life are not simply vulgar ostentation. Rather, they represent a twenty-first-century manifestation of characteristic Russian traits: expansive generosity and fatalism.

Historical extravagances

The communal table has long been an important site for the enactment of social relations in Russia. Historically, Russians have celebrated the moment and aestheticized their otherwise often deprived lives by dramatizing the quotidian meal. The performance of a meal also serves as a vivid means of self-promotion and advertisement. In the past, as today, a shared meal – whether a magnificent feast staged by a nobleman to consolidate political power or a restaurant debauch orchestrated by an oil-rich oligarch – is a means of publicly announcing a host's power and prestige and a useful way to manipulate social standing.

Restaurants provide an ideal arena for projecting one's desired image, but even before restaurant culture developed in Russia in the nineteenth century, a climate favoring entertainment and pleasure reigned among the upper classes. For those of means in Russia, when it came to regalement, the attitude was quite distant from the "waste not, want not" mentality that has prevailed in much of Western culture. The rigid Russian Orthodox sequence of feast and fast days, in which roughly two hundred days a year are designated as fasts, meant that even wealthy Russians were continually aware of imminent (if only relative) deprivation. When they had to fast, they fasted.[2] Feasting represented a fleeting opportunity for celebration, and because feast days were built into the Church calendar, this excursion into excess was sanctioned. A cautious and parsimonious approach to life held little sway over

Russians.[3] When feasting was allowed, they went to extremes, with seemingly total disregard for restraint, experiencing glee at their own wantonness. As elsewhere in Europe, the aristocracy delighted in dining in the presence of the plebes, to whom they literally threw table scraps at the end of their meal.

What we find in Moscow today is a new iteration of a way of thinking that is engrained in the national psyche; the spectacles continue, only in new form. While it is true that in the new Russia, as elsewhere in the developed world, a certain Bakhtinian ideal has been lost,[4] the memory of a forced collective is still all too close for Russians, and certainly nothing to aspire to. Nevertheless, the focus on pleasure is not merely a reaction against seventy-odd years of Communist rule.

Contemporary Russian attitudes toward regalement are best understood by first considering the changes that took place over the course of the eighteenth century in the wake of Peter the Great's radical reforms. It was then that food in the households of upper-class Russians moved from the realm of sacrament (feasts held on Church holidays) to that of *byt* or everyday life (Sipovskaia 2003: 59). As the century progressed, this change was accompanied by a newfound delight in illusion as part of the French aesthetics the Russians sought eagerly to emulate: faux fruits in bowls, *trompe l'oeil* table settings. A new social type appeared, the so-called *petimetr* (from the French "petit-maître"), a dissolute young man evincing passion for all things French. Although wealthy Russians historically had regaled with excess on feast days, the new, more secular mode enabled them to follow their inclination to live life in general outside of prudence. With few financial constraints, the nobility and gentry held "open tables" at which anyone of the proper class was welcome to appear.

As prime markers of social change, meals were an easy target for conservative ire. Prince Mikhail Shcherbatov, in his late-eighteenth-century treatise *On the Corruption of Morals in Russia* (1969), disdained the new focus on pleasure and artifice and rued the loss of the meal's sacred character. He complained of Russia's moral deterioration, as evidenced by the newly fashionable style of dining that admitted outsiders into a formerly closed realm. The introduction of exotic ingredients also disturbed him:

> The meals were not of the traditional kind, that is, when only household products were used; now they tried to improve the flavor of the meat and fish with foreign seasonings. And, of course, in a nation in which hospitality has always been a characteristic virtue, it was not hard for the custom of these open tables to become a habit; uniting as it did the special pleasure of society and the improved flavor of the food as compared with the traditional kind, it established itself as a pleasure in its own right.
>
> (Shcherbatov 1969: 143)

What troubled Shcherbatov most was the idea of the table as "a pleasure in its own right," with no thought given to the moral and religious obligations of the meal. But his voice was largely ignored. The nobility continued to revel in novelty, transporting flash-frozen fish on sledges from Arkhangelsk to St. Petersburg and Moscow in winter (a good two hundred years before mechanical freezing was perfected), and ordering pies, breads, and sweets directly from Paris, which arrived in St. Petersburg within six days (Zabelin 1852: 274). Those who were not content with mail order simply took themselves to Paris, returning with news of the latest dining trends and inspiring their friends and neighbors to ever greater heights of one-upmanship and excess.

Before the invention of restaurants, the nobility indulged their gastronomic fantasies within the privacy of their own homes. Their needs were taken care of by the many "souls" (serfs) they owned, which left the less resourceful among them with too much spare time and prompted them to seek ever more novel diversions. Ennui may be endemic to wealth, but the idea of *pokazukha* or illusion is especially appealing to Russians, whose lives have long been defined by a severe climate and isolation. At the least, simulated environments offered an antidote to otherwise bleak routine. The eighteenth-century nobility especially liked to create magical, neoclassical settings that transported guests to distant places and times. For one famous party Count Grigorii Potemkin transformed his dining room into a Caucasian grotto, complete with a fully engineered stream spilling down an artificial mountainside. Roses and other fragrant flowers grew in profusion; myrtle and laurel trees were resplendent with fruits crafted of gems. On Catherine the Great's arrival a chorus broke into song, limning her praises in ancient Greek (Lotman and Pogosian 1996: 28–30). Count Aleksandr Stroganov turned his dining room into a Roman triclinium, with tables of marble and mosaic, and mattresses stuffed with swans' down so the guests could recline. Each guest was served by a beautiful young boy, who brought in one exquisite dish after another, including herring cheeks – for which more than one thousand herrings were required to compose a single plate – salmon lips, boiled bears' paws, roast lynx, cuckoos roasted in honey and butter, cod milt and fresh turbot liver, oysters, wildfowl stuffed with nuts and fresh figs, salted peaches, and pickled pineapples, which were, of course, unknown in ancient Rome but were such a desirable novelty in Russia that their inauthenticity was overlooked (Pyliaev 1897: 11).

With money no object, too many Russian noblemen led idle lives, their interest piqued only by excessive behavior. The nineteenth-century Count Musin-Pushkin is said to have spent more than 100,000 rubles a year on the pleasures of his table, with at least 30,000 expended on confections alone. His profligacy was so great that he raised his turkeys on truffles and his calves on cream, and even ordered them kept in cradles like infants. Musin-Pushkin's chickens enjoyed cedar nuts and walnuts rather than oats and grains; instead of water they drank heavy cream and Rhine wine. With 40,000 serfs, it was easy enough for the count to lavish this sort of attention on his domestic animals (Pyliaev 1897: 15).

Yet, immoderate as the nobility's behavior may have been, it paled in comparison to that of the merchants, who found themselves newly, and often fabulously, rich as the nineteenth century wore on; in many ways they can be seen as the precursors of today's New Russians. The merchants chose to entertain in restaurants rather than at home, frequently reserving private rooms for their festivities and spending exorbitant amounts on dishes like *ukha* made of sterlet poached in imported champagne, which could cost up to 300 gold rubles. But, as is true today, the food was generally secondary to the mealtime amusements (Ivanov 1982: 286, 288). In an oral history, Ivan Pavlov, a seasoned waiter who often attended the merchant carousals at the Nizhny Novgorod fair, confessed that some of the merchants' recreations were too appalling to mention (Ivanov 1982: 288). Their more benign pastimes included performances of a "mermaid's funeral," for which the host ordered a coffin in which a nubile "mermaid" would lie down. Candles were lit to make the atmosphere properly macabre, and as a Gypsy chorus sang mournful songs, the drunken merchants would sob. A more upbeat diversion required that the maître d' bring in a large tray of food garnished with flowers and greens. On a bed of napkins lay the centerpiece – a naked woman, the exotic dish of the day. While an orchestra played, the merchants showered the woman with rubles and poured wine and champagne over her, nibbling all the while on the surrounding food. At nearly 5,000 rubles, such entertainment did not come cheaply (Ivanov 1982: 287–8). Naked women also figured in a variation on the mermaid theme, in which a girl was thrown into a large tub of champagne for the merchants to enjoy watching her float. Or she could be used in "living swings," for which the men tossed her, naked, from arm to arm, sometimes until she lost consciousness.

This sort of carousing came to an abrupt end with the 1917 Revolution, after which even the best restaurants experienced food shortages. As Il'ia Erenburg remembers it, the once-luxurious restaurant in Moscow's Metropol Hotel served "thin soup, millet gruel or frozen potatoes. When you left the restaurant you had to hand in your spoon and fork, otherwise they did not let you out" (Ehrenburg 1962: 139). Equally difficult was the new attitude toward pleasure that took root by the mid-1920s. This new model demanded that good Soviet citizens not indulge in excess or caprice. Individual gratification was frowned upon in favor of asceticism, and every action became morally fraught. Sex and overeating came under official disapproval as forms of personal indulgence. A puritanical discourse took root in which desire, both sexual and gastronomic, became equated with bourgeois decadence. Young communists were encouraged to engage only in healthy, collective forms of pleasure, eschewing the consumption of rich or luxury foods.[5]

A dreary conformity took hold, and apart from forays into the ethnic cuisines of the "brother republics," the Soviet era was marked by a continual narrowing of the range of available ingredients, a reduction of dishes to their most prosaic forms, and a pervasive coarsening of the national palate, all of which resulted in a loss of connoisseurship. Although the ideological purity of the 1920s was, by the 1930s, a thing of the past, public dining never really recovered. Apart from the ubiquitous and largely grim "zakusochnye" [snack bars], "stolovye, pel'mennye" [dumpling houses], "chainye" [tea rooms], and "kafeterii" [cafeterias], by the late Soviet period the good restaurants of Moscow could be counted on one hand. Going out to a restaurant was still a mark of prestige, but the terms had changed. It was not enough to have money, which in any case was not the real currency; the issue was whether you were deemed worthy of a table at all. Not everyone was allowed into the few desirable places, even when they were virtually empty. Aragvi, with its tasty Georgian cuisine and balcony musicians, was a favored spot for the *nomenklatura.* Members of the Writers' Union could eat at the ultra-chic TsDL dining room, where the food was excellent, even if less exquisite than as Mikhail Bulgakov recalled in *The Master and Margarita.* These Soviet-era restaurants still served up illusion, but of a different kind. Now the pretense was of abundance and plenty at a time when very few products were for sale in the stores. This was especially true during the Stagnation era under Brezhnev, when good food most often could only be "obtained" [dostat'] rather than bought. This illusion went only as far as the printed menu, however. Even into the late twentieth century, only one or two dishes were typically available at restaurants, though the menus listed dozens.

One of the first indications of loosening governmental control was the 1987 opening in Moscow of Kropotkinskaya 36, a cooperative café boasting creatively prepared food and attentive service – attributes so astonishing at the time that one critic has likened its culturally transformative power to Yuri Gagarin's voyage into outer space (Nazarov 2006).[6] He was only half joking. In a kind of culinary perestroika, the success of Kropotkinskaya 36 led to a rash of new, independent restaurants. However, these eateries remained accessible only to those with plenty of money. What truly changed Moscow's restaurant culture was the opening of a more-or-less affordable restaurant where everything on the menu was always available, where quality was controlled, and where service was quick and friendly. This was Russia's first McDonald's, for which 30,000 people showed up on the opening day in January 1990.[7] Suddenly, a new standard was set for service and quality. And in this new environment, the ritual Soviet-era restaurant meal as a marker of important occasions like weddings gave way to a new style of eating out simply for pleasure, on ordinary days. This reversal called for a new psychology, a new ideological framework, one that harked back to the old Russia, when those who had means engaged in pleasurable activity for its own sake.

Which brings us to the present. Eighteen years after the collapse of the Soviet Union, Moscow is transformed. After decades of deprivation people are hungry for pleasure, and those who have money are willing to spend virtually any amount on it. Wealthy Russians now frequent restaurants less for a meal, which could be prepared at home by their private chefs, than for something far greater: the opportunity for public display. Restaurants make possible the centuries-old Russian practice of simultaneously flaunting wealth and demonstrating largesse. At Moscow's tables, Russia poses and performs.

Social power

What, then, constitutes glamour in Moscow's recreation of itself as a world-class city for dining, as befits the capital of Russia's commercial and political life? At first glance, glamour in the city's trendiest restaurants seems to be merely about surface, façade: the restaurant's ambience, the faces of those dining therein. But, in fact, the essence of Russian glamour is at once more nuanced and more corrupt. Zhenia Mikulina, former deputy editor of the Russian edition of *Architectural Digest* and now cultural director of *In Style* magazine, explains that, ultimately, it is not enough just to have a beautiful face (though that certainly helps),

> It's all about connections, about being included, whether as a mistress or by dint of having a job, like journalism, that can get you into the right places. Once you're 'in,' the money follows. What is now chic was previously disdained as part of a decadent western lifestyle – the focus on spas, on beauty, on sports. The difference in Russia is that as long as you're part of the gang, you're considered glamorous, even if you're ugly and fat. Alla Verber [vice-president of an influential real-estate holding company], for instance, is quite fat. But she rules the system.[8]

To be "in," Mikulina contends, you must either have new money (which characterizes businessmen and managers, honest and dishonest alike) or belong to old families, generally those who were part of the artistic intelligentsia during Soviet times and who now have gone into business. This second category includes the film world's Mikhalkovs and Bondarchuks. For example, Stepan Mikhalkov, son of director Nikita Mikhalkov – his celebrity status is discussed in Chapter 5 – and actress Anastasiya Vertinskaya, now owns the restaurants Vertinsky and Indus. The friends of these families, their children, their ex-wives and schoolmates all, by association, carry the mark of glamour. The third group that qualifies among the new Moscow chic are the restaurant owners, chefs, actors, editors, and journalists who know everyone and are therefore influential. Tellingly, when members of any of these groups eat out, they follow not the chefs but *svoi* – people of their own kind. The French sociologist Claude Grignon has commented on this stick-to-your-own-kind mentality in regard to public dining, noting that "[c]ommensality is a result and a manifestation of a pre-existing social group" (qtd. in Scholliers 2001: 24). Thus, by dint of their very presence, the beautiful people make the restaurants they visit glamorous. And once they are at the table, the "politics of signification rule" (Gigante 2005: 8).

It follows, then, that some observers would criticize the restaurant as a site of incivility, seeing the intrinsically performative nature of the communal meal as leading to uncivilized behavior because it discourages meaningful interpersonal communication and instead creates an environment in which people are encouraged to play roles and thus relate less sincerely to their companions (a word that, not incidentally, comes from the Latin *com* + *panis*, to break bread together). Joanne Finkelstein writes that "[t]he artifice of the restaurant makes dining out a mannered exercise disciplined by customs that locate us in a framework of prefigured actions" (Finkelstein 1989). However, while a regulated environment may be emblematic of fine dining establishments in Europe and the United States, it is less so in Russia, where the rules of engagement and etiquette are, as we have seen, differently construed than in the West. As a possible sign of awareness of this difference, etiquette classes are springing up in schools throughout Russia. Perhaps, as outside observers, we need to relinquish our preconceptions about what constitutes civility and "appropriate" behavior. Nevertheless, critical distance enabling a more objective response can empower the outside observer. From such a vantage point, what appears to be taking place in Moscow now, as in past times of radical change, is a heightened search for both individual and national identity that is, in part, being played out in the city's restaurants. The individual, once scorned in favor of the collective, is now sacrosanct. The nation, too, has moved from a fraternal brotherhood of diverse peoples to a single Slavic entity with a strong sense of history and pride.

In the early years of the post-Soviet restaurant revolution, new dining venues focused on the mythical and the nostalgic. The presentation of "authentic" Russian food in an "authentic" atmosphere served to affirm the idea of Russianness and the importance of national identity. Significantly, several American fast-food chains that appeared early on gave way rather quickly to Russian chains, such as Russkoe Bistro, where the food was friendly and fast but distinctly Russian.[9] Other popular chains like Elki-Palki and Mu-Mu accentuate their Russianness by serving hearty comfort food in *izba*-like interiors; the Mu-Mu sites are even decorated with artificial birch trees, long a symbol of Mother Russia. These chains were founded, respectively, by Moscow's two great restaurant moguls: Arkadii Novikov, who began his career as a chef with the support of oil tycoon Roman Abramovich,[10] and Andrei Dellos, a former artist and art conservator.[11] It is not surprising that these down-home-style cafeterias should announce Russian identity through cuisine. But even the high-end restaurants that opened in the first burst of the 1990s revealed an uncommon connection to Russia's cultural past. The best restaurants in New York, London, or Paris are almost never named after literary, artistic, or historical figures. Yet among Moscow's top restaurants in the 1990s were Godunov, Yermak, Café Pushkin, Petrov-Vodkin, and Oblomov (named after historical and literary figures); Vechera na khutore, Taras Bul'ba, and Balaganchik (titles of works by Nikolai Gogol and Aleksandr Blok); Carré Blanc and Krasnyi bar (both named in homage to Kazimir Malevich), and Beloe solntse pustyni and Kavkazskaia plennitsa (the titles of two cult films). In this way Moscow's restaurants were reminders of the country's cultural heritage, which in itself represents a kind of glamour (and self-orientalizing) on the world stage (à la Ballets Russes).

These restaurants also presented creative dishes that tapped into a deep longing for national pride, and it is here that the evolution of a new gastronomic sensibility began. The first fine restaurants (1, Red Square and Tsarskaia Okhota) evoked pre-revolutionary Russia, whether through historical menus or by celebrating the glory days of the great Russian hunt. Yet, within a few years, the locus of nostalgia for the past moved from Old Russia to the Soviet era in restaurants like Petrovich (named after the popular Soviet cartoon character),[12] whose décor bespoke Soviet style: the walls were covered with items of kitsch and the menus were *papki*, bureaucratic folders. As in Soviet days, it was nearly impossible to get into Petrovich without having some "blat" [pull]. Today, the immediate Russian past no longer spells glamour – the trendsetters now consider such evocations passé. But, as happens with elite trends, there has been a trickle-down effect, and the emerging middle class now frequents Soviet-chic places like Borshchev (which specializes in borshch) and Glavpivtorg (the Soviet acronym for the beer distribution agency) on Lubianka Square near the former KGB headquarters, where an erstwhile apparatchik can still dine in style.

Moscow today

In 1997 Boris Yeltsin entertained French president Jacques Chirac at Tsarskaia Okhota; today, Vladimir Putin prefers to regale his guests at Turandot, Andrei Dellos's $50 million recreation of a French Rococo palace that opened in December 2005. It serves mainly Asian food. The new generation of affluent Russians has traveled more, has more money, and is not wedded to things Russian. Thus the trendiest places, such as GQ Bar, Turandot, Vogue Café, Bon, Not Far East, China Club, Peperoni, and Yapona Mama announce their foreignness, and the real signs of the times are sushi and hookahs. Even in avowedly French or Russian or Italian kitchens, sushi is ubiquitous, a phenomenon the Russians call *sushimania*.[13] As for the hookahs, they represent a realm in which connoisseurship is evident, even though it is still lacking in regard to food. At Café Pavilion, for instance,

> Pavilion's hookah menu is a sumptuous fairyland [roskoshnaia feeriia] of tastes and aromas. Fifteen types of hookahs based on original recipes, fifteen types of tobacco, are capable of making relaxation truly magical. The best hookah master, brought specially to Pavilion from the Arab Emirates, will advise you and tell you about the subtleties of smoking.[14]

This focus on extra-prandial affairs encourages pretense and ostentation. As in medieval feasts, the food is the pretext for the events that unfold around it. Gathered around their hookahs, today's New Russians actively construct their public image, not unlike the hyperbolic hosts of earlier eras. In this way Moscow's restaurants are complicit in the construction of identity, at both the individual and national levels, offering ever-new strategies for distinction based on the rise of an inordinately wealthy new elite, which is marked by hedonism and a "capacity for consumption."[15] Through the act of public dining and the consumption of food, class differences are vividly articulated – perhaps all the more so in a visibly striving society that was only recently ostensibly classless.

As consciously created spaces, restaurants hold additional allure in their promise of escape. Particularly in the aftermath of the Soviet experience, they offer patrons the opportunity to experience entertainment devoid of the kind of political meaning that was injected into nearly every Russian art form throughout most of the twentieth century. There is also the appeal of novelty, the discovery of hitherto unknown worlds, the sense of *trouvaille*. The willingness to try new foods and exclusive new places is an important way to distinguish oneself from the masses,[16] and Arkadii Novikov goes to great lengths to help his patrons learn what it means to exercise discrimination, to display distinction. At almost all of his restaurants he makes available free copies of exclusive lifestyle magazines that promote the glamorous life. Printed on extraordinarily heavy paper (no recycled content here), some have predictable titles like *Yachting*, *Gala*, and *Golf Style*. Others reveal a more specifically Russian mentality: *Chelovek-brend* [Man – the brand], *Luxury* (titled in English, though the content is Russian), and *Burzhuaznyi zhurnal* [Bourgeois Journal], all presented without irony.

At least for the moment, this glamorous life is concentrated in two places in Russia: within the Moscow city limits and just beyond, in the prestigious dacha villages along the Rublevskoe Chaussée (for the connection between glamour and Rublevka, see Mikhailova's discussion of Robski in Chapter 4). The hierarchies that have always defined Russia still persist; only the terms of belonging have changed. Because St. Petersburg has not yet succumbed to the omnipresent branding found in Moscow, it does not register high on the glamour scale. As Mikulina notes, "Moscow is like Monte Carlo. It is a state of its own, so different from the rest of Russia."[17] The comparison is apt. As in Monte Carlo, gambling and fast cars hold sway in Moscow (though Putin has signed a law consigning all casinos to just four locations in Russia, all outside Moscow, by July 2009). In place of Grace Kelly, Moscow offers up Svetlana Bondarchuk, the dazzling television anchor and editor-in-chief of *Hello!* magazine's Russian edition ("a celebrity magazine about celebrities"). Bondarchuk regularly lends her beauty to restaurant openings, polo championships, golf classics, and supercar rallies – events that attract people of money and leisure.[18] The difference is that Moscow enjoys no Prince Rainier, no nobility old enough to relax in their roles. Instead, it is a strivers' society.

The restaurant moguls

Russia's premier ubiquitous restaurateur, Novikov, claims that his restaurants will educate people and give rise to a new generation of epicures who, like those of the past, understand and appreciate fine food. His mission is not immediately apparent, for the restaurants in his empire seem to be all about setting. Beloe Soltntse Pustyni beckons with the sands of Central Asia, where a harem of waitresses serve up lamb pilaf rivaling them in succulence. Sirena [The Siren] entices with a watery subterranean kingdom of sturgeon swimming beneath a glass floor as diners savor their less fortunate cousins. Ju-Ju, with its animal trophies and reproduction crafts, is designed to recall colonial Africa, with a menu heavy on meat.

Novikov's competitor, Andrei Dellos, has created fantasylands of his own. Early on, in the period of nostalgia and nationalism, he opened Shinok, a Ukrainian tavern where the dining experience comes straight out of Gogol by way of *Alice in Wonderland*: the tables look out on a third-floor interior farmyard with a horse, goat, rooster, chickens, rabbits, and even a *babushka* to tend to them all. Dellos is also the mastermind behind what are arguably Moscow's most talked-about restaurants, Café Pushkin and Turandot. The former, which takes up an entire townhouse on elegant Tverskoi Boulevard, appears to be a beautifully renovated eighteenth-century mansion. But, in fact, the original buildings were demolished and a new one constructed in 1999. Dellos's attention to detail is legendary; so convincing are his interiors that patrons are easily fooled into thinking that they have actually stepped into the past. Dellos devoted a full six years to the creation of Turandot, located next door to Café Pushkin. Again he succeeded in tearing down a neoclassical ensemble of eighteenth- and nineteenth-century mansions that had once belonged to Ivan Rimsky-Korsakov, a lover of Catherine the Great, despite the buildings' listing on the registry of historic buildings. Obvious corruption was involved (Kishkovsky 2006; Cecil 2007). This new site is an eerily faithful reproduction of an eighteenth-century French palace. To create the requisite atmosphere, Dellos hired Moscow art students to meticulously paint bucolic frescos and fashion gilded moldings and chinoiserie,[19] then hired lighting and set designers from the Bolshoi Theater to complete the magic. The restaurant's circular main dining room rises up to a cupola depicting the sky in French blue. Puffy clouds add a lightness that offsets the room's massive rock crystal chandelier. The tables and chairs are hand painted; the toilets are crafted of porcelain. Numerous private dining rooms – no two alike – promise even more elite dining and allow for discreet assignations. All guests are greeted at the door by restaurant staff wearing period costumes, including powdered wigs, who usher them into a marble foyer flanked by two Gianmaria Buccellati boutiques, where post-prandial jeweled confections can be purchased for tens of thousands of dollars. Visitors are then led through a corridor into the dining room, graced by a chamber orchestra that plays on a slowly rotating stage. In a nod to the legendary Princess Turandot, made famous by Puccini's opera, the menu, created by London's Alan Yau, is – rather jarringly for the surroundings – pan-Asian and European, and includes such politically incorrect dishes as shark-fin soup and turtle soup (aka "exotic Japanese soup") – which prove not to be delicacies in the hands of the chef.

Because Dellos's "shiny sham re-creations of a glamorous Tsarist past" (Cecil 2007) play into the expectations of contemporary visitors, they appear more real than the original buildings and beg the question of authenticity. Both Café Pushkin and Turandot are representations of the real; within the context of twenty-first-century Moscow, for the clientele their reality is genuine enough. In architectural actuality, however, both restaurants are fakes, imitations, and the conjunctions of fact and fantasy are simultaneously wondrous and awful. As *New York Times* architecture critic Paul Goldberger wrote of Warner LeRoy's extreme renovation of New York City's Tavern on the Green (a good twenty years before LeRoy tackled the Russian Tea Room), "It is all, on one level, absurd; and yet it is all, on another level, quite wonderful. Mr. LeRoy's creation, as a piece of design, goes beyond the conventional limits of taste to create a new and altogether convincing world of its own" (qtd. in Asimov 2001). The same can be said of Dellos's and Novikov's creations, though a more recent critic, commenting on Philippe Starck's design for the Novikov restaurant Bon, reacted more critically to its over-the-top décor – the Kalashnikov lamps, the stuffed owls sporting rhinestones,

> The project of Moscow perhaps posed a moral challenge – on one hand, he doesn't particularly like the city (or didn't before) for its gross excesses, but on the other he's friends with the owners of Billionaire, who convinced him to open this third Bon restaurant next door. In the end, he had to be true to his values. The two Paris venues evoke a sense of timeless elegance – Moscow's is done, admittedly, in the aesthetic of "rich man with no taste." Essentially, Bon is New Russian camp.
>
> (Rinkus 2006)

Another commentator situates Starck's values in his "dark shrine to the Moscow excesses of sex, violence, and food … Bon's design is surprisingly effective and feels somewhat disturbing, like being awake during a vivid nightmare. Such is the overwhelming nature of the design, it's easy to forget that this is a restaurant, not a theatre set" ("Hideously Kinky" 2006).[20]

Such totality of experience is evident in Moscow's restaurants (and nightclubs),[21] the arenas in which the Russian propensity for lavish spending and preoccupation with illusion are played out. Whether or not they are tasteful by Western standards is beside the point. What is important is the diner's opportunity for total immersion in another realm. To this end, it helps if the restaurant boasts a "secure and discreet ambience with respect for customers' privacy, whether it is friends enjoying a dinner or business partners meeting discreetly in a private setting"[22] – crucial for business deals and liaisons alike. Of course, the most sought-after restaurants further promise the spectacle of beautiful women and rich men, with the implicit expectation that the twain will eventually meet. When Isaac Correa was still chef at Ulei [The Hive],[23] his remarkably fine food was not the main draw. Ulei gained notoriety for its "Moscow's Most Beautiful Ladies" celebration and a promise to

> pamper every stunner who struts through the door during the month of September with mirrors strategically placed at flattering angles, gauzy, seductive decor and a menu designed around sweet pink watermelon flesh. After receiving a 50 per cent discount on meals between 4pm and 8pm, the loveliest ladies are also promised a complimentary decadent dessert served on a mirror – so they can admire their sweet reflection.[24]

In the dozens of restaurants he oversees, from fine dining to chains like Elki-Palki, Kish-Mish, and Prime Star, Novikov avoids such crass gimmicks. Tat'iana Mel'nikova, the general manager at the ultra-trendy Art-Café Galereia, who has worked for Novikov for years, has made a careful study of what makes a restaurant click (or clique). It all comes down to the clientele, she argues, who bring glamour and cachet to the places they frequent.[25] Galereia is visited largely by Moscow's golden youth and by foreigners. The café does not advertise – it succeeds entirely by means of the "sarafannoe radio" [word of mouth]. Mel'nikova admits that the practice of face control keeps the café exclusive, but contends that "elite" diners must be protected from hangers-on and wannabes.

Exclusivity here can be understood as both a process and a result. The process of exclusion is a means of attracting the kind of clientele that the restaurant desires through the elimination of those it does not want. Consequently, the café becomes an exclusive place to dine because only the select have been admitted. The desired clientele, for their part, are assured of their desirability by the presence of professional excluders – discerning bouncers. Face control is an art, Mel'nikova believes. She maintains that there are only ten truly excellent face controllers in Moscow, and Galereia boasts one of them.[26] She is quick to point out, however, that face control is practiced only on Fridays and Saturdays; otherwise, Mel'nikova says, it's business as usual at the café, "a place where capital and culture meet."

Because the ante is always being upped, it is not easy to be glamorous in Moscow. It used to be enough to have a car; then a Mercedes or Audi or BMW was needed. Now Maseratis and Bentleys and Maybachs are de rigueur, and more than a few armored Hummers prowl the streets. And since so many people have fancy cars, the only way to demonstrate true importance and celebrity is to have a "migalka" [a flashing light] so that you can literally stop traffic and arrive at your destination in style. One reviewer summed up the tony clientele of GQ Bar (a Novikov property opened in partnership with Condé Nast Publications) by wryly commenting on its location near the fashionable Baltschug Kempinski Hotel, "It doesn't matter that it's about 10 blocks from the metro because no one should be going there by metro" (Ortega and Borden).

Another requisite for the glamorous life is maintaining a certain elusiveness – playing hard to get. According to Mel'nikova, Novikov changes his cell phone number every ten days so that he cannot easily be found (she has his home phone number in case there is a fire at the restaurant). Elusiveness leads to exclusivity, which in turn engenders a perception of celebrity. Within the realm of food, exclusiveness is communicated in numerous ways. For one, Novikov regularly invites celebrity chefs from abroad to cook in his kitchens. Only those who have traveled widely and are already in the know will recognize the names of Charlie Trotter, Pierre Gagnaire, and Pierre Hermé, all of whom have been guest chefs at Galereia. Another way to weed out non-sophisticates is to give restaurants foreign names that appear in roman script (Carré Blanc, Bon, Next Door), or to mix Cyrillic and roman letters (бараshка, Ваниль, Золотой). In both cases a familiarity with languages other than Russian is presupposed. Menus can be particularly difficult to parse, transliterating as they do food terms from numerous other languages, usually without explanation.

Yet the allure of the foreign is, we must remind ourselves, nothing new in Russia. We need only recall the stanza from Pushkin's *Evgenii Onegin* (1999) in which Onegin goes out for a night on the town,

> He mounts the sledge, with daylight fading:
> "Make way, make way," goes up the shout;
> his collar in its beaver braiding
> glitters with hoar-frost all about.
> He's flown to Talon's, calculating
> that there his friend Kaverin's waiting;
> he arrives – the cork goes flying up,
> wine of the Comet fills the cup;
> before him roast beef, red and gory,
> and truffles, which have ever been
> youth's choice, the flower of French cuisine:
> and pâté, Strasbourg's deathless glory,
> sits with Limburg's vivacious cheese
> and ananas, the gold of trees.[27]

Talon's restaurant, where Chef Pierre Talon presided over the kitchens until his return to France in 1825, was a favorite Nevsky Prospekt gathering place for young men of Onegin's means – the dandies of the era – and its offerings demonstrate the overriding influence of Western European tastes on nineteenth-century Russian cuisine. The bloody roast beef is, of course, as symbolically English as possible; the truffle-scented Strasbourg pie is purely French; and the Limburger cheese is a surface-ripened, cow's milk cheese from Belgium. The meal ends with pineapples, at that time still a rarity in Russia and thus very chic. Onegin celebrates by popping the cork of an 1811 vintage French Champagne, called "Comet wine" after the year in which the Great Comet appeared.

A half-century later, foreign foods were still alluring, as evidenced by the famous scene from Chapter 10 of Tolstoy's *Anna Karenina*, where the worldly Oblonskii and the salt-of-the-earth Levin meet in a St. Petersburg restaurant,

> "This way, your Excellency, please. Your excellency won't be disturbed here," said a particularly pertinacious, white-headed old Tatar with immense hips and coattails gaping widely behind …

> "If you prefer it, your Excellency, a private room will be free directly; Prince Golitsin is with a lady. Fresh oysters have come in …"

> "How if we were to change our program, Levin?" he said, keeping his finger on the bill of fare. And his face expressed serious hesitation. "Are the oysters good? Mind now."

> "They're Flensburg, your Excellency. We've no Ostend."

> "Flensburg will do, but are they fresh?"

> "Only arrived yesterday."

> "Well, then, how if we were to begin with oysters, and so change the whole program? Eh?"

> "It's all the same to me. I should like cabbage soup and porridge better than anything; but of course there's nothing like that here."

> "Porridge à la russe, your honor would like?" said the Tatar, bending down to Levin, like a nurse speaking to a child …

> "Well, then, my friend, you give us two – or better say three – dozen oysters, clear soup with vegetables …"

> The Tatar, recollecting that it was Stepan Arkadyevitch's way not to call the dishes by the names in the French bill of fare, did not repeat them after him,

but could not resist rehearsing the whole menu to himself according to the bill: – "Soupe printanière, turbot, sauce Beaumarchais, poulard àl'estragon, macédoine de fruits … etc …"

"Yes, sir. And what table wine?"

"You can give us Nuits. Oh, no, better the classic Chablis."

"Yes, sir. And *your* cheese, your Excellency?"

"Oh, yes, Parmesan. Or would you like another?"

"No, it's all the same to me," said Levin, unable to suppress a smile.

The menu at Novikov's Next Door restaurant echoes this Tolstoyan menu, the main difference being that today's dishes are listed in Russian and English, the latter having become the new French. Here we find fresh oysters (the waiter, like Tolstoy's Tatar, will presumably inform patrons of their provenance), Parmesan cheese (in addition to a selection of French cheeses), turbot, and Chablis. A "Lyon" onion soup takes the place of Tolstoy's *soupe printanière*, while a pear and black-currant coupe flavored with maple syrup replaces the similar *macédoine*.

In *Anna Karenina*, the artless Levin is offended by glamour. On entering the St. Petersburg restaurant, he feels troubled at the sight of a "painted Frenchwoman decked in ribbons, lace, and ringlets" standing by the sideboard. For him, Frenchness (as opposed to Russianness) and fashion sully the world. By contrast, Moscow's current beau monde embraces things Western and then ratchets them all up a notch. For instance, celebrity chefs' cookbooks have been big business in the West for a good decade now, presenting recipes and beautiful photographs of artfully constructed dishes demanding a kitchen brigade to execute properly. No matter for star-struck consumers; simply owning the book brings readers close to the chef by allowing them to peek into his kitchen. The Russian approach differs. Here, the books are less about celebrity chefs than about celebrity restaurants, which is not surprising, given the lesser importance ascribed to food than to atmosphere. Galereia promotes its image through a beautiful publication (printed partly in a limited edition) that is less a recipe book than a celebration of the café's style. It features photographs of the movers and shakers and often sultry women who frequent the café; the text boldly states (in English) that "The Gallery is a place where the probability of bumping into a celebrity is up to 99.9 per cent."[28] One photograph shows a beautiful woman talking on a cell phone during her meal, signaling importance and prestige.

The German sociologist Norbert Elias has posited "the civilizing process" as involving an awareness of others that led to increased self-control at the table (Elias 1994). Elias, of course, was not referring to the distracting din of cell-phone conversations but to such refinements as using one's own eating utensils instead of a shared implement or the hands. Still, sensitivity to the wellbeing of others was part of the evolution in Western societies from medieval ideals of *courtoisie* to early modern *civilité*. If we accept civility to mean controlled behavior, we could conclude that Russia is not yet fully civilized, at least according to contemporary Western norms of etiquette. Using cell phones at fine restaurants is definitely *mauvais ton* in the West, but in Russia it proclaims celebrity and status. Some visitors to Moscow today might concur with Adam Olearius, who on his seventeenth-century travels found the Russians "arrogant" and "self-interested" (Olearius 1967: 163).

Such Russians can be found at three other Novikov restaurants, which, in addition to Galereia, Mel'nikova considers among the most glamorous in Moscow: Bon, Aist [Stork], and GQ Bar. The only outside property to make her list is Café Pavilion, whose internet site declares, "If you aspire to behold the best representatives of glamour face [sic] with your own eyes, you absolutely must come to Pavilion..."[29] Interestingly, Novikov's Vogue Café did not make Mel'nikova's list, even though after its 2003 opening it was one of the first restaurants to be dubbed *glamurno* – everyone wanted to be seen there. Its New York-style business lunch [biznes lanch] soon became the hot ticket in town, and additional chairs were sold for $300 apiece to diners desperate to get in.[30] Even now, Vogue Café registers an ambience of mixed hopefulness and despair as long-legged beauties leisurely sip cappuccinos while chatting on their cell phones, periodically glancing around the room to see whether they have caught some tycoon's eye.

Because of its climate, Moscow has not developed a year-round sidewalk-café culture as have other, more temperate European capitals. One exception is found on the newly facelifted Stoleshnikov pereulok, where the ultra-cool fashion designer Denis Simachev opened a restaurant decorated with flea-market finds on the ground floor of his boutique. In warm weather, Moscow's golden youth while away their time on the sidewalk terrace, drinking fresh berry mojitos and watching the fashionistas parade by. A somewhat older crowd heads to the new Barvikha Luxury Village just outside the Moscow city limits, not far from Putin's dacha, which caters to mega-millionaires like those who participate in the annual Bentley party for Bentley owners from around the world. Alla Verber, the vice-president of the Mercury Company behind Barvikha, explains the choice of stores invited to open in the Village, "We realized that we want to sell not simply what's most trendy/fashionable, but what is namely *lakshere*" ("Butik").

This luxury is apparent at the Village's restaurant, A.V.E.N.U.E., sister to T.R.E.T.I.A.K.O.V. Lounge in the equally upscale Tretyakov Passage near Red Square. Here, style reigns over substance. The menu is eclectic, with something for every expensive taste: French, Italian, a little Russian, and, of course, the requisite sushi. In a shopping center where not a single homegrown brand is to be found, it is not surprising that, as in eras past, "gourmet" is defined at A.V.E.N.U.E as imported. Even the *pâte feuilleté* is brought in, frozen, from Belgium and France. Unlike in Europe and the USA, "locally grown" is not yet a buzzword in Russia. If the food comes from someplace else, then it must necessarily be more exotic and certainly more expensive – therefore better. Such traditional (and beloved) native fruits as Antonov apples are less likely to find a place on Russian menus these days than are Muscat grapes flown in from Spain. Strictly local food has become the food of the poor – the opposite of the trend in affluent Western society.

One prominent exception is wild strawberry [zemlianika] soup, the signature dessert prepared by chef Yuri Rozhkov at Vogue Café. In fact, this dessert appears on the menu at almost all of Novikov's restaurants, both in season and out; the tiny berries beloved by Russians are grown in Novikov's own greenhouses in Gorky-10, on the outskirts of Moscow. The soup costs 750 rubles, which at the dollar's weak conversion rate in September 2007 amounted to $30. The berries lacked the sun-kissed intensity of those picked in the wild, yet they were a joy nonetheless. I willy-nilly felt kinship with those profligate Russians of times past who served fresh hothouse strawberries in December to spite the elements and enchant their guests. I thought, too, of Princess Zinaida Yusupova, who created the wintertime illusion of blossom-laden orange trees growing right through her dining table by covering the entire length of the table with mirrored glass encasing the tree trunks – a victory over seasonal darkness (Kamenskaia 1894: 254). Novikov understands the psychology of his countrymen well.

Conclusion

The current dining scene in Moscow raises an important question. Does the proliferation of restaurants serving nontraditional foods mean that Russian culinary culture is at risk from the twenty-first-century manifestation of globalization, with its near-instantaneous transport of goods throughout the world – particularly since Russia, being less assured of the distinctiveness of its cuisine than, say, France or Italy, is more vulnerable to outside influences?[31] The answer is no. Culture is infinitely malleable, and in Russia's case, ever since Peter the Great's forced program of westernization, the country has actively absorbed outside influences. Notably, however, in every instance the Russians have rendered these influences their own through assimilation and adaptation. By the end of the eighteenth century, the wholesale importation of foreign foods and cooking methods had made the traditional Russian cuisine both more sophisticated and complex, and this process continued as leading chefs were lured to Russia to cook in the latest European style. By the 1880s Moscow's Hermitage was considered one of the great restaurants of the world (Chamberlain 1982: 293), and its chef, the Frenchman Olivier, gave his name to *salat Oliv'e*, a mixed meat, potato, and vegetable salad that became a hallmark of Russian (even Soviet) cuisine. Today, the Frenchman David Dessaux is chef at A.V.E.N.U.E, Italian Uilliam Lamberti presides over the stoves at Galereia, and German Heinz Winkler, recipient of three Michelin stars for his restaurant Residenz, near Munich, cooks at the newly opened Moscow Ritz-Carlton. They are only a few of the foreign chefs bringing their culinary sensibilities to bear on the Russian palate.

Paradoxically, the Russians' embrace of foreignness ultimately serves to promote their own national aspirations. Unlike elsewhere in the world, the Russians have never protested the symbolic presence of McDonald's so close to their own potent national symbol, the Kremlin.[32] Their embrace of the first McDonald's is understandable – after all, it represented freedom and liberation from the fetters of Soviet life. Yet even now, when America has fallen from grace and Muscovites have a vast range of restaurants to choose from, McDonald's remains a popular place to eat; it does not serve as a symbol of Western hegemony. The original McDonald's on Tverskaya Street remains extraordinarily busy, and, significantly, its style of service has led to the creation of homegrown chains like Blindonald's, which serve fast, but identifiably Russian fare (including bliny, hence its name). As in the great nineteenth-century debates about Russia's destiny, Russians today evince both an insecurity about their position as parvenus on the world market and a certainty in the rightness of Russia – a deep belief that, among other things, allows for culinary transformations. Thus we find at Novikov's Not Far East achingly fresh sushi alongside *stroganina*, a traditional Siberian preparation of shaved frozen fish, which had virtually disappeared during the Soviet years. The whitefish (muksun; Coregonus muksun), sparkling with ice crystals, is accompanied by soy sauce and a relish of lime, pickled red onion, orange, and ginger. Once connoisseurship develops, such a juxtaposition of dishes should lead interested diners to explore the resonances between Russian and Asian cuisines.

The consumption of food inevitably carries cultural and social meaning. Because food choices reinforce what we believe ourselves to be or what we wish to become, nourishment is more than a matter of feeding. Eating out creates a hub for social interaction and represents a locus of power: who eats what and with whom; whose appetites are satisfied and whose are not. Through these group dynamics, both identities and relationships are forged. Priscilla Ferguson sees in this social phenomenon the establishment of an "eating order."[33] Or, as Claude Grignon puts it, "To study commensality is therefore to study social morphology, but in a particularly concrete way ... group relationships take the practical shape of drink and food exchange, and of everything that is exchanged through this exchange" (Scholliers 2001: 24–5). As in the world of fashion, commensal practices spotlight how a society construes itself at any given moment in time. The food that gives rise to these practices is ephemeral and fleeting; the practices themselves may be unstable and continually shifting. Nevertheless, dining habits can reveal deeper meanings that are often obscured in less capricious social manifestations. Transitory though it may be, food has the power to act as a dynamic social agent and shape the culture of a locality, particularly one that is itself in transition.[34] By examining the restaurant culture of post-Soviet Moscow and the way it literally feeds an ethos of privilege and glamour, we see deeply into Russia itself.

Notes

1 Tellingly, during my September 2007 visit, *effektnost'* (literally, "showiness") was the word most often used to describe glamour. This term was chosen over other words of Slavonic origin that can also denote glamour, such as *obaianie, ocharovanie, chary, volshebstvo*. These words all have at their root the idea of "enchantment" or "magic," which accords with the original English association of "glamour" with "grammar," considered an attribute of occult knowledge. Thus, when the term *glamour* first appeared in English, it referred to a sort of magic spell or bewitchment because the erudition

associated with learning and grammar was linked to occult practices. See "Word for the Wise" (2007).

In an essay titled "The Power and the Glamour," Arthur Miller describes glamour as "that trans-human aura or power to attract imitation" and goes on to say that "Glamour [is] the power to rearrange people's emotions, which, in effect, is the power to control one's environment" – something attributed to witches in the past (Miller 2002: 120–4).

2 Even on designated fast days wealthy Russians managed to feast, simply by avoiding meat products. A fast-day meal enjoyed on Palm Sunday, 1656, by Boyar Boris Ivanovich Morozov, head of the Treasury under Tsar Alexei Mikhailovich, included the following dishes: "Fine wheat bread, cabbage with herring, pressed caviar, black caviar, red cisco roe, sturgeon marrow [viziga] with horseradish, steamed herring, boned salted pike with horseradish. Backbone of spawning [narostovye] sterlet, fresh sturgeon garnished with cucumbers. Fish filet [telo] with cucumbers. Salmon [losos'] with lemons. Fresh salmon [semga] with lemons, pike, steamed bream, steamed pike-perch, steamed sterlet, half a head of sturgeon, pancakes; salmon back, white salmon back, beluga belly, white salmon entrails, red pike, fish pie [prosypnoi], black sterlet, pie with fish filets in brine. Pike soup, pie with filets of [fish] [s telesy so mnevymi], perch soup, pie with sturgeon milt, crucian soup, white salmon pie, tench soup, a large sturgeon [osetra] pie, bream in brine, sour fish pies; [fish] [kolotka], small pancakes, perch in brine, long pies with dried peas, half heads of fresh sturgeon, fresh herring in pastry, white salmon backbone, crucian with fish filets [s telom], lateral backbone [zvena bocheshnye] of beluga, fritters, central backbone [zvena stupishnye] of sturgeon, whitefish with sauce, Ladoga whitefish [ladoga] with horseradish, soup with fish belly and tongue. 2 fish bellies, 2 sturgeon vertebrae. For the [derzhal'niki]: cabbage with herring, sturgeon marrow, sturgeon with cucumbers, buckwheat groats with fish, perch soup [ukha], long pies. Whitefish, Ladoga whitefish, *five dishes*. For the servants, *six dishes*. For the [podacha], 20 beluga and sturgeon vertebrae" ("Rospisi": 53–4).

3 Of course, the majority of Russians did not have the luxury to feast in style; more often than not, feast days meant simply the addition of a bit of lard to the cabbage soup, or a measure of vodka. These comments apply only to Russians of some means.

4 As one contemporary critic puts it, "the modern feast has lost its material connection with the struggle against adversity" and "simply represent[s] a gluttonous celebration of abundance, rather than a collective celebration of the achievements of productive labor" (Ashley *et al.* 2004: 44).

5 Tarasov-Rodionov's classic socialist realist novel *Shokolad* [Chocolate] chronicles the downfall of the stalwart functionary Zudin through the twin temptations of lust and chocolate. See LeBlanc (2003) and also Naiman (1997): 210, 214).

6 No one seems to know what has happened to Andrei Fedorov, the mastermind behind Kropotkinskaya 36.

7 In short order, Pizza Hut, Dunkin' Donuts, and Baskin-Robbins all appeared, although Pizza Hut and Dunkin' Donuts subsequently pulled out of the Russian market.

8 Interview in Moscow, September 2007.

9 Russkoe Bistro was established in 1995 but failed after the financial crisis of 1998. It was sold at auction in 2005.

10 That, at least, is the rumor. Abramovich is said to have financed Novikov's first restaurant, Sirena, which opened in 1993. For information on Novikov's empire see the website of his restaurant at: www.novikovgroup.ru (accessed 20 December 2009).

11 Dellos's restaurants include Café Pushkin, Bochka, Shinok, TsDL, Turandot, and the Mu-Mu chain.

12 Petrovich is the creation of Andrei Bil'zho, who first depicted him around 1990 in the pages of *Kommersant*. In Bil'zho's words, "Petrovich is a city lunatic. He is, in many ways, a composite character – an optimist who finds himself in many embarrassing situations, as does everyone in our country. But in spite of all the difficulties he faces, he maintains his self-respect. Sure, he may break his arms and legs occasionally, but

he recuperates quite quickly. He is a strange fellow" (Patina 2000).

13   How things have changed! Until the 1990s the only restaurant serving sushi in Moscow was located in the hulking Russian World Trade Center, which was off-limits to ordinary Soviet citizens. There, sushi could be purchased with hard currency, but it was rumored to be made from fish caught in the polluted Moscow River, which would make you sick.

14   This information is taken from the restaurant's website: www.restoran-oblomov.ru/index.php?target=rest&id=1 (accessed 29 August 2007).

15   As Bourdieu has shown, the same was true of the rising Parisian middle class of the 1960s (Bourdieu 1984: 310).

16   As noted above, social scientists like Bourdieu have shown that the quest for novelty is often associated with the rise of new social classes. See also Deborah Lupton, who argues that "Trying new foods and cuisine is also a sign of sophistication and distinction, of a willingness to be innovative and different from the masses" (Lupton 1996: 127).

17   Zhenia Mikulina, interview, September 2007, Moscow.

18   For a full list of Bondarchuk's appearances see the following website "Sur la terre: Moscow high-life and society" available online at: www.surlaterre.ru/en/people/person/svetlana-bondarchuk (accessed 20 December 2009). The tagline for the Russian edition of *Hello!* reads "Znamenityi zhurnal o znamenitykh liudiakh" ["A famous magazine about famous people"].

19   An interesting account said to be based on Dellos's own story can be found in the blog (see "New York Social Diary" 2006), Las Vegas was apparently interested in having Dellos open a restaurant, but so far he has demurred.

Las Vegas has been to visit and offers have been made for him to do the same out in the Nevada desert. He was intrigued, especially intrigued by Las Vegas, but decided that he couldn't run 26 restaurants in Russia and another one in Las Vegas. Besides, he knew that as much as Las Vegas hotel developers would pay for his services – and the sums they quoted him were stratospheric and impressive – Las Vegas businessmen would never tolerate five or seven years creating the Andrey Dellos version of an eighteenth-century palace. The Las Vegas businessman might be willing to spend a lot but ultimately only for what Andrey calls "the approximate." Andrey has a passion for the real thing.

In recounting this he explained the process of decorating another private dining room at Turandot. "He wanted a room of boiserie that looked eighteenth century, but was nineteenth century. The reason for the nineteenth century was that he knew he could never afford actual eighteenth-century boiserie but that they made some very good reproductions in France in the late nineteenth. Finally one day a dealer from Paris called to say he had the boiserie. Andrey went to look. It was eighteenth-century. He knew it was. No, said the dealer, as much as he would have wanted it to be. It was just very good nineteenth century. And so for $100,000 it would go into Turandot."

20   Starck himself sees things somewhat differently. In an interview with the *London Times*, he explained his "dark" approach, "I am, in my way, depressed, but so deeply and so continuously that you don't see the difference. I'm of Russian stock, and Russian people always have a bullet from a gun one centimetre from the brain. I am one of those people who live more in death than in life, or who appreciate life only if they think about death. I am a dark person, very dark." How does this square with the Starck who quaffs champagne and whips up delicious dinners for 30? "You know, only deeply depressed people try to have fun non-stop," he says sagely. "The others don't need it" (Shepherd 2005).

21   Nightclubs warrant separate examination; they are even more out of control. For a description of Moscow nightlife see Forrest (2006).

22   The restaurant's website is www.carreblanc.ru/en/restaurant (accessed 26 October 2007).

23   He has since moved on to his own eponymous restaurant and catering business, Correa's, with four cafés and food shops selling his own line of products.

24 From a 2004 notice in the *Moscow Times*, Available online at: www.kokian.com/article. php3?id_article=190 (accessed 20 December 2009).
25 Tat'iana Mel'nikova, interview, September 2007, Moscow.
26 The story goes that one night Novikov went to Galereia Club, which used to occupy the site. When the face controller refused to let him in, he bought the place and turned it into Art-Café Galereia.
27 Chapter 1, Stanza 16, translated by Charles H. Johnson (Pushkin 1999).
28 The restaurant's promotional leaflet read in Russian: "'Галерея' – то место, где вероятность появления гламурных персонажей максимальна" (*Uilliam Lamberti* 2005). See also the restaurant publication from A.V.E.N.U.E (Dessaux).
29 This information is taken from the restaurant's website, available online at: www. restoran-oblomov.ru/index.php?target=rest&id=1 (accessed 29 August 2007).
30 As may be clear by now, money is no object at the restaurants discussed here. Several of them offer "air catering"; Galereia alone prepares vacuum-packed meals for up to 150 private jet flights a month.
31 For more on globalization and vulnerability see Ferguson (2005: 695).
32 Quite the opposite: in 2003 *Argumenty i Fakty* reported that the McDonald's chains in Russia served 300,000 customers daily, and that over the course of a month they consumed 2,550,000 portions of fries. See "Podsevshie na Mak" (2003).
33 This term is Priscilla Ferguson's (Ferguson 2005: 689).
34 For more on food as a social agent see, for instance, Bell and Valentine (1997) and Humphrey and Lin (1998).

Bibliography

Ashley, B., Hollows, J., Jones, S., and Taylor, B. (2004) *Food and Cultural Studies*, London and New York: Routledge.
Asimov, E. (2001) "Warner LeRoy, Restaurant Impresario, is Dead at 65," *New York Times*, 24 Feb: A11.
Bell, D. and Valentine, V. (1997) *Consuming Geographies: We Are Where We Eat*, London and New York: Routledge.
Bourdieu, P. (1984) *Distinction: A Social Critique of the Judgement of Taste*, trans. R. Nice, Cambridge, MA: Harvard University Press.
"Butik v sel'skoi mestnosti. Proekt Luxury Village," *Kommersant*, 27 Oct. Available online at: www.zya.ru/article/article_570_3.asp (accessed 20 December 2009).
Cecil, C. (2007) "Letter from Moscow," *Prospect*, no. 136, July. Available online at: www. prospectmagazine.co.uk/2007/07/9675-letterfrommoscow/ (accessed 20 December 2009).
Chamberlain, L. (1982) *The Food and Cooking of Russia*, London: Allen Lane.
de Segur, A. (1865) "Zapiski" reprinted in N. N. Rusov (ed.) *Pomeshchich'ia Rossiia* (1911), Moscow: Izd. mosk. knigoizd. T-va "Obrazovanie."
Dessaux, D. (2005) *Kogda fua-gra vstrechaet ikru/A la rencontre du foie gras et du caviar*, Moscow: Katharsis.
Ehrenburg, I. (1962) *First Years of Revolution 1918–21*, London: MacGibbon & Kee.
Elias, N. (1994) *The Civilizing Process: Sociogenetic and Psychogenetic Investigations*, trans. by E. Jephcott, rev. edn. ed. E. Duning *et al.*, London: Blackwell Publishers.
Ferguson, P. (2005) "Eating Orders: Markets, Menus, and Meals," *Journal of Modern History* 77, no. 3 (Sept): 679–700.
Finkelstein, J. (1989) *Dining Out: A Sociology of Modern Manners*, New York: New York University Press.

Firat, A. F. and Nikhilesh, D. (1998) *Consuming People: From Political Economy to Theaters of Consumption*, London and New York: Routledge.

Forrest, B. (2006) "Midnight in Moscow," *Vanity Fair*, July. Available online at: www.brettforrest.com/articles/midnight-in-moscow-2/ (accessed 20 December 2009).

Gigante, D. (2005) *Taste: A Literary History*, New Haven: Yale University Press.

Grimes, W. (1999) "First the New Russia, Now the New Tea Room," *New York Times*, 15 Dec: F1.

Hakluyt, R. *The New Navigation and Discovery of the Kingdom of Muscovy by the North-East in the Year 1553: Enterprised by Sir Hugh Willoughbie, Knight, Performed by Richard Chanceler, Pilot-Major of the Voyage*, trans. out of Latin into English, in R. Hakluyt *Discovery of Muscovy, etc.* Available online at: http://infomotions.com/etexts/gutenberg/dirs/etext03/dsmsw10.htm (accessed 20 December 2009).

"Hideously Kinky", on Snowsquare: Urban postings from Moscow, Russia (2006) 27 Aug. Available online at: http://snow-square.blogspot.com/2006/08/hideously-kinky.html (accessed 29 August 2007).

Humphrey, T. C. and Lin, T. H. (eds) (1988) *"We Gather Together": Food and Festival in American Life*, Ann Arbor: UMI Research Press.

Ivanov, E. (1982) *Metkoe moskovskoe slovo*, Moscow: Moskovskii rabochii.

Kamenskaia, M. F. (1894) *Vospominaniia*, repr. Moscow: Khudozhestvennaia literatura, 1991.

Kishkovsky, S. (2006) "Letter from Moscow: Where the High Rollers Dine," *New York Times*, 25 May. Available online at: http://travel2.nytimes.com/2006/05/25/travel/25webletter.html (accessed 20 December 2009).

LeBlanc, R. D. (2003) "The Sweet Seduction of Sin: Food, Sexual Desire, and Ideological Purity in Tarasov-Rodionov's *Shokolad*," *Gastronomica: The Journal of Food and Culture* 3, no. 4 (Nov): 31–41.

Lotman, Iu. M. and Pogosian, E. A. (1996) *Velikosvetskie obedy*, St. Peterburg: Pushkinskii fond.

Lupton, D. (1996) *Food Body and the Self*, London: Sage Publications.

Meakin, A. M. B. (1906) *Russia: Travels and Studies*, Philadelphia: J. B. Lippincott.

Miller, A. (2002) "The Power and the Glamour," *Allure* (Apr): 120–4.

Naiman, E. (1997) *Sex in Public: The Incarnation of Early Soviet Ideology*, Princeton: Princeton University Press.

Nazarov, O. (2006) "Predislovie" reprinted in *Luchshie restorannye 'fishki' mira*, Moscow: izd. dom Restorannye vedmosti. Available online at: www.restoved.ru/boooks/48.html (accessed 20 December 2009).

"New York Social Diary" [Blog of David Patrick Columbia] (2006) Entry for 25 May. Available online at: www.newyorksocialdiary.com/socialdiary/2006/05_25_06/socialdiary05_25_06.php (accessed 20 December 2009).

Olearius (1967) *The Travels of Olearius in Seventeenth-Century Russia*, trans. and ed. S. H. Baron, Stanford, CA: Stanford University Press.

Ortega, J. and Borden C. W. "Gentleman's Quarterly Not Just for Gentlemen," Available online at: www.passportmagazine.ru/article/730/ (accessed 20 December 2009).

Patina, T. (2000) "Country's Chief Brain Prefers Life as Cartoonist," *St. Petersburg Times* 621, no. 0, 17 Nov. Available online at: www.sptimes.ru/index.php?action_id=2&story_id=13301 (accessed 20 December 2009).

"Podsevshie na 'Mak'" (2003) *Argumenty i Fakty* 32, no. 1189, 6 Aug. Available online at: http://gazeta.aif.ru/online/aif/1189/18_01 (accessed 20 December 2009).

Pushkin, A. (1999) *Eugene Onegin and Other Poems*, trans. Charles Johnson, New York: Alfred A. Knopf.

Pyliaev, M. I. (1897) *Staroe zhit'e: ocherki i razskazy*, St. Petersburg: Tipografiia A. S. Suvorina.

Rinkus, S. (2006) "Starck Strikes," *Element* 19, no. 150, 25–31 May. Available online at: http://elementmoscow.ru/articles.php?i=150000&s=07-deep-dish (accessed 20 December 2009).

Robinson, J. (2005) "The Exploding Restaurant Scene in Moscow," Available online at: www.jancisrobinson.com/articles/nick051217.html (accessed 20 December 2009).

"Rospisi kushan'iu boiarina Borisa Ivanovicha Morozova," in I. Zabelina (ed.) *Vremennik imperatorskogo moskovskogo obshchestva istorii i drevnostei rossiiskikh*, kn. 6, Moscow: v un. tip., 1850.

Scholliers, P. (ed.) (2001) *Food, Drink and Identity: Cooking, Eating and Drinking in Europe Since the Middle Ages*, Oxford and New York: Berg.

Shepherd R. (2005) "Starck Raving about Everything," *London Times*, 2 Apr. Available online at: www.timesonline.co.uk/tol/life_and_style/health/features/article441525.ece?print=yes&randnum=1151003209000 (accessed 20 December 2009).

Shcherbatov, M. (1969) *O povrezhdenii nravov v Rossii*, in A. Lentin (ed.) *On the Corruption of Morals in Russia*, Cambridge: Cambridge University Press.

Sipovskaia, N. (2003) "Vkus prazdnika," in *4 chuvstva: Prazdnik v Peterburge XVIII veka* [Exhibition Catalogue] Moscow: Khudozhnik i kniga, pp. 57–78.

Tolstoy, L. (2003) *Anna Karenina*, trans. C. Garnett, New York: Noble Classics.

Uilliam Lamberti: Kafe Galereia s ekskliuzivnymi fotografiiami Armina Zogbauma (2005) Moscow: izd. Kartush.

"Word for the Wise, Topic: Glamour" (2007) [Online Broadcast] 17 Oct. Available online at: www.m-w.com/cgi-bin/wftwarch.pl?101707 (accessed 20 December 2009).

Zabelin, I. (1852) *Khronika obshchestvennoi zhizni v Moskve s poloviny XVII stoletiia*, Zhurn. Voenno-uchebnykh zavedenii, vol. 98, nos. 388–9.

Index

Entries for figures are in *italics*.

Robski, Oksana, glam novels of 7, 8, 66, 102–3; happiness equated with wealth 90–3; magic of shared consumption 95–9; ownership in 99–102
Rockefeller, John D. 59
Rodnia [Kinfolk] (Mikhalkov film, 1981) 110
Rogachevskii, Andrei 69n11
Rojek, Chris 14, 15, 17, 18; on achieved celebrity 196, 204, 214; on celebrity and decline of religion 173; on celebrity as modern phenomenon 221; definitions of celebrity 107; on fans of celebrities 35; on social distance and celebrity 225; on staging of celebrity 175, 177; taxonomy of 30; on transgression 222; on veridical self 208
Roman-Kino [Novel-film] series (Akunin) 76
Romanov dynasty 110, 111
Roosevelt, Franklin D. 234
Rosman Press 90
Ross, A. 207
Rossiiskaia Gazeta (newspaper) 234
Rozhdestvenskaia, Ekaterina 17, 242, 243, 250n53
Rozhkov, Yuri 272
Rublevskaia kukhnia [Rublevka Cuisine] (Robski) 90
Runet (Russian internet) 156, 157, 158, 162
Russia, Imperial 4
Russia Blog 67
Russia/Russians, post-Soviet (Russian Federation) 2, 213, 236; black market economy 165; comparisons with West in Zadornov's humor 128, 130–1; democratization 140; demographic crisis 1–2; dining culture as social power 261–3; financial crisis (1998) 1, 7, 22, 24n7; high literature and identity of 75; media under state control 37, 39, 45; oil industry 35; poverty and homelessness among 4–5; Russian tourists 1; sexualized "new man" 14; Soviet legacies 14, 22
Russia Today (digital TV channel) 1
Russian language 7, 82, 94, 138–9, 214n2; English influence on 129, 256; glamour terminology 2–4, 256, 273n1; internet and 155, 159, 165, 166; in Latvia 137; new media and 148; Russian/Soviet empire and 139; Surzhik hybrid with Ukrainian 202, 206, 216n29; Western magazines in editions of 6, 7, 185

Russian Tea Room (New York restaurant) 255–6, 266
Russkie bez Rossii [Russians without Russia] (TV series) 118
Russkii Zemel'nyi Bank (Russian Land Bank) 58, 64
Russkoe Bistro restaurant chain 263
Rutka, Vasilii 181
Ryder, Winona 222

Sadko (Ptushko film, 1952) 236, 250n42
"safari-style" galas 64
Safronov, Nikas 42–3, 51n35
St. Petersburg, city of 10, 234; as "artificial" place 116; Moscow compared with 265; Putin cult in 34; restaurant/dining culture 258–9, 269–70; Silver Age 108; Tsereteli statue of Peter the Great 237, *238*
Salakhov, Takhir 49n7
Samoilova, Tat'iana 109
Sarkisian, David 233
Satarov, Georgii 41
scandals 60–1, 178, 185, 186; American celebrities and 221–2; Danilko/Serdiuchka and 195, 201–204, 212, 213–14
Science and Education to the World, or Prometheus (Tsereteli monument) 224
Scythians 139
"Seks-Mashina" (Sex-Machine/Sex-Car) 12
self, public and private 17
Semnadtsat' mgnovenii vesny [Seventeen Moments of Spring] (TV series) 49n12
Sennett, Robert 77, 80
Sentimental'noe puteshestvie na rodinu [Sentimental Journeys to the Motherland] (Mikhalkov film, 1996) 115–16, 119
Serdiuchka, Verka (fictional character) 14, 17, 195–6; community roots as moral anchor 209–14; drag performance and Ukrainian identity 205–7; Eurovision and 195, *196, 203,* 204–5, *205*; evolution of 197–201; internet postings about 215n23; Pugacheva and 207–9; scandals and 195, 201–4, 212, 213–14. *See also* Danilko, Andrei
Serdtse na palitre: Khudozhnik Zurab Tsereteli [Heart on the Palette: The Artist Zurab Tsereteli] (Kolodnyi) 230
Sex and the City (cable TV series) 7

Printed in Great Britain
by Amazon